Battles In Britain

and their political background

1066-1746

William Seymour

BOOK CLUB ASSOCIATES
LONDON

Front endpapers: Assault on a castle in 15th century, source unknown

First published in two separate volumes in Great Britain in 1975
by Sidgwick and Jackson Limited

This edition published 1979 by
Book Club Associates
by arrangement with Sidgwick and Jackson Limited

Printed in Great Britain by The Anchor Press Ltd,
and bound by Wm Brendon & Son Ltd,
both of Tiptree, Essex
for Sidgwick and Jackson Limited
1 Tavistock Chambers, Bloomsbury Way
London WC1A 2SG

Battles
In Britain
and their political background

Volume 1

1066-1547

William Seymour

Drawings and Battle Plans by W. F. N. Watson

BOOK CLUB ASSOCIATES
LONDON

By the same author
ORDEAL BY AMBITION
An English family
in the shadow
of
the Tudors

Illustration on page 2: Bayeux Tapestry, William is told that Harold is near

To Jenny
Whose map-reading passeth all understanding

This edition published 1979 by Book Club Associates
by arrangement with Sidgwick and Jackson Limited

Copyright © 1975 William Seymour and Sidgwick & Jackson Limited

Design by Bob Burroughs

Picture research by Mary Walsh

Typesetting by Watkins Repro Service, London, EC1

Printed in Great Britain by The Anchor Press Ltd,
and bound by Wm Brendon & Son Ltd,
both of Tiptree, Essex

Contents

TABLE OF BATTLES BY COUNTIES

Preface

To cover adequately the more important British battles in one volume requires a book that would be too large for convenience, and so it has been decided to produce this work in two volumes. The division falls conveniently after the battle of Pinkie Cleuch (1547), for there was a gap of almost 100 years before any further major fighting took place in Britain, and by that time there had been considerable weapon development. The second volume will cover battles from the Civil War to Culloden.

Several useful books have been written about British battles, but very few of them attempt to give the reader in any detail the reasons why the battles were fought, what motivated the principal protagonists and what right, if any, they had in taking up arms. I have devoted a good deal of space in trying to present the background to the battles without, I hope, obscuring the main purpose of the book, which is the reconstruction of the actual fights. Similarly, although any book on battles must inevitably be chiefly concerned with a description of the fighting and some account of strategy, tactics and military principles, whenever possible I have endeavoured to bring out the human side and give thumb-nail character sketches of the commanders.

No apology is made for the frequent reminder that our knowledge of many of the battles is far from precise. Half the enjoyment of visiting the battlefields and walking the actual site of conflict is to decide for ourselves, with what information is available, just how it happened, and in some cases exactly where. It would be very wrong to be dogmatic about events that took place up to a thousand years ago; even where we have reliable eye-witness accounts we cannot be certain that facts and information that have not come down to us over the centuries may have made decisions we now think should have been taken appear hazardous, if not impossible, to the commanders at the time. It is all too easy to pass judgement in the certain knowledge of what subsequently occurred, but a more difficult task, although an intriguing one, is to try to understand the problems as they presented themselves to the commanders at the time.

In the 700 years of military history covered by the two volumes of this book there were many changes in weapons and tactics, but all the battles were fought by men like ourselves, who experienced the same emotions of fear, boredom, weariness, despair (and sometimes defiance) in defeat and exhilaration in victory, for basically the deep springs of human action have remained fairly constant down the ages. There are few, if any, new facts to be found in these chapters; the ground has been well covered before and the contemporary and near-contemporary accounts of each battle carefully sifted and narrated. My object has been to retell them in a straightforward and I hope easily understandable manner, and wherever the facts are open to more than one interpretation, or the exact site of any battle cannot be certainly determined, I have tried to piece together the mosaic of these long-forgotten fights in a way that may stimulate the reader to further personal investigation. I have also avoided the temptation to forecast the possible outcome of any battle had the losing side been the victors; it is a fascinating, but usually fruitless, undertaking for which—perhaps fortunately—there was no space.

It only remains for me to offer my thanks to those who have helped me with advice, encouragement, hospitality and, in some cases, hard work in the preparation of this book. It is not possible to mention all of these kind people individually, but to some I owe a special debt of gratitude. First to my secretary, Miss M. H. L. Taylor, who has not only typed and re-typed the manuscript many times, but has undertaken part of the research and made many useful suggestions. Lt. Colonel W. F. N. Watson has embellished the book with his superb illustrations, helped me in the annotation of the photographs and master-minded the weapons development table; the battle maps that he has drawn were based on the appropriate Ordnance Survey sheets, by permission of the Director of Ordnance Survey.

Many people have read through parts of the manuscript and given me the benefit of their advice, and of these I should particularly mention Mr Ivan Roe, Doctor David Cox, Mr G. C. Baugh, Mr Alan Young and Mr Michael Lynch. The staffs of the London Library and the Dorset County Library have taken enormous trouble to produce books and information.

During my visit to St Albans Miss Muriel Wilson and Miss Wells, of the City of St Albans Public Library, gave me great assistance. To all of these I am most grateful. Finally, I am indebted to William Armstrong of Sidgwick & Jackson for his patience, understanding and advice.

William Seymour
Falconer's House
Crichel
Wimborne
Dorset.

CHAPTER 1

Norsemen

Fulford and Stamford Bridge

20 September 1066 and 25 September 1066

Stamford Bridge is eight miles east of York on the A 166. In 1066 the actual bridge was some 400 yards upstream from the present one and about twenty yards below the modern cut in the river. Part of the site is now occupied by caravans, and on the left (or eastern) bank the ground rises fairly steeply to Danes Well garage. The main fight took place just south of the A 166 on what is now private property. The farm is called Battle Flats Farm.

King Edward the Confessor died on 5 January 1066, and almost immediately the Witan, or Great Council, elected Harold Godwinson, Earl of Wessex, to be their king. Harold ascended the throne uneasily: he had scarcely a drop of royal blood in his veins; the Earls of Mercia and Northumbria, Edwin and Morcar, had no love for him; and there were two foreign claimants to the throne who had been anxiously watching and waiting. Earls Edwin and Morcar, who were brothers, do not appear to have opposed Harold's election, but he had to make a journey north before Northumbria would give him her allegiance. By marrying the Earl's sister Aldyth Harold gained the acceptance of these powerful men and their thanes, but on account of the long enmity between his house and theirs he could never be entirely confident of their loyalty.

When the Anglo-Danish King Hardicanute died in 1042 the Danish male line came to an end, and Magnus King of Norway laid claim to the English and Danish thrones under an agreement made between him and Hardicanute. He invaded Denmark, and had he not died in 1047 would almost certainly have attempted to wrest the English crown by force from Edward the Confessor. Magnus's successor, King Harald Hardrada, was a man in every way built upon a scale larger than the usual run; six feet six inches tall with a massive frame, he was reckoned the greatest captain of his day; he had pursued glory and risked every hazard from his own shores to the gates of Constantinople. In 1066 this fearsome Norseman was ready to revive Magnus's claim to the English throne. The fact that

9

that claim was flimsy in the extreme mattered little, for he saw the possibility of England once more entering upon a period of profound decline, such as had many times before opened the floodgates to a Viking invasion. He was confident that as in the past the islanders would be unable to withstand the foray.

Duke William of Normandy's claim to the English throne had slightly more substance than Hardrada's. Through his great-aunt Emma, who married first the disastrous Ethelred the Redeless and then the truly splendid Canute, he was first cousin once removed to Edward the Confessor. There is also good reason to believe that Edward, who had spent some years in exile in Normandy and was very pro-Norman, had, as long ago as 1051, promised William the succession – although he had no right to promise the crown of England to anyone. Moreover, quite recently, when Harold had been shipwrecked on the French coast, William had rescued him from the unscrupulous clutches of the Count of Ponthieu who held him captive, and, after treating him with the utmost respect and favour as an honoured guest and comrade in arms, had induced him to swear an oath that he would not oppose William's accession to the English throne. In those days an oath was a much more binding affair than it later became, and for good measure William concealed some holy relics beneath the cloth covering the table when William's half-brother, Bishop Odo of Bayeux, administered the oath.

This artifice was to strengthen William's cause in Rome, for, the sanctity of the oath apart, Harold was already at a grave disadvantage with the papacy. Ever since Robert of Jumièges had been unlawfully replaced in the see of Canterbury by Archbishop Stigand, the Roman curia had regarded the church in England with considerable displeasure if not hostility. Furthermore, the new pope, Alexander II, had been elected with Norman support, and so William had little difficulty in ensuring that when he marched he did so with the Holy Father's blessing and under the papal banner.

So much then for the two iron-willed foreign princes who were making ready with ruthless determination to fight for England. What of the Saxon earl, recently elected king, who was preparing to defend his kingdom against this two-pronged threat?

In the time of Edward the Confessor there were three great earldoms, Wessex, Mercia and Northumbria. Godwin Earl of Wessex had risen to prominence through the favour of Canute, whose cousin he had married, and during Edward's reign he became the most powerful man in the land – not excluding the king who under pressure had married his daughter. Godwin's eldest son Sweyn, an unpleasant man, died on a pilgrimage to the Holy

Coins: 1: Edward the Confessor, 2: Harold II, 3: William I, at the British Museum. Below: Canute and Edmund Ironside in equal combat, from Chronica Majora I by Matthew Paris, at Corpus Christi College, Cambridge

Land, and so when the Earl died in 1053 he was succeeded in the earldom by his second son Harold – a golden youth of much promise and in high favour with the King.

Edward the Confessor was a good and pious man, but a weak, vacillating king; he would have been better suited to a monastery than a palace. Shortly after promising the throne to William he was forced to dismiss many of the Norman faction from his court, and in 1054 he seems to have had a change of heart. He sent for Edmund Ironside's son, Edward the Atheling, who had been in exile in Hungary and had married the King of Hungary's daughter. Edward arrived in England, but died before he reached the court – some said in mysterious circumstances – leaving a young boy, his son Edgar, as the only surviving member of the ancient royal house. Earl Harold was the most powerful man at court, and probably persuaded the dying King Edward to promise him the crown. In any event the Witan was not prepared to entrust the kingdom at this time to a boy, and Harold met with little opposition. He was certainly the best man England could have found. Nevertheless, it was a coup d'état; he had seized the throne with speed and resolution not only from the two foreigners who thought it belonged to them but also from the legitimate royal line of England. This was an added burden amongst the immense difficulties and pressures that beset the newly elected warrior king.

Harold's troublesome younger brother Tostig had been banished from the earldom of Northumbria, and it was he who opened the fight against Harold. He had taken refuge with his wife's half-brother, Count Baldwin of Flanders (whose daughter Matilda married William), and in May 1066 he set sail from the French coast, certainly with William's blessing if not with Norman aid. His attempt at invasion was a hopeless failure: having raided the Isle of Wight and briefly occupied Sandwich, his force was cut to pieces in Lincolnshire by Edwin of Mercia and he sailed on with his few remaining ships to join the King of Scotland, and from Scotland he promptly got in touch with Harald Hardrada.

Harold did not need his brother's traitorous actions to realize that he would soon be called upon to face sterner opposition; but he realized the vulnerability of the southern coast and accordingly moved down to the Isle of Wight to supervise defence preparations. He was not unaware of Harald Hardrada's ambitions, but he may have thought that the threat from Normandy was greater, or perhaps more imminent; he therefore mustered all his ships and concentrated his military strength in the south. Harold's corps d'élite were known as house-carls; they were of Danish origin, having been raised by Canute as a royal bodyguard. Armed principally with shields and long double-handed battle-axes they were perhaps the finest infantry in Europe at that time; they were in fact mounted infantry capable of covering great distances quickly on their shaggy ponies, but they invariably dismounted to fight.

The house-carls were the kernel of Harold's army, but they were a comparatively small force of around 3,000 men, and for weight of numbers he depended on the fyrd. This was a levy of free men raised from each hundred* and liable to serve for a period of two months annually. During that time they were paid and provisioned by the shires, but if their period of service had to be extended (and this was seldom practicable) they became a charge on the state. It was possible to assemble about 12,000 of these irregulars at any one time, and although they are sometimes described as nothing better than an ill disciplined rabble this is not true. Certainly they carried a curious assortment of weapons, ranging from spears, axes, stone slings and javelins to scythes and even pitchforks, but many of them were well led by their thanes and capable of giving an excellent account of themselves. A part of this force could be transported on ponies. The English army was without cavalry, and virtually without archers.

Harold must have called out the southern fyrd immediately after Tostig's attempted invasion, and retained them and his fleet under arms for most of the summer; but by the first week in September their rations and pay were running out and being mostly subsistence farmers they were sorely needed on their own holdings. And so on about 8 September Harold was forced to disband his levies and sail his fleet back to London. It was an unavoidable but desperate situation, for he knew very well that William was by now ready and only awaiting a favourable wind.

However, the first camp fires of an invading army were to be seen not in the south, as Harold had expected, but in Yorkshire. The King had not been back in his capital more than a few days when he learned that Harald Hardrada and the egregious Tostig had sailed up the Ouse and disembarked at Riccall. Harald Hardrada, taking advantage of the north wind that had kept William in harbour, had sailed via the Orkneys – then a part of the Norseman's dominion – where his liegemen the Orkney earls had ships and men to join him. Tostig may have sailed with Hardrada from Norway, or more likely met him at some point off the Northumbrian coast,

*At this time the English shire was divided into districts known as hundreds (varying in size) for fiscal and administrative purposes.

and together they proceeded south sacking Scarborough and penetrating Yorkshire from the mouth of the Humber. Accounts vary as to the numbers of the combined fleet, but certainly no fewer than 200 longships sailed up the Ouse. These open boats, averaging about seventy-five feet in length and seventeen feet in beam, were rowed by thirty men. They could sail far up rivers on account of their shallow draught, and their usual complement was around sixty men. It seems reasonable to suppose, therefore, that this armada brought rather more than 10,000 fighting Norsemen to plunder and pillage the northern part of the kingdom. Even with William only waiting for a wind, Harold could scarcely afford to disregard so formidable a host.

Northumbria and Mercia between them comprised the whole of the north and Midlands; their earls, Morcar and Edwin respectively, were able to command a very considerable force. They had prudently anchored their small fleet at Tadcaster, which probably determined the Norsemen to disembark at Riccall: if they had sailed beyond the junction of the rivers Ouse and Wharfe the English fleet might have been able to come between them and the sea. Leaving perhaps as much as a third of his men with the longships, Harald Hardrada advanced on York, some ten miles to the north. This is a part of Yorkshire that is very flat, and although the

Norse longships

fields are now well drained and neatly cultivated 900 years ago this whole area was wet and swampy, even after a dry summer. There was also at this time a large water-filled ditch to the east of the road.

The Earls could not have known whether Harold would march to their aid; indeed, they may have considered this unlikely in view of the Norman threat. They decided not to wait behind the inadequate defences of York, and on 20 September they advanced and gave battle. The two armies met at Fulford, now a suburb of York but then an open and very wet field. The battle, which lasted for most of the day, was a hard slogging match. At first the English gained considerable success on their left flank, but Harald Hard-rada was an experienced commander quite capable of delivering a decisive blow at the right moment. When the English army in the centre and left were most hotly engaged he swung his left away from the river and before long had rolled his enemy into the ditch, slaughtering many and drowning even more. The Earls' army was cut to pieces, and the conqueror's standard, the famous *Land-waster*, fluttered triumphant over a field strewn with the bodies of fighting men that England could ill afford to lose.

Fulford is often dismissed as a minor affair, but it was a battle of great importance. Had Harold been able to communicate with the Earls in time, and instruct them to remain upon the defensive until he could arrive, this large northern army would not have been decimated and the combined force available to oppose William might quite likely have thrust the Norman invasion back into the sea. Neither Edwin nor Morcar took any part in the Battle of Hastings, and there is no evidence that this was for any reason other than that they could not assemble fresh levies and reach the rendezvous in time.

For some reason, perhaps because Tostig wished to preserve the city, the victorious Norsemen did not march on York. Instead they fell back on their ships and entered into negotiations with the vanquished for the surrender of the city and delivery of hostages. We do not know for certain what occurred, but it seems that the people of York, and even the Earls, may have agreed to terms that were both humiliating and treacherous. No satisfactory reason has been put forward for the selection of the site for the reception of the hostages. Stamford Bridge is eight miles east of York and all of twelve miles from the Norsemen's base camp at Riccall; it is a place where four Roman roads met at a crossing of the Derwent, and one of these led direct to the coast. The royal palace of Aldby was nearby, which may have appealed to Tostig, but the choice of venue cannot be explained on these grounds.

Additional supplies of food, negotiations for the hostages and the movement of the main army from Riccall to Stamford Bridge would have occupied a little time, and it is unlikely that the Norsemen would have arrived on the Derwent before 24 September. The next day they must have received an unpleasant shock. Incredibly, as they were relaxing in the meadows, they suddenly saw, a mile or so to the west, the glint of sunshine off many helmets, and as they looked more closely through the clearing dust the standard of Wessex and the banner of the Fighting Man (see p. 29) told them that Harold of England was upon them. The King had been faced with an agonizing decision, but he did not hesitate and, with the same rapidity of movement with which a few years earlier he had broken the power of the Welsh prince Griffith ap Llywelyn, he raced his house-carls up the straight Roman road – long since grassed over – to the north, calling out the shire levies as he went. The men of England responded to their king's valour and vigour, and by the time he reached Tadcaster on 24 September his army must have been quite considerable, and may have been further enlarged by some of the survivors of Fulford.

In the space of four days Harold and his army had covered 180 miles: it was one of the great marches of history. We can be fairly sure that the night of 24 September was spent in Tadcaster. The men and ponies must have been incredibly weary, and Harold himself had risen from his sick-bed only a few days earlier, but before dawn they were under way again and into York. Here Harold may have intended to pause a while to allow his troops time to regain their strength, but hearing that the enemy were only eight miles off and blissfully unaware of their peril he ordered the march to continue. We may imagine that there was much grumbling, and it is a measure of the greatness of the man, and the excellence of his troops, that he was able to infuse such discipline into a rapidly assembled and ill assorted force as to bring them to the point of battle in such a condition that they were able to defeat an army reckoned by many to be the best in Europe, and led by a legendary, unconquerable giant.

The allied army – for such it must be called, as it consisted of Norwegians, Flemings, Scots and even some English – was caught completely unprepared for battle. The two leaders, King Harald Hardrada and Earl Tostig, probably thought the English king was fully occupied in the south, and certainly unable to be anywhere near York. It is true that Hardrada, as a normal routine measure, had outposts on the west bank of the river Derwent, but the main body of troops were taking their ease on the east bank in the fields around the present site of Danes Well garage and Battle Flats Farm. So warm was the weather and so unsuspecting were these warriors that many had discarded their mail tunics. A mile to the west of Stamford Bridge the ground rises at a village called Gate Helmsley and Harold's army could not have been visible to the enemy outposts until they had topped the ridge, so there could not have been much time to organize the defence. The outposts were ordered to stand firm on the west bank for at least sufficient time to allow the main body to don their mail and take up the best position available, and a messenger was urgently despatched to Eyestein Orre, commanding the troops at Riccall, to march with all speed to the battle.

The ground slopes fairly gently to the river, and those few Norsemen fighting with their backs to the water were in an unenviable position. Nowadays the banks are not steep at this place (although they are just below the present bridge), but it is fairly safe to assume that they were before the river course was altered, and there is no doubt that only strong swimmers lightly equipped could have escaped other than by the narrow wooden bridge. Tired though they must have been the house-carls and fyrd men showed few signs of it during the battle, and the sheer weight of their attack was altogether too much for the small body of men holding the river; they were swept aside like autumn leaves, and many who were not killed by Saxon weapons perished in the Derwent.

However, one Viking hero, unknown in name but glorious in repute, held the bridge alone, steadfast in the face of every Saxon assault. He stood at the west end of the bridge taunting the house-carls to hazard themselves and match his skill; and as they fell beneath his powerfully plied axe his comrades on the east bank raised a mighty cheer. For a little while this great berserk held the bridge, and many a Saxon body was despatched downstream by his bloodstained axe, but the end came quite suddenly, and rather ingloriously. A short way upstream a house-carl found a swill-tub which he managed to paddle, under cover of overhanging willows, to beneath the bridge. Here he was able to manoeuvre his craft to immediately below the spot where the Viking stood, and through one of the chinks in the planks of the bridge he thrust his spear into a particularly vital and unprotected part of the Norseman's body. With a piercing scream the Norseman fell, and the Saxon army was soon across the bridge.*

*The *Heimskringla Saga* of Snorri Sturluson (an unreliable guide for the actual battle) curiously makes no mention of this magnificent feat of one of its own compatriots; but English chroniclers, who do mention it, are unlikely to have invented an enemy hero.

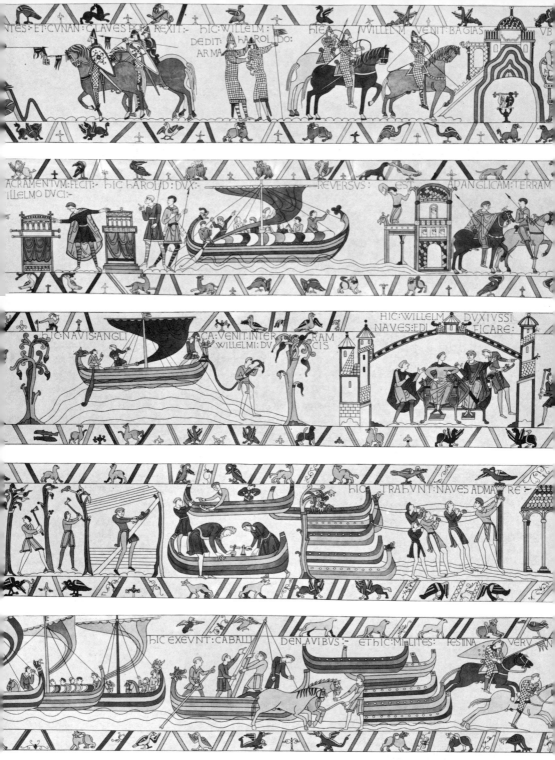

Left to right: Row 1: Harold knighted by William, William arrives at Bayeux. 2: Harold's oath before William, Harold returns to England and arrives at Westminster. 3: An English ship goes to Normandy, William holds a council. 4: Trees felled to build ships, the fleet built and dragged to the sea. 5: Fleet nears England, horses landed at Pevensey, invaders gallop to Hastings

Unlike the Battle of Hastings, about which we know quite a lot, thanks to the Bayeux Tapestry and certain French chroniclers, accurate details of the fight at Stamford Bridge, if they were ever written down, have not survived the centuries. We know that the Vikings in defence adopted the shield wall, a formation later to be used, with certain modifications, by the Saxon army at Hastings. The allied commanders probably had their men drawn up shoulder to shoulder in the shape of a hollow triangle with its apex presenting a comparatively narrow front. Once across the river and formed up the English would have had but one objective, to smash the shield wall, for there could be no retreat except into the dark and swirling waters of the Derwent.

At some time during the day – it may have been before the fight began, or more probably not until the river had been crossed – we are told that Harold offered his brother peace and the restitution of his earldom if he and his men would return to their allegiance; but rascal though Tostig was it is to his credit that he had sufficient honour not to turn traitor twice.

As to how well matched for numbers the two armies were we cannot tell. Probably the English had the advantage initially because the day was far gone before Eyestein Orre and the Riccall contingent joined the fight. It was to be a trial of strength between the house-carls and the Vikings, each vying with the other for

Battle of Stamford Bridge

pride of place as Europe's foremost infantrymen. Both knew that the clash would be savage and the slaughter great.

The Saxon army could not have arrived at the Derwent much before 11 a.m., and it would have been well past midday before the first assault against the shield wall. Those accounts, therefore, that say the fighting lasted until dusk are very probably right, because the Norsemen stood their ground magnificently, and only inch by inch could the Saxon axes, slings and javelins perform their remorseless task. As men fell others took their places, and every time a wedge was made it was quickly closed. But when the day was nearly over the Norwegian king, a heroic figure who had dominated the battle, was felled by a well aimed English missile. Earl Tostig tried to rally what was left of the polyglot army, but those were the days when the loss of their king struck a chill into the hearts of soldiers who so long as he lived would bravely withstand the most murderous onslaughts. The shield wall began to crumble, and the men from Riccall found they had arrived only to die. Soon Tostig and Eyestein Orre had joined the fallen, and there was no one left to rally the survivors round the *Landwaster*.

Briefly, and for the last time in history, that proud raven surveyed the carnage of a British battlefield; and then the dreaded emblem was trodden underfoot as the Norsemen fled the field, pursued all the way to Riccall by the utterly exhausted but triumphant Saxons. In victory Harold proved magnanimous; he allowed Harald Hardrada's young son Olaf and the equally young Orkney earls who had remained with the longships throughout to leave without ransom – but under oath not to invade England again. The defeated enemy required only twenty-four ships in which to return to their homes. As they sailed away down the Ouse it was the end of an era, for they were the remnants of the last Scandinavian army ever to harass the shores of England. Harold, never a vindictive man, buried his brother in York, which is where he would have wished to lie. The bones of King Harald Hardrada may still rest beneath Battle Flats Farm, for his namesake kept the promise he is said to have made, that all he would get was seven foot of English soil.

It was a decisive victory, but not won without cost. The housecarls and the levies had been sadly depleted. Harold retired on York, but although the fickle inhabitants of that city greeted him as a conquering hero the King's mind was sombre. He knew that an even sterner task lay ahead, and that somehow he must fill his thinning ranks and once again be prepared to stake his crown, his reputation, and indeed his very life upon the terrible hazards of war.

20

CHAPTER 2

Normans

Hastings

14 October 1066

The site of some of the fiercest fighting in the Battle of Hastings is in the grounds of Battle Abbey and Battle Abbey Park, which lie just to the south of the town of Battle on the A 2100 road to Hastings. Battle is some six miles north-west of Hastings and sixty miles from the centre of London. Most of the battle took place on what is now private property, but every point of importance can be viewed from the public grounds of Battle Abbey, or from the roads and public footpaths surrounding the area.

Points of interest outside the grounds of Battle Abbey are the primary school, which was approximately the left of the Saxon line, and from where the visitor can appreciate the steepness of the neck of land on its east side; the hedge bordering Powdermill Lane from where the site of the fighting round the hillock is best seen; the grounds of Glengorse School (if permission can be obtained) from where the Senlac position first became visible to William; and the windmill on Caldbec Hill, which offers the best viewpoint for Harold's approach march and the line of pursuit after the battle.

Duke William of Normandy was about to set out on a day's hunting in his park at Quevilly, near Rouen, when a messenger from England arrived to tell him that Edward the Confessor was dead and that Harold had been proclaimed King of England by the Witan. William was exceedingly angry, and for some time only William FitzOsbern, perhaps his closest friend, dared reason with him. The Duke was a fiery man not likely to be serene in disappointment, but once his anger had cooled he was capable of comprehensive judgment. He knew that if he was to get the English throne he would almost certainly have to fight for it, but though his prime bent was military he was also something of a diplomat, and he was well aware that his case as well as his army would need strengthening before the venture could take place. Messages were therefore exchanged between William and Harold, in which the Norman reminded the English king of his oath and called upon him to honour it. Predictably Harold refused; William made ready for war.

At a meeting of his innermost council William received much encouragement, but when the larger gathering of his barons was assembled at Lillebonne and asked to ratify the inner council's resolve that William should right the wrong done to him by Harold through force of arms, he met with considerable opposition. For a time it looked as though the necessary support would not be forthcoming, but once again it was William FitzOsbern who gave the lead. As the barons' elected spokesman he compromised them to such an extent that it was difficult for any of them to avoid the commitment, and their loyal support was finally achieved through the personal approach of William to each of them individually with words of high resolve, reward and reassurance. Soon news spread throughout western Europe that William of Normandy was about to undertake a holy mission against England blessed by the Pope, and that in the event of success those who offered their services would be assured of rich rewards. Volunteers flocked to Normandy from all parts of France and even Italy.

The system of military service in Normandy was entirely different from that prevailing in Saxon England; the Norman army was a feudal army. Each baron, or bishop, held his land on the understanding that he raised and equipped a prescribed number of mounted knights for the ducal service, and on this occasion William and his friend FitzOsbern had prevailed upon the barons to bring twice the number of men prescribed for their particular holdings, and to assist with materials and money for the building of the fleet. Most of the men now being conscripted by their feudal overlords would fight as infantry, for problems of transport would restrict the number of horses that could be brought across the Channel. The mounted knights probably did not exceed 2,000.

Although this was before the days of armour for horses the knights themselves wore long coats of mail slit at the bottom to fall over the saddle, cone-shaped helmets fitted with nose-pieces, and neck-guards of fine mail which were usually attached to the hauberk. Their weapon was a lance or sword – occasionally a mace – and they carried kite-shaped shields. The infantrymen wore leather hauberks covered with flat iron rings and quilted; their helmets were similar to those of the knights and their stockinged legs were bound with leather thongs. They carried shields large enough to protect most of the body and fought with swords, spears or short axes. The archers wore no mail, and their headgear was a cap; they used the short bow which had a maximum range of 150 yards.

The question that has never been satisfactorily answered is how large was the force that William transported across the Channel. Some of the chroniclers mention the staggering figure of 50–60,000, but most modern writers consider this to be a gross exaggeration.* There is not space to discuss the various known factors that have to be considered when trying to arrive at a reasonably accurate figure for the total force, but it seems most likely that it would have been around 8,000 and certainly not more than 10,000. While this host was being assembled on the hills above the small town of Dives, the ring of the woodcutter's axe could be heard throughout the surrounding forests, for there was no Norman fleet of any consequence and most of the transports (open single-masted boats) had to be hewn from the round log and put together in an incredibly short time. It is unlikely that these small craft could have held more than twenty men, so William would have needed about 1,000 to carry the army and necessary non-combatants, 2,000 or so horses and a certain quantity of provisions and war materials.

All through the summer the work proceeded, and gradually the small harbour at the mouth of the river Dives filled up with newly made craft. By August sufficient ships had been assembled. Throughout this long period of waiting only William's iron discipline and inspired leadership had kept his large army from deserting or looting. Harold, as we have seen, was unable to keep his men together, and when at the beginning of September news reached William that the fyrd had been disbanded he sailed his fleet – not without loss – to St Valery, at the mouth of the Somme, where he would get fresh provisions and have a shorter voyage to the now unguarded south coast of England. Here then at St Valery the destiny of two men – and indeed of two peoples – waited upon the veering of the wind.

At last, on 27 September, two days after Harold's victory at Stamford Bridge (see pp. 16-20), the wind moved into the south. Embarkation lasted for most of the day and towards evening William, in the *Mora*, a ship presented to him by his wife, led the fleet out of harbour. On the morning of the 28th the invaders were off Beachy Head and William steered for the old Roman castle at Pevensey, whose landlocked harbour has long since been reclaimed from the sea. Here the army disembarked completely unopposed, and on the next day William removed both men and ships to Hastings. At that time Hastings, situated on a narrow peninsula and protected by the Brede and Bulverhythe estuaries, was an ideal

*However, Piers Compton in his *Harold the King* supports the high figure of the early chroniclers.

place for a covering action in the event of a withdrawal on the fleet becoming necessary; it also had an excellent harbour. The road to London was barred by no soldiers, but William dared not move too far from his base. Instead he erected a wooden fortress with materials brought over for the purpose, and waited – with increasing uneasiness – upon events.

It is usually accepted that Harold received news of William's landing while at a banquet in York on the evening of 1 October; only Guy of Amiens states that the news reached him while on the march south, but this account may well be correct. Even allowing for the fact that there were problems requiring attention in the north and that the soldiers badly needed a rest, it would have been a grave dereliction of duty on the part of the English king – and a most uncharacteristic action – had he dallied in York for four whole days after he must have known that at last William had got the wind he wanted. He returned as he had come, down Ermine Street, and may himself have ridden ahead of his army, for there was much to be done: fresh levies had to be hastily assembled, and either on his way to London, or while there, we know that he paid a visit to Waltham. Here, in the beautiful abbey that he had founded, and which was dedicated to the Holy Cross that worked such miracles and had become the battle-cry of the Saxon army, the attendant monks echoed the prayers of a suppliant monarch.

By the time Harold reached London, if not before, he would have learned of the devastation of the countryside around Hastings. William deliberately set his men to scourge and pillage and burn. He knew Harold's impetuous nature, and guessed rightly that the proud dynamism of the English king would never allow him to play a waiting game while part of his kingdom was burning. It would have been better had Harold done so, for the further William marched from his ships (and he certainly couldn't play a waiting game) the greater became his perils and his problems; while Harold needed time for the fresh levies to rally and the valiant veterans of Stamford Bridge to recover from the rigours of their forced march. While the King was in London his brother Gyrth tried to persuade him not to march against William, but to leave the fighting to him and his other brother Leofwine, who were bound by no oath; but Harold, conscious of his kingship and aware of the magical aura of the crown, would not hear of it. Besides, he looked upon a fight with zest and thrill.

We do not know for certain the day that Harold left London, nor the number of troops that marched with him. It seems most likely that he delayed his departure until 12 October, and there may

Bayeux Tapestry: Harold is shown to the people after his coronation at Westminster

W·F·N·WATSON·

Above: The Fyrd 1066. Saxon armies usually fought on foot but house-carls and many of the fyrd rode on ponies.
Below: Norman knights 1066

W·F·N·WATSON

have been no more than 5,000 men with him, for some contingents would have met him en route and others would have been ordered to march direct to the appointed rendezvous. Harold was marching into his home county and would be fighting on ground he knew well. We know that the selected rendezvous was a hoar apple tree and that it stood just beyond the southern boundary of that massive forest called the Andredsweald. Such trees were often prominent land and boundary marks; this one may have been situated on Caldbec Hill (three-quarters of a mile north of Battle), then the junction of two or three local roads, or it may have been on the actual ridge where Harold took up his defensive position. It is yet another detail of which we cannot be sure, but in either case the distance from London was some sixty miles.

Harold would have reached the rendezvous on the evening of the 13th, and much of his army, well strung out and utterly exhausted from trudging miles over rough and rutted tracks, would trickle in throughout the night, finding their way by the light of a waning moon – it was twenty-two days old. There would be no roistering; instead, as each party arrived they would throw themselves upon the dew-soaked ground and, with the stolid indifference of the soldier to what the morrow might bring, quickly fall asleep.

The writings of French chroniclers are almost our only window on this long forgotten past, and they are an unreliable guide to any interpretation of Harold's intentions. There has been much argument over the years as to whether Harold always intended to fight a defensive battle, or whether this was forced upon him by the rapid advance of the Norman army from its base camp at Hastings. The present writer is of the opinion that the English king, with foreknowledge of the ground, said to himself, 'This is the place where I shall defeat the French.' A purely defensive battle hardly fits with what we know of Harold's character, and his previous campaigns had been the embodiment of the offensive spirit. But if occasionally hasty in judgement he was a competent and experienced general. At Hastings Harold was facing for the first time in England a body of determined and well armed cavalry; he had had the opportunity of seeing cavalry in operation while campaigning with Duke William a short while back, and he must have realized that before he could achieve a decisive victory he would have to blunt the cavalry weapon. What better way of doing this than to invite them to attack a difficult position, and at the appropriate time to counter-attack with part or all of his force and roll back a tired and dispirited enemy.

That Harold intended to go over to the offensive, and was confident of victory, is borne out by the fact that he ordered what few ships could be manned in time to leave London and sail round the North Foreland to ensure that William's fleet, now beached under the protection of Hastings Castle, would not put to sea without a fight. But first there would have to be a battle of attrition. The alternative would have been to catch the Normans off balance, as he had done the Norsemen, but here there could have been little hope of surprise and he might well have given William the chance to make use of ground of his own choosing and more suitable for his cavalry.

A general faced with the necessity of taking up a strong defensive position could not have selected a better site than that chosen by Harold. From Caldbec Hill there runs a narrow neck of land (now largely occupied by Battle High Street) and from this isthmus the ground drops away steeply on both sides – particularly to the east. At the point where this narrow ridge begins to dip into the marshy area, called in medieval days Sandlake, or Santlache, and known to history as Senlac through the French pronunciation of 'Sand-lake', there is a fairly level cross ridge stretching for approximately half a mile east and west. The slopes down from this Senlac ridge were not nearly so steep as those from the neck of land connecting it with Caldbec Hill – indeed the slope at the west end is only one in thirty-three* – but troops attacking the centre and east end of the ridge would be severely handicapped by the climb. On the other side of the slightly undulating valley the ground rises gradually to Telham Hill, the summit of which is a mile from the Senlac ridge and nearly 200 feet higher. The ground between these two high points, especially that on the west, must have been very wet and marshy even in October, for it was intersected by a number of streams – one of them now dammed to make a chain of fishponds – and by the Asten brook. The southern slopes of the Senlac position may have been cultivated, but it is more likely that the whole ridge was rough, open ground covered by gorse, bracken and bramble. The Bayeux Tapestry depicts a few trees, as was to be expected in a well timbered area.

In addition to its being a natural defensive position, across the ridge and the land behind it there ran not actually the Roman road but the ancient trackway from the coast which eventually joined the Lewes–London Roman road; Harold, therefore, effectively barred William's direct advance upon London. Even if the rendez-vous, as seems likely, was a little way back at Caldbec Hill, Harold

*C. H. Lemmon, *The Field of Hastings*, p.37.

would have been on the Senlac ridge soon after first light (approximately 5.30 a.m.) and here he would have received word of William's advance. The *Anglo-Saxon Chronicle*, although of no assistance with the battle, assures us that Harold was taken by surprise, and it seems, therefore, that he would have had little time to erect any effective defence works. We can be fairly certain that reinforcements for the English army would continue to come in at any rate during the early hours of the battle, so the line when first drawn up may have been comparatively thin. Almost all accounts agree as to the site of Harold's command post and the fact that the English fought in a very dense formation. The flanks may have been extended as the levies came in, but more likely these were sent to strengthen the existing front.

The Saxon left extended to the area of the present primary school, and the line cut diagonally across the east-west abbey ruin with the right flank close to the wire fence now dividing the abbey grounds from the park. It was thus a little over 600 yards long and although at an angle to the present Hastings road was almost square to the ancient trackway which left the metal road at the abbey lodge gates and continued straight up the hill to the spot near the Norman stone where Harold had his headquarters. Here, close-guarded by devoted house-carls, stood the standard of Wessex – a golden dragon on a red or purple background, which was certainly carried by Edmund Ironside at the Battle of Assingdon in 1016, and was probably the royal standard of all Alfred's line. Harold had a personal banner that was also carried in battle, and known as the Fighting Man. Legend had it that it had been woven by his mother Gytha, and that the helmet, mail and weapons were sewn with sparkling gems. Harold himself chose the design and it is not impossible that the Cerne giant, or the larger figure of a fighting man on the Sussex downs above Wilmington, both of which are probably pre-Saxon, inspired his choice.

The most reliable accounts of the battle are those written by William of Poitiers and William of Jumièges; both were living at the time and wrote their story in the early 1070s. William of Poitiers, who was chaplain to Duke William, was not present at the battle but in earlier life he had been a soldier, and although he, like most of the other earlier writers, greatly exaggerated the numbers of soldiers taking part on both sides, his account of the fighting is, together with the Bayeux Tapestry, our best guide to the battle.

We know from these sources that in the first phase of the battle the Norman infantry were overwhelmed by the weight of missiles hurled at them by the Saxons. Now most authorities place the house-carls in the forefront of the Saxon line, but it was the fyrd who were armed with missiles and javelins. Even if the house-carls were placed slightly lower down the slope these tall hand-picked men would have felt distinctly uneasy at having to stand with their backs to a bunch of over-excited shire levies hurling stones and javelins just above their heads. It seems reasonable to assume, therefore, that some of the levies were placed in front of the house-carls with orders to withdraw through the ranks after they had discharged their missiles – in the early stages their place may even have been taken by a second line of 'slingers'.

Thus by nine in the morning the English army was drawn up on this famous ridge under command of its king, who had with him his two able and courageous brothers. But what of the Normans? William had staked everything on being able to put all to the test in an early battle, and it must have been with considerable relief that he learned on 13 October that his formidable adversary was about to oblige him. The Norman leader had been agitated, morose and unsure of himself in the days since the landing at Pevensey, but now we see him with all doubts and fears vanished and in their place determination and resolution. He gave orders for the army to be ready to leave the Hastings camp at dawn the next day – Saturday 14 October.

The head of the column (which stretched for about three miles) would have been on the march by 5.30 a.m., and we are told that William himself had reached Telham Hill by the time news was brought to him of the Saxon position. Telham Hill was some six miles from the Norman camp and the rear of the column could scarcely have reached it much before 8.30. While the army closed up and prepared for battle the Duke would have ridden forward to the point, now occupied by Glengorse School, from where the Senlac position first became visible, and decided upon his plan of attack. Nevertheless, the army still had to descend into the valley and deploy across difficult ground before battle could begin. It is generally stated that the first Norman assault went in at nine o'clock, but it is difficult to see how a long column could form line in less than an hour, so it would appear doutbful that any attack could have been made before 9.30 at the earliest.

The Norman army, which may have numbered very slightly less than Harold's when his was fully assembled, was to attack in line on a three-division front. The right was given to the Franco-Flemish mercenary contingent under the command of Roger of Montgomery, with Robert of Beaumont, William FitzOsbern and Eustace of Boulogne. Their section of the Saxon line lay in the area

House-carl. The blade of his axe was as much as a foot across, with a 5-foot helve. It was held in a left-handed grip to strike a foe's unshielded right side

WFN WATSON

now covered by the Chequers Hotel and the primary school. On the left were the Bretons and men from Maine and Poitou who were commanded by Alan of Britanny. Originally their left probably rested on the small hillock* which was to be the scene of much heavy fighting, but during the battle they appear to have extended their line to the west somewhat in order to allow more room for the Norman centre, which was larger than both the two wings put together, and perhaps to enable them to deliver a flank attack. The Bretons had the easiest part of the slope up which to attack, but the wettest part of the field on which to deploy and manoeuvre. The Norman centre was under the personal command of William, who rode into battle carrying a mace, and from his neck hung some of the relics upon which Harold had sworn his famous oath. He was supported by his two half-brothers, Robert of Mortain and Odo Bishop of Bayeux, and they were faced with a fairly steep ascent to the centre of the Saxon line, now a part of Battle Abbey garden. Each division was drawn up in three echelons: archers, heavy infantry and cavalry.

The battle lasted all day, and we can safely assume that there were certain definite pauses – possibly between each of the distinct phases into which the battle fell – for no troops wearing chain mail and attacking uphill could keep up a sustained effort over a period of almost nine hours. William opened the fight with his archers. These troops made little impression on the Saxon phalanx, and when they came in range proved very vulnerable to the shower of well aimed missiles, which accounted for many of them. Moreover, as Harold was virtually without archers, the Normans were soon left with no arrows. This first phase in the battle could not have lasted much more than an hour.

It was now the turn of the infantry, and as is so often the case it was they who bore the brunt of the fighting throughout the day. The whole line advanced to the attack, and although they suffered grievously before they reached the English these were tough men, most of them schooled by many seasons of campaigning in their native lands. Their struggle with the house-carls was a bloody one and both sides fought bravely. The footsoldiers made a dent here and there, but the Saxons remained steadfast, shouting 'Out, out' and 'Holy Cross' as they laid about them with their huge axes. Thus the second phase.

The heavy infantry now fell back in a perfectly orderly manoeuvre to allow the cavalry, the corps d'élite of William's army, to

*Clearly recognizable from the hedge bordering the road called Powdermill Lane.

32

pass through into the attack, with the infantry keeping close behind ready to exploit the expected success. But the cavalry were at a disadvantage: the boggy ground on the left of the Norman line was by no means ideal for forming up, and in the centre and on the right they were faced almost immediately with a steep slope which greatly lessened the impetus of the attack. It was not possible for the unprotected horses to be ridden at any speed against the still intact Saxon line, and losses were suffered in the attack. But it was about now that a vitally important incident took place.

The Breton knights on the left may have been less courageous than their allies, or perhaps they faced opposition even fiercer than that which assailed the other cavalry. In any event they gave way, and in their retreat not only rolled back their own infantry, but by exposing the Norman left flank forced that division to retire precipitately. It was a crisis moment for both sides. Before the battle Harold had given strict instructions that on no account was any man to quit his position without orders; yet a number of men on the Saxon right charged down the slope after the fleeing Bretons. We must suspect that these were a body of ill disciplined shire levies who thought they had stood their ground long enough and could not resist the chance to chase and chastise the hated invader. But it is just possible that they left the Senlac ridge as part of a prepared counter-attack under the orders of Gyrth or Leofwine. Whatever the cause the result was the same. For a moment the whole Norman line was in confusion, and to make matters worse William was unhorsed and a shout went up that he was dead.

There are those ready to condemn Harold for not advancing his whole force at this critical moment, but at this distance of time we should not attempt to criticize a man who was undoubtedly a great general, and to whom the field of battle on that autumn day in 1066 must have appeared quite different from what it does to us who stroll around the pleasant abbey grounds 900 years later. At any rate the chance, if it ever was there, was fleeting: William rose to the occasion by removing his helmet so that all could see him, and exhorting his men to greater efforts. Not only that, but he immediately rallied the cavalry and swung them onto the now hopelessly vulnerable English. Much slaughter took place around the hillock and where the fishpond now is, and although the Norman cavalry floundered in the mud and many riders were unseated, not a single Englishman regained the Senlac ridge. But by the time all this had taken place Harold's army would have reached its full strength and he would have had men to fill the gap. William of Poitiers assures us that when the next Norman attack went in they

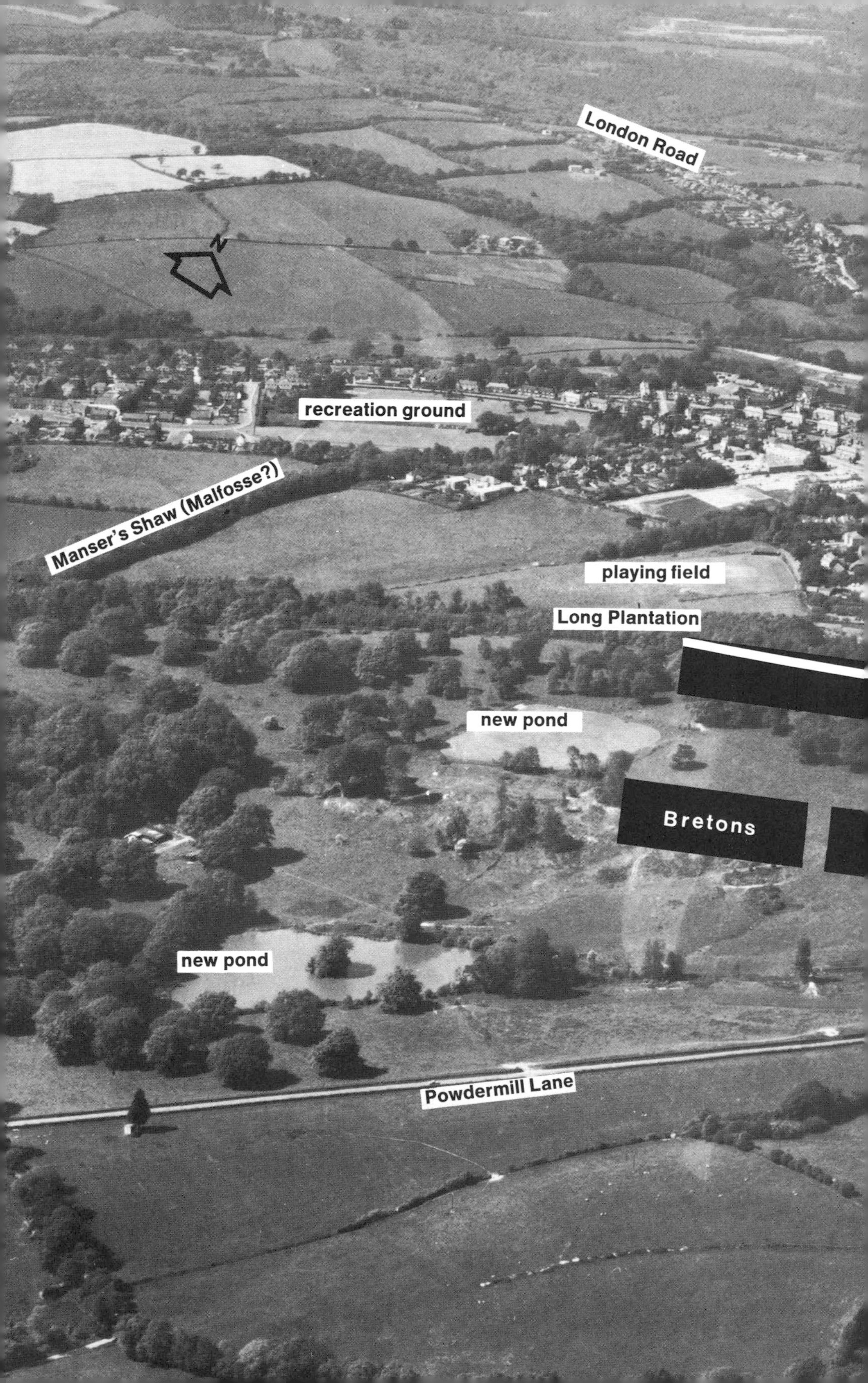

London Road

recreation ground

Manser's Shaw (Malfosse?)

playing field

Long Plantation

new pond

Bretons

new pond

Powdermill Lane

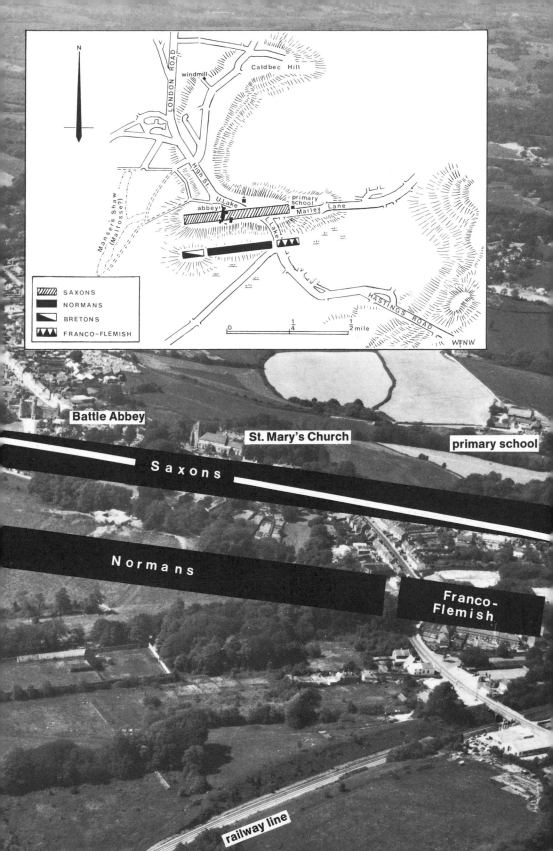

N

LONDON ROAD

windmill

Caldbec Hill

High St.

Manser's Shaw
(Malfosse?)

abbey

U.Lake

Lake

primary
school

Marley Lane

HASTINGS ROAD

SAXONS
NORMANS
BRETONS
FRANCO-FLEMISH

0   1/4   1/2 mile

WFNW

Battle Abbey

St. Mary's Church

primary school

S a x o n s

N o r m a n s

Franco-
Flemish

railway line

CECI ... DE ... RVNT QVIERAN

Pages 34–5: Town of Battle from south-east showing battle of Hastings. Inset shows modern town of Battle and estimated position of armies at 9.30 a.m.

found the Saxon line almost intact.

At this stage it is almost certain that there was a considerable pause in the fighting; both sides had taken a severe battering and there was much reorganizing and replenishing of weapons to be carried out. The day would have been more than half spent by the time William sent his knights once more into the breach. Again they could make little impression on the valiant house-carls, supported by the sturdy men from the shires, and again men and horses floundered in vain among the dead and dying. Undoubtedly they weakened the phalanx, but the greatest damage to the English was caused by a repetition of the Breton incident, this time on the French right. William of Poitiers says that there were two feigned retreats inspired by the excellent – albeit fortuitous – results of the Breton rout. He may be reporting correctly, for during the pauses in the battle there would have been an opportunity for William to coordinate such a manoeuvre. But it has to be remembered that a feigned retreat is a very difficult operation of war to control, and it can have dangerous consequences. It is more likely that the retreats were genuine, but that William, profiting from the first one, was quick to swing in reserve cavalry which, aided by a downhill charge, dealt swift destruction to the pursuing Saxons.

Somewhere around four o'clock in the afternoon the last, most crucial and bloodiest phase of the battle began. Time was running short, not much more than two hours of daylight remained, and Harold's army still stood rocklike upon the ridge, defiant and full

36

Above: Bayeux Tapestry: Harold is wounded by an arrow and his men slain

of fight. William risked all on this last attempt. Each of the three
arms were to combine in one final push. The archers were ordered
to increase the trajectory of their arrows, which might not cause
many casualties but would have the effect of raising the shield wall;
under cover of this fire what was left of the cavalry (some would
have been held in reserve) and the still numerous infantry were to
join with the enemy. Once more the house-carls fought valiantly
under an avalanche of iron and steel, but the solid phalanx of
Saxon soldiers had started to crack. The gaps made by those who
had left their posts and died on the slopes below could no longer be
filled; the Normans were able to gain a footing on the plateau, and
once upon level ground the few remaining knights, closely supported by the heavy infantry, began to drive wedges into troops now
assailed even from the sky.

The Bayeux Tapestry depicts Harold's brothers as being slain at
a comparatively early stage in the battle, while some chroniclers
say that they were still fighting in the last assault and that
William, by now always in the thick of the battle, actually slew
Gyrth himself. We do not know the hour of their death, but we can
be fairly certain that Harold died a little after sunset on that
memorable day. At a time when the chaos and confusion of the
close hand-to-hand fighting were at their height, and the Normans
were putting in all that they had to force an issue while there was
still light, the English king was seen to stagger and clutch an
arrow that had pierced his eye. As he leant upon his shield in fear-

37

ful agony, a body of four Norman knights charged home and cut him down before the house-carls could close around the standard and drive them back.

It was very nearly the end. The house-carls fought on devotedly as yard by yard the Normans strengthened their foothold upon the ridge. The English king and his equally brave brothers lay dead; the position could no longer be defended and the levies had had enough. They broke and fled, hoping that night and the great forest would cast a concealing cloak upon them. William let loose what cavalry he had kept in reserve. The light was almost gone and the country difficult to ride over with steep, treacherous slopes on either side of the neck of land over which the beaten English were hurrying. What exactly occurred will never be known – four chroniclers writing at various times in the hundred years after the battle give differing accounts – but somewhere between the Senlac ridge and the Andredsweald the last act in the tragedy was played out. It seems as though, in the failing light, a number of horsemen overrode a steep ravine, or covered ditch, and those who survived the tumble found themselves confronted by a party of retreating Saxons. In the ensuing mêlée some of the French were killed and Count Eustace of Boulogne was wounded. It was no more than a delaying action, for William soon got the pursuit under way again, but the French were sufficiently impressed by the magnitude of the disaster to call the place Malfosse.

William the Bastard, Duke of Normandy, had won the battle, and the Norman dynasty was born. But there was great glory for England that day as the few remaining house-carls closed their ranks and died with their king under the golden dragon of Wessex and the banner of the Fighting Man. Legend has it that Harold's body had been so mutilated that it could not be found for some time, and that it was eventually recognized by his devoted mistress Edith Swan-neck. This may or may not be true, but the body was certainly found, and was – at first – denied a Christian burial. William had staked his claim to the throne principally on a perjured oath; he could not therefore accede to Gytha's request that she might be given her son's body for burial in hallowed ground.

However, the Conqueror paid due honour to a courageous foe; he gave the English king a soldier's farewell upon the cliffs of the coast that he had striven so valiantly to defend. Later, when William was secure upon the throne, the body of King Harold II, accompanied by Normans and Saxons alike, went in solemn procession to Waltham to be buried beneath the high altar of the church that he had founded and loved so well.

38

CHAPTER 3

The Barons' War

Lewes

14 May 1264

Simon de Montfort's army at Lewes took up a position before the battle that extended approximately from the present derelict grandstand of Lewes racecourse eastwards to the edge of the chalk pits on Offham Hill. This position can be reached by walking up the sunken track (almost certainly the same one over which Simon led his army) which leads immediately off the A 275 road at the village of Offham, a mile north of Lewes, and runs due south-west up to the extensive plateau where the army was deployed. The main fighting probably took place in the vicinity of the Offham chalk pits and towards the end of the two spurs which run south-east from the plateau towards the castle and the prison respectively. There was also some mopping up in the town itself.

The visitor wishing to study the battle, and perhaps draw his own conclusions as to how it was fought, should view the field from Simon de Montfort's position on the downs above Offham; from the keep of Lewes Castle, where Prince Edward would have had his first view of the baronial army, and from the remains of the Priory of St Pancras (marked on the one-inch Ordnance Survey map, sheet 183, just to the south of the town), from where he can appreciate the difficult position in which King Henry found himself at the outset of the battle.

By 1258 it had become clear to almost everyone that Henry III was a disaster as a king. He had come to the throne in 1216 as a boy of nine, but not until 1232 (five years after he had officially declared himself of an age to rule the kingdom) did he feel himself strong enough to challenge the prestige of his great justiciar, Hubert de Burgh. From then on he had moved from one crisis to another: conflicts with his prelates and barons (not with all of them, for much of the time not even with most of them, but with a powerful minority) who were determined that he should rule without the help of his foreign friends and in accordance with the terms of the Great Charter forced upon his father King John; a disastrous

Above: Seal of Simon de Montfort at the British Museum. Left: Effigy of Henry III in Westminster Abbey. Below: Seal of Henry III

campaign in France to regain the French possessions his father had lost; punitive expeditions against the Welsh princes; and in 1254, worst of all follies, an entanglement with the Pope over an offer (with exorbitant financial liabilities attached) of the Sicilian crown for his second son Edmund.

Henry's appearance is known to us from the superb effigy in Westminster Abbey and the description left by William de Rishanger. He was a man of medium height and strong build with delicate hands and a handsome head, enhanced by a prominent nose; his otherwise fine features were spoilt by a drooping eyelid – a defect that he passed on to his eldest son. He was capable of great charm, although his affection was chiefly reserved for those who flattered him; his piety was absolutely genuine and because of his love of art and architecture we are indebted to Henry for the rebuilding of Westminster Abbey. But there was much to dislike about him. He was weak, and like so many weak men he was obstinate; he was quick-tempered, vainglorious and a decided sybarite. At a time when the country needed a strong hand and dominant personality he was too easily influenced by bad advice and too inclined to surround himself with his wife's Savoyard and Provençal relations, as well as his obnoxious French half-brothers. Frequently forced to bow to the passions of the hour, he was incapable of honouring any pledge.

Quite different was the man soon to raise the standard of revolt against him. Simon de Montfort, Earl of Leicester, was perhaps a year or so younger than the King, and through his marriage to Henry's sister Eleanor in 1238 had become his brother-in-law. When Simon arrived in England in 1231 to claim his inheritance of the honour of the earldom of Leicester and stewardship of England he and Henry were the greatest friends, but although the de Montforts were a most devoted couple Simon's marriage to the King's sister soon became the cause of many petty acerbities between him and the King.

There is no contemporary effigy of Simon that can be trusted, but his deeds have been recorded, and his praises sung or his actions condemned, down the ages. He was a man uplifted above the crowd, and in a generation that was not short of great men he was perhaps the greatest of them all. He was not as saintly as Louis IX, he may not even have been as pious as Henry, although he was a consistent and conscientious Christian, but far outstripping his faults and peccadilloes there were many qualities that make for nobility in a man.

Simon de Montfort has been accused of arrogance, ambition,

spite and ill-temper. He certainly had a quick temper, and perhaps like many great men he possessed some ambition and displayed some hubris; but he did not champion the baronial cause on account of his enmity for the King; nor can he be accused of responsibility for the civil war, or for the destruction of the baronial plan of reform. It was Henry, not Simon, who brought civil war to the country, and having once agreed to the plan of reform Simon's only fault was that he was one of the few determined to stick to it. At a time when the English and French nobility were beginning to draw apart it must be remembered that Simon de Montfort was born and bred a Frenchman, and although a highly intelligent man who numbered among his friends some of the leading English clerics of the time he probably never spoke English. But he was in the forefront of those who recognized a nascent nationalism and he genuinely wished to bring England to a juster and better way of life.

The crisis of 1258 orginated as a financial one, brought about by the absolute refusal of the Great Council to advance any money for the ridiculous Sicilian venture in which Henry had become involved. The King had always maintained the closest relationship with Rome, much to the annoyance of his own clergy, who greatly resented the papal place-men and extortions. He must therefore have been deeply distressed when his ally the Pope, weary of his weakness and vacillation, threatened to excommunicate him and bring the whole land under an interdict unless the money for the expedition was quickly forthcoming. Clearly something had to be done; but the barons had had enough of foreign interlopers and illusory empires and demanded certain safeguards as the price of rescuing their king from his stubborn ineptitude. About the end of April a small cabal of the more powerful of their number, which included the Earls of Gloucester, Norfolk and Leicester, headed a party of knights who arrived armed at the Palace of Westminster and so frightened the King that he agreed that a committee of twenty-four (half to be nominated by his council and half by the barons) should meet at Oxford on 11 June to draw up terms for what was to become a constitutional revolution.

The barons had at last realized that the trouble went deeper than the presence of incompetent foreign favourites and exorbitant extravagance; the foreigners would have to go, but there would also have to be total administrative reform. Government in future could not be conducted by the king alone, but by the king in council. The Provisions of Oxford provided for conciliar government that was cumbersome and complex, but in that summer of 1258 England took

42

an important step forward along the road to constitutional monarchy; and through the Provisions of Westminster, which came into force a year later, important changes were affected in land tenure and a much needed curb was put on ecclesiastical and baronial jurisdiction. Magna Carta was a lengthy document of some sixty-three clauses most of which dealt with points of dispute between the king and his barons; the Provisions of Oxford were a form of written constitution which laid down the method whereby the clergy and the barons were to play their part in the running of the country. The magnates, as well as the king, were called upon to fulfil certain obligations towards their tenants, and all took an oath in 1258 to uphold the terms of the Provisions.

It was never intended that the Provisions should be permanent, but in providing for them to last twelve years the barons hoped that their king would be held in leash for the rest of his life. Henry chewed the thongs of thraldom sourly, took the oath and bided his time; but Prince Edward reacted strongly against the new arrangements and was with difficulty persuaded to swear, perhaps by his father, who never could understand why anyone regarded an oath as binding. Simon de Montfort does not appear to have been over-enthusiastic about the terms hammered out at Oxford, and was certainly not the leader of the barons at this time. Only when many of them began to weaken and Henry set about undermining the Provisions did he stand out as the most steadfast and determined of them all. He had not long to wait, for events marched forward remorselessly and in anger and bitterness the country fell into anarchy.

There was a cleavage in the baronial ranks in 1260. The powerful Earl of Gloucester had quarrelled with Simon, and Henry, an adept at dividing his enemies, quickly made capital out of this split. By May 1261 he had obtained a bull from the Pope absolving him from his oath on the grounds that it had been taken under duress, and by May 1262 – when Simon de Montfort was in voluntary exile in France – he felt strong enough to formally revoke the Provisions and revert to personal government with the aid of his foreign friends. But a force had been set in motion that could be arrested only by wise and conciliatory government on the part of the king, and of this Henry was incapable. The county knights had been given responsibilities under the Provisions which they were loath to surrender, and even the common people had been stirred by the promises of reform which now seemed about to elude them. Moreover, the barons may have been temporarily divided by a conflict of interests, but they were not unmindful of their former triumph, nor disposed to surrender the fruits of that long, wearisome struggle.

WFN WATSON

Left: Infantry. Left: chain mail hauberk with long sleeves ending in bag-mittens, kettle-hat. Right cervellière over leather coif, quilted gambeson. Below: 13th-century knights or mounted men-at-arms. 12th and 13th-century innovations included closed helms, calf-length surcoat, sometimes reinforced with plates on the inside, gamboised cuisses to protect the thigh and plate jamberis or schynbalds on the lower leg, and the flat-topped shield

W.F.N. WATSON

In that July, while Henry was on a prolonged visit to France, Simon's rival the Earl of Gloucester died; his young heir, Gilbert de Clare, threw in his lot with the barons. During the King's absence his newly appointed ministers proved totally unable to cope with a deteriorating situation, and by December, when Henry at last arrived home, the whole of the Welsh border was aflame. Llywelyn ap Gruffydd was rampaging along the northern and middle march and his Welshmen had threatened Chester and Shrewsbury, while the marcher lords were far too busy squabbling among themselves, and alternatively laying waste estates belonging to the King's friends, to interfere with Llywelyn.

In April 1263 Simon returned from France, either on his own initiative or more probably at the invitation of the barons. The country was crumbling into civil war and from now on Simon assumed the leadership of the diminishing band of magnates who were still prepared to honour their binding pledge. Having won over the principal towns and castles in the west and gained the support of Llywelyn, he marched eastward along the Thames valley carefully avoiding any clash with Prince Edward, now at Windsor, and reached Kent. The Queen (with the crown jewels) and her Savoyard uncle the Archbishop of Canterbury made their escape to France, but as Simon had secured the Cinque Ports the mercenary force that they hoped to raise would have difficulty in entering the country. In Kent Simon gained many supporters and the King, who had shut himself up in the Tower among a hostile population, was in no position to resist Simon's demand for the restitution of the Provisions of Oxford.

A truce was arranged for the purpose of mediation, which Henry broke not once but twice. The second time, in December, he all but succeeded in trapping Simon as he lay with a small force outside London at Southwark, but the Londoners succeeded in opening their gates just in time. Although Simon had a large 'country' following the barons were far less united now than they were in 1258; we do not know the exact figures, but many held aloof and a good number supported the King. Having under his command only a minority of the baronage undoubtedly influenced Simon in agreeing that both parties should put their case to arbitration by King Louis and swear to abide by his award. Simon may have believed that under the terms of the arbitration the Provisions of Oxford could be only amended and not abrogated; but we can hardly credit him with not realizing that kings stood for absolute monarchy.

The Mise of Amiens, as Louis's award of January 1264 was called, was completely predictable: the total overthrow of the Provisions and a reversion to the status quo of 1258. It could have but one result: England would be engulfed by civil war. Simon was not present at Amiens, for on setting out for France from his castle at Kenilworth he fractured a leg bone when his horse stumbled, but this did not incapacitate him from taking the field almost as soon as he learned of the award. The campaign which was to culminate in the Battle of Lewes had begun. As is so often the case in war, the side that was ultimately to gain the victory met with early disasters.

Simon divided his army into three, giving his sons Henry and Simon their first taste of command. Henry he despatched into the West Country, where he failed to take Worcester and allowed himself to be tricked by Prince Edward. The Prince, after reluctantly taking the Oxford oath, had for a time showed sympathy towards the cause of reform, but by now his allegiance was firmly to his father. He had managed to get himself shut up in Gloucester Castle, but Simon ordered his son to allow him his freedom on the understanding that he took no part in any fighting. This condition he accepted but soon repudiated, and after securing Gloucester he marched his army to join the King at Oxford, leaving William de Valence to ravage the western marches and prevent Henry de Montfort (who had retired on Kenilworth) from joining forces with his ally Llywelyn. Worse still befell young Simon, who had shut himself up in Northampton. Although at first he repulsed the royal army that marched against him from Oxford, the treacherous Prior of St Andrew's guided the royalists into the city, and after some severe street fighting, in which victors and vanquished performed prodigies of valour, Simon's army was defeated and he himself made prisoner.

Meanwhile, the elder Simon, who had reached St Albans on his way to relieve Northampton, realized that he was too late, retraced his steps to London and marched from there to Rochester, whose position astride the London to Dover road made it of some strategic importance. He soon took the town, but the castle held out. Not wishing to put himself in the position of besieger being besieged, he returned to London on learning that the royalist army – which had made an incredible forced march of 156 miles in five days – was upon him. During these dismal days of April and early May 1264 both sides conducted themselves with that degree of fury and savagery so often associated with civil war. Land was devastated, churches were pillaged, houses were fired, and many innocent men, women and children perished by the sword or in the flames.

No doubt the march to Rochester was a splendid feat, but it is difficult to understand King Henry's overall strategic plan at this time. Why race for Rochester? Would not London have been a more worthy prize? No army could have withstood the rigours of such an ordeal: horses must have died in hundreds and stragglers been left littered along the roads of Kent. But almost at once they were on the move again, and marching still further from London; Tonbridge fell and then Winchelsea. True, Henry was heading for country where the great castles were mainly held by his supporters, but the dark forests of the Weald, ideally suited for ambuscades, were full of hostile bowmen and the army that eventually reached Lewes on 11 May must have been in a sorry plight. There was little enough time to recuperate before further exertions were required, and problems of provender were formidable. Henry, who loved his creature comforts, made his headquarters in the Cluniac Priory of St Pancras, which lies just to the south of the hill on which Lewes is built; Prince Edward, with most of the cavalry, occupied the more advantageously sited castle.

Earl Simon and his army left London on 6 May. Even when battles were of short duration and often conducted almost as set-piece affairs it was important to have a good intelligence system. Gentlemen known as 'espials' were employed by both sides, and those working for Simon seem to have been efficient in their duties, for he was well informed of the royalist army's movements. It was of the utmost importance for him to bring the King to battle, for unless his army was destroyed quickly it would increase in size at the expense of Simon's potential followers, and the disparity in numbers would become even greater than it was already. We do not know the exact route he took, nor does it greatly matter, but by the time the King reached Lewes Simon's army was pitching camp in the densely wooded area around Fletching, a small village some nine miles to the north of Lewes.

There are many conflicting accounts of the numbers engaged in the Battle of Lewes. The chroniclers, as usual, offer fantastic figures ranging upwards to 60,000. The *Chronicle of St Pancras Priory*, however, puts the number of royalists killed at 2,700. But even if this was fairly accurate – and it may well have been, for counting corpses is an easier task than estimating military formations – it does not help us very much, except that we are told that the number of casualties in relation to the total combatants engaged was not noticeably high. Wild statements are often made about the number of knights taking part, and it is interesting that modern research* reveals that at the time of which we are treating there were not many more than 400 knights on the active list – as opposed to those

Collected Papers of N. Denholm-Young, pp.83–94.

who were too old to fight. Here again we are not greatly helped, because knights comprised only a very small part of an army, and many fought on horseback (sometimes erroneously called knights) who were either young men aspiring to knighthood, but who had not yet received the accolade, or retainers of one sort or another owing mounted service to their feudal overlord. The King may have had a continental contingent fighting for him, and he was certainly aided by some Scottish barons and their vassals. The most usual estimate made by modern writers puts the royalist army at around 10,000, including some 3,000 cavalry, and the barons' army at half that number with perhaps only 5–600 horsemen. Furthermore, the men from London, who formed a fair part of their army, may have been ardent supporters of the cause, but were inexperienced and ill disciplined soldiers.

There had not been any spectacular changes in arms and equipment since those used by William the Conqueror and described in the previous chapter. The shape of the helmet had altered a little and now completely enclosed the head; the richer knights would wear fine mail with plate reinforcements, and surcoat – in some cases emblazoned with their arms. Plate armour for horses was still in its infancy, but some was being brought in, at great expense, from Poitou and Aquitaine. The cavalryman's principal weapons were the lance, the sword (broad or pointed) and occasionally the mace. The infantry wielded a variety of weapons; they had spears, slings and short bows and by now there were quite a few crossbows in use. The hauberk of mail armour was an expensive item of equipment, and it is fair to assume that many of the infantrymen (especially among Simon's men, for a rebel army always attracted a number of hangers-on) wore quilted leather jackets. The kite-shaped shield was still in use, although it had become shorter.

It is sometimes suggested that to offset his inferior numbers Simon de Montfort hoped to surprise the royalist force. It is difficult to see how this could be so, for on the day before the battle Simon sent the Bishops of London and Worcester to the King with one final appeal for peace. This letter, signed by Simon and Gilbert de Clare, ended with the words 'Given in the Weald, near Lewes, on the first Tuesday after the feast of St Pancras'. If the King did not already know (which is most unlikely) that the rebel army was close at hand, this letter told him so. Simon was no doubt worried by the overwhelming superiority of his enemy, but it was also almost a sacrilegious act to take up arms against your anointed sovereign, and Simon could be expected to make every effort to avoid bloodshed. The letter from the barons was short and most

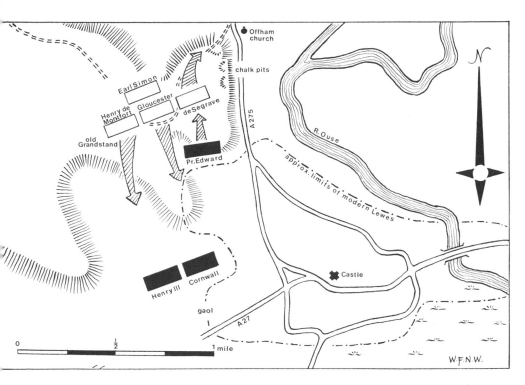

Battle of Lewes. Above: arrows denote Prince Edward's successful charge against the Londoners. Note chalk pits where large quantities of human bones have since been found

conciliatory, begging that the King should be guided by those who had his interests at heart and not by roguish counsellors. We may now detect some spark of grandeur in Henry, shining forth amid the stresses and strains of impending battle – a spark that did not entirely desert him until the day was lost. He returned a blunt refusal: 'Since it manifestly appears by the war and general disturbance already raised by you in our kingdom . . . that you do not observe your allegiance to us, nor have any regard to the security of our person, inasmuch as you have lawlessly oppressed those barons and other our lieges, who adhere with constancy to their truth towards us . . . We, therefore, value not your faith or love, and defy you, as their enemies.' The vials of wrath were overflowing; Lewes was about to be drenched with their lamentable outpourings.

In trying to piece together the story of an ancient battle the historian has to rely principally on the accounts in the various chronicles. Sometimes the chroniclers' tales are tendentious, wisely eulogizing the tactics and behaviour of the victors, but they certainly bring to light in a vivid way the pattern of a long forgotten past, from which we can draw our own conclusions. The reconstruction of the Battle of Lewes is fraught with imponderables, many interpretations are possible, but fortunately certain principles of war have not changed over the centuries and we have two incontrovertible facts upon which to build. We know the approximate position of both armies immediately before battle began, and within the last hundred years or so large quantities of human bones have been unearthed in pits around the site of the present gaol, in the chalk pits of Offham Hill, and in one or two other sites in or near the present town. These mortal remains of some massive disaster are unlikely to have been those of plague victims, for no plague pit would have been left unsealed long enough to contain so many bodies from a small town. Their discovery has helped us to determine those parts of the field where the fighting was fiercest.

The Monk of Lewes records in his chronicle that the battle took place between Prime and noon. Some prominent military historians consider that this account is wrong, for it would have involved the baronial army in the additional strain of a night march through the densely wooded country that lay between Fletching and Lewes. But if, as they suggest, the barons delayed their departure from Fletching to first light (sunrise on 14 May was at 4 a.m.) they could not have reached the top of Offham Hill before 7 a.m. at the earliest. Now almost all the chroniclers agree that the royalists had an outpost at the top of Offham Hill which was withdrawn on the evening of the 13th, except for one man who was surprised asleep at his post by the baronial army. Three hours after sunrise, in a dew-soaked field, the ground reverberating with the thud of a thousand tramping troops? Some soldier, some sleep. No, if these almost unanimous reports are correct it surely means that Simon's army did arrive on Offham Hill in the early hours of the morning; although that is not to say that battle began as early as Prime (about 5.30 a.m.) – indeed the indications are that the first clash was at least two hours later.

But we go too fast. At the village of Offham Simon had the choice of making straight for Lewes or ascending Offham Hill and deploying his army on the broad plateau at its top. He would have been well informed on the local topography, even if he had not personal knowledge of the grounds. Simon was a most able commander and would have dismissed the direct route immediately, for it necessitated a march in column through a fairly narrow defile flanked by an escarpment to the west and the tidal marshes of the river Ouse that protected the town on its eastern and southern flanks. He would, therefore, have climbed Offham Hill by the sunken track that still exists.

Offham Hill is crowned by a plateau which stretches for about 1,000 yards from the chalk pits at its eastern end to the now dilapidated grandstand of the old Lewes racecourse on the west side; two prominent spurs extend from this plateau almost to the town, divided by fairly shallow re-entrants. Simon drew up his army on the plateau in four divisions, or 'battles' as they were sometimes called, and if we are right about the number of men he had under command he could have covered the whole front of 1,000 yards with his three forward battles five lines deep. This is a further example of Simon's military proficiency, for it was unusual at this time to have a formation in reserve. He took command of the reserve himself, and probably stationed it on the right rear of the army. On his left flank he placed the Londoners under Nicholas de Segrave, a veteran soldier who had escaped from Northampton; he was assisted by Henry de Hastings. The young Earl of Gloucester was in command of the centre battle and the right flank was entrusted to Henry de Montfort, who had with him his brother Guy and Humphrey de Bohun, whose father the Earl of Hereford was fighting on the royalist side. Before leaving Fletching the rebel army had sewn white crosses on the backs and fronts of their tunics, no doubt chiefly for ease in recognition; but as they knelt in prayer, following the usual pre-battle exhortation of their commander, this spiritual symbol may have stirred some into believing that in fighting for their liberties they were also honouring their God.

It is said that the alarm was first given in the royalist camp by a party of grooms who were foraging their horses in the meadows before the town; but surely Prince Edward must have had a watch in the keep of the castle, from where he would have seen the enemy array as soon as they topped the hill, or at first light. There was no element of surprise, nor was any intended, but the hill on which Lewes is built completely obscured the enemy's position from the King. Not only did he have to rely on the castle for information, but it would take a little time for him to lead the bulk of the royalist army round the hill and deploy in front of the town.

On the battle itself we are very short of reliable facts. We only know that Prince Edward, at the head of the cavalry, routed the Londoners on Simon's left flank. He bore a particular grudge against these men for the insults they had heaped upon his mother the Queen when she had attempted to leave the Tower to join him at Windsor the year before; and either on this account, or flushed with the exuberance of inexperienced youth, he pursued them for an unwarrantable distance, not returning to the battlefield until after his father's army had been defeated. Prince Edward was impetuous, but it is unlikely that he advanced upon the enemy without having first informed his father what he proposed doing, and possibly having received permission. That he was in advance of the main royalist army is certain, but probably the King and his brother Earl Richard of Cornwall had deployed for battle at the foot of the two spurs by the time the Londoners and the royalist cavalry left the field after a savage encounter in the area of the Offham Hill chalk pits.

But what would have been Simon's reaction to the departure of the Londoners? No commander with his flank exposed likes to await upon attack from that quarter, and Simon was not to know that Edward was still galloping towards Croydon. He could either fill the gap with the reserve and await the advance of the King in a favourable defensive position, or he could himself advance to the attack on a two-battle front, keeping his reserve intact and partly concealed behind the westernmost spur. The present writer is of the opinion that he adopted the second course. So long as Edward remained off the field the balance in numbers was slightly more favourable to Simon, and his small cavalry force now looked much more dangerous; Simon would certainly have understood the psychological value of attack to any army obviously slightly demoralized by the disappearance of its left flank; and finally we have the evidence of the burial pits round the gaol, which leads one to think that the heaviest, and in this case decisive, fighting took

52

place somewhere in that area.

It seems that contrary to usual practice the King commanded the royalist left, and that his brother (with his son Henry of Almain) led the centre and was opposed by the Earl of Gloucester.* After a short but fierce fight Earl Richard's centre gave way and he was forced to take refuge in a windmill, from which he was later evicted amid ignominious scenes. This left the King facing the full fury of the de Montforts, for Henry and Guy came at him from the front, and it seems probable that victory was clenched when Simon swung the reserve in against the King's left flank. Poor Henry always got himself involved in battles when he would far rather have been building churches, and it is pleasant to record that on this occasion he fought with the utmost gallantry.

Before victory was complete intermittent fighting went on in the town itself and the marshy outskirts to the south, where it is said many lost their lives in trying to escape across the river Ouse. When Prince Edward eventually returned he was too late to rally the royalist forces and the town was already occupied by the rebels. The Prince, like his father and uncle, was made prisoner, but a number of important royalists fled and got to France.

We do not know how many perished on the battlefield or in the swampy marshes of the river. Probably no more than 3,000 men were killed on both sides, and stories of horsemen being sucked to their death in the mud while still in the saddle were certainly exaggerated and probably fabricated. Not many of the barons and knights on either side were killed.

This incident certainly did not delay the Prince's return to the field of battle, as is sometimes suggested, but had he contented himself with the partial rout of his hated Londoners and brought his cavalry back to take part in the main battle would the result have been different? Perhaps we are faced with enough imponderables as it is without having to pose this one, but it is tempting to think that with the weight of numbers and the preponderance of cavalry so greatly in their favour the royalists could have got the rebel army off balance with a flank and frontal attack from which they might not have recovered. If so Simon de Montfort's task would have been left unfinished, for he still had something to offer England.

*Thus Charles Oman, *A History of the Art of War in the Middle Ages*, p.427. Most accounts of the battle give the command of the centre to the King, but Oman's research has led him to a different conclusion. The change from the usual positions was probably due to the hurry and haste of the muster.

CHAPTER 4

The Barons' War

The Evesham Campaign

June–August 1265

The field of Evesham is not an easy one for visitors to see, because the battle was fought on what is now private, and for the most part intensively cultivated, ground. The obelisk marked on the Ordnance Survey one-inch map, sheet 144, a mile to the north of Evesham, is in the grounds of Abbey Manor House. The owner will often give permission for it to be inspected, but it almost certainly does not mark the site of the battle. This probably took place around Battle Well, now an overgrown tangle of grass and rubbish which lies off a rough track running due west, 100 yards south of Twyford House. Permission can usually be obtained to walk down this track and from it one gets a very good view of the ground over which the battle was fought. Today a part of the site is covered with fruit trees, and although these would not have been there in 1265 the open, cultivated ground may well have been sparsely clad with larger trees, for Green Hill was on the edge of Feckenham Forest.

A panoramic view of the battlefield, and the line of approach to it for part of Prince Edward's army, can be obtained by climbing the Bell Tower in the old abbey grounds, but this can only be done by appointment with the Vicar of Evesham. The site of the old ford across the river Avon at Offenham and the clump of willows growing at Dead Men's Ait, where it is generally thought that many of the fallen were buried, can be reached by a short walk down Blayney's Lane, which runs due east just by Twyford House.

After his decisive victory at Lewes (see chapter 3), Simon de Montfort probably took up his headquarters at the Grey Friars, a recent foundation situated just to the south-east of the town wall. Now he was master of the King and much of the kingdom. He had reached this pinnacle of power through his superiority in the profession of arms. His prowess as a ruler was about to be tried.

Simon knew very well that although he had won England by the sword he could only rule her through the King and with the consent of the clergy and nobility. Above all his regime would have to be royal and respectable. It was a task beyond the reach of almost any man not invested with the aura of monarchy; Simon was never able to impose his will on any but a few of his closest confederates, and some of these turned against him. As the months unfolded he more and more assumed the role of a dictator, and many personal defects could be decried; but there were undoubted bursts of beneficent activity, and if in the end his military talent seemed to desert him we must remember that he was around sixty years old, quite an age for those days.

No sooner had the battle been won than emissaries from both sides met to negotiate peace terms. These were hammered out all through the night of 14–15 May, and were known as the Mise of Lewes. We cannot tell what was arranged that night at the Grey Friars, for if a document was drawn up it has not survived, but the release of the Northampton prisoners (which included young Simon de Montfort) without ransom and the imprisonment of Prince Edward and Henry of Almain as hostages for their respective fathers seem certain to have been included in the terms. Once the immediate and important points had been settled in outline Simon left Lewes, taking the King with him. Indeed Henry, now little more than a puppet king with his court circle dismissed, was to accompany Simon on most of his journeys and all the orders were sent out under the royal seal, for it was important to make it appear that they came with the King's full authority, freely exercised.

Simon's power was massive, but so were his problems. The country was a long way from being settled, especially in the north and west, where most of the barons brooded sullenly, awaiting time and opportunity. In France a hostile faction gathered round the English queen, and the threat of invasion – to meet which it was necessary to keep a large force under arms for many months – did not evaporate until the autumn gales made a Channel crossing too hazardous. There was constant correspondence with the French court, for in spite of the lesson learned from Amiens Simon thought it necessary to get French support for his regime – after all Henry was Louis's liegeman – by referring the terms worked out at Lewes to arbitration by Louis. Presumably this time the barons were careful to impose limitations on the points to be settled, but in the event nothing came of the arbitration because of papal hostility towards the baronial cause and the intransigence of the papal legate.

Early in June writs were issued for a parliament to be held in London. Four knights to be elected from each shire were to attend, together with the bishops and magnates. At this parliament 'the community of the realm' were required to give their assent to a provisional form of government that should continue until the peace terms had been finally settled. A triumvirate was established consisting of the Earls of Leicester (Simon) and Gloucester, and Simon's staunch supporter Stephen Berksted, Bishop of Chichester. These three appointed nine councillors by whose advice the King should reign, but the triumvirate, through their ability to dismiss any of the nine, made sure in whose hands the real power resided – and Simon's position was always greater than first among equals, a fact resented by Gilbert de Clare, the young Earl of Gloucester.

Two of the most powerful marcher lords were Roger Mortimer and Roger Leyburn; both had fought against the barons at Lewes and both withdrew to the comparative safety of their border fastnesses on the defeat of the royalist army. From here they were soon in almost open rebellion, refusing to attend the June parliament, or to release their Northampton prisoners, and in the autumn organizing an abortive attempt to rescue Prince Edward from Wallingford Castle. Simon and Gloucester forced them to submit and they were made to surrender the royal castles they held and hand over their prisoners; but in November they again proved contumacious and thinking to make themselves safer destroyed the Severn bridges, including the important one at Worcester. By now Gloucester had become disillusioned with Simon and was inclined to sympathize with his neighbouring marcher lords, but Simon obtained assistance from his Welsh ally Llywelyn and the marchers, fearing to be crushed, sued for peace.

By the end of 1264 Simon seemed almost secure. The north remained unsettled, but the French threat had subsided, at least temporarily, and the more important marcher lords were awaiting deportation to Ireland – to which country in fact they never went. Simon had greatly increased his landed possessions, and he and his family kept Christmas in almost regal style at Kenilworth, while the King celebrated the feast in comparatively humble circumstances at Woodstock. But the winter sun shines with spasmodic brightness, and even as Simon was preparing for his greatest contribution to English history the storm clouds were fast approaching.

The importance of the parliament summoned to meet at London on 20 January 1265 was not in its deliberations – for its principal purpose was to arrange for the liberation of Prince Edward and Henry of Almain, although other matters of national importance became its concern – but in its composition. The calling of a parliament was a long established custom, and knights had often been summoned to attend, but they came mostly to bring information, or receive instruction, and not to take part in important business. On this occasion the writ was broadened to include two burgesses from every city and town as well as two knights from every shire. It was, therefore, a fairly representative assembly, although the higher echelons were carefully chosen. The clergy, who on the whole supported Simon, sent 120 representatives, but only some twenty-three barons known to be favourable to the revolution were summoned. We may suspect that the commons were called because Simon needed their support, but the very fact that they were necessary shows a growing awareness that representatives of shires and boroughs had an integral part to play in the management of the country's affairs. Probably, had Simon survived Evesham, he would not have summoned them to every parliament – for one thing their constant attendance would have proved costly – but the seed had been sown that Edward was to nurture, and from which the modern polity of England would eventually emerge.

It was now that the signs of a widening chasm in the baronial ranks became openly apparent. The Earl of Gloucester was an arrogant young man who resented criticism, such as he received from this parliament for his support for the marcher lords. Moreover, he had been somewhat shaken by the imprisonment of the Earl of Derby – whose numerous offences quite justified Simon's action – and he began to feel insecure. When in February Simon refused permission for the de Clares and the young de Montforts to take part in one of those highly dangerous field exercises that in those days passed for tournaments, Earl Gilbert, accompanied by a number of knights, rode away from Westminster to join up with the dissident marcher lords. It was a quarrel that Simon tried hard to patch up, but although Gloucester made it clear, when later he offered his allegiance to Prince Edward, that he supported much of what Simon stood for politically, mistrust and envy prevented any personal reconciliation.

In May Edward gave Simon the slip. The Prince had been taken to Dover Castle directly after Lewes, and from there to Wallingford; after the rescue attempt at that castle Simon moved him to the greater security of his lake-fortress at Kenilworth. On 11 March, in Westminster Hall, Edward and his cousin Henry of Almain were formally given their liberty in the presence of the King. The ceremony was something of a mockery, for both men remained under close surveillance. However, at Hereford Simon gave Edward permission to take exercise outside the town walls. On 28 May, through a carefully prepared ruse, and some equine prowess, Edward outwitted his guards and galloped to the safety of Roger Mortimer's castle at Wigmore. Under his banner a ring of royalist steel would soon to be forged to contract remorselessly round Simon.

The Battle of Evesham was to last for little more than two hours, but looked at in depth it was merely the culminating episode in a campaign that lasted two months. The actual engagement was aptly summed up by the chronicler Robert of Gloucester: 'Such was the murder of Evesham, for battle it was none.' Prince Edward first outwitted the opposition and then smothered them by sheer weight of numbers. But the interest of the battle lies in Edward's sound strategy, which contrasted so favourably with his rash tactics at Lewes, and the incredible ineptitude of the two Simons, father and son. This extraordinary irresolution and incompetence on the part of the elder Simon started at the end of May when he found himself trapped to the west of the Severn. By this time he knew he would have to fight to retain his position, and he probably realized that the dice were loaded against him. A recent attempt to win back the Earl of Gloucester was clearly seen to have failed when that nobleman welcomed Edward on his escape from captivity; William de Valence and John de Warenne had landed in Pembroke with a small force in early May, and although London was still loyal many of the shires – particularly those on the Welsh border – had declared for Edward.

Simon seems to have been stupefied by the situation in which he found himself. For many days he remained at Hereford doing little except ordering the Bishop of London in the King's name to excommunicate Edward, while all around him the proud, aggressive marcher lords prowled menacingly. The Prince was the first to move, quickly securing Chester, Shrewsbury and Bridgnorth; he then set up his headquarters at Worcester. From here he moved down to attack Gloucester; Simon had reinforced the garrison with some 300 men under Robert de Ros, for it was almost the last place open to him for crossing the Severn. The town soon fell to the royalists, but de Ros held out in the castle for fifteen days. Between 10 and 22 June Simon made a treaty with Llywelyn, whereby in return for many advantageous concessions the Welshman agreed to help him with 5,000 spearmen. This treaty was ratified by the King on 22 June and immediately afterwards Simon decided to march on Monmouth, taking Henry with him.

It is not easy to understand this manoeuvre, unless Simon was interested principally in a personal vendetta against the de Clares, whose lands quickly became a prey to ravage and spoliation. Had he marched direct for Gloucester he might conceivably have relieved the castle before de Ros was forced to capitulate at the end of June. As it was he made for Newport after Monmouth, where he summoned boats from the inhabitants of Bristol, who were still

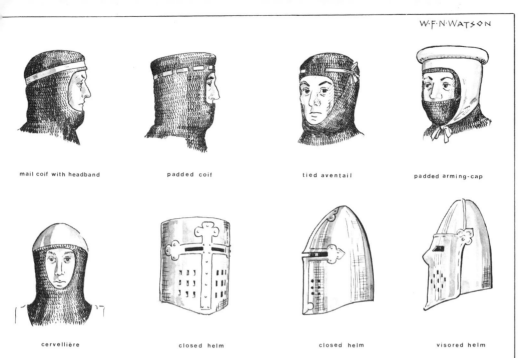

mail coif with headband   padded coif   tied aventail   padded arming-cap

cervellière   closed helm   closed helm   visored helm

12th and 13th-century head armour

loyal to him, even though their castle had remained in royalist hands since Lewes. When the boats were sunk in Newport harbour by ships despatched from Gloucester, Simon was forced to make a circuitous march back to Hereford through a wild piece of country whose primitive agriculture could scarcely support an invading army. It was a sullen and dispirited body of men, grumbling at the lack of bread and the quality of the Welsh mutton, that reached the comparative safety of Hereford somewhere about 20 July.

Prince Edward, having failed to bring Simon to battle in Glamorgan (although he nearly caught up with him at Newport), withdrew up the Severn and concentrated his now considerable force at Worcester, from where he positioned patrols along the river to give warning of any attempt on Simon's part to force a crossing. Towards the end of June Simon had sent word to his son Simon, who was Warden of the Peace for Surrey and Sussex and currently besieging the royalist castle at Pevensey, to join him immediately. There is a difference of opinion as to the exact date on which the order to raise the siege and march to his father's assistance reached Simon at Pevensey, but authorities agree that if the urgency was conveyed to him correctly he showed unforgivable tardiness.

It is understandable that he would seek reinforcements en route to Kenilworth (which town was presumably the rendezvous), and

59

it is just possible that he made the considerable diversion to London, where he is said to have been on 6 July, for this purpose. Certainly he wasted time in a cruel and wanton attack on Winchester on 16 July, and then he made for Oxford. From here it is alleged that he marched to Northampton. If this is correct – and not all accounts agree – he would have added some thirty miles to his march, and the delay involved could be excused only by a considerable recruitment of men-at-arms from that town. Nearly every account puts his eventual arrival at Kenilworth at 31 July – at least a month after he had received his marching orders. But, as one notable military historian has pointed out,* this date seems very unlikely and, for reasons that will appear shortly, he was almost certainly at Kenilworth by 30 July and probably a day or two earlier.

It is difficult to condemn completely this young commander for his marplot peregrinations round half of southern England, for although they could have further imperilled his father's position they appear to have greatly strengthened his own force, judging by the imposing list of baronial leaders who arrived with him at Kenilworth, not all of whom were at Pevensey. The younger Simon's worst offence was yet to come. He must have known that Prince Edward's army was in the neighbourhood – indeed he might have supposed it to be closer than it actually was – and yet for perhaps two days he took no precautions to safeguard his army. Kenilworth Castle at this time was a very different place from the ruin we know now. John of Gaunt converted it from a fortress to a palace, and in the seventeenth century the lakes were drained and the fortifications dismantled. Then, entirely surrounded by water with access only through well protected drawbridges, and with four massive towers and a keep commanding the inner and outer wards, the castle was virtually inexpugnable. Instead of sheltering the bulk of his army within this great fortress and maintaining outlying picquets, Simon elected to disperse his troops in the town, which with the priory offered more comfortable billets.

By the end of July Prince Edward was in the enviable position of being able to deal with his adversaries one at a time. He chose to march against the smaller army first. Numerically young Simon was almost certainly the weaker, but had his troops been on the alert and within the castle Edward would have put himself at a grave disadvantage in attacking him. However, he received information (some say from a spy called Margot, who posed as a man

*A. H. Burne, *Battlefields of England*, p.47.

in Simon's camp) that his enemy was quartered outside the castle and that no special precautions were being taken. He immediately prepared to march against him, and in the early hours of 1 August completely surprised the sleeping barons, killing or capturing many of their most important leaders. Some, half-naked, managed to escape this merciless slaughter in the streets; Simon was among their number, and finding a boat he gained the safety of the castle. But the royalists took not only important prisoners, but also fresh horses, many banners and a complete supply train which they caught entering the town.

The distance from Worcester to Kenilworth is some thirty-four miles, and with an army that comprised a considerable number of infantry – and there is no reason to suppose that he risked a cavalry raid only – this would have taken Edward at least fourteen hours. It would therefore have been impossible for him to have received the report from his spy and mounted an attack on Kenilworth in the early hours of 1 August if Simon's army had only reached that place on 31 July.

Edward was powerless against those who had taken refuge in the castle, and so, after resting his men for a day, he returned to Worcester on 2 August. It may have been a coincidence – although more likely he had received information – that on the same day as Edward left Worcester for Kenilworth Simon, bear-leading the King as usual, left Hereford. The royalist picquets had been withdrawn for the expedition and so Simon was able to ferry his army across the Severn four miles south of Worcester at Kempsey, where the manor belonged to Simon's old friend Walter de Cantilupe, Bishop of Worcester. This operation took up most of 2 August, and although Edward may have learned about it as he re-entered Worcester his troops would have been far too tired to attack. Simon was therefore allowed to spend the night in peace, and by the morning of the 3rd he had gone.

Now, as always when reliving these early battles, we are again to a great extent in the realms of conjecture. Certain dates and certain facts are assured, but nobody knows what was going through the minds of the two commanders. We can only try to put ourselves in their positions. In saying that Simon may well have been brought to battle at Evesham against his will, and by the superior generalship of Prince Edward, we are on fairly safe ground, and it seems almost certain that, unaware of the disaster at Kenilworth, he was trying to link up with his son, to whom he had sent a message. It is usually assumed that he took the longer route to Kenilworth via Pershore and Evesham in order to put as much distance as possible between himself and his enemy until he could join forces with his son and come nearer to parity in numbers with the royalist army.

On the day before the battle Prince Edward was not to know what was in Simon's mind, but he almost certainly knew that he had taken the Pershore route and that with the delay caused by having to cross the river there he would lie in the Evesham area on the night of 3 August. The river Avon surrounds Evesham on three sides in the form of a U, and the only entrance or exit from the south was by the fairly narrow bridge at Bengeworth. It is hard to understand why Simon led his army across this bridge (itself quite a time-consuming operation) and settled down in the trap. One can only assume that he misjudged the speed with which Edward would move, and perhaps Henry's piety and love of ease led him to the abbey in preference to a night in the open on the safer and strategically sounder left bank of the river.

It seems that Edward was just as surprised as we are that Simon put his army to such a hazard, for if it is true that he marched two columns (his own and Roger Mortimer's) down the left bank of the river he must have thought it more probable that he would have to fight there than in Evesham, which he covered with only one column – Gloucester's. A glance at an old map clearly shows that in those days the road to Stratford and Kenilworth ran to the east of the river past Offenham, Cleeve Prior and Marcliff, then up Buckle Street to Bidford – the present Norton–Harvington road was then at best a small track. Now if Edward had known for certain that Simon had shut himself up in the town, Roger Mortimer's column would have been sufficient to close the gap at Bengeworth and at the same time seal the Kenilworth road. There would have been no point in Edward carrying out the complicated manoeuvre that the chroniclers describe of crossing the river at Cleeve Prior and recrossing it again at Offenham to make a difficult junction with Gloucester's troops, who were marching parallel, but hidden from view, down the Alcester–Evesham road, unless he thought that the enemy might well be met with on the left bank. By the time he reached Offenham he would have learned the true position, and left Mortimer to close the southern exit.

It has been suggested that Edward split his army for the approach march from Worcester and advanced along three different routes; another suggestion is that in order to mislead the enemy he left Worcester by the north and then wheeled right-handed in a wide half circle. We can dismiss this last suggestion at once, for no sensible commander would waste time and energy on such a futile attempt at deception. To advance into battle with columns widely

62

separated presents coordinating problems even with modern methods of communication, but when the only means of communicating was by messenger and the army was moving through fairly close country the difficulty would be immense. Moreover, there was no need for it, because in those days there was no disadvantage in large concentrations of troops. It therefore seems fairly certain that until he reached Dunnington (some seven miles north of Evesham) Edward kept his force concentrated, and then, as mentioned above, divided it into three columns with two crossing the Avon at Cleeve Prior, where the river is only a few feet deep, and the third advancing down the Alcester road.

Once again the royalist army was subjected to a night march. They must have reached Dunnington while it was still dark, for we are told that they were in position on Green Hill by 9 a.m., and the crossing at Cleeve, the march down the east side of the river and the recrossing at Offenham would have taken several hours. Once across the river Edward would have conferred with Gloucester, and as the overriding necessity now was to prevent Simon from breaking out of the trap the royalist line would have been stretched to the utmost to cover the 2,000 yards that separate the two arms of the river. This meant a thin line covering the width of Green Hill and even down to the river on both sides, but a plan would have been

Evesham. The approach of Prince Edward and Simon de Montfort

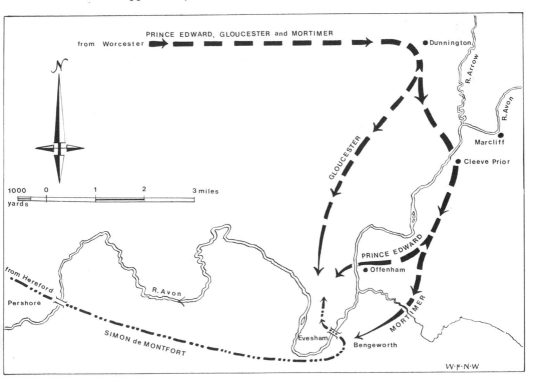

made to swing in the flanks as soon as it was seen at which point Simon would attempt to break through.

On the morning of Tuesday 4 August, while the royalist troops were nearing Evesham, Simon's army was preparing to move out across the bridge and onto the Kenilworth road. Some say that the delay in getting on the move was due to the King insisting on hearing mass first. This may be so, we cannot tell, but whatever caused the delay it was fatal to the slender chance that Simon's soldiers ever had of escaping the slaughter of that day. The tower of the abbey was almost certainly much higher than the present bell tower (built towards the middle of the sixteenth century), and from it a look-out could see far up the river valley and beyond Green Hill. But if the country to the north of Green Hill was wooded an approaching army might have reached the summit of the hill undetected. It was Simon's scouts who first reported the enemy's advance; but Edward marched into battle carrying the standards captured at Kenilworth, and this caused some initial confusion among the scouts. The look-out on the tower would merely have seen a dense column of men advancing along the Kenilworth road, and it seems possible that the delay in standing to arms may have been because for a little while – until the scouts had brought more definite news – these men were thought to belong to young Simon's army. By the time the situation was clarified the royalists were almost in position along Green Hill, and Roger Mortimer's column had closed the bridge.

It was now that Simon realized the full implications of his disastrous decision to enter Evesham, and according to William de Rishanger he was heard to say: 'Let us commend our souls to God, because our bodies are theirs.' But Simon's audacious spirit did not desert him in this hour of crisis. He decided that the best, indeed the only, chance to break through this iron ring was to pack a punch at the centre of the enemy line. Accordingly he drew up his army in a compact, deep column with a frontage that may not have exceeded 100 horsemen, cavalry in the van, followed by the English infantry and Llywelyn's spearmen bringing up the rear. It was about 9 a.m. when the head of the column marched out of Evesham towards Green Hill. The morning sky was loaded with black clouds, and across the darkening countryside the trees stood motionless in the lull that comes before a great storm.

The northernmost ridge of Green Hill, which the royalist army occupied, slopes gently down to a narrow valley and then the ground rises again and there is a slightly undulating plateau for half a mile before the hill descends to Evesham. Prince Edward's

64

position on the furthermost crest would not have been apparent to Simon until his army had gained the plateau, but it would have been no different to what an experienced commander such as Simon would have anticipated. It was in fact an ideal defensive site, for the enemy had to approach in full view for half a mile, which enabled the royalists to see exactly what their intention was and to prepare their encircling movement, and action could be delayed until the rebel army was ascending the final slope. We do not know the numbers engaged on either side, but on the obelisk the battle casualties (which agree roughly with the *Chronicle of Lanercost* figures) are given as 18 barons, 160 knights and 4,000 soldiers. Most of them came from Simon's army, so he probably marched out of Evesham some 6,000 strong, but this number would have been at least halved when the Welsh contingent deserted before the battle was joined. The royalists, even without Roger Mortimer's column, probably numbered nearly 10,000.

At first Simon's punch, delivered at about the junction of Gloucester's and Prince Edward's battles, made some headway; but as soon as the Prince was able to swing in his two wings an avalanche of men, utterly irresistible, swept down upon the barons and the affair became a massacre. No quarter was asked for and none was given. As wounded horses limped from the field, their riders – among them Simon himself – continued to fight on foot until eventually, overwhelmed by the weight of numbers, they sank to the ground in quivering, writhing heaps. Simon had brought the King into battle clad in armour and completely unrecognizable; he only saved himself by constantly shouting until dragged from the fray: 'I am Henry of Winchester, your King. Do not harm me.' In two hours it was all over and some of the bravest and noblest men in England lay dead or dying in the tangled scrub of that tiny valley. Around the body of Earl Simon there lay his son Henry, Hugh le Despenser the Justiciar, Simon's friend Peter de Montfort, Ralph Basset, William Mandeville, John Beauchamp and many others bearing household names. Guy de Montfort was dragged from the field a mass of wounds, and his life was spared. The Welshmen's flight availed them nothing, for they were cut down in hundreds as they made for the river, or drowned in its waters.

As the battle raged the threatening storm broke overhead, and to the clash of arms and screams of wounded men and horses there was added the crash of thunder and the flash of lightning. The countryside trembled in almost total darkness, and later, when

Overleaf: Battle of Evesham with plan inset

65

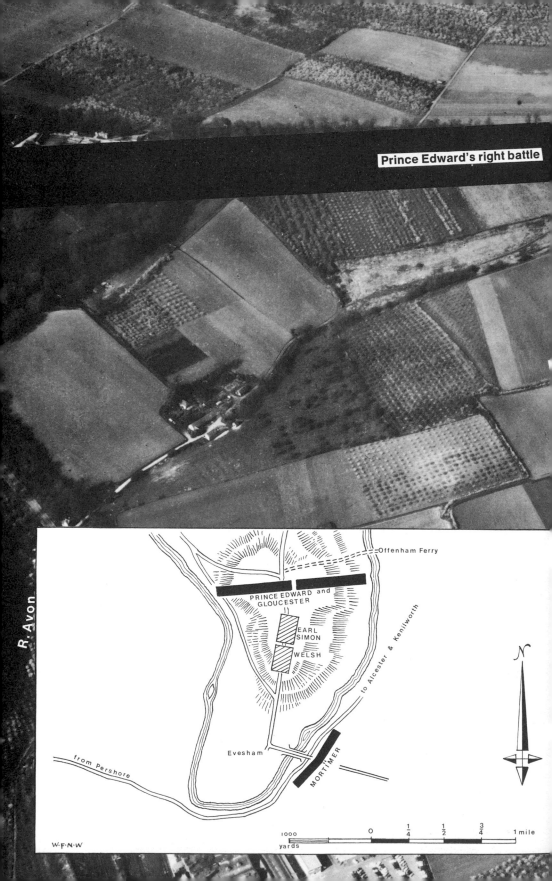

Prince Edward's right battle

R.Avon

Offenham Ferry

PRINCE EDWARD and
GLOUCESTER

EARL
SIMON

WELSH

to Alcester & Kenilworth

Evesham

MORTIMER

from Pershore

N

1000
yards

0   ¼   ½   ¾   1 mile

W·F·N·W

Twyford House

left battle

lane to Offenham ferry

Green Hill

Welsh

Simon's tomb became a holy place, there were those who recalled another such occasion when nature herself seemed to shudder at the time of a great catastrophe.

The fury of the royalists knew no bounds; they butchered the corpses with insensate violence. Simon's body was completely dismembered, the head – according to some accounts – being sent to Roger Mortimer's wife at Wigmore and the limbs distributed in other parts of the country. After the battle the monks of Evesham Abbey were ordered by Edward to bury the dead, and recognizing Simon's mutilated torso they laid it, along with the body of Hugh le Despenser, in the abbey church. What happened to the common soldiery of his army, who although defeated, dead and discredited had in fact shed their blood in a cause that was far from lost, we do not know. Probably they found a mass grave by the river at a place which is called to this day Dead Men's Ait.

The Barons' War smouldered on until the middle of 1267, when the King and Prince Edward made peace with Earl Gilbert, who had once more turned his coat and with a strong force taken possession of London, and the men in the Isle of Ely – always a popular resort for rebels – had been induced to surrender.

The younger Simon had belatedly answered his father's summons for help, but before his troops reached Alcester he learned of the disaster at Evesham and returned sadly to Kenilworth. Before the castle was besieged he left to join other magnates of the baronial party who had escaped from custody, and together they conducted a short and forlorn resistance in the Isle of Axholme. Ordered to abjure the realm, he took up arms once again before leaving the country, when he fought at Winchelsea alongside the men of the Cinque Ports. His subsequent career abroad, and that of his brother Guy, did no credit to the family name. Kenilworth, as might be expected, resisted all attempts at reduction. The garrison scorned the efforts of the most modern siege engines and when in December 1266, near to starvation, they surrendered, secure in their honour, the great fortress remained battered but defiant.

On that fatal morning before Evesham, when he saw the enemy array, Simon is credited with saying (although we do not know who recorded these alleged utterances, for nearly all his close companions were killed), 'They come on well: they learned that from me.' And indeed Prince Edward's conduct of the campaign showed that he was already a fine commander. But he had learned more than the art of war from Simon de Montfort; soon he would become a great king, who understood and espoused the more important causes for which his uncle had fought and died.

68

CHAPTER 5

The Scottish Struggle for Independence

Stirling Bridge and Falkirk

11 September 1297 and 22 July 1298

The Battle of Stirling Bridge took place on ground that is now entirely built over. The actual bridge was a wooden one thought to have stood about fifty yards upstream from the 'old bridge' that was built about the beginning of the sixteenth century and is still in use for pedestrians. From this bridge the old causeway ran northwards in much the same direction as the present A 9 – only slightly to its west – and the battle took place on either side of this causeway and around the bridge. The best place from which to view the area is Stirling Castle.

The Falkirk site is a matter of conjecture. A possible position (and the one adopted in the following account) for Wallace's troops, which seems to be hinted at by some of the chroniclers and which is a natural defensive position, is to the south of the town and immediately to the south of Callendar Wood. Here the ground slopes down to the Westquarter burn (although the canal would not, of course, have been there in 1298) and was obviously partly a morass in those days. A good viewpoint for this position is from the high ground immediately to the south of Glen Village on the B 8028 road – Ordnance Survey one-inch map, sheet 61. Another possible site for the battle is right in the middle of the present town and cannot be defined.

So utterly vile was the weather on 18 March 1286 that the Chronicler of Lanercost assures us that most men took care to stay indoors. But only five months before King Alexander III of Scotland had married as his second wife the beautiful Yolande, daughter of the Count of Dreux, and after his council meeting in Edinburgh the King was anxious to join her at Kinghorn. His councillors strove, to no avail, to dissuade him from so imprudent a journey, and when he reached Dalmeny, where the sleet swept like a curtain down the Firth and the wind whipped the water to a fury, the boatman added his plea. Alexander little recked his warning and landed safely at Inverkeithing. But by now it was dark and the uniform blackness of the night made riding along that rugged coast perilous in the extreme. The King became separated from his guides; no one knows what happened, for no eye could pierce the darkness. The next morning they found his body lying just above the tide line.

The Scottish throne passed to a three-year-old girl, known to history as the Maid of Norway. Alexander's daughter Margaret was married to Eric King of Norway; she died in 1283 giving birth to the Maid, who was also called Margaret, and less than a year later Alexander's only surviving son followed her to the grave childless. The Great Council had at once accepted the Maid of Norway as the heir to the throne, but in 1285 when the King, who was only forty-two, took a young bride there seemed every chance of another prince. But destiny chose otherwise.

On the death of their king the Scots appointed a regency of six noblemen and prelates – three to rule on each side of the Forth – and for three years, while their young queen was still in Norway, nothing outwardly disturbed the general peace with England that had flourished now for almost exactly 100 years. But Edward I was quick to realize his opportunity. He assiduously courted the friendship of the King of Norway and set about obtaining papal dispensation for a contract of marriage between his son and Margaret of Norway, since the relationship between them was within the prohibited degrees. At a meeting in Salisbury in October 1289 between the representatives of the Scottish, Norwegian and English courts nothing was said about this marriage, although it was agreed that Margaret should come to Scotland and that the Scots would not marry their queen without Edward's prior consent. This was just a short step to a formal contract of marriage between these richly endowed young people.

The Scots, while accepting the marriage, were careful to impose upon Edward certain safeguards affecting their independence. The English king, with the gleaming prospect of the two kingdoms becoming united under one crown – and that the English crown – was prepared to make concessions. He agreed to ensure that the kingdom of Scotland should remain separate from England (although in a saving clause he reserved the right of the King of England 'in the marches or elsewhere'), that Scottish laws, liberties and customs should continue inviolate, and that failing any issue from the union of Margaret and his son Edward the Scottish crown should revert to the nearest heirs, without interference from the English king. These and other rash promises were signed and sealed under the Treaty of Birgham in 1290. Edward was confident; he could afford to wait for a long cherished design.

But the wheel of fortune turns with infuriating caprice. The seven-year-old Maid of Norway left her father's court in September 1290. Great preparations had been made for her arrival in Scotland, and many precious wedding gifts awaited her. But Margaret was never to receive them. On reaching the Orkneys she became very ill, and within a few days she was dead. Scotland was thrown into confusion; the guardians – as the regents were called – found it difficult to avert faction springing up among a dozen or so claimants to the throne, mostly basing their claims on dubious descent from distant monarchs.

Edward was asked to arbitrate and, as the only thing upon which the competitors could agree was their need to remain on the best of terms with the English king, he saw clearly that the path to arbitration led directly to overlordship. There was considerable resistance from the Scottish magnates to his attempt to get them to recognize his suzerainty, for, as they very properly pointed out, only their king could make such a promise; but the competitors had perforce to make concessions, otherwise – as Edward made it very plain – there would be no award. Having thus gained their individual fealty and homage to himself as their overlord, Edward launched himself into the long and tortuous business of arbitration. He was careful to be scrupulously fair and to allow the various cases to be fully postulated before the courts set up for that purpose. It soon became clear that two men had superior claims to any of their rivals – with the possible exception of John Hastings of Abergavenny. They were Robert Bruce, Lord of Annandale, and John Balliol of Barnard Castle. Both were descended in the female line from David Earl of Huntingdon, the younger brother of William the Lion.

Judgement was eventually given – at the end of 1292 – in favour of Balliol, whose case was based on the indisputable fact that through the rule of primogeniture he was the senior descendant of Earl David. Balliol was crowned at Scone on St Andrew's Day 1292. His reign lasted nominally until 1306, although most of it was spent as a prisoner in England or in papal custody. Once he had made judgement Edward quickly showed the Scottish king and people that he regarded King John as no better than his vassal, and he lost no opportunity of humiliating the King before his people. Balliol was summoned to London to hear appeals taken to Westminster from the Scottish courts, and it was even suggested that he should sit as a justice in Yorkshire in his capacity as an English baron. At first Balliol meekly submitted to these power politics, and when at the beginning of 1293 he revoked the Treaty of Birgham and released Edward from his commitments he probably sealed his doom. However, he was not an entirely ineffectual king, nor a complete puppet. He carried through some much needed administrative reforms in western Scotland, and he was at least the nominal head of Scottish affairs – even if, placed between the hammer and the anvil, he allowed himself to be manipulated by his barons – when the nation first commenced its struggle for independence.

In 1294 Philip IV of France and Edward I went to war over Gascony. King John was not only ordered to prohibit all sea communication between Scotland and France, but his personal service, together with a number of his earls and barons, was demanded for the war. Although the country was bedevilled by rival factions with conflicting interests there was sufficient unity to resist this summons to march with Edward, and indeed the 'Auld Alliance' with France, which went back 100 years or more, was reaffirmed in a fresh treaty with Philip – ratified by the Scottish parliament in February 1296.

Rebellion of this sort clearly surprised Edward, who lost no time in putting it down. Leaving French affairs to his brother Edmund of Lancaster, he ordered the levies to assemble at Newcastle in March. Berwick was sacked with a savagery reminiscent of a more barbarous age, and in April old John de Warenne, Earl of Surrey (a veteran of Lewes (see chapter 3)), utterly defeated the Scots at Dunbar. A haul of prisoners, impressive in name and rank, were taken at Dunbar, but King John retired to the north. The English king progressed leisurely through Scotland, demonstrating his puissance by such acts as the removal to England of the Black Rood of St Margaret from Edinburgh and the Stone of Destiny from Scone, and showing his strength in every important town between the border and Elgin. In June Balliol sued for peace. He was summoned to Brechin, where Edward dictated terms that were, not surprisingly, astringent, as a result of which the Scottish king joined the important Dunbar prisoners in England.

Scotland was occupied; her king and many of the most powerful baronial families were in exile or discredited, and of the original guardians only two, James the Steward and Robert Wishart Bishop of Glasgow, were left in the country. The outlook was bleak indeed, but from adversity painful efforts were extorted; a national uprising produced a leader worthy of the embittered and resolute men who rallied to his banner, many of whom were those who had supported the Bruce competitor against Balliol seven years before.

William Wallace was a feudal vassal of James the Steward (or Stewart), a man utterly devoid of fear, of great physical strength and energy, and capable of inspiring men through his enthusiasm for the cause of ridding Scotland of the English. Although he possessed considerable military talent, Wallace was perfectly content to share command of the army with Andrew Murray until the latter's death. He did not attempt to arrogate national leadership to himself, but was as ready to assume responsibility when it was thrust upon him as he was to relinquish it when fortune deserted him.

Wallace raised the standard of revolt in June 1297, and soon most of Scotland north of the Forth was aflame. Many of the higher baronage held land in England as well as Scotland and had much to lose if things went wrong, but their patriotism was never in doubt and in any case there were sufficient of the lesser gentry to hasten the English from this region. Moreover, this was a difficult time for Edward, who was at loggerheads with his clergy over a matter of taxation and in almost open conflict with two powerful nobles, the Earls of Hereford and Norfolk. Much of the onus, therefore, fell on Surrey at Berwick, a man who was no longer capable of speedy and decisive action. He wavered for a long time, but at last realized that he must advance deep into Scotland and force the insurgents to give battle. In the first week of September the English army under Surrey and the greatly hated treasurer, Hugh Cressingham, reached Stirling.

Wallace and Murray had taken up a strong position about a mile north-east of the wooden Stirling bridge on the south-facing lower slope of Abbey Craig. Their left was protected by the loop in the river Forth at that place, and before them a causeway ran to the bridge, flanked by meadows that were passable but wet. There was some delay while the Earl of Lennox and James Stewart volunteered their services to try to persuade Wallace and Murray to disband their force, and again when two Dominican friars were sent – with equal lack of success – on a similar mission. By the morning of 11 September Wallace's defiance made battle unavoidable. But Surrey treated the whole business with unpardonable insouciance. He had already sent away one contingent, because the Treasurer had complained of the expense, and now he held up proceedings through oversleeping.

The bridge was only wide enough for two horses to cross abreast, but two miles upriver, where the Forth meets the Teith, there was a ford where sixty men could cross simultaneously. Making use of

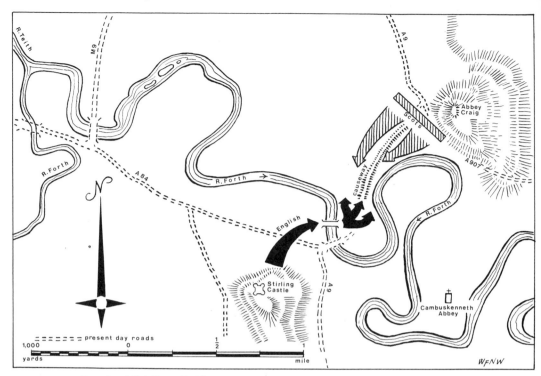

Battle of Stirling Bridge

this crossing to deliver a flank attack was virtually the Englishmen's only hope of success, but when Sir Richard Lundy suggested it the egregious Cressingham persuaded Surrey that it would be a completely unnecessary waste of time. Accordingly the men-at-arms were sent over the bridge. With what feelings of exultation must the Scots have witnessed this incredible piece of folly; and no sooner had a fair proportion (faultlessly adjudged by the Scottish leaders) of Surrey's knights crossed the bridge than Wallace and Murray unleashed their men along the causeway and over the meadows. The confusion was indescribable, for the attack succeeded brilliantly in cutting the English army in two. The men on the far bank were insufficient to cope with the weight of attack, and Surrey was powerless to reinforce them at a rate greater than two by two. Some of the more lightly clad Welshmen escaped by swimming the river, and a few knights fought their way back before the bridge was destroyed – either by the Scots or on Surrey's orders – but most of the men who had crossed perished in the fray, including Cressingham, who chose the path of repentance like a true knight. The Scots did not get off unscathed, and Andrew Murray can probably be numbered among their casualties, for his death

74

shortly afterwards seems to have been due to a wound received in this battle.

Surrey then entrusted Stirling Castle to Sir Marmaduke Tweng, who was one of those who had fought his way back over the bridge, and made all haste himself to Berwick. The Earl of Lennox and James Stewart, who with commendable foresight had sat quietly on the fence, now seeing which way matters had gone called out their men in time to intercept the heavily laden baggage train, which they plundered close to the place that was soon to be the scene of a more disastrous English defeat.

Stirling Bridge decided very little. The English had been smitten, but not too grievously, and the battle showed them two things. First, that heavy cavalry were vulnerable to determined and resolute infantrymen, making proper use of their pikes* and bills, and, second, that the Scots were not only in deadly earnest, but were a force to be taken seriously. The lessons of this rebellion were not lost on Edward: he determined to tame these troublesome clansmen to their yoke.

Not long after Stirling Bridge William Wallace was knighted and raised to the position of sole guardian. An honourable, but unenviable, post in the circumstances. In the summer of 1298 Edward set up his headquarters at York and ordered the host to assemble on the borders ready for the advance into Scotland. Although there was no Marshal's Register for that year we have a better idea than is often the case, from horse-lists that have survived and the Scottish Roll for the year, of the numbers involved in the English army. Edward would seem to have mustered some 2,500 heavy cavalry (almost all the cavalry of Edward I's reign was armoured, only a few light horse being used in his battles) and the April infantry levies were for 12,500 men – 1,000 each from Cheshire and Lancashire and the rest from Wales. However, it seems probable that there were also some levies, or volunteers, from the border garrisons, making the infantry total a little in excess of 15,000. These figures are for the campaign, and by the time detachments had been hived off for special duties, such as garrisoning captured castles, the numbers for the actual Battle of Falkirk would be slightly less.

*At this time the pike, which was not quite such a long-handled weapon as that to be used by the Scots at Flodden (see pp. 203-4), was usually called a spear; but as this may conjure up the picture of a short-handled weapon of the type hurled by some Zulu warrior, premature use has been made of the words pike and pikemen. The bill was a kind of halberd, wielded like a two-handed axe, and was used more by the English than the Scots.

At the beginning of July the army crossed the border and marched through Lauderdale to Fala, the Braid Hills and Temple Liston,* a few miles to the west of Edinburgh. Feeding an army of this size in a land that the Scots (and English) had largely laid waste presented a formidable problem, for regular supply trains were not yet a feature of the commissariat, and supply by sea was most uncertain. The English and Welsh soldiers suffered great hardship, and there was at least one ugly incident, involving casualties and much bitterness, when Edward rashly permitted the Welsh contingent to enjoy a shipment of wine that had unfortunately arrived unsupported by more solid substance. Although Wallace could hardly be expected to take to the hills and leave Scotland south of Stirling at the mercy of the invader, no one seemed to know where his army was. Dirleton and two other castles were taken by that militant prelate Anthony Bek, Bishop of Durham, in the interlude; but so grave was the supply position that Edward was on the point of turning back when news was brought to him by the Earls of Angus and March† that the Scottish army was in Callendar Wood beside Falkirk, only fifteen miles away. Edward immediately advanced and the English bivouacked that night (21 July) just east of Linlithgow.

Wallace has sometimes been criticized for offering battle with considerably inferior numbers, but he really had little alternative, and having decided to fight he took up a strong position on the southern slope of Callendar Wood with the Westquarter burn running below him.‡ Another burn ran down from Glen Village; where the two met they overspilled, and in the naturally boggy ground a fair-sized sheet of water was formed which was not immediately visible to the English troops. In spite of Stirling Bridge the Scots were still very fearful of the English armoured horse, and Wallace (who was possibly the first man to adopt the formation) organized his troops into what later became the famous schiltron. This was a tight circle or square of perhaps as many as 1,500 pikemen, with the front ranks kneeling, their pikes at an angle of forty-five degrees. The whole formation bristled like a porcupine

*Now called Hallyards.
†This was before the days when the Douglases held the title of Angus, and this earl was Gilbert de Umfraville; March was Earl Patrick, also of Dunbar, who had been an adherent of the English cause for some while.
‡See description of battlefield at beginning of chapter. The chroniclers give very scanty information as to the site of the battle; the present writer agrees with the location favoured by Professor G. W. S. Barrow.

Scottish clansman c. 1300. He wore a mantle (or plaid), saffron shirt, and sometimes a ring or chain mail byrnie, or quilted gambeson

and presented a living *cheval de frise*. In between the schiltrons were positioned the archers under Sir John Stewart and in the rear the cavalry. The schiltrons were further protected by wooden stakes, but it is hardly likely that in the time available anything could have been constructed that would seriously have hindered heavy cavalry. Edward, who may have been somewhat shaken from being trodden on by his charger during the night, and was anyway unimpressed by the strength of the opposition, wished to send men and horses into battle fed and rested, but his barons

*English longbowman.
Wearing chapelle-de-fer
and quilted gambeson*

W.F.N. WATSON

were fearful of being taken unprepared,* so he gave orders for the vanguard, under his adversaries of the previous year Norfolk and Hereford, to advance to the attack. The Bishop of Durham commanded the second battle and the third, under Edward himself, was held in reserve.

On meeting the boggy ground the Earls felt round to their left and the Bishop did likewise to the right. Bek, probably with better military intuition than his impetuous second-in-command Ralph Bassett, wanted to hold back in order to synchronize his attack with that of the left, and allow the reserve to come forward. Such foresight was met with some uncanonical advice from Bassett and the attacks duly went in. Considerable success was achieved early on, for the Scottish cavalry left the field having hardly struck a blow, and the archers were ridden down and most of them, including their commander Sir John Stewart, killed. But when the English horse turned upon the schiltrons, now hopelessly isolated, they failed to pierce the steel wall. However, Edward's army was strong in archers using the comparatively new and formidable weapon, the longbow. This weapon took a dreadful toll of the closely packed Scottish infantry, and as the gaps in the ranks increased from the inexorable hail of arrows and sling missiles the cavalry were able to crash their way through the crumbling ranks and complete the discomfiture of the Scottish foot. The schiltrons had proved their worth against armoured horse, for we know that there were more than 100 horses killed, but they were no match for the combined attack of horse and bow, and as yet they had not learned to be effective on the move. Wallace and most of the Scots magnates escaped into the great forest behind, but they left a vast number of the rank and file dead or dying on the field of battle. Casualties among the English were comparatively few, and they lost only two knights of rank.

Edward first used the longbow in his Welsh campaign, in which country longbows made from elm were known to have been in use as early as 1150, but Falkirk was the first battle of importance in which the power of this weapon was felt. As it dominated the European battlefield for the next 200 years and gave the English (who curiously enough were the only nation to make full use of it) a superiority in firepower over all her adversaries, we should pause to examine its characteristics.

The bow was made from yew – Spanish or Italian yew being

*In fact it was the Scots who were unprepared. Wallace himself was away on patrol when the English were first sighted.

Overleaf: Battle of Falkirk with plan inset

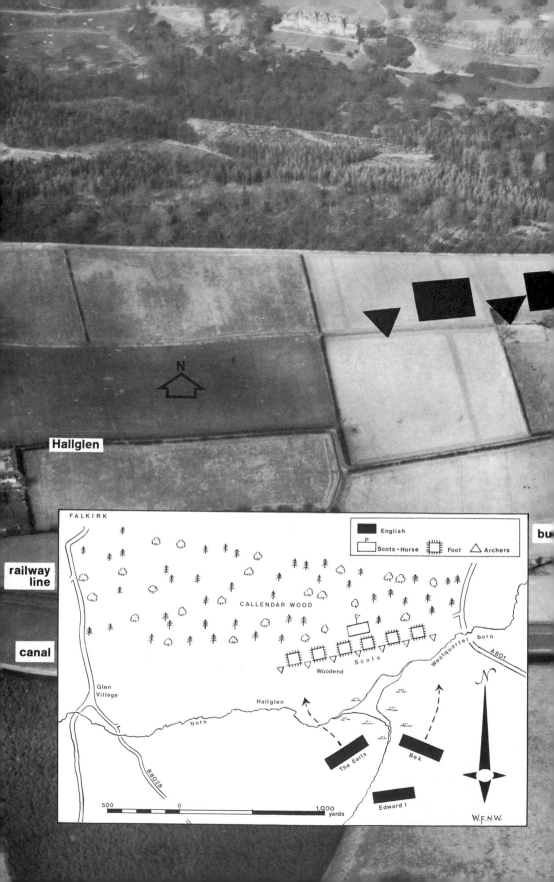

Hallglen

railway
line

canal

bu

FALKIRK

English
Scots-Horse   Foot   Archers

CALLENDAR WOOD

Scots

Westquarter burn

A801

Woodend

Glen
Village

Hallglen

burn

B8028

The Earls   Bek

Edward I

500   0   1,000
yards

N

W.F.N.W.

CALLENDAR WOOD

SCOTS

Woodend

Westquarter burn

The Earls

Bek

Edward I

preferred to the native species – and was five foot six inches to over six foot in length. The draw weight of a military bow (when drawn thirty-six inches to the ear) would not have been under sixty pounds and could have reached ninety according to the user. The normal practice range was 220 yards, but arrows could be fired much further when the bow was elevated. Arrows were about three feet long with a triangular broad head; the fletching was of goose feather, or preferably peacock feather, which was stiffer than goose; the feathers of crane, swan and other birds were also used. The strings of bows were of hemp, or silk, and at a later date than Falkirk would have been dressed with some waterproofing glue.

Archers wore quilted jackets – very seldom mail – and they carried from a dozen to twenty-four arrows bound together in a sheaf suspended from the belt. They were also usually armed with a dagger or short sword for in-fighting. A good archer would discharge twelve arrows in a minute with considerable accuracy up to 220 yards. At a range of more than 200 yards arrows would not easily penetrate a mail hauberk, and certainly not plate, but at shorter ranges their penetration power was very considerable. Much of the destruction was wrought among the horses, for even the large and valuable Spanish destriers ridden by the great men of the time could not be entirely protected, and a grounded knight was as helpless as a tortoise on its back.

With defeat in battle the strident voices of discontented vilipenders are quickly raised, and yesterday's hero becomes tomorrow's galoot. So it was to a great extent with William Wallace. From being the sole guardian of the realm, elected to rule the country on behalf of the exiled king, he became little better than a guerilla captain. Nevertheless, for the next seven years, whether leading Scotsmen in their homeland or championing their cause on the continent, he steadfastly refused to submit, and the name of Wallace became synonymous with nationalism. Finally, a hunted fugitive with a price upon his head, he was basely betrayed. He was led captive through the streets of London to be butchered under Smithfield's trees.

But the torch that Wallace had lit was soon to be carried by another, whose courage and tenacity of purpose qualified him in every respect to become the ruler of a race of men as tough and determined as any on earth. Robert Bruce was a young man of divided loyalties; but when at last, albeit through a deed of shame, he seized the reins that fate had thrown him, Scotland was to rediscover the true spirit of her people.

82

CHAPTER 6

The Scottish Struggle for Independence

Bannockburn

23–4 June 1314

The greater part of the battle area is now built over and it is very difficult to get a clear idea of what happened from walking the ground. However, from the higher ground around Foot o' Green (one mile south-west of Bannockburn) the visitor can visualize the Scots' position on 23 June and the English attack across the Bannock burn – although at the time of writing (January 1973) it is not possible to say whether the new motorway now under construction will interfere with this view. Again one can get a fair idea of the Carse (now cultivated farmland lying to the east of the railway) and Broomridge by going down the side road in Bannockburn that leads north from the A 9 towards the A 905 (Ordnance Survey one-inch map, sheet 54). There is a track running parallel to the railway line which leads almost to the burn somewhere near the place at which the English army must have crossed on the night of 23–4 June.

Fortunately, it is not necessary (although very pleasant on a fine day) to drive, or walk, all round the battlefield, because the National Trust for Scotland have an excellent exhibition at the monument, which is just off the Glasgow road (A 80) at Bannockburn. Here they have a very good model of the field of battle and they also have an audio-visual account of the lead-up to Bannockburn and of the battle itself. This exhibition is open during the months of April to September inclusive.

The Bruces, who were of Norman origin, gained favour and considerable property under Henry I of England and David I of Scotland. The Robert Bruce, known as the Competitor, who was the future king's grandfather, was not only a large English landowner, but had been for a time Governor of Carlisle. This accounts for the fact that the family, like many others in the same position, were often found fighting for the English king although they may have held Scottish land and titles. King David had given the Robert Bruce of his day the lordship of Annandale, and through marriage the family later acquired the earldom of Carrick.

The Competitor's grandson, also called Robert Bruce, was born – probably at Turnberry Castle – on 11 July 1274. This Bruce, the son of an undistinguished father, was born and reared a Scot, and after early years of double allegiance, doubts and disappointments was to gain through conquest the throne denied to his grandfather through arbitration. We have evidence from the opening of his tomb at the beginning of the last century that he was six feet tall – which was very tall for those days – and powerfully built; concerning his features we know nothing, but of his character we are well informed. In the early days there was clear evidence of a hasty temper and lack of control, but on assuming a position of responsibility he kept in leash this dark and explosive side. Instead there developed qualities that fitted him to bring his country safely through some of the most desperate years of her history: a belated but sincere patriotism, a steel-like composure in the face of all dangers, an ability to bear defeat with fortitude and a resilience to rebound to victory, and above all and in great measure the human touch, combined with a willingness to share and endure all that he asked of his men.

Shortly after Falkirk (see pp. 75-82) Edward had to leave Scotland, and the nationalist party had a chance to gather up the pieces and make a fresh appraisal of their position. Robert Bruce and John Comyn, the younger of Badenoch, were elected guardians. We do not know if Bruce fought at Falkirk; two years previously his family were known to be loyal to Edward, but in 1297 he had thrown in his lot with the nationalists, so he could well have been under arms against the English at Falkirk. Certainly he learned some lessons from the way that battle was fought. However, we are still in the period of Bruce's double allegiance. When at the beginning of 1300 it was decided to take action against dissidents in his own part of the country – where his father had always remained pro-English – he resigned the guardianship, but did not immediately offer his sword to Edward.

The fate of the border Scot had been for some time now – and indeed was to continue to be with little respite for a further 300 years – one of involvement in acts of terrorism, guerilla warfare and large-scale raids. But for the first three years of the new century it might be said that the Scots succeeded in holding their own, and with a reversion to a single guardian (Sir John de Soules) diplomatic activity supplemented, if it did not actually replace,

*Engraving from impression in British Museum of Robert the Bruce's
second great seal*

strife in an attempt to bring King John back to his own. In 1301 a
strong incursion into the south-west of the country under the
Prince of Wales, to coincide with an advance into Selkirk by his
father, met with only limited success – largely due to the efforts of
Robert Bruce, whose castle of Turnberry held out until the late
autumn.

But the year 1302 was one of gloom for Scotland, heralding the
disasters of 1303 and 1304. Early in that year Bruce turned his
coat yet again, and from being a passive supporter of the patriots
became an active opponent, offering the English king the assistance
of his armed retainers. At almost the same time the French defeat
at Courtrai lost the Scots the assistance of King Philip, and Pope
Boniface VIII also withdrew his support for the nationalist cause.

Edward's invasion of 1303–4, which took him once more as far
north as Elgin, was at first by no means a triumphal progress.
John Comyn and Simon Fraser seriously mauled the English

army south of Edinburgh and both Stirling and Brechin Castles put up a stern and resolute defence against the most powerful siege engines. Not long after the fall of Stirling peace terms were arranged from which the Scots emerged quite favourably. They were to be allowed their own laws and customs (Edward reserving the right to be consulted on any alterations), prisoners were to be released free of ransom, and no reprisals were to be taken. One man only was beyond any act of mercy: William Wallace was proscribed and his life when captured was forfeit. But in spite of these fairly generous terms and a willingness on the part of Edward to meet the Scots in full consultation on their form of government the country was to all intents and purposes occupied and under the tutelage of English administrators: a position not very different to that pertaining directly after Falkirk.

Edward's nephew, John of Brittany, was appointed Governor of Scotland, and he was advised by a Scottish council which included both Bruce and Comyn of Badenoch. In 1304 Bruce's father died in England and Edward at once conferred upon the son the family titles and lands, for he felt assured of the young man's loyalty. But in that very summer, quite unknown to Edward, Bruce was in communication with William Lamberton, Bishop of St Andrews, who although a member of the ruling council was a completely dedicated nationalist. These secret negotiations, in which the two men formed a compact to help each other in case of need, almost certainly ranged over a possible successor to King John in the interest of the nationalist cause. Now Comyn was John Balliol's nephew and in default of any children his heir apparent; here was an obvious stumbling block to any aspirations that Bruce may have had to the crown. However, we may be fairly sure that what happened in the church of the Friars Minors at Dumfries two years later was not premeditated murder.

It is a measure of Robert Bruce's courage and daring that just at a time when everything seemed to be going his way – a second marriage to an influential Irish lady, great possessions in England and Scotland, the trust and favour of the English king – he should suddenly decide to hazard all for a prize which, although the most dazzling gift that fortune could bestow, might be grasped, if at all, only on the other side of a river of blood both wide and deep that most would fear to cross. To achieve his object the full cooperation of John Comyn was essential. The two met in the church at Dumfries while Edward's justices were in session at the castle. What exactly happened before the high altar in that church we shall never know; but it is reasonable to suppose that Comyn, as many other Scottish noblemen would have been, was appalled at any idea of overthrowing his legitimate sovereign, no matter how ineffectual that sovereign might be. There had never been more than a thin veneer of friendship between the two, and high words may have been spoken when suddenly Bruce lunged his dagger into the unsuspecting Comyn, and before his uncle Sir Robert Comyn could come to his rescue Bruce's companions had completed the woeful deed. They then slew Sir Robert as well. The Bruce faction, who seem to have ensured themselves of adequate support, now took possession of the town and seized the castle, in which the terrified justices were still assembled.

Having imperilled his immortal soul in the eyes of friend and foe, Bruce must have realized that there could be no turning back. The speed and success with which he consolidated his position in the south-west of the country between 10 February 1306 when he slew the Red Comyn and 27 March when he had himself crowned at Scone show that although he may have intended to delay action until after Edward I (who was clearly on the way out) had died, his plans for a coup d'état were well advanced. He, or his supporters, succeeded in capturing five important castles, and only the refusal of Sir John Menteith to surrender Dumbarton prevented him from having complete control of the Firth of Clyde, the door through which succour could come from Ireland.

Only hazy details survive of the coronation of King Robert I; it seems that there were two ceremonies, one on 25 and another on 27 March. Three bishops, Wishart – in whose diocese the murder had been committed and who had absolved Bruce from spiritual damnation – Lamberton and Murray, the Bishop of Moray, were present, together with at least three earls, – Lennox, Atholl and Menteith.*

The Earl of Fife, whose presence was most needed (because by tradition the Earls of Fife had the privilege of placing the Scottish kings on the Coronation Stone), was completely under Edward's control, but his sister the Countess of Buchan – whose husband was a cousin of the Red Comyn's – inspired by loyalty to an ancestral duty put pride of race above petty faction and hastened to Scone in time to crown the new sovereign on 27 March.

Edward reacted strongly, appointing Aymer de Valence (Comyn's brother-in-law) as his representative in Scotland with wide and ferocious powers. De Valence soon captured, and sent to England, the troublesome bishops Lamberton and Wishart, and in June he

*Alan Earl of Menteith, not to be confused with Sir John Menteith the keeper of Dumbarton Castle.

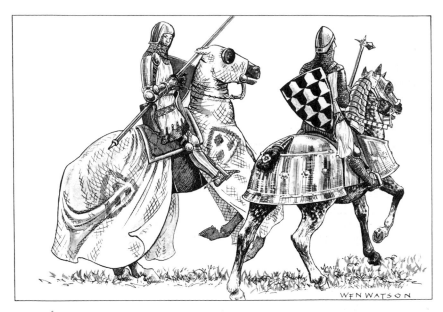

Horse armour (bards). Trappers (left) of mail, or cloth, sometimes quilted or studded, were worn from the 12th century. By early 14th century all-round defences of solid plate had been developed (right). Costly and weighty, they appear not to have been much used in war apart from the testière or chamfron protecting the horse's head

caught Bruce's army unprepared at Methven, near Perth, and completely destroyed it, forcing Bruce to fly with but a hundred or two supporters. Travelling west and south into Argyll and then Ayr, his small band suffered a further defeat at Dalry, after which his queen, and certain other ladies, were sent off in the care of Bruce's brother Nigel, the Earl of Athol and James Douglas to the supposed safety of Kildrummy Castle on Donside. But this place fell to de Valance in September and the party made off northwards to seek sanctuary at St Duthac at Tain in Ross-shire. This availed them little, for they were seized by the Earl of Ross, a staunch supporter of Balliol, and sent to England. Edward's infamous behaviour towards these ladies was one of the most discreditable acts of his reign. It is true that the Queen was placed in honourable captivity, but her sister-in-law and the Countess of Buchan were confined to iron cages and hung from the walls of Roxburgh and Berwick Castles respectively, while Bruce's daughter, a very young girl, was for a while similarly treated in the Tower of London. Nigel Bruce was hanged at Berwick, and to complete the family discomfiture two other brothers, Thomas and Alexander, were captured a few months later and suffered a similar fate.

The defeat at Methven had one redeeming feature for Bruce,

which was that it forced him to adopt the guerilla tactics that from now on served him so well right up to the time when through his brother's over-chivalrous conduct he was obliged to give battle at Bannockburn. We cannot trace in detail the long years of endeavour and endurance during which Bruce's resilient spirit and sturdy body kept the flame of revolt alive. Slowly but surely, through a series of small-scale engagements based on surprise and mobility, large areas of Scotland were won to his cause. There are months early on when we lose all trace of Bruce's movements; hunted from one hiding place to another he seems to have left the country, or at least the mainland, for a while. Then in the summer of 1307 came the first taste of victory at Loudoun Hill, where his men defeated de Valence in a small engagement, and a few days later Sir Ralph de Monthermer was roughly handled and forced to take refuge with his men in Ayr Castle.

The death of Edward I in 1307 brought a welcome respite, for his son, although a brave fighter with campaign experience, was not cast in the warrior mould of his father. He preferred less arduous pursuits to warfare and it was not long before he had troubles and difficulties that kept him at home. However, he had no intention of relinquishing the pressure upon Scotland, which was maintained, as before, first through the governorship of John of Brittany, and then by Aymer de Valence. But from 1308 the tide gradually began to turn in Bruce's favour. By the end of that year he was in control of Scotland north of the Tay, and had won recognition from Philip IV of France, and in March of the following year Bruce was able to hold his first parliament at St Andrews. Edward II stirred himself into action in 1310 and 1311, but the considerable armies that he brought into Scotland were unable to achieve anything except to infuriate Bruce and his now considerable following, who replied with devastating raids into most of the northern counties, where Bruce was able to raise huge sums of protection money.

By 1313 the reduction of Lothian was almost completed and it could be said that with the exception of a few strategically important castles Bruce was in control of almost all Scotland, and a truce with the northern counties had been proclaimed. The year preceding Bannockburn might be called the year of the castles, when with reckless heroism, and a commando style worthy of the best Achnacarry* tradition, Bruce himself and a few of his more daring captains waded moats and scaled walls at the head of small bands

*Lochiel's seat was used as the commando training centre in the 1939–45 war.

of picked men. Falling upon the enemy from their scaling ladders and forcing them to surrender after fierce hand-to-hand combat, they took by stealth and storm Perth, Roxburgh, Linlithgow and Edinburgh Castles. Here was leadership of the highest quality from men hardened by constant fighting, in command of troops trained by example and not by precept. At this time the English had none to match them.

By the spring of 1314 the only castle of any real importance still in English hands was Stirling. Edward Bruce had laid siege to this castle for almost three months in 1313, and had then agreed to a proposition by its hard pressed castellan Sir Philip Mowbray that if an English army had not relieved him by midsummer's day 1314 – which was then a year ahead – he would surrender the castle.* This chivalrous, but unwise, gesture had no doubt been prompted in part by the difficulties that Edward was known to be having with his barons – some of whom had recently killed the hated favourite Piers Gaveston – which might be expected to keep him at home. But it was a challenge that no English king could afford to neglect, and was to give Edward the necessary spur to attempt the reconquest of Scotland. It was a piece of folly that earned for its instigator a severe rebuke from his elder brother, because it committed the Scottish king to an open conflict with the might of England, which was something that for the past six years he had been studiously avoiding.

As the deadline approached Edward made preparation to cross the border with a formidable host, drawn mostly from the northern and Midland counties and many parts of Wales. Orders also went out for a large number of ships and sailors to mobilize for the purpose of transporting supplies and troops north, and to ferry men over from Ireland – Bruce's father-in-law, the Earl of Ulster, commanded the Irish contingent. We have considerable information concerning the extent of this call-up, but we do not know exactly how many men responded – although the death of Gaveston had rallied many barons to the King's side who were now prepared to send their full feudal muster – nor how many deserted before the battle was joined. It seems probable that the English king eventually arrived at Bannockburn† with a force not far short of 20,000

*By the custom of those times a castle was considered to have been relieved when the relieving army had come within three leagues (nine miles) of it.

†In those days the scene of the battle was within the parish of St Ninians and Bannok was a sub-division of this parish. The battle was eventually to be called after this small place, and *not* after the famous burn.

90

0   40   80 miles

Aberdeen

GRAMPIAN MOUNTAINS

Perth

Stirling Bridge

Bannockburn

Falkirk
1298

Edinburgh

Pinkie Cleuch

SOUTHERN UPLANDS

W.F.N.W.

men, of which 2,500 were heavy cavalry. Of the 16–17,000 infantry we have no means of telling how many were archers, although in the first writs (subsequently cancelled) 5,000 had been summoned from a total of five counties, and more from Wales. Undoubtedly Edward was well supplied in this important arm, which makes it all the more astonishing that he made such little use of it. The baggage train was immense in size and value; for Edward, confident of victory, had brought into Scotland every kind of aid to a life of luxury.

We are in the realms of conjecture when trying to put a figure on the number of men with which King Robert could meet this great English array. It has to be remembered that even now not all of Scotland was behind their king; there were those prudent enough to hold off and a few bold enough to oppose. Moreover, the guerilla tactics adopted hitherto would not have required a large force. We may therefore place some confidence in Barbour's* figure and say that the Scottish infantry numbered no more than 7,000 and was probably nearer 6,000, and that there were 500 Horse (smaller and carrying lighter armour than their English counterpart) under the Earl Marischal, Sir Robert Keith. In addition there were perhaps as many as 3,000 men known as the 'small folk', who possessed the enthusiasm but not the training of the more regular soldiers and whose discipline might be suspect.

Edward followed the route taken by his father before Falkirk, but he seems to have allowed too little time in which to move so vast a host, for we find the army being hustled along in the great heat of that June in order to keep the tryst with Sir Philip Mowbray within the allotted time. Some twenty miles was covered on Saturday 22 June, and by that night the army had reached Falkirk. Bruce had ordered his troops to assemble in Torwood, which forest stretched from a point north and west of Falkirk almost to the Bannock burn, and was separated from the New Park only by the cultivated ground in the valley of the burn. Here he drew them up in four battles, with his own forming the rearguard as he fell back to a strong defensive position.

This was in New Park, an extension of the older King's Park, which had been fenced by Alexander III in 1264. It was a fairly well wooded area rising not too steeply to a broad plateau. The actual park was about a mile long and almost two wide, and we must presume that there was an entrance on the south side not far up from the Bannock burn. The road from Edinburgh to Stirling ran

*John Barbour of Aberdeen, *The Bruce*, 198.

through Torwood and passed just to the east of New Park. The Scottish king adopted a somewhat irregular formation, for he had to be prepared for more than one contingency. Edward could not outflank him to the west on account of the denseness of the woodland, but he could attempt a frontal attack, or he might pass below the escarpment and either try to turn the position from that flank or make straight for Stirling Castle. Bruce therefore placed his own battle on the right, occupying the ground from near the burn to about where the present monument stands; on his left was Edward Bruce whose own left was turned back overlooking the low ground below; the Earl of Moray's men were positioned still further back near St Ninians Church to guard the road, and in reserve were the cavalry and the battle nominally commanded by Walter the Steward, but as he was only a youth it was actually commanded by James Douglas. The 'small folk' were left in a valley between Coxethill and Gillies Hill. Against the possibility of a frontal attack the position had been further strengthened by a series of pits, or pots as they were called, which were camouflaged and in which sharpened stakes awaited horse and man.

From this position the Scottish king despatched Sir Robert Keith to spy out the English host. The Earl Marischal was greatly perturbed at the overwhelming strength of the enemy; the whole chivalry of England seemed to be moving through the forest. The knights, sitting their great war horses with the sun glinting off their basinets and burnished armour, their colourful banners caught in the light summer's breeze, made a deep impression which Sir Robert anxiously conveyed to his king. Bruce wisely suppressed such a disturbing report and told his soldiers that the English were advancing in disarray.

At some place near to present-day Bannockburn Sir Philip Mowbray joined Edward and pointed out to the King that technically the army had relieved Stirling Castle, and that not only was there no need for the garrison to surrender, but in all probability Bruce, whose force was very small, would not risk a fight. However, Edward was in no mood to stand on technicalities; he was there with a huge army to subdue the turbulent Scot once and for all. Edward's van was commanded jointly by the Earls of Hereford and Gloucester* (a tactless arrangement, for the two were usually

*Gilbert de Clare, Earl of Gloucester, was Edward's nephew and only in his early twenties. It is easy to confuse him with his stepfather Ralph de Monthermer, who from 1298 until the death of his wife Joan (Edward's sister) in 1307 was given the style and title of Earl of Gloucester.

at loggerheads) and they appear to have wasted no time in going into the attack. If they did not act under orders it was certainly Edward's intention that they should attack, for although the afternoon was by now far advanced he would not have wanted the foe to escape overnight, and to guard against this – and perhaps with the alternative task of relieving the castle garrison – he sent Sir Robert Clifford and Sir Henry Beaumont, with about 600 horse, along the foot of the escarpment to cut off the expected retreat of the Scots.

As every schoolboy knows, the Battle of Bannockburn opened with the English knight Sir Henry de Bohun (who was in the van with his uncle the Earl of Hereford) tilting his lance at the Scottish king. Bruce mounted on 'ane gray palfray litill and joly', and easily distinguished by the gold circlet or small crown worn above his helmet, was examining the forward positions of his battle, when the English van came up the wooded slope. Eager for personal glory, Sir Henry spurred his charger forward, but Bruce on the more nimble, smaller animal had no difficulty in side-stepping the thrust, and, in Barbour's immortal sentence, 'Scher Henry myssit the nobill Kyng'. But the noble king did not miss Sir Henry; turning in his saddle he 'cleft de Bohun to the brisket'. Thus the battle started on a sorry note for the English. Soon the whole of their force that had crossed the burn was hotly engaged by King Robert's battle, possibly helped by that of his brother Edward. The fight was no minor skirmish, but a savage encounter in which the English were worsted. Gloucester was unhorsed, and narrowly escaped capture, and perhaps in the withdrawal the pots took some toll. But the force regained the main English army without much loss and Bruce recalled the pursuing Scots – which speaks highly for his control and their discipline.

Meanwhile, Clifford's cavalry had got almost opposite St Ninians Church without Moray taking any action. The King, with whom he was standing at the time, chided his nephew 'that ane rose of his chaplet was faldyn'; stung by the rebuke Moray at once advanced his small infantry force down the hill towards the cavalry. According to the chronicler Sir Thomas Gray,* Clifford was delighted by their coming and was heard to say, 'Let them come on, give them some ground.' But Moray's schiltron remained steady in the face of repeated charges and took heavy toll of horse and men – including the chronicler's father, also called Sir Thomas Gray, who was captured, and Sir William Deyncourt who was killed.

*Sir Thomas Gray of Heton, *Scalacronica*, p.141.

94

*Bannockburn: detail
from mural by William
Hole in Scottish National
Portrait Gallery*

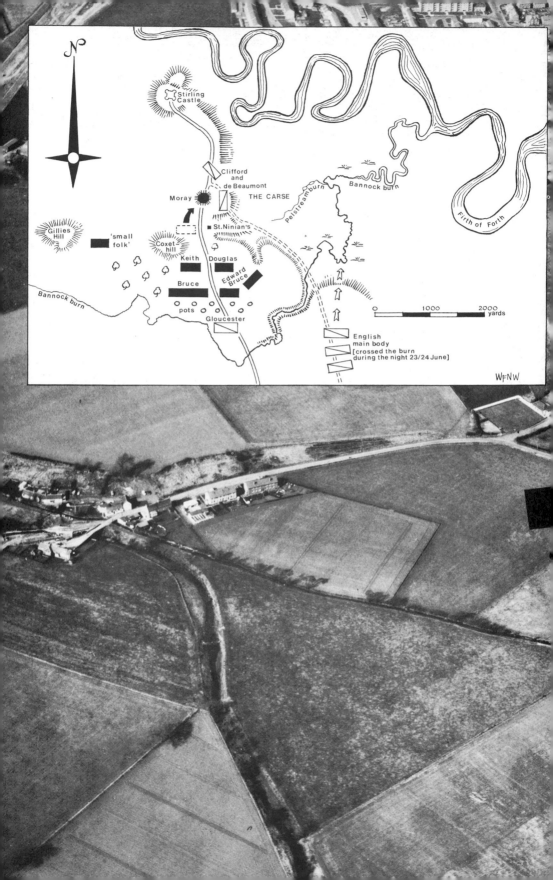

N

Stirling Castle

Clifford and de Beaumont

Moray

THE CARSE

Gillies Hill

'small folk'

St. Ninian's

Pelstreamburn

Bannock burn

Firth of Forth

Coxet hill

Keith   Douglas

Bruce   Edward Bruce

pots

Gloucester

Bannock burn

0   1000   2000
yards

English main body
[crossed the burn during the night 23/24 June]

WFNW

Moray

Keith

Douglas

monument

Edw.Bruce

Edw.Bruce

Bruce

0   0

pots

Gloucester

Eventually, unable to break this solid phalanx, Clifford's men drew off badly mauled; some rode back to the English lines, while others made for the castle.

The first day of the Battle of Bannockburn was over. It had been one of triumph for the Scots, for they could congratulate themselves on two important achievements. The teaching they had received from their king, that the schiltron if properly handled and resolutely manned could resist cavalry, had been gloriously vindicated; and the repulse of the English on two fronts had raised their morale to a high pitch, while at the same time reducing that of their opponents to a dangerously low level. Later that night, as the weary, dispirited English were floundering across the Bannock burn, the Scottish leaders were to learn that the chance to stem the tide of invasion was now within their grasp.

What could Edward do? He now realized that a frontal attack against that strong position must fail, nor could he ride round the flank with impunity. But below the escarpment was a large plain called the Carse. It is now known that the Carse was not a huge, swampy morass in those days, although where it bordered the Forth it may have been impassable for cavalry; but for the most part there was a good depth of clay above the soggy peat, and in spite of scattered pools and wet patches there was no reason why a battle could not be fought there. Edward argued that if the Scots were so foolish as to offer battle on this plain they would be devoured by his huge army, and anyway he was assured that the sight of it deployed for battle would be enough to disperse them leaving the road to Stirling clear. Moreover, the great heat of the day had made it imperative to water the horses, and so in the evening of 23 June he made for the burn and prepared to cross.

The Bannock burn and its tributary the Pelstream were tidal higher up their course than they are now, and the banks of the burn were in some parts much steeper. Here was a formidable obstacle, and the crossing place had to be chosen with care and at low tide if possible. We hear accounts of doors and beams being brought to assist the horses over the pools; but clearly it would have been impossible in that scarcely populated area to find sufficient timber in time to enable a huge cavalry host to ride dry shod. If any timber was brought it must have been with a view to helping the baggage train across wet areas, but in the event it is much more likely that the baggage never crossed the burn. For most of that short night the crossing would have continued, and we can readily imagine what a long, tedious process it must have been, with horses slithering and falling in the mud, their riders exhausted almost beyond endurance.

Maybe Bruce was wondering whether he was strong enough to meet the English in open battle in the plain, although it seems improbable that his courage and constancy should have deserted him at this hour. However, Sir Alexander Seton, for reasons we do not know, deserted the English camp that night to tell the Scottish king of the plight of Edward's army, and that he only had to attack to gain the victory. Advice that must have seemed bold indeed as with the coming of the dawn the Scots looked down upon the assembled array of English might drawn up in all its clanking panoply of war. But Bruce knew that a grave risk must be run, for now was his only chance of victory. We must admire the spirit of the man as he contemplated the peril that impended, convinced of the justice of his cause. It was Monday 24 June, St John's Day, and after he had addressed his army – a speech that comes down to us from the Abbot of Arbroath, and well calculated to stir the hearts of all those who could have heard it – he gave the order to advance.

Exactly where the Battle of Bannockburn was fought will never be known. Ever since Doctor W. M. Mackenzie produced convincing reasons as to why it was not fought on the traditional site (the original Scottish position in New Park), but somewhere on the Carse, historians have been striving to pinpoint the location. It is possible to argue a case for two or three sites. An examination of the ground seems to indicate that the fight must have taken place to the east of Broombridge, and from what we know of the battle from the various chroniclers it seems to have been fought in a very restricted area. This brings us to the site suggested by General Sir Philip Christison,* and if we say that Edward's army was drawn up in the land lying between the Bannock burn and the Pelstream, near the railway line and just north-west of the Skeoch steading, we may not be far wrong.

King Robert advanced his battles in echelon with Edward Bruce leading on the right. As they came forward the Scotsmen knelt briefly in prayer. Edward appears to have been astonished even at this late hour that they meant to offer battle, and is reported to have said, 'Those men kneel to ask for mercy', to which Sir Ingram de Umfraville replied, 'You are right, they ask for mercy, but not from you. They ask it from God for their sins.' Not only the King but the whole English army appear to have been taken unawares,

*Bannockburn: A Soldier's Appreciation of the Battle, p.19.

and there was a hasty scramble to get to horse. The young Earl of Gloucester, impetuous as ever, rode into battle without his surcoat, which may have cost him his life. As on the day before, the mailed knights of the English van could make no impression on the bristling hedgehog of pikes. But the fighting on this right flank must have been very fierce and Bruce found it necessary to bring Moray's battle into line alongside Edward Bruce's. A little later Douglas was brought into line and so the Scots were fighting on a three-battle front with the King's force in reserve.

The slaughter in the English van was heavy. Gloucester was among the first to be killed, but before the leading troops retired in confusion many another knight lay dead on the field, including Sir Robert Clifford and Sir John Comyn, the son of him whom Bruce had slain at Dumfries. Much the same was happening all along the line: at no place could the English break through the schiltrons, and at every attempt the Scottish pikes took a heavy toll, especially among the horses. Whenever an English division – and there were ten of them – broke, the confusion among the infantry as loose and wounded horses surged around was considerable. Edward II did not lack courage; he was a brave fighter, but unlike his father he was no general, and he had not learnt the lesson of Falkirk, that cavalry needed supporting fire if they were to break the Scottish schiltrons. Not until his horse had been sorely bent and almost broken did he bring up archers on the Scottish left – they were probably firing from the north bank of the Pelstream. Then a dangerous situation developed for Douglas's men. But this was the great chance for Bruce to use his small band of cavalry. He ordered Keith into the attack, and the archers were soon swept back into the now sadly struggling English army. The cry went up among the Scots to press on; the English were unable to manoeuvre in the circumscribed area in which they had been caught and the Scottish schiltrons were rolling them up remorselessly.

When he saw the plight of the enemy, some of whom had already begun to attempt the difficult escape across pools and burn, Bruce ordered the Highlanders and Islesmen, comprising his own battle and hitherto held in reserve, to go forward. The result was almost decisive; the demoralized English had already begun to waver when they saw the royal standard leave the field. Edward had no wish to desert his army, but the Earl of Pembroke (Aymer de Valence) and Sir Giles d'Argentine, who were responsible for his safety, insisted that he made haste for Stirling Castle. The Earl went with him, but once his king was safely off the field the gallant Sir Giles, recognized as one of the leading knights of his day, rode back into the fray to be killed. With their king and their fighting spirit gone the English army was ready to break; at that moment the 'small folk', utterly unable to restrain themselves any longer, emerged from their position over Coxethill. For the English this was the end; they would not stay to fight what appeared to them to be fresh reinforcements. It was now every man for himself and the army broke up in all directions. Many perished in the burn desperately striving to avoid the Scottish pikes; a strongish party managed to reach the high ground round Stirling Castle and others fled towards Falkirk and home, but terrible casualties were inflicted and all the baggage fell intact into Scottish hands. A vast army, reckoned by many to hold the professional primacy of Europe, had been brought to its knees by the skill and daring of a small, determined force, led by one of the great captains of history.

Sir Philip Mowbray refused King Edward sanctuary in Stirling Castle, for the excellent reason that it could now no longer hold out, and so the King with a fairly strong escort made his escape through the King's Park and behind the Scottish army. Bruce was more interested in dealing with the large body of fugitives who had made towards the castle, and so the pursuit of Edward was left to Douglas and a small force. They failed to catch him, and from Dunbar Edward took boat to Berwick. The English losses in the battle were grievous, not so much in numbers as in the men of high rank who rode with the cavalry. There were probably 300 or more men-at-arms slain, and besides these knights, squires and mounted retainers many infantrymen were killed in the battle, drowned in the Forth, or perished on the way home. Some important prisoners, including the Earl of Hereford, were taken, in Bothwell Castle on the Clyde. Escaping from the battlefield they sought sanctuary with the constable, who having admitted them promptly made them prisoner. Hereford was exchanged for the Scottish queen, her daughter, her sister-in-law and the Bishop of Glasgow. Sir Marmaduke Tweng and Ralph de Monthermer were returned without ransom, but there were around 500 for whom ransom was demanded. After Sir Philip Mowbray had surrendered Stirling Castle he changed sides and followed Bruce. Of the Scottish casualties in the battle little is known, but the ratio of men killed to the numbers engaged would certainly have been considerably smaller than with the English army.

'Robert de Bruce was commonly called King of Scotland by all men, because he had acquired Scotland by force of arms.' Thus the

Overleaf: Bannockburn, second day's battle, plan inset

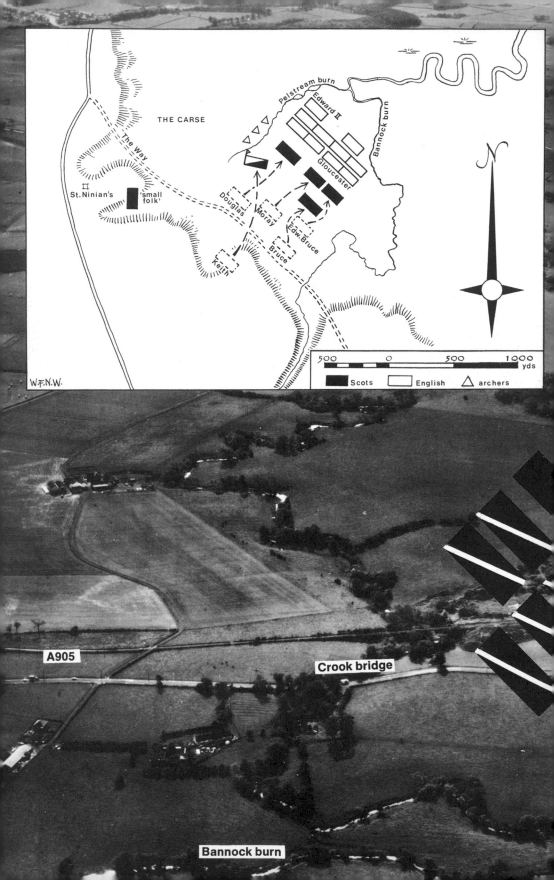

THE CARSE

Pelstream burn

Edward II

Bannock burn

The Way

St. Ninian's

'small folk'

Douglas

Moray

Gloucester

Keith

Bruce

Edw. Bruce

N

W.F.N.W.

500   0   500   1000 yds

■ Scots   ☐ English   △ archers

A905

Crook bridge

Bannock burn

N

BANNOCKBURN

Bruce

Keith

Edw. Bruce

Moray

Douglas

Gloucester

Pelstream burn

archers

Chronicle of Lanercost. Certainly Bruce had won Scotland by the sword, but until his sovereignty was recognized by all his task was not complete. The English king and the Pope steadfastly refused him recognition; his great victory at Bannockburn had yet to be consummated.

The story of the next fourteen years is mainly one of plunder and pillage, fire and sword, throughout the border areas and northern counties of England, for Bruce came to realize that these were the methods by which he would most speedily gain his ends. The principal exponents of these acts of terrorism were Sir James Douglas and the Earl of Moray; so devastating were their attacks that as in earlier years a large sum of money was raised through blackmail, and many northern Englishmen who could not buy the raiders off changed their allegiance and became 'Scottish'. To begin with Edward Bruce was also among the raiders; but the Irish, inspired by Bannockburn, sought help from King Robert to free them from the English, and it suited the Scottish king well to send them his brother. Edward met with some small success, but soon after being crowned king he was killed fighting at Dundalk in 1318.

Edward II's only large-scale attempt to avenge Bannockburn in 1322 was a dismal failure. An ill-found, unmounted force with few archers was quite unable to bring the mobile Scots to battle, and a near starving army was forced to sue for peace. A thirteen-year truce was arranged at York in 1323, and soon afterwards the Pope was persuaded to recognize the Scottish king.

Edward III, on his accession in 1327, offered a more lasting peace but, like his father, would not hear of Scottish sovereignty. It was not until after a further hopelessly abortive campaign that the English realized the need for more subtle tactics. In the spring of 1328 a marriage was agreed upon between King Robert's son David and Joan, King Edward's six-year-old sister, and in May of that year the English king recognized Scotland's absolute independence. The treaty, which had been framed in Edinburgh, was ratified by the English parliament on 4 May at Northampton. In July of that year the young couple were formally married at Berwick, and in June 1329 Pope John XXII granted to Robert Bruce and his successors the right, long in abeyance, to receive anointing and coronation.

Thus at last all that this great man had fought for had been achieved; but the papal bull came six days too late, for on 7 June 1329 the strife and struggle of a lifetime ended. King Robert I died at his palace at Cardross. His going left a void that would soon prove serious.

CHAPTER 7

The Wars of the Roses

A General Survey

1455–71

The story of the Wars of the Roses is one of the most complicated in all our history. The great families of England, with their large bands of armed retainers, often clouded the main issue with personal feuds. The fact that they constantly intermarried and that titles and estates frequently passed through the female line is a further cause of confusion to the student of those times. The dynastic quarrel between the houses of York and Lancaster spanned more than thirty-five years, during twelve of which there were fought as many battles as there were years, and the English nobility scowled upon each other with lineaments of fury, while the great slaughter on battlefield and block left their hatreds and vendettas behind. This chapter endeavours to trace in outline the events that led us to this period of turmoil and distress, and to present the principal facts. In subsequent chapters five of the more important battles will be discussed in detail. See table giving brief descriptions in chronological order of the principal battles of the Wars of the Roses on p. 186 and map of England and Wales showing the sites of the battles on p.187.

Edward III had seven sons. The Wars of the Roses chiefly concerned the descendants of the second (surviving) son, Lionel Duke of Clarence; those of the third, John Duke of Lancaster; and the fourth, Edmund Duke of York. Edward was succeeded by his grandson Richard II, but in 1399 Henry Earl of Derby, the eldest son of the Duke of Lancaster, seized the throne, had Richard murdered, and established the ruling dynasty of Lancaster. Like most usurpers he did not have matters entirely his own way and had to fight to retain his throne, notably against Owen Glendower in Wales and the lords of the northern marches. His most serious clash was with the old Earl of Northumberland's warrior son, Henry Hotspur; the Percys, having helped Henry to the throne, had become disaffected to him after the Battle of Homildon Hill (1402), and decided to ally themselves to Glendower and the Duke of Clarence's grandson Edmund Mortimer. However, on 21 July 1403

105

the King successfully defeated and killed Hotspur just north of Shrewsbury in a battle memorable for being the first in which both sides used the longbow. A little later Glendower was forced back into his Welsh mountains and eliminated as a serious threat. In due course Henry was succeeded by his son Henry V, who dying in 1422 left an infant as his heir, and England was faced with a long minority.

Henry VI was born in 1421 and during the years immediately following his father's death affairs in England and France were managed by his uncles the Dukes of Bedford and Gloucester. In 1437, two years after Bedford's death, Henry began to assume personal control. He proved over the years to be a kindly, pious man, who was easily led; but he was not unintelligent, and at brief intervals showed that he had a will of his own. His misfortune was that in this age of rule by kings he was mistakenly loyal to a faction who constantly mismanaged affairs of state. He stands condemned as the man chiefly responsible for the Wars of the Roses, because he headed an administration that was incompetent and untrustworthy, while he himself was too weak to cope with the passions and artifices of these fierce and dangerous times.

We are not concerned with the early years of Henry's reign. One by one the men who led the nation – Gloucester, Cardinal Beaufort, the first Duke of Somerset, the Duke of Suffolk – disappeared by fair means or foul, until in 1450 the King's principal counsellor was Edmund Beaufort, second Duke of Somerset, who for the past few years had been busy losing every important town and province in France which Henry's father had so gloriously conquered. By August 1450 the whole of Normandy had gone and only Gascony remained. In twelve months' time that too would be lost and by 1453 the English were left with just a precarious foothold in Calais.

The country was full of bewildered, discontented ex-soldiers, who had been driven out of France and disbanded; robbers roamed the roads and woods, and the evils of unlawful 'livery and maintenance' were weakening traditional loyalty to the crown and binding the lesser nobles and their tenants to their more powerful neighbours, who thus formed independent armies. The King ruled not so much through Parliament as through his chosen council – dominated largely by the Beauforts. In 1455 a bride had been found for him from France, and Margaret of Anjou was already exhibiting signs of that courage, determination and masterful spirit which were the hallmarks of her character. She greatly favoured Somerset, and was said to have been responsible for Richard Duke of York's removal from France and banishment to the lieutenancy of Ireland.

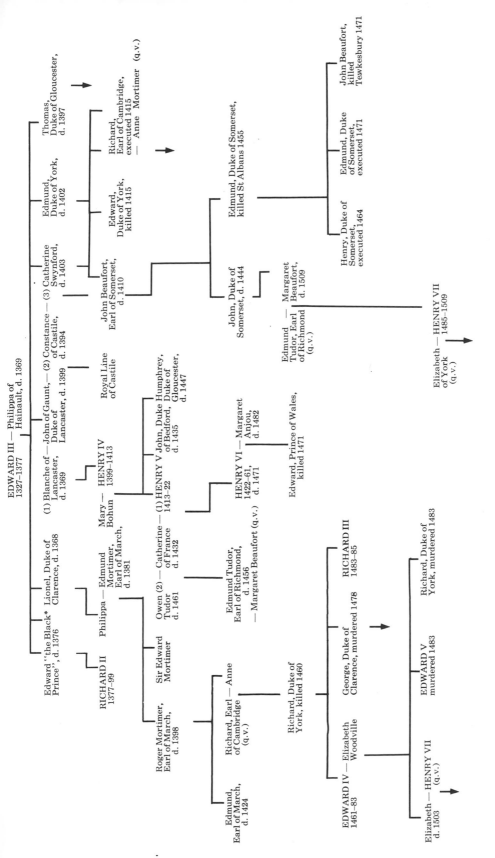

EDWARD III — Philippa of
1327–1377   Hainault, d. 1369

Edward "the Black*
Prince", d. 1376

Lionel, Duke of
Clarence, d. 1368

John of Gaunt,—
Duke of
Lancaster, d. 1399

(1) Blanche of
Lancaster,
d. 1369

(2) Constance —
of Castile,
d. 1394

(3) Catherine
Swynford,
d. 1403

Edmund,
Duke of York,
d. 1402

Thomas,
Duke of Gloucester,
d. 1397

RICHARD II
1377–99

Philippa — Edmund
Mortimer,
Earl of March,
d. 1381

Mary —
Bohun

HENRY IV
1399–1413

Royal Line
of Castile

Richard,
Earl of Cambridge,
executed 1415
— Anne Mortimer (q.v.)

Edward,
Duke of York,
killed 1415

John Beaufort,
Earl of Somerset,
d. 1410

Roger Mortimer,
Earl of March,
d. 1398

Sir Edward
Mortimer

Owen (2) — Catherine —
Tudor   of France
d. 1461   d. 1432

(1) HENRY V
1413–22

John, Duke
of Bedford,
d. 1435

Humphrey,
Duke of
Gloucester,
d. 1447

HENRY VI — Margaret
1422–61,   Anjou,
d. 1471   d. 1482

Edmund, Duke of Somerset,
killed St Albans 1455

John, Duke of
Somerset, d. 1444

Margaret
Beaufort,
d. 1509

John Beaufort,
killed
Tewkesbury 1471

Edmund, Duke
of Somerset,
executed 1471

Henry, Duke of
Somerset,
executed 1464

Edmund,
Earl of March,
d. 1424

Richard, Earl — Anne
of Cambridge
(q.v.)

Edmund Tudor,
Earl of Richmond,
d. 1456
— Margaret Beaufort (q.v.)

Edward, Prince of
Wales, killed 1471

Edmund Tudor, Earl
of Richmond
(q.v.)

Elizabeth — HENRY VII
of York   1485–1509
(q.v.)

Richard, Duke of
York, killed 1460

George, Duke of
Clarence, murdered 1478

RICHARD III
1483–85

EDWARD IV — Elizabeth
1461–83   Woodville

Richard, Duke of
York, murdered 1483

EDWARD V
murdered 1483

Elizabeth — HENRY VII
d. 1503   (q.v.)

THE HOUSES OF YORK AND LANCASTER

* Edward III's second son
William died in infancy

Political agitators and military adventurers found ready material to hand in these dark days. One such man, calling himself Jack Cade, marched on London at the head of a large band of Kentish men in the summer of 1450. His army was eventually dispersed and he himself killed, but it was a typical example of the lawlessness of the times. Possibly Cade had Yorkist backing; certainly his Articles of Complaint included a demand for the expulsion of the ruling clique and the recall of the Duke of York. Anyway, with the present government discredited both at home and abroad, the Duke felt strongly the need for action.

He left Ireland in August 1450 and landed in Wales. Henry recalled the Duke of Somerset from Calia and made half-hearted attempts to intercept York, but on these failings he weakly submitted to receiving him and listening to his complaints and demands – without, however, acceding to them. Although York's open enmity for Somerset could have sparked off civil war at any moment, it seems almost certain that neither now, nor when fifteen months later he led a more threatening march on London, did he seek the kingdom. He was, however, head of the house that finally prevailed in the Wars, and we should look briefly at his strong claim to the throne (see chart on p. 107).

Richard II left no issue. As early as 1385, however, he may have recognized his cousin's son Roger Mortimer, fourth Earl of March, as his heir apparent; such at any rate was the substance of a later Yorkist legend. March's claims were inherited from his mother Philippa, daughter and heiress of the Duke of Clarence, who in the year of her father's death (1368) had married the third Earl of March (died 1381). Roger was killed in Ireland in 1398, leaving a son of only six and two daughters, the elder of whom (Anne) married the Earl of Cambridge, son and heir of Edward III's fifth son, the Duke of York. Early next year the death of the King's uncle the Duke of Lancaster precipitated the events that were to lead to Richard II's deposition and the destruction of any hopes the young Earl of March may have had of succeeding to the throne. On Lancaster's death Richard sentenced his son and heir Henry of Bolingbroke (then in temporary banishment from England) to perpetual exile, at the same time confiscating the enormous Lancastrian inheritance. Faced with a choice of poverty-stricken exile or rebellion, Henry chose the latter, and in a rapid campaign seized the kingdom and the crown. By 1450 the Lancastrian dynasty was represented only by the childless Henry VI. The Mortimer claim to the

Henry VI, artist unknown, National Portrait Gallery

throne had descended, after the death of the fifth Earl of March (1424), to the son of his elder sister Anne – Richard Duke of York.

His claim *de jure* was probably superior to the King's, but the Lancastrians had won the throne, and York at this time only wished to dispute the way in which the exercise of royal power had fallen into the hands of a clique or faction. His mistrust and dislike for Somerset, however, went deeper. In 1407 Henry IV had carefully regulated the descent of the crown in an Act of Parliament which had never been repealed, and while recognizing the legitimacy of his Beaufort half-brothers he had specifically debarred their line from any claim to the throne. Save for the childless king, Henry IV's line was extinct, and Richard of York was unquestionably his heir. But Somerset was in direct male descent, through the Duke of Lancaster, from Edward III, and all that was needed was for the favourite to slip an Act through Parliament repealing Henry IV's prohibitory clause. Thus the two men glowered upon each other suspiciously with a cold, enduring antagonism.

York had good reason to feel aggrieved at being excluded from the King's council, for his talents as an administrator and soldier were probably superior to Somerset's. He saw clearly what was wrong with the country, and he believed himself capable of putting those wrongs to right. For a little while he took no overt action, but having failed to move the King by constant supplication he determined to rid the country of Somerset and purge the government, if need be by force. Early in 1452 he marched south from his castle at Ludlow at the head of a large army. London closed its gates against him so he camped at Dartford. The King, with a much bigger army, moved to Blackheath. Civil war seemed imminent, but neither side wanted it and York realized that he was in no position to fight. He had committed high treason, but he was far too strong to be punished. On taking a solemn pledge not to disturb the peace again he was given his freedom, and the country gained a short respite from the horrors of internecine strife.

The following year, 1453, was crowded with momentous events. While further and final disasters in France – which culminated in October with the surrender of Bordeaux – were being inflicted upon his armies, the King was dramatically released from his troubles. A sudden start plunged his feeble mind into oblivion, and for fifteen months he remained in this state of suspended animation, declaring on his recovery that he remembered nothing. Parliament was faced with having to appoint a regent. The court favourite, Somerset, had been successfully impeached by the Duke of Norfolk for the French catastrophes and was in the Tower, but Queen Margaret felt that her claim was paramount. She was, however, somewhat preoccupied, for on 13 October 1453 – after eight barren years – she produced a son. Parliament hesitated and procrastinated, but eventually the Yorkists won the day and in March 1454 the Duke was appointed Protector and Defender of the Realm. He was also given the captaincy of Calais, recently held by Somerset.

The country remained comparatively quiet until at Christmas 1454 the King recovered his senses. He wasted little time in reversing most of what York had done and in restoring Somerset to freedom and responsibility – including the captaincy of Calais. York retired to his castle of Sandal, near Wakefield, where he and the Yorkist lords brooded sullenly upon the scene. All the evils that Somerset had inflicted upon the country seemed about to be repeated; moreover, not only all that York stood for, but his very life, was now only prey to time and occasion. He determined upon a resort to arms. In the middle of May 1455, at the head of 3,000 men, he marched south. The first blood in the Wars of the Roses was about to be shed. But we should pause to examine the composition of the forces which were soon to sear England with the flame of war.

The pernicious effect of unlawful livery and maintenance – which has already been touched upon – meant that the Wars of the Roses were fought between private armies under the command of the more important barons supporting one side or the other – and occasionally changing their allegiance. The heads of these great families were virtually petty kings within their own domains, and by giving their badge and livery to almost any rascal who applied they could command large armies – the Duke of Norfolk put 3,000 men and cannon into the field during a private quarrel in 1469, and at about the same time the Earl of Warwick had very many more armed retainers proudly flaunting his badge of the Bear and Ragged Staff. There was frequently a bitter rivalry, and sometimes private warring, between these great families; this was largely responsible for the ruthless extermination of important prisoners that was such an unpleasant aftermath of most of the battles, but on the other hand it tended to make the Wars mainly an affair of the aristocracy. Both sides were, for obvious reasons, usually anxious to spare the common man as far as possible; hence reprisals were few and far between and although there were inevitably cases of sack and plunder these were comparatively rare.

These great lords of the land did not march to war at the head of ill armed rabbles; for the most part their retainers were equipped with up-to-date arms and armour. There had been many changes since Bannockburn, which was fought more than a hundred years earlier. Although the longbow had a further span of sixty years to run, already the improvement in armour – especially the completeness of plate – had considerably lessened its destructive power. Until tackled at close quarters the man-at-arms was almost invulnerable, for gunpowder was still in its infancy. Both sides – particularly Warwick, who employed Burgundian mercenaries at the Second Battle of St Albans – used a limited number of hand-guns. These were very primitive and unreliable weapons, fired by means of a touch-hole on the top of the barrel near the breech. Cannon, which was soon to end the rule of feudal despotism, was at this time still very unwieldy, and although employed in many of the battles by both armies it was really only the heavy ordnance, such as the great bombards used at the siege of the northern castles, that made any mark. Probably the most useful weapon was the halberd, introduced into England at the end of the fourteenth century, although it and the bill were now giving way to the pike.

Horse armour had undergone little recent change, but the man-at-arms (who in the Wars of the Roses mostly fought on foot) now wore a new style of helmet; the basinet with its close-fitting visor had been replaced by a continental introduction called the salade. This was a curious-shaped helmet with a long projection at the back and a movable visor; it was worn with a mentonnière, which was a plate fastened to the breastplate and moulded to cover the lower part of the face. Towards the end of the Wars the more orthodox-shaped armet was used as a helmet. The breastplate was still globular, but was stronger, being reinforced by what was called a demi-placcate and with gussets of plate adapted to the movement of the arms. The shield was no longer carried, which necessitated greater protection by plate armour on the left, or vulnerable, side of the man. The ordinary infantryman was some-what less well protected; a longbowman usually wore a hat and gorget of banded mail, and a hauberk of overlapping scales of leather, but the arbalester might expect to be given a helmet and complete plates for his legs.

Mention has been made of the great families, and something must be said concerning the man who more than any other was responsible for putting Edward Duke of York on the throne – Richard Neville, Earl of Warwick, known to history as the Kingmaker. His father was the second son of the Earl of Westmorland by his second marriage with Alice de Montacute, through whom he inherited the lands and title of his father-in-law the Earl of Salisbury. These lands were mostly in Wiltshire and Hampshire, and it is interesting to note that in general the Yorkist support came mainly

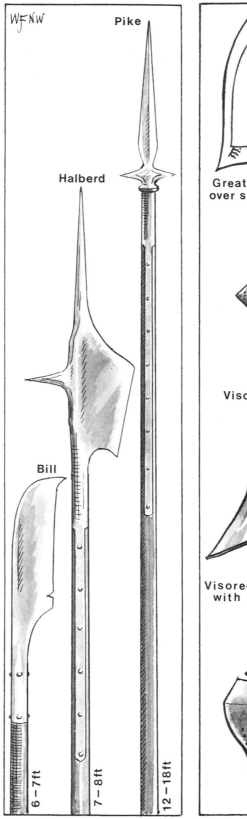

WFNW

Pike

Halberd

Bill

15th-century
pole arms and
head armour

6 – 7ft

7 – 8ft

12 – 18ft

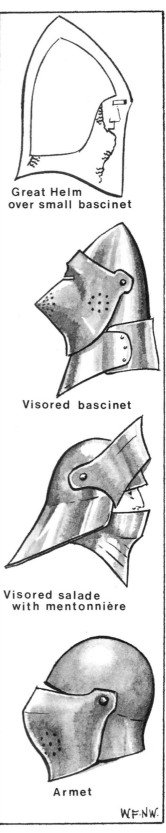

Great Helm
over small bascinet

Visored bascinet

Visored salade
with mentonnière

Armet

WF·NW.

from the south and from Wales and the marches, while the Lancastrians drew their strength from the north. Richard Neville was Salisbury's eldest son, and following the wise example of his father he too married an heiress, Anne Beauchamp, daughter of Henry, fourteenth Earl of Warwick. Richard, therefore, in due course succeeded not only to the vast possessions of his father and father-in-law, but also to both titles, Warwick being the premier earldom of England. Furthermore, his aunt Cicely Neville had married the Duke of York, and so Warwick was fighting first for his uncle and then – until he turned against him – for his first cousin.

We know little enough about Warwick's private life, but his public record stamps him clearly as a man built upon a larger scale than almost all his contemporaries. He was a fearless fighter and tireless organizer, although not a conspicuously talented general. His excursions into diplomacy were often successful, for he was a courteous man of much charm, but they were not always wisely undertaken. Immensely popular with the rank and file, he was at first loyal to the cause he championed; but in the end injured pride proved stronger than loyalty.

This was the man, now aged twenty-seven, chiefly responsible for his uncle's victory at St Albans on 22 May 1455. We left Richard Duke of York, with Salisbury and Warwick, marching south at the head of 3,000 men. On 20 May they sent a letter from Royston to the Chancellor explaining their reasons and demanding the removal of Somerset, and a similar letter, but couched in deferential terms, was sent to the King from Ware. However, Henry never received it, for on learning of the Yorkist approach he had moved out of London (which was pro-Yorkist) and headed for Leicester. With the King were the Dukes of Somerset and Buckingham and the Earls of Pembroke, Northumberland and Devon – the last named having recently deserted York, with whom he had marched in 1452.

The King halted at St Albans on learning that York was at hand. He set up the royal standard in St Peter's Street, and after some unsatisfactory parleying awaited the Yorkist attack. He had under command little more than 2,000 men, so the Duke of York held the advantage in numbers. St Albans was an open town, being at that time still under the jurisdiction of the abbot. Only a partially filled-in ditch presented any obstacle, and this was not properly manned by the Lancastrians, who preferred to rely principally on barricading the two roads leading from the south into St Peter's Street. These barricades were under the command of Lord Clifford, and the Duke of York obliged him by a frontal attack, which made no headway. But Warwick, acting either on information or intuition,

Petardier. A petard contained inflammable material and explosives. It was thrown into the faces of the advancing enemy

crossed the ditch at an undefended spot and forcing his way through the back of the houses in Hollywell Street gained access to the main street, where he fanned out and took both the barriers in their flank. The Lancastrians were thus divided and the troops manning the barriers being attacked from two sides soon fell back, allowing the Yorkists to pour into the town.

The whole affair was little more than a street scuffle lasting only half an hour. The total casualties were probably less than 150, but the Duke of Somerset, the Earl of Northumberland, Lord Clifford and many other Lancastrian noblemen lay dead; the Yorkists lost Lord Clinton and Sir Robert Ogle. The Duke of Buckingham had been wounded by an arrow in the face, and the King, standing forlornly by his standard, received a flesh wound in the neck before taking refuge in a tradesman's house, where the Duke of York found him and immediately assured him of his fealty and devotion. The time of bitter hatreds and savage reprisals among the families of the nobility was still five years away; now the victors behaved with moderation. York caused a parliament to be summoned within four days of his victory, and many of the important offices of state were given to men of his faction. Warwick became Captain of Calais in place of Somerset, and was the only man to retain his posi-

115

tion when Margaret of Anjou and the court party once more gained the ascendancy at the end of 1456. He was thus available to succour the Yorkists with his garrison troops when hostilities broke out in earnest in 1460.

The four years following the First Battle of St Albans saw an uneasy truce in the land. The Yorkist government, which was terminated in October 1456, struggled with the problems of the time. The Lancastrian power was always formidable, and apart from a short period when Henry was again incapacitated by illness they had the magic of the crown on their side. In 1457 York was once more given the lieutenancy of Ireland for a period of ten years. Presumably this was to get him out of the way, but if so the attempt failed, for when at last in 1459 Margaret felt herself strong enough to act and sent out writs in the King's name for an armed assembly to gather at Leicester on 10 May York was at Ludlow – although apparently in no hurry to arm.

All that summer Margaret was busy raising troops in the counties of Lancashire and Cheshire, but there was no action before September. By then York had realized his peril and sent urgent messages to his brother-in-law Salisbury, who was at his Yorkshire estate of Middleham, and to Warwick in Calais, to join him at once. Soon armies were marching throughout England: Warwick north-west from Kent, Somerset north-east from Wessex (the two nearly clashed), Salisbury from Yorkshire to Ludlow, and when the Queen learned that Salisbury was on the move she dispatched Lord Audley to intercept him. This he did on 23 September at a place called Blore Heath, just east of Market Drayton (see also p. 186). Salisbury had but 3,000 men and was outnumbered by perhaps as much as three to one, but he was forced to fight. He took up a strong defensive position with one flank resting on a wood and the other protected by baggage carts; Audley's first attack was mounted and repulsed with heavy loss, and so were two subsequent ones made with dismounted troops. The battle lasted for most of the afternoon, but when Audley had been slain and his lieutenant Lord Dudley captured the Lancastrians had had enough; 500 deserted to the enemy, the remainder fled the field.

Salisbury, although victorious, was in a dangerous position between two superior Lancastrian armies. Thanks to the antics of a crazy friar, who kept firing a cannon all night, he managed to leave Blore Heath undetected and join York at Ludlow. A few days later Warwick arrived with a contingent of trained soldiers from Calais. But Henry displayed unwonted determination and vigour. He was now in the area of Worcester with an army that may have numbered 30,000 men, with which he planned to deal swift and exemplary chastisement to all who would not accept his pardon. York faced this vast host behind the river Teme at Ludford, but the peril of his situation was plain for all to see; soon Andrew Trollope, with many of the Calais men, deserted, and the disheartened Yorkist army dispersed in the night. The Duke and his youngest son made for Ireland, while Warwick and his father, together with York's eldest son, struck south and took ship from Devon to Calais. No longer officially its captain, Warwick nevertheless gained entry to the town and was soon holding it against his nominated successor Henry Duke of Somerset, who had inherited much of his father's puissance at the Lancastrian court.

On 26 June 1460 Warwick, who had visited Ireland at Easter to concert plans with York, left Calais with Salisbury and the Earl of March (York's son). They landed near Sandwich with 1,500 men and were unopposed, for the Lancastrian army was centred mostly in the Midlands. On 10 July Warwick's force encountered Henry's army encamped in a strong position just outside Northampton (see also p.186). The Earl attacked on a three-battle front, and his task was made considerably easier by the treachery of Lord Grey of Ruthen, whose soldiers were ordered to help Lord March's right battle over the fortified ditch and mound. With these men across the ditch the Lancastrian position was untenable. Once again the total casualties (about 300) were small compared with the loss in the higher echelons: the Duke of Buckingham, the Earl of Shrewsbury, and Lords Beaumont and Egremont (Northumberland's brother) were among the Lancastrian fallen. The King, who appears to have taken no part in the battle, was conducted back to London with every mark of respect; his wife, on learning of the defeat, retreated north with her son.

York was still in Ireland, but when Warwick had won the greater part of the kingdom for his cause he came to London. Here at last he declared his true colours and claimed the crown. But he had acted prematurely: neither the lords temporal nor spiritual wished to change the dynasty at this time. A compromise was reached whereby Henry should rule for his lifetime, and should be succeeded by York. It seemed an admirable expedient, but it failed to take into account one important factor. Henry might agree to disinherit his son, but Margaret certainly would not.

The indefatigable queen, helped by the Duke of Somerset (now back from his abortive attempt on Calais), the Earl of Northumberland and other northern noblemen, immediately set to work organizing another army based on York. They soon had a force of 15,000

15th-century plate armour

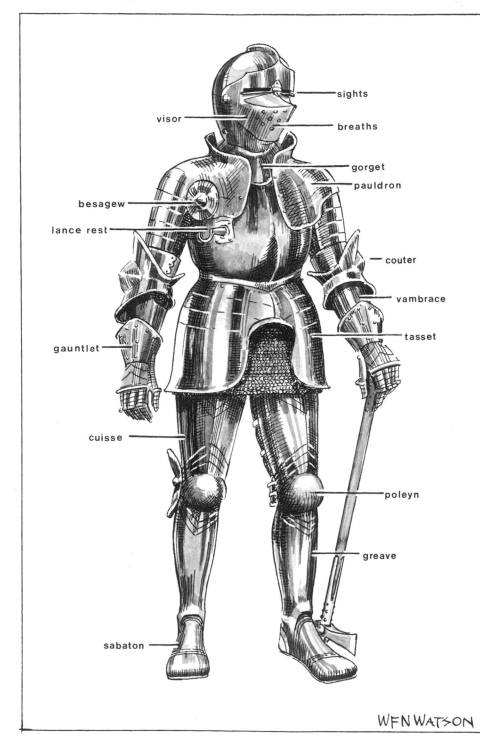

sights

visor

breaths

gorget

pauldron

besagew

lance rest

couter

vambrace

tasset

gauntlet

cuisse

poleyn

greave

sabaton

WFN WATSON

armed men. York hurried north and spent Christmas at Sandal.
Five days later the Lancastrians with superior numbers fell upon
his army (see also p.186). Details of the Battle of Wakefield no
longer exist. Possibly the Yorkists were taken by surprise; certainly
they suffered a crushing defeat and both in the mêlée and after the
battle was over their enemies took a fearful revenge. Richard Duke
of York fell in battle; his young son the Earl of Rutland was caught
fleeing the field by Lord Clifford, who personally stabbed him to
death; Salisbury was captured that night and executed the next
day. Their three heads were sent to adorn the walls of York, that of
the Duke being exposed to mockery and malice by the adornment of
a paper crown. It is said that the Yorkists lost 2,000 men to the
Lancastrian 200. There were to be other disasters, but none so great
as this. However, the cause was not lost, for Edward Earl of March
(now Duke of York) was to prove himself a fine soldier and a popular prince. But the struggle now became far more bitter, for a new
generation took over the ugly business of avenging their fathers:
Lord Clifford had already opened his account.

Warwick was not present at Wakefield, but lay at his castle on
the Avon; on learning of the disaster he at once made for London
with his troops. The Queen's army was marching south towards the
capital and on the way committed what were by far the worst rav-
ages of the war, sacking Stamford, Grantham, Peterborough, Royston and later St Albans. In so doing the Lancastrians alienated
their cause still further with the common people of the south, and
there was much sympathy for the Yorkists gathering to defend the
capital. However, Warwick marched from London to meet the
Queen's army and allowed himself to be surprised near St Albans:
'the prickers came not home to bring tidings, how near the Queen
was, save one, who said that she was yet nine miles off.' This time
he himself was taken in the flank and his army soundly beaten (see
p.188 or chapter 8 for a detailed account). The way to London lay
open – there was no occasion throughout the Wars on which any
town closed its gates to a victorious army. But Henry, whom Warwick had taken from London to witness the battle and who had as a
result been united with his queen, forbade the Lancastrians to
advance on the city, having been sickened by the sack of St Albans.
It was an honourable decision but fatal to his chances, for when at
last he did dispatch a force to seize Westminster it was too late.

The Second Battle of St Albans was fought on 17 February 1461.
On 2 February the young Duke of York, now just three months
short of his nineteenth birthday, had taken the first steps in a tale
of broadening glory that led him to the throne. In a battle of whose

details we know nothing he defeated the army of the Earls of Pembroke and Wiltshire at Mortimer's Cross (see p.188). The beaten army was pursued to Hereford and the Lancastrian losses were said to have been heavy. The two earls escaped, but in the ceaseless bloodletting that was now to become such an unpleasant feature of these rancorous times Owen Tudor (who had married Henry V's widow), Sir John Throckmorton and eight other important prisoners were beheaded. Young Edward of York then marched to meet Warwick, and although he was too late for St Albans he joined the Earl in time for them to re-enter London ahead of the Lancastrian force.

The Yorkists had now crossed the Rubicon; there could no longer be any pretence that their loyalty still lay with the King, for the King was firmly in the hands of the Queen and in no circumstances could they treat with Margaret. There had to be a new dynasty. On 4 March Edward Duke of York rode from the family home of Baynards Castle to Westminster, where he was officially acclaimed King Edward IV. England now had a man on the throne cast in the true mould of a king. Tall (he stood six feet four inches), handsome and of a pleasing disposition, he was to prove himself a brave fighter and a very capable general. Possessed of considerable intelligence he was capable when he exerted himself of governing wisely, but he had a broad streak of indolence and hedonism. He much preferred to leave matters of state to his cousin Warwick, and to enjoy the fruits of his kingdom. It was a mistake that nearly cost him his throne.

The new king had no time for dalliance in London; he had to march north to subdue the unconquered Lancastrians who were assembling in large numbers around York. On 29 March 1461 there was fought at Towton (see p.188 or chapter 9 for a detailed account) the bloodiest, and perhaps the most decisive, of all the battles of the Wars of the Roses. The Yorkists gained a complete victory in that part of the country where the Lancastrian strength was greatest. Edward, whom we must now call the King, spent the next three weeks in York. After the battle there were plenty of noble Lancastrian heads to replace those of his father and others that had grinned down upon the city since Wakefield.

The next three years belong in a special way to Queen Margaret. We can only condone her behaviour if we remember that she was a princess of France, and although a queen of England she was without a throne; her interests centred round her husband and her son, for England she cared not a straw. Nevertheless, we can have nothing but praise for her indomitable courage in the face of

15th-century hand-gun and hand-culverin

defeat, anxiety and extreme hardships, for her determination, her
perseverance and her skill. The royal fugitives hovered between
Scotland and northern England; in Scotland and in France she
had two allies, for it was the policy of these countries to keep
England divided by backing the weaker cause. Margaret's peregrinations cannot be gone into here; sufficient to say that for
Scottish aid she gave away Berwick, and for French she mortgaged
Calais. She became a supplicant at the French and Burgundian
courts, and with the aid of the devoted and competent Pierre de
Brézé, and a slice of English treachery, she gained the important
northern castles of Alnwick, Bamburgh and Dunstanburgh. To
regain them Edward was forced to ship his heavy ordnance – the
pride of his military arm – north, and the Earl of Warwick took
charge of the siege operations (see p.189).

Edward, although ruthless when occasion demanded, could also
be magnanimous. In 1462 he not only pardoned the Duke of Somerset, but took him into his confidence and showed him great favour.
Such generosity was ill received by his supporters and ill repaid by
the recipient, who at the end of 1463 renegued with his followers to

Henry. Warwick's brother Lord Montagu, who was Warden of the East March, was escorting the Scottish envoys to York to treat with Edward when Somerset and Sir Ralph Percy confronted him on 25 April 1464 at Hedgeley Moor, between Morpeth and Wooler; it was a small affair in which the Lancastrians were worsted, and Percy, who disdained flight, was killed (see p.189). But on 15 May a more serious engagement was fought near Hexham in a meadow on the south side of the Tyne (see p.189). Here the Lancastrians had taken up a position that offered no hope of escape, and in a short, sharp encounter Montagu virtually surrounded them, and those who were not killed had no alternative but surrender. Somerset was among those who were taken and executed on that same day; Lords Hungerford and Roos suffered the same fate two days later.

The war in the north was now virtually at an end; it was left to John Tiptoft, Earl of Worcester and Constable of England – a man as cruel as he was cultured – to bring Lancastrian nobles and knights to trial by the score with a view to execution. Henry, who was in nearby Bywell Castle during the fight at Hexham, made good his escape and wandered about the Lake District for the next year before being betrayed. He arrived as a prisoner at the Tower on 24 July 1465.

Edward was a valiant man of war, but he loved peace; he loved it for what he could get from it by way of ease and enjoyment. So far, for the most part, he had been content to let the powerful Neville family run the kingdom for him, and had he let matters go on in this way the Wars of the Roses might now have been over. But the King had a will of his own; he would not be thwarted and when he was he could quickly slough off his indolence and let it be known that he was the master, a soldier with a sword in his hand and a man to be reckoned with. His quarrel with the Nevilles lasted six years, but in the end he triumphed.

It concerned first his marriage to Elizabeth Woodville, or Wydvile, which had occurred in 1464 and been kept a carefully guarded secret. To Warwick and other magnates, who thought that this was just another harmless flirtation, the announcement that he had actually married this comparatively lowborn Lancastrian widow came as a deep shock – especially to Warwick who had plans for a French bride. But more damaging was their difference over foreign affairs, for here the matter was raised above a purely family quarrel. Warwick was convinced that a French alliance was essential to forestall any possibility of a Lancastrian revival borne upon French arms; while he was working hard to this end, Edward was all the time negotiating behind his back with the Duke of Burgundy.

Just as Warwick was bringing his negotiations to a successful conclusion Edward, in 1468, announced his pact with the Burgundian court, which included the marriage of his sister Margaret to Charles the Bold.

Such public humiliation could not be tolerated. Warwick laid his plans with care. He won over the King's brother the Duke of Clarence, to whom he married his daughter and co-heiress Isabella. Next he stirred up trouble in the north, where a man calling himself Robin of Redesdale headed a tiresome insurrection that necessitated the King marching against him. As soon as he learned that the King had left London, Warwick and his new son-in-law crossed from Calais with a number of trained soldiers and entered London in something like a triumph. Edward, learning of Warwick's landing, now became seriously alarmed; he fell back on Nottingham to await reinforcements from Wales under the Earl of Pembroke.* But these were cleverly intercepted by the northern rebels, who getting between them and the King met Pembroke at Edgcote – some five miles north-east of Banbury – on 26 July 1469 (see also p.189). The previous day Pembroke had had a disagreement with the Earl of Devon,† who had gone off with all his archers, and so Pembroke fought at a grave disadvantage. Even so although at first repulsed he rallied his Welshmen and might have won the day had not an advance party of Warwick's troops joined the fight at the critical moment. The slaughter was considerable, both sides losing men of consequence. Pembroke, and later Devon, were among those of the defeated army to be executed.

The King found himself unable to rally his scattered forces, and at Olney was made to realize that he was Warwick's prisoner. He was conveyed to Middleham, where he was treated with the respect due to his high rank, although left in no doubt as to where the power now lay. Edward decided to dissemble; he professed himself penitent and ready to mend his ways. In due course he was liberated. However, any outward healing of the breach between these two powerful men was only on the surface. Warwick continued to plot and another insurrection – this time in Lincolnshire – required the King once again to march north. In a battle near Empingham on 12 March 1470 – known as Losecoat Field from the way in which the rebels hastened their flight – the King defeated Sir Robert Welles before Warwick could join him (see p.189). The

*Sir William Herbert, recently created Earl of Pembroke in place of Jasper Tudor.
†Sir Humphrey Stafford, recently created Earl of Devon, in place of Thomas Courtenay who had been beheaded after Towton.

defeated leader then confessed that Warwick was the instigator of the revolt and that he had intended to place Clarence on the throne. Warwick fled the country, and being refused entry into Calais he eventually landed at Honfleur.

Louis XI saw his chance. Here was Warwick crippled, beaten and discredited; in Anjou were Margaret and her son mortified, moneyless but indomitable. If he could but persuade these two deadly enemies that together their cause could triumph he would at the same time relieve the pressure on France. A wide and bloodstained gulf separated Warwick and Margaret, but eventually Margaret accepted Warwick's plea for forgiveness, and as a pledge of his new found allegiance to the house of Lancaster his daughter and co-heiress Anne was to marry the Prince of Wales. Louis supplied money and ships for the invasion of England.

In only six months after Empingham the wheel of fortune had turned full circle. Edward, from being supreme and seemingly secure in his kingdom, with his dangerous rival a fugitive abroad, was himself scurrying to safety in Friesland. Warwick's landing in Devonshire had taken the King by surprise; he was without support in the north and the force that was with him in Yorkshire was small and not entirely reliable. He was wise to seek safety in flight. Henry VI, resigned to whatever fate might impose, was restored to the throne at Michaelmas 1470 by the man who five years before had led him to the Tower crying 'Treason, treason and behold the traitor'.

Edward's return to England in March 1471 and his defeat of the Lancastrian armies first at Barnet and then at Tewkesbury were prodigies of daring and determination that clearly portray the dynamic force of the man. No sooner had Charles of Burgundy realized that Warwick's policy was to aid France against him than he readily supplied Edward with money, ships and more than a thousand German mercenaries. Landing at Ravenspur,* he overcame the sullen resistance of the citizens of York by declaring that he came only to claim his paternal inheritance, upon which assurance they opened their gates to him. His march south, gathering reinforcements as he went, was swift and skilful. Montagu had 4,000 men assembled at Tadcaster ready to oppose him, but Edward evaded this force and when he reached Nottingham he was strong enough to declare his real intention and reassume the royal title.

Warwick learned when he was at Coventry what Edward had known for some time, that the treacherous Clarence had reaffirmed his loyalty to the King (Edward). With Clarence against him and

*This port at the mouth of the Humber, where Henry IV also landed, has long since been swallowed by the sea.

Montagu still in Yorkshire, Warwick felt himself unable to offer battle at Coventry. This suited Edward admirably. He marched on to London, where he was admitted virtually unopposed. He left it again the next day, Easter Saturday 13 April, to fight the Battle of Barnet (see p.189 or chapter 10 for a full account). With him went the wretched Henry, once more bereft of everything but his simple dignity and moral virtue, to witness the death in battle of his recent champion the Earl of Warwick, together with Montagu and many other lords and knights of both factions. It was an expensive victory for Edward, but with the death of Warwick the hopes of Lancaster were all but gone.

Queen Margaret had shown considerable reluctance in answering Henry's and Warwick's constant calls to join them. We do not know her reasons, but contrary winds could not be the full explanation, although they certainly delayed her in the end. She eventually landed at Weymouth on the day that Barnet was fought. The news of that disaster – brought by Somerset – temporarily overwhelmed this dauntless woman; she wished to return to France immediately. But her son, who had perhaps inherited his grandfather's military qualities, soon rallied her flagging spirit. The Lancastrians were not without hope of reinforcements in the west and Jasper Tudor – once more Earl of Pembroke – commanded a large force. And so she agreed that the army should march for the Welsh border. It was a race against time; both armies covered long distances in a day, and the Lancastrians, brought to battle at Tewkesbury, were in a badly exhausted state (see p.190 or chapter 11 for a full account of the battle). Here they were shattered and scattered; the Prince of Wales was cut down together with many other noblemen. The Duke of Somerset* sought sanctuary in Tewkesbury Abbey, from where he was removed for execution. Jasper Tudor, who was not at the battle, skulked in Wales before escaping to Brittany with his nephew Henry, who would one day return.

Edward IV was now triumphant. An attempt by the Earl of Kent's bastard to take London had been forestalled, and a rising in the north had been quickly subdued by the Earl of Northumberland. On 21 May the King entered London in state with Queen Margaret his prisoner. That very day Henry VI was reported to have died 'of pure displeasure and melancholy'; Richard Duke of Gloucester is often thought to have been the particular cause of this 'displeasure'. The Wars of the Roses were not quite over; but for fourteen years the sword slept in the scabbard.

*He was a brother of the duke executed after Hexham, and the third holder of the title to die in the Wars.

CHAPTER 8

The Second Battle of St Albans

17 February 1461

The battle was fought in three distinct phases. The first phase took place in the centre of the town around the fifteenth-century watch tower, which still stands, and over much the same ground as the First Battle of St Albans. It is impossible to be certain about the exact site for phases two and three, but the second and principal battle was fought either on Bernard's Heath (a northern suburb of the town), or more probably on ground to the west of Sandridge. Warwick's rearguard action took place south of Nomansland Common.

Bernard's Heath is now very much built over, although a part of the great ditch constructed by the Belgae is unspoilt. But the Sandridge–Nomansland area is still mostly open country. A good idea of the ground over which the fighting took place can be obtained by driving along the B 651 road to Nomansland Common, and along the minor roads leading off the B 651 west from Sandridge. The watch tower can usually be ascended on application to the museum (situated near the Roman town), and from the top a very good view of the city is obtained. The Lancastrian approach march and the first phase of the battle can be studied from this vantage point, but the rising ground to the north obstructs any view of Bernard's Heath and the land beyond.

The Second Battle of St Albans (see also pp. 119-20 is perhaps the most interesting of all the battles of the Wars of the Roses; not from a tactical standpoint, for we know all too little as to how it was fought, but from the point of view of strategic appraisal of both commanders. It also presents a fascinating exercise in trying to make a credible picture of a whole fight from a few clearly established facts.

The overwhelming Lancastrian victory at Wakefield in December 1460 (see pp. 117-19) and the subsequent elimination of Richard Duke of York, came too late to have a decisive influence on the war. By now the quarrel had bitten too deep; anger and hatred, far from being subdued at the death of the Yorkist leader, strengthened the arm of strife. And anyway there could be no Lancastrian victory while King Henry, captured at Northampton, remained a puppet king in Yorkist hands. In fact Wakefield merely gave fresh impetus to the struggle. Queen Margaret hastened from Scotland to York, where her council were unanimous in calling for a march on London to free the King; and the Earls of March and Warwick – both with fathers to avenge – who were on the Welsh border and in Warwickshire respectively, at the same time realized the urgency of securing the capital. Thus we see the two sides girding themselves for yet another trial of strength.

Warwick received the news of Wakefield on or about 3 January and lost no time in getting to London. But once there a strange inertia seems to have come upon him; for a whole month he did virtually nothing. He does not seem to have been in touch with his protégé, the nineteen-year-old new Duke of York, Edward, until after Edward had defeated Jasper Tudor, Earl of Pembroke, at Mortimer's Cross on 2 February (see p. 120); he made no personal attempt to settle certain disaffected areas in the home counties; and he issued no commissions of array, nor took any steps to recruit men in the important Midland counties, but relied chiefly on his large Kentish following. On the other hand he does seem to have taken infinite pains in procuring many strange devices for a defensive battle. When Warwick eventually marched out of London he certainly had a formidable and well armed force, but the total – and surprising – lack of intelligence concerning his enemy's progress obviously inhibited him from making a constructive plan.

Warwick was not normally a sluggish and incompetent commander, and his performance immediately before and at the Second Battle of St Albans seems to have been out of character; but it could well have extinguished Edward of York's prospects of ever becoming king, and it was largely responsible for the poor opinion that Edward always held of his cousin the Kingmaker as a military commander. Edward himself set about raising men for his march on London as soon as he learned of Wakefield; he had in fact started at the head of some 10,000 troops when news reached him of the Lancastrian rising in Wales. He turned back to defeat Pembroke, but then he would have been better employed hastening to join Warwick (his victory was gained more than a fortnight before St Albans) than chasing his opponents and chopping off their heads.

Queen Margaret left York somewhere around 20 January at

the head of an army that may at first have numbered 40,000 men. The northern Lancastrians had rallied to her in good numbers, but the bulk of her army comprised moss-troopers from the borders – rascally ruffians in the game solely for what they could get from it. Andrew Trollope, who it will be remembered deserted to the Lancastrians after Blore Heath (see p. 116), is usually credited with having the overall command. This may seem strange, for he was certainly not in command a month later at Towton, and there were such distinguished persons as the Duke of Somerset (a favourite and not an insignificant commander), the Duke of Exeter, the Earls of Northumberland, Devon and Shrewsbury and Lord Clifford also in the field. But, together with the Queen, this distinguished soldier may well have formulated the Lancastrian plan, which was bold, imaginative and, for those times, unorthodox. We know the army's route as far as Royston from the trail of pillage and destruction and the burning towns it left behind. From Royston the Lancastrians probably marched down Icknield Way to Luton, and on learning of a 200-strong Yorkist contingent in Dunstable they made a short detour in order to wipe out the whole force. This was completed by the afternoon of 16 February.

The Earl of Warwick left London on 12 February, accompanied by, among others, the Dukes of Norfolk and Suffolk, the Earl of Arundel, Lords Bourchier, Bonville and Montagu and Sir Thomas Kyriell. He did not consider it safe to leave Henry in London, so the King was brought along, eventually to be placed under a tree from where he could brood agreeably upon the discomfiture of his enemies. The size of Warwick's army is given variously as between 9,000 and 30,000 men. The figure of 30,000 is probably much too high, but as is so often the case we have only the haziest idea of the numbers engaged. Almost certainly the Lancastrians had the edge, although by the time the Queen's army reached Dunstable the majority of the wild northerners had amassed their quota of loot and gone off home. Gregory* says that she went into battle only 5,000 strong; it is unusual for a chronicler to err on the low side, but this is surely too few. Perhaps some 20,000 men fought at St Albans, of which Warwick had rather less than half.

On reaching St Albans on the evening of the 12th Warwick halted. His intelligence was sadly lacking, for although there is reason to believe that he knew the Lancastrians were crossing his front from east to west, the first real intimation he got of the enemy's whereabouts was when they attacked his flank. He

*The Historical Collections of a Citizen of London in the fifteenth century, ed. James Gairdner, p.212.

128

apparently spent four days in preparing a defensive position (which in the event had to be hastily altered), confident that his enemy would oblige him with the usual frontal attack. But this was to be a most unusual battle, and Warwick himself – no doubt partly on account of his lack of information – was the first to abandon orthodoxy.

He took up a position that stretched from St Albans to Nomansland Common, which lies four miles to the north; he did not, of course, hold an unbroken line, but covered this long front with four unconnected defensive positions. The right flank probably rested on the high ground immediately south of Nomansland Common; the centre on the ridge west of Sandridge; the left either in Beech Bottom or on the high ground of Bernard's Heath; and on the extreme left in the town by the watch tower he stationed a strong body of archers. There remains the question of the troops at Dunstable. Quite likely these were a small band of local volunteers hastily brought together, for the chroniclers tell us that they were commanded by a butcher, who appears to have escaped the slaughter and later hanged himself out of shame.

We have a very full description of the devices used to protect at least some of these positions. On the ground were placed huge caltrops, which were spiked lattices that would effectively break up a cavalry charge, while the infantry were taken care of by stout nets measuring twenty-four feet long by four feet wide, fixed upright by iron rods with a nail standing upright at every second knot – the meshes being wide enough to allow the defenders to fire arrows through them. In addition there were many hundreds of pavises (door-shaped shields of thick wood) supported by stakes, from behind which archers and arbalesters discharged arrows and quarrels through holes pierced for that purpose. Warwick had some cannon and his Burgundian mercenaries were using the hand-gun, a weapon little known in England then, that 'wolde schute bothe pellettys of ledde and arowys of elle lengthe with VI fetherys, III in myddys and III at the other ende, with grete myghty hedde of yryn'.* These hand-guns were in fact more lethal to the operator than to the enemy. A section of the Burgundians called petardiers were employed throwing 'wylde fyre', which belched from an ignited earthenware pot that they flung in the faces of their enemy – another hideously unreliable weapon.

In those days when communications were of a most primitive kind, why did Warwick abandon one of the most important prin-

*ibid., p.213.

ciples – concentration of effort – and disperse his force in so dangerous a way as to invite defeat in detail? One eminent military historian* asserts that from Harpenden two roads led to London, one via St Albans and the other via Hatfield, and that Warwick wanted to cover them both. But a look through some old maps reveals no sign of a road running from Harpenden through Nomansland to Hatfield, nor does one seem to be mentioned by the chroniclers. Possibly, not knowing the exact line of the enemy's advance, he wanted to ensure that he was not bypassed, and by throwing out strongly defended positions on a wide front he hoped that the one eventually attacked could hold out long enough for him to bring up support. In fact when one of his positions was attacked he was unable to succour it in time to save it. There is little point in trying to guess Warwick's reasons when we have only fragmentary – and often contradictory – accounts of the actual sites he occupied and the part that his defensive works played in the battle; but the latter were on a big enough scale to indicate that, apart from the uncertainty born of bad intelligence, the Yorkist commander was sadly lacking in the offensive spirit.

The Lancastrian plan of attack – and, as I have suggested, we may perhaps see the Queen's questing mind at work here – was almost as unorthodox as Warwick's defensive position. Throughout the Wars of the Roses well laid plans were frequently vitiated by the presence of a traitor in one or other camp; so it was at St Albans. A Kentish squire by name of Lovelace (whom the French chronicler Jehan de Waurin states had been captured at Wakefield and only released in order to play the traitor†) sent Queen Margaret the Yorkist plan of defence, and indicated his intention of bringing his men over at the decisive moment of the battle. Armed with this information the Lancastrians rejected the customary thrust at the heart, and determined upon a flank attack – as unprecedented as it was unsporting. The initial point of attack would be the archers in St Albans, and once they had been disposed of the army was to swing left against the Bernard's Heath position. Dunstable to St Albans is twelve miles, and in order to gain surprise the approach march was to be made at night.

The hard core of the Lancastrian army still remaining under arms had had a lot of marching, and on 16 February a tough skirmish in Dunstable. All this was now followed by a night march down Watling Street, which was no longer a nice paved way, and by

*A. H. Burne, *Battlefields of England*, p.84.
†*Anciennes Chronicques d'Engleterre*, II, p.264.

130

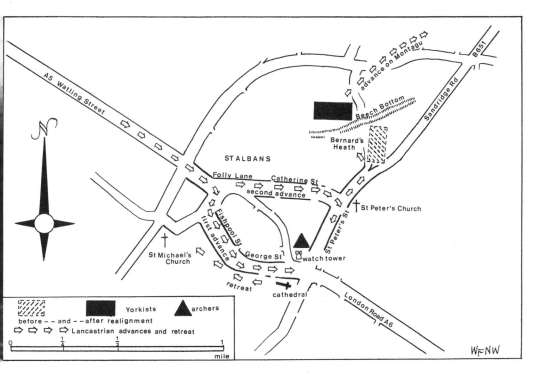

Above: The second battle of St Albans (first phase). Below: The second
battle of St Albans (second phase, note east-west orientation)

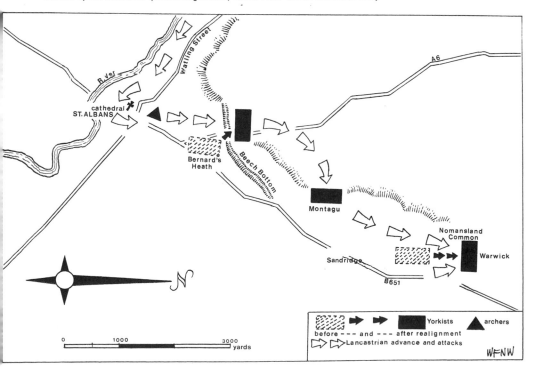

dawn on 17 February, as the troops crossed the river Ver and ascended what are now Fishpool Street and George Street, they must have been feeling far from fresh. The town barriers were not manned, but round the watch tower and Eleanor Cross the archers, although a comparatively small force, resisted with such spirit that they pushed back the Lancastrian advanced guard, who retreated precipitately on the main body by St Michael's Church. Clearly this narrow way could not be forced; a scouting party was sent out who soon reported that the archers could be outflanked by an advance up Folly Lane and into St Peter's Street via Catherine Street. This was successfully accomplished, and presented the archers with an unpleasant situation, for the rear of the Lancastrians was only moving away from St Michael's Church when the van was in St Peter's Street; the Yorkists had therefore to watch two fronts. But the second phase of the Lancastrian plan, to roll up the Yorkist left flank, could not be put into operation until the archers had been liquidated as a fighting force. For the second time in less than six years the streets of St Albans became a battleground; and in a restricted area where deployment was difficult these highly skilled bowmen were able to give so good an account of themselves that the morning was well advanced before they were done with.

Thus far, with the exception of the exact sitings of Warwick's positions, we are on firm ground. All of it has been recounted by one or more contemporary, or near contemporary, chroniclers. But now we are forced into the realms of conjecture. No detailed account of the rest of the fight exists, and one can only be constructed from the few threads of surviving evidence. The student of military history has the chance to open his own window upon the past, for the official one has long since been closed.

We have seen that Warwick's left-hand defensive position was in the Bernard's Heath area, immediately north of the town. At the bottom of this small patch of heath there is still a length of the great ditch that the Belgae dug before the Roman occupation; at one time it stretched from the town through Sandridge almost to Wheat-hampstead, and the portion still extant is even now some thirty feet deep. It was of course a natural defensive position, and it is possible – as some historians assert – that Warwick's men held it in the first instance, and on learning of the Lancastrian attack in St Albans pulled out onto the high ground facing south instead of west, and that the main fight took place there.

We know that the Bernard's Heath troops did not go to the aid of the archers, who were left to their fate, and most contemporary accounts refer to only one further main engagement and a rearguard

132

action. The main engagement must have been fought either on Bernard's Heath or on the high ground above Sandridge a mile or so to the north. In spite of Gregory's inference that the complicated defensive equipment was rendered useless through the flank attack, we have Andrew Trollope's word that he was incapacitated by a wound received from a caltrop, so at any rate some of the protective devices must have been re-aligned in time to receive the attack. If the Bernard's Heath contingent held the line of the ditch they may not have had any further artificial protection – and anyway they would have had little time to dismantle it and drag it to the high ground. It therefore seems more likely that they withdrew behind the limited protection of the Sandridge post which, under Warwick's brother Lord Montagu, bore the brunt of the main attack.

The precise spot on which the battle was fought cannot be known for certain, but we have sufficient information about the fighting to enable us to make a reasonable reconstruction of events. The February air was chill and keen; and as the Lancastrian host, each man wearing besides his lord's livery the white ostrich feather on crimson and black (the badge of the young Prince of Wales), advanced upon the Yorkist ranks, snowflakes began to fall from a leaden sky. We are told that the buffeting wind sweeping flurries of snow into the eyes of the Yorkists played havoc with their shooting, and made the task of their hand-gunners more perilous than ever. These troops were, of course, outnumbered, but relied upon what they hoped would be their superior firepower to hold the enemy at bay until Warwick could strengthen their ranks with the men from Nomansland. But amid the falling snow and yellow fog of powder smoke, loud explosions followed by jagged pieces of metal that tore through the Yorkists ranks told a tale of exploded guns. Soon the fire from these unreliable weapons ceased altogether, and as the opposing ranks closed the fighting was sword to sword, axe to axe, with Montagu trying to shore up his wavering line and Trollope trying to crush him before reinforcements could arrive.

The Abbot Whethamstede asserts that the Yorkists would have won had their endurance equalled their valour at the outset; but there is a limit as to how much battering the smaller army can withstand in close quarter fighting, and Montagu's men fought for many hours before, judging themselves abandoned as the archers had been, the last bonds of discipline snapped. What, meanwhile, was Warwick doing? He certainly never lacked physical courage and the one account that credits him with leading a cavalry charge with fresh troops may well be true, but much of his time seems to have

133

been spent in striving to hold his timorous lieutenants in leash. There were those who argued that to reinforce failure was foolish, and that it would be wiser to withdraw the right wing from the field while it was still intact, and march to join the Duke of York. But Warwick eventually managed to overcome such caitiff counsel and set off with these fresh troops to relieve his hard-pressed brother.

It was at this stage of the battle, just as Warwick had managed to get the right wing on the move to reinforce his centre, that the Kentish squire Lovelace went over to the enemy with his troops. Naturally this had a most demoralizing effect, and in any event it was by now too late to save Montagu. His men, who had resisted with the utmost constancy against superior numbers, had already broken, leaving their commander to be captured. As they poured back in disorder, closely pursued by the victorious Lancastrians slashing and thrusting with intent to kill and destroy, the atmosphere was heavy with defeat. However, Warwick, whose nerves were of steel and who seemed unaffected by the strain of the day and the imminent peril, now managed to save the Yorkists from utter rout and ruin. Somehow he stabilized a line above Nomansland Common, and here until dusk he stood at bay against the howling Lancastrian wolves. No doubt the enemy, who had marched all night, had had a stern fight and were without their wounded commander, preferred to hunt Yorkist fugitives along the patchwork of hedges to tackling a fairly formidable force of fresh troops; but in any case Warwick's final stand, and his orderly withdrawal from the field with 4,000 fighting men, went some way to atone for his lamentable lack of generalship in the early stages of the battle.

Throughout the Wars of the Roses both sides so often owed their victory to the odium of military treachery that one hesitates to predict what the result might have been had the losing commander not been betrayed. At St Albans the defection of Lovelace may have hastened the end, but Warwick never seemed to have a grip on the battle, and in hoping for victory from an already inferior force rendered more so by his curious dispositions he was asking his men to perform a prodigy of war.

The chroniclers are fairly consistent in estimating the numbers killed in this battle, and a figure of about 2,300 is usually accepted. On this occasion very few men of importance fell in the battle; however, the unpleasant practice of slaughtering prominent prisoners of war was now becoming commonplace. King Henry had been placed in the care of Lord Bonville and Sir Thomas Kyriell, who after the battle conducted him to Lord Clifford's tent,* where amid scenes of much joy he was reunited with his queen. It is said that his guardians had been offered a safe conduct, but they were brave men to place themselves in the empoisoned hands of Queen Margaret on such a tenuous understanding. Their fate was probably inevitable, but the manner of it – if correctly recounted by the chroniclers – was particularly loathsome. The Queen had them brought before the Prince of Wales, and said: 'Fair son, what manner of death should these knights, whom ye see here, die?' to which the boy, not yet eight years old but clearly aware of what was expected of him, replied, 'Let them have their heads taken off.' Lord Montagu's life was spared, possibly because he had been Henry's chamberlain, but more likely because Somerset's brother was a prisoner of the Neville faction in Calais. The only Lancastrian of distinction killed was Sir John Grey of Groby, whose widow Elizabeth was soon to become Queen of England.

At St Albans Warwick may have lost his reputation for victory, but he retained his courage and resolution. He accepted responsibility, made no accusations, levelled no reproaches; intent only on continuing the struggle, he led the remnants of his army across the miry roads and tracks that led, not to London, for that would have been hopeless, but westward to Chipping Norton, where he joined the Duke of York.

From the ashes of defeat would come a new flood of strength welling from depths as yet unplumbed. Warwick determined that he would palter no longer with a puppet king in whose name a plundering horde had recently ravaged many of the principal towns of England. There was no sense in striving to prop up a broken reed. Only a year before he had been vehement in opposing any change of dynasty, now he saw the need for a new effulgence to dazzle and to dominate. A fortnight after the Yorkist defeat at St Albans the young man whose badge the losing army had worn was proclaimed Edward IV at Westminster.

Before March was out the stigma of St Albans was to be expunged; Warwick wasted no time in assembling a new army reforged on the anvil of monarchy and ready to strike hard and swiftly at the enemy. Queen Margaret had withdrawn her army to Yorkshire; the new king was eager for pursuit, and the heavy hand of vengeance was to be laid upon the Lancastrians in the slaughter of Towton (see p.120 or chapter 9 for a full account).

*In some accounts Lord Clifford is said to have commanded the Lancastrian army, but this is most unlikely. There is, however, no reason why he should not have received the King.

DEVELOPMENT OF WEAPONS

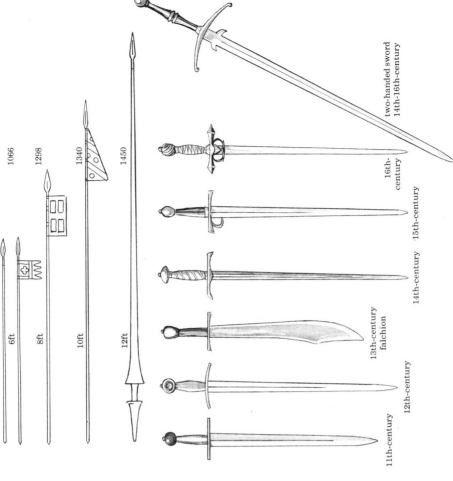

1066
1298
1340
1450

6ft
8ft
10ft
12ft

two-handed sword
14th-16th-century

16th-century

15th-century

14th-century

13th-century
falchion

12th-century

11th-century

Spears and Lances (above right)
The spear or javelin used by both Saxon infantry and Norman cavalry appears from the Bayeux Tapestry to have been 5 to 6 feet long, and to have been used both for thrusting and casting. 13th and 14th-century illuminated manuscripts show spears lengthening and developing by the 15th century into the heavy, tournament-type spear or lance

Longbow and Shortbow (above)
The shortbow used until Edward I's time (c. 1270) was about 3 or 4 feet long. The 6-foot longbow with a pull of 60 to 90 pounds, developed first in Wales, became by the 14th century the national weapon of the English. Arrows were 3 feet long and had heads of various shapes: broad, leaf-shaped for use against horses, long and narrow for piercing armour. The longbow was used from the 14th to 16th century. Short, hunting bows were still used by some Scottish clansmen during the Civil War

Swords (right)
Beginning as a fairly short weapon mainly for cutting and slashing, the sword tended to grow steadily stiffer, longer and more pointed through the centuries, and so better suited for thrusting as well as cutting. There were many minor variations within the main development, but the 13th-century falchion was a particularly unusual weapon designed to increase the weight and penetrating power of the cut, as armour improved. The 6-foot long two-handed broadsword was a 14th-century invention. It achieved little popularity in England but found great favour in Scotland in the 14th to 16th century, being called

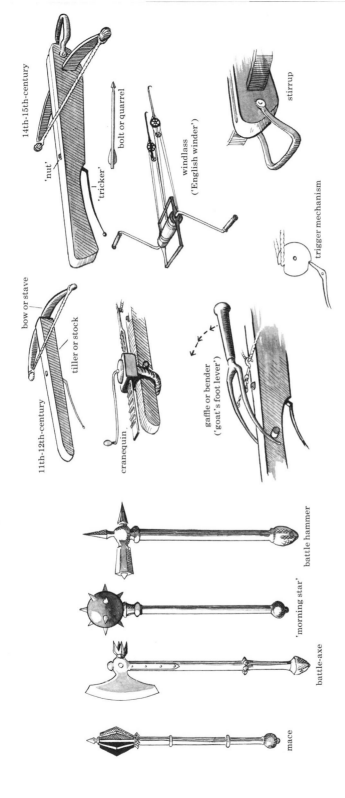

14th-15th-century

'nut'

'tricker'

bolt or quarrel

windlass
('English winder')

stirrup

trigger mechanism

bow or stave

11th-12th-century

tiller or stock

cranequin

gaffle or bender
('goat's foot lever')

battle hammer

'morning star'

battle-axe

mace

Arbalest or Crossbow

The crossbow was spanned by pulling the cord back with both hands while the archer's foot steadied the front end on the ground, in later models with the aid of a stirrup. These later more powerful bows required first a hook attached to the belt and eventually spanning devices such as the windlass, the cranequin and the simpler 'goat's foot lever'. The bolt or quarrel was a stout, heavy missile about a foot long, fletched with vanes of parchment, wood or leather, often angled to impart spin. Little used in England as a military weapon after the development of the longbow, the crossbow reappeared during the Wars of the Roses when foreign mercenary troops were brought in

Maces, Battle-Axes and Battle Hammers

Heavy maces with flanged or spiked heads, battle-axes and battle hammers were used by horsemen from the 11th to 15th centuries. For crushing or piercing heavily helmeted heads, they must have been useful weapons in a mêlée

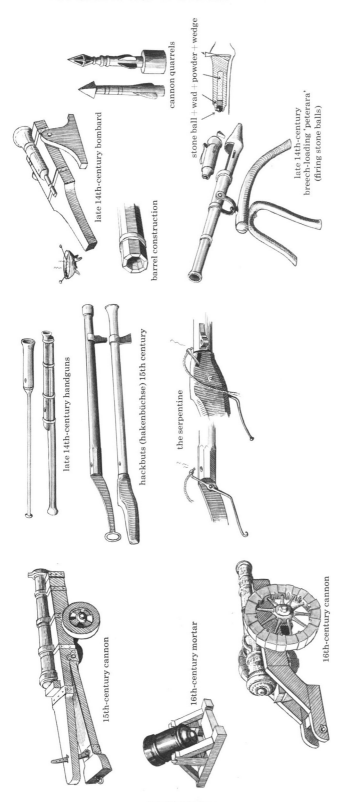

late 14th-century bombard

cannon quarrels

barrel construction

stone ball + wad + powder + wedge

late 14th-century breech-loading 'peterara' (firing stone balls)

late 14th-century handguns

hackbuts (hakenbüchse) 15th century

the serpentine

15th-century cannon

16th-century mortar

16th-century cannon

Hackbuts (hakenbüchse) 15th century

The hackbut was a larger and more advanced handgun, which could presumably be hooked over a wall or other cover to absorb recoil. The stock was of iron or wood. Developed in the early 15th century, it appears to have still been in use at Pinkie Cleuch, though it is possible that the name persisted after the invention of the slow match, which soon led to the addition of a simple device, the serpentine, to carry the lighted match to the touch-hole, and so to the development of the arquebus or matchlock musket

Handguns

Late 14th century handguns

The earliest handgun was essentially a miniature cannon, a barrel as short even as 8 inches, fixed to a wooden or iron stock or tiller which was held against the chest or tucked under the arm. Some required 2 men to handle them. Like the cannon, the handgun was fired by means of a red hot wire or coal. It was in use from the late 14th century until the end of the 15th

Guns

Cannon were used from the mid-14th century onwards. Early ones were constructed of a series of wrought-iron bars welded together longitudinally. They fired stone balls or cannon-arrows (quarrels) which were a natural development from the crossbow bolt and the ballista missile. Many early cannon were breech-loaders: the chamber containing powder, wad and ball was plugged into the breech, being held firm with wedges. The guns were fired by means of a red hot iron rod or wire, or a live coal, heated in a brazier. Breech-loaders were soon abandoned in favour of the doubtless safer and more efficient muzzle-loader

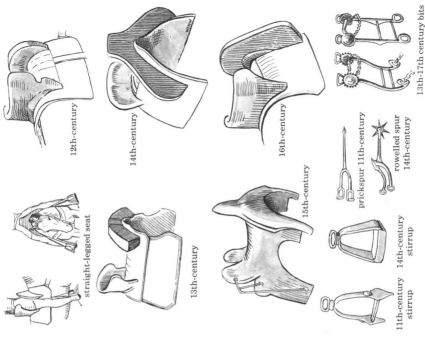

12th-century

14th-century

16th-century

13th-17th century bits

straight-legged seat

13th-century

15th-century

prickspur 11th-century

rowelled spur 14th-century

11th-century stirrup

14th-century stirrup

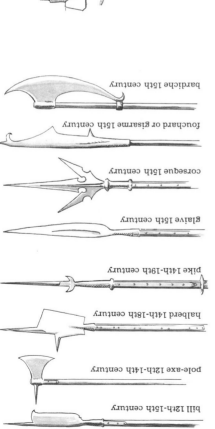

bardiche 15th century

fouchard or glsarme 15th century

corseque 15th century

glaive 15th century

pike 14th-19th century

halberd 14th-18th century

pole-axe 12th-14th century

bill 12th-15th century

Pole-Arms

Originating from agricultural and hedging implements (axes, scythes, bills) mounted on poles, pole-arms were in use by infantry throughout the 11th to 18th centuries, becoming steadily longer, more elaborate and more varied. Most of the 13th to 16th century ones included a point for thrusting, a heavy blade for cutting and a rear spike or hook for dragging horsemen from their saddles. A feature of most is the long steel straps or 'langets' from the head down the shaft, to prevent the lopping off of the head by enemy horsemen

Saddles (right)

The medieval knight rode with a straight leg. His saddle had a high pommel and cantle, of which there were many varieties, both for protection of the lower trunk and thighs, and for assistance in resisting the shock and pressure of an opponent's weapons and body. A straight legged seat necessitates long spurs. These were originally prickspurs, but rowels were introduced in the early 14th century. Bits were very long cheeked and extremely severe

CHAPTER 9

The Battle of Towton

29 March 1461

*Towton is two and a half miles south of Tadcaster on the A 162 road.
Immediately south of Towton the road forks, and about a mile along
the right fork (B 1217) there stands, on the right of the road, the
battle monument. It is usually held that the Lancastrian line was
just to the south of the monument, stretching from the edge of the high
ground on the west to a little way across the A 162 road on the east.
The Yorkist battle line was on the cross ridge beyond the slight
depression that runs directly in front of the Lancastrian position in an
east-west direction.*

*The land, which is much as it was at the time of the battle, except
that then it was open heath land and now it is neatly cultivated but
still mainly unenclosed, is all privately owned. A public footpath
runs across the southern part of the battlefield, but probably the best
view is obtained from the highest point of the B 1217 road in the area
of the monument. A bridle path leads from Towton to Stutton (it
follows the line of the old London road), and about half a mile along
it the river Cock is bridged at the same spot as where the great
slaughter took place in 1461. Very little is changed here. On the
north side of Saxton Church can be seen Lord Dacre's tomb; he was
buried there after the battle, together with his horse.*

At the beginning of his reign Edward was undoubtedly much under
Warwick's influence. It was Warwick who first put kingship into
Edward's head, and it was he who organized the great military and
civilian gathering in St John's Fields, Clerkenwell, two days after
their entry into London, at which the people loudly acclaimed their
new sovereign. But Edward, although only nineteen years old, was
by no means Warwick's puppet; he had a mind of his own, and when
he stirred himself to use it – particularly in military matters – he
showed what a keen instrument it was. Moreover, as we have seen,
his confidence in Warwick as a commander had been somewhat
shaken by St Albans, and there is evidence that he placed more
reliance in his (and Warwick's) uncle, William Lord Fauconberg,
during the forthcoming Towton campaign.

There were two strangely contrasting pleasures in Edward's life:

the pursuit of leisure and the pursuit of war. When there was no fighting to be done he was foremost among the lotus-eaters; but the slightest smell of battle stimulated him to tireless industry. The speed with which he made the journey from Chipping Norton to London, and the exertions he made to mobilize an army after he had reached the city, were manifestations not only of his readiness to assume his new responsibilities, but also of his determination to stake all on building a reputation worthy of his kingly office. Warwick, who had received another contingent of Burgundians under the Seigneur de la Barde, was dispatched on 7 March to recruit men from the western Midlands; the Duke of Norfolk went to East Anglia to levy his formidable number of retainers; on 11 March Lord Fauconberg left London at the head of a strong infantry force, and on the 12th or 13th Edward himself set out for the north.

The Lancastrian army which, against all advice, King Henry had prevented from marching on London until it was too late, began its withdrawal to the north on 26 February. The holocaust from which Henry had saved London was reserved for numerous smaller towns; for the large, unruly section of mosstroopers among the Lancastrian soldiery, who had been deprived of what they regarded as the legitimate spoils of victory, considered all land south of the Trent as foreign and therefore fair game. Queen Margaret was well aware that without a triumphal entry into London to take possession of the city her army's effort at St Albans was but a hollow victory. Warwick had been deeply smitten, but she was herself too well endowed with the attributes of the warrior mind not to know that he would soon be burning for revenge. The Lancastrian leaders had the choice of three great rivers behind which they could select a strong position that would afford the army reasonable prospects of success, the Don, the Aire and the Wharfe. They chose the Aire. But in the first instance Margaret, whose guiding hand was probably still at the helm, directed them to the Tadcaster–York area, there to await the arrival of reinforcements from those northern counties which most favoured the Lancastrian cause.

Somewhere north of the Trent (we do not know exactly where) Edward, who had been following the trail of ravaged towns and burnt out homesteads blazed by the Lancastrians, was reunited with the advance elements of his army. The Don was crossed unopposed, but soon afterwards news was received that the enemy were massing behind the Aire. On Friday 27 March, from his camp at Pontefract, Edward sent a detachment under Lord Fitzwalter to reconnoitre the river crossing at Ferrybridge and if possible to seize and hold it.

Towton (see also p.120) is often considered to have been the most decisive battle of the Wars of the Roses, for this overwhelming Yorkist victory was gained in the heart of Lancastrian country, and the melancholy toll of Lancastrians who perished on the field or by the axe made serious inroads into their leadership. This assertion is open to argument; but what bears no contradiction is that it was the bloodiest battle, with the greatest number of combatants engaged, ever to be fought on British soil. And yet it is a battle upon which the contemporary chroniclers bestowed only a few lines. Perhaps the best account comes from the pen of Edward Hall, written some seventy years later. The principal facts stand out clearly from the meagre accounts, but there are many contradictions in detail, not least in respect of the numbers of men who fought and of those who were killed. Hall, in computing a figure of 48,660 Yorkist soldiers, states that he took this from the pay roll – an impeccable source, but there were many on the pay roll who were non-combatants. His estimate of 60,000 for the Lancastrian army is probably too high. Edward may have started the battle with just under 40,000 fighting soldiers, against an enemy numbering a few thousand more.

King Henry and his queen, together with their son, remained in York. Unlike at St Albans, where we do not know for certain who commanded the army, it seems that now the Duke of Somerset, although only twenty-four years old, was put in overall command. It could not have been a very enviable post with such as the veteran Earl of Northumberland, Andrew Trollope, the Duke of Exeter and Lord Dacre breathing down his neck. It was never a part of the grand design to hold the Yorkists on the line of the river; in those days it was usually better tactics to harass the enemy while he attempted a river crossing and then allow him to come up against a strongly held position with the river at his back in the event of defeat. Accordingly the main army was drawn up on the ridge that rises from the York plain between the villages of Towton and Saxton, while Lord Clifford was sent forward to dispute the crossing of the river.

The Yorkist detachment commanded by Lord Fitzwalter found the Ferrybridge crossing unguarded. The wooden bridge had been broken down, and much of that day was spent in repairing it. The night of Friday 27–8 March was passed by Fitzwalter's troops on the north bank of the river, but clearly proper precautions against surprise had not been taken. On the Saturday morning, as a cold, translucent green sky was gradually extinguishing the stars, Lord Clifford and his men swooped down upon the unsuspecting Yorkists and swept them back across the bridge they had so laboriously re-built. Lord Fitzwalter was asleep when the enemy pounced, and coming out of his lodging to investigate the noise was promptly killed.

The contemporary chronicler William Gregory states that War-wick was present at this skirmish and slightly wounded in the leg. Hall casts him in the highly dramatic and somewhat uncharacter-istic role of the hysterical messenger of defeat: hastening back to the King with the tidings, he dismounted, drew his sword and hav-ing cut his horse's throat with it proceeded to kiss the hilt and ex-claim, 'Let him fly that will, I will tarry with him that will tarry with me.'* The story must remain apocryphal; it is most unlikely that Warwick was present at this fight, although his bastard brother was killed with Fitzwalter.

Edward, at any rate, remained absolutely calm. As soon as he learned that Clifford commanded only a strong raiding force he ordered Lord Fauconberg to cross the river four miles upstream at Castleford and cut off the Lancastrians' retreat. Fauconberg's column comprised troops led by Sir Walter Blount and the re-nowned Kentish captain Robert Horne. Their mission was entirely successful. Clifford, realizing his predicament, made a hasty re-treat, with Fauconberg always at his heels. The Yorkists finally closed on their prey in the picturesquely named Dintingdale valley.†
Here a sharp fight ensued and before the Lancastrians could regain their main body they had suffered many casualties including Clifford (who for some reason had removed his gorget and received an arrow in the neck) and John Neville.‡ The death of these two men would have cast considerable gloom over the Lancastrian host, for they were both experienced and valued leaders.

Lord Clifford and his men had almost gained the safety of their own lines, for Somerset had decided to make his stand on the low plateau south of Towton, which rises to 100 feet above sea level out of the vast York plain. The rise is scarcely perceptible on all sides except the west, where from the valley of the Cock Beck the ground ascends steeply and parts of the slopes are wooded. At its top this plateau is crossed by the east–west depression of Towton Dale,

*Hall's Chronicle, p.258.
†This valley, which is marked on the 1850 Ordnance Survey six-inch
  map, lies between Saxton village and the A 162 Tadcaster–Ferrybridge
  road.
‡Brother of Ralph, second Earl of Westmorland; this branch of the
  family were mainly Lancastrians.

which on the east side is little more than a dip, but where it drops into the river it forms a considerable gulley. At the time of the battle, when populations were small and only the best land in the immediate vicinity of the villages was cultivated, all this ground was open heath land. The little river was then a more formidable obstacle, for besides being in spate at the time of the battle and therefore in parts up to five feet deep and fast-flowing, the banks were lined with marshy ground, which near the bridge north-west of Towton assumed the proportions of a treacherous quagmire.

The Duke of Somerset awaited the enemy somewhere along the top of this plateau. In order to follow the course of the battle and the appalling slaughter that ensued it is not essential to know the exact position of the two armies, and there is no contemporary account that pinpoints these. Most historians are agreed that the Lancastrian line was situated immediately south of the battle monument, stretching from the bluff that falls sharply down to the river on the west side to a point a little way across the main Tad-caster–Ferrybridge road on the east; and that the Yorkists drew up for battle at the top of the ridge immediately south of the dip. There-fore the opposing forces faced each other across this shallow (except at the extreme west end) depression.

This opinion among historians may well be right, but it was for the Lancastrians almost what we would now call a reverse slope position, and the time was some way on before this became an accepted battle position. The forward slope of the depression was insignificant, except in one small area. It must also be remembered that Somerset had more than 40,000 men to draw up in battle order, and even allowing for the fact that both armies almost certainly fought in column of divisions he would have needed a good deal of space. The accepted position denied him some 400 yards of ground that would have been available 300 yards further south with his right resting on Castle Hill Wood, and here he would definitely have had a forward slope position.

The evidence for the generally accepted site of the battle rests almost entirely on legend: a field known as Bloody Meadow, on the west of Towton Dale, grave pits, and a 'bur tree' behind which the arrow that killed Lord Dacre was fired. The grave pits are authen-tic, but they do not necessarily indicate the initial position of either army; neither for that matter does the name given later to a field – although it helps – and the 'bur' or elder tree has long since disappeared and then, as now, there must have been a great many in the area. In accepting the majority opinion, therefore, it must be realized that there is at least one alternative site for

144

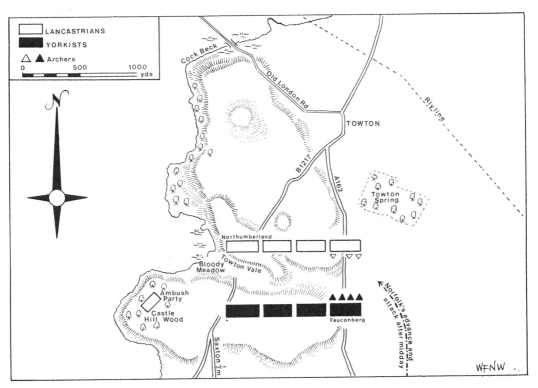

Battle of Towton. Note Bloody Meadow: Slaughter here was extremely
heavy and survivors escaped across the Cock over the bodies of the fallen

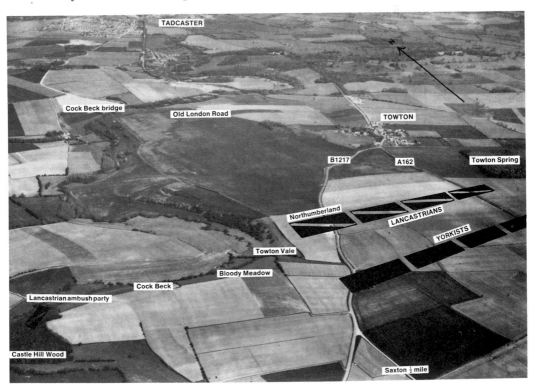

this murderous battle. However, having accepted it, it is logical also to agree that Somerset may well have placed a strong ambush in Castle Hill Wood: there would have been no very great risk in doing this and a resolutely led force on the enemy's flank could do much damage.

The Lancastrians made no attempt to support Lord Clifford, or in any way cover his withdrawal; instead they remained inactive for the whole of Saturday 28 March, awaiting the arrival of the Yorkist army. Edward had left Pontefract and crossed the river as soon as he had learned that Clifford's force had withdrawn with Fauconberg in pursuit. The main body probably crossed the river at Castleford, for the bridge at Ferrybridge was being either rebuilt or greatly strengthened to take the cannon and supply wagons. In this approach march of nine miles no doubt Edward and Warwick led the way, but later in the day Fauconberg and his victorious troops would have rejoined the army and Fauconberg then assumed command of the vanguard.

The head of the Yorkist army reached Saxton village well before dark, but a large army always has stragglers and the wagon train was still far back. Edward wisely decided to postpone the issue until the following day. The Yorkists advanced to within half a mile of their foe, but it was a wild and bitter night with a whiff of snow in the air and the wind – then from the north – deadened the sound of their approach. The men of both armies lay down on the cold ground with no protection from the elements. Sentries were posted, and as darkness gradually enveloped the landscape straining eyes would seem to detect parties of enemy stealthily approaching. But soon the few trees, which stood in elemental solitude on that windswept plateau, surrendered their weird shapes to the night, and all was quiet, save for the whine of the wind.

The morning of 29 March, which was Palm Sunday, dawned cold and cloudy. The wind had now gone round to the south and as the Yorkists prepared to advance to the crest of the plateau it began to snow. Edward was in no hurry to engage, for he was still short of the Duke of Norfolk's contingent,* but he would not have waited too long with so powerful an army to his front. The chroniclers mostly agree that the fight, including the immediate

*The Duke of Norfolk was a sick man; he died the following November. He may or may not have fought in person, but certainly his troops arrived on the scene late in the day and had a decisive influence on the battle. Some accounts say that Norfolk was left at Pontefract to follow on with the reserve; but it seems more probable that his contingent was always a day's march behind.

pursuit, lasted for ten hours – a long time for those days – so it must have started before 10 a.m., for by 8 p.m. it would have been almost pitch dark. We do not know the order of battle, nor the formations adopted, but from the meagre accounts of the fighting, and the knowledge that vast numbers were employed in a limited space, it is reasonable to assume that both armies fought in column of divisions (or battles) and not in extended order as was usual. And we do know that Lord Fauconberg commanded the Yorkist van and was responsible for the first successful phase of the battle.

The strong south wind that blew snow into the Lancastrians' faces put them at a grave disadvantage, the full significance of which seems to have escaped even so experienced a soldier as Andrew Trollope who, together with Northumberland, commanded the Lancastrian van. Fauconberg advanced his archers a few paces and ordered them to fire a single volley into the enemy and then withdraw to the main body. The volley took some effect and the Lancastrians immediately returned the fire, but the combination of a headwind and the withdrawal of the Yorkist archers caused their arrows to fall short by '40 tailor's yards'. However, so bad was their fire discipline that they continued to loose off arrows until their quivers were empty. Fauconberg then advanced his archers again, this time to keep up a steady fire not only with their own arrows, but also with the many that had fallen harmlessly from enemy bows. Those they did not return were stuck in the ground to impede the oncoming troops, for the Lancastrians were the first to advance.

Cannon appears to have played no part in this battle – indeed the Yorkist guns may not even have arrived on the field in time – but the archery was a sufficient irritation to the Lancastrians to cause them to close with their enemy. As they entered the depression, and marched steadily up the slope towards the inexorable firing line, their casualties were heavy – especially on the west above Bloody Meadow where the slope was at its steepest – but once the two armies were joined in the savagery of hand-to-hand combat their very weight of numbers gave them some advantage, and the wind and snow were of less worry to them. This desperate contest was fought upon an unprecedented scale between at least 80,000 men in a very circumscribed area. It was a soldiers' battle, for there was little that the commanders could do, except to keep feeding fresh men into the fray to take the place of wounded or fallen comrades. A dreadful ardour inspired all ranks; men thirsted to be at their enemy's throats to kill and be killed. It was said that in places the dead lay so thick on the ground that the troops from the rear divisions were marching over a carpet of bodies to get at their foe.

. For three hours the struggle continued thus. Some pauses were inevitable, but for the rival commanders there was no respite. Casualties among the leaders were heavy, and those still fighting had the constant task of shoring up the front lines with ever-dwindling reserves. The Yorkist left may have felt the effects of the Castle Hill Wood ambush, while the centre and right were holding on grimly, but by around midday fortune, indifferent to sacrifice though smiling upon numbers, clearly favoured the Lancastrians. Edward remained cool and resolute; he was everywhere to encourage by word and example; although only nineteen he displayed a nerve of steel. The Yorkists were indeed lucky in their leaders, for the young king had invaluable support from such as Warwick and Fauconberg. But by now only one man's name could have been on all lips. Where was the Duke of Norfolk?

Slowly, but surely, the Yorkists were giving ground; back now nearly to the southern edge of the plateau, hacking and thrusting with sword and bill amid gaps that were gradually widening, for it was becoming increasingly difficult to fill them. But just as the battle had reached its crisis, the spirit of hope was rekindled throughout Edward's rapidly weakening army: out of the gloom there appeared the Duke of Norfolk's banners. Marching through the ancient hamlet of Sherburn in Elmet with what speed they could muster in the slush and snow, his men had arrived on the right of the Yorkist army and they wasted no time in taking up position. It was now a little after midday and Norfolk's arrival marked the turning point in the battle. But it did not cause any immediate panic or disintegration among the Lancastrian soldiers; stubbornly they fought on, still almost shoulder to shoulder, and the issue remained in doubt until the now extended Yorkist line could turn the Lancastrian left. At first, almost imperceptibly, the Yorkists regained their lost ground, and then more noticeably the Lancastrians began to give way. A trickle to the rear gradually spread into mass flight. By the late afternoon this tremendous trial of strength was over. The Lancastrian army was in full retreat.

As always in those days, when men attempted to flee encumbered by armour or heavy equipment, it was in the retreat that the heaviest losses occurred, and the nature of the terrain played a decisive part in this. We can therefore believe that the slaughter in the field known as Bloody Meadow would have been very heavy, for it was a veritable trap with the river on one side and on the other a steep slope that left only a narrow, marshy passage of flat ground. The obvious line of retreat was towards Towton and along the old London road, which had been the Lancastrian line of advance; but this involved the crossing of the swollen stream by a small wooden bridge surrounded by a marshy quagmire. So long as they were on the plateau we hear of pockets of Lancastrians turning at bay and fighting with great courage and desperation to stave off defeat, but as soon as the steep decline to the London road and the river was reached all semblance of discipline seems to have disappeared, and men rushed headlong to the crossing. The ghastly scene of destruction by steel and water has often been described; men were slaughtered, or trampled into a watery grave, in such thousands that the chroniclers probably did not exaggerate when they said that the survivors crossed the Cock over the bodies of the fallen, and that the water still ran red when it joined the river Wharfe three miles downstream.

Not all the Lancastrians would have converged on the bridge at Towton; no doubt some of those fighting on the left would have tried to reach Tadcaster across country, but accounts of further fighting on the 30th between Towton and Tadcaster would seem to be inaccurate. Mopping up went on almost to the gates of York; Sir John Denham and Sir John Wenlock were sent in pursuit with a strong cavalry force and killed many with little resistance.

The numbers of those who perished on the field of battle, in the waters of the Cock, or in the pursuit beyond its banks will never be accurately known. Polydore Vergil, writing some fifty years after the battle, gives a figure for both armies of 20,000, of which he says 10,000 were wounded and made prisoner (some of whom died). This is the lowest estimate and is of interest in mentioning prisoners, for most authorities say that there was no quarter given. The Monk of Croyland heads the list with a figure of 38,000 and Hall is not far behind with 36,776; in the Paston letters we get a total of 28,000 of which 20,000 were Lancastrians, and this latter figure is supported by another contemporary writer, the Abbot Whethamstede. The truth may lie somewhere between Polydore Vergil's and Paston's figures, and is sufficiently horrifying without accepting the probably exaggerated higher numbers.

Particular attention was paid, as in most of these battles, to cutting down men of rank. The list of Lancastrian peers and knights who fell is formidable indeed. The Earl of Northumberland was carried off the field badly wounded, only to die the next day; Lords Dacre, Clifford, Neville, de Maulay, and Welles were killed, and among the knights to perish were Sir Andrew Trollope, Sir

Henry Stafford, Sir John Heyton and Sir Richard Percy. Thomas Courtenay, Earl of Devon, was made prisoner, and on the Monday when Edward rode into York the Earl's head was needed to replace that of Edward's father, which had adorned the walls since the Battle of Wakefield (see p. 119). Later in the month the Earl of Wiltshire was captured and he too was executed. Henry and Margaret were hustled out of York with a small escort and headed for the safety of the Scottish border; the Dukes of Somerset and Exeter also made good their escape. The Yorkists lost few men of rank. Lord Fitzwalter, Sir Richard Jenney, Warwick's bastard brother, and Robert Horne were the only prominent men to be killed, while Lord Scrope of Bolton was severely wounded.

Edward had won this, his first major engagement, on merit. There seems little doubt that although well supported by more experienced men he was not content to act as their parade ground fugleman, but was in active command of the army from the day of assembly until the march into York. The Lancastrians may have suffered from divided leadership; certainly the affair at Ferry-bridge and the subsequent fate of Lord Clifford and his men showed a lamentable lack of generalship, and the first phase of the battle was lost through inexperience or indifference on the part of the vanguard commanders.

In the space of ten hours a sizable slice of the English aristocracy and gentry had been dealt a crippling blow. But if the limbs are lopped the trunk remains. Despite the devastation to their ranks during the Wars of the Roses scarcely an English peerage became extinct,* and fifty years later when a similar disaster overtook the Scots at Flodden (see chapter 13) their ancient nobility showed the same powers of recovery. The fact remains that the total casualties in this one battle were almost a third of those suffered throughout the Wars of the Roses. Lurking foes across the Scotish border and the Channel must have wished that they had been in a position to take advantage of this cataclysm. No one could be certain that they were not. For this reason Edward left Warwick and his brother to guard the north, while he and most of the other magnates went south to London for the happier duty of preparing for his coronation.

*Succession through the female line was partly responsible for this survival.

CHAPTER 10

The Battle of Barnet

14 April 1471

Although the actual site of this battle is surprisingly free from buildings, there are, unfortunately, sufficient to make it difficult to view the complete positions of the rival armies from the ground. However, it is fairly easy to trace these, and the course of the battle, piecemeal, by driving and walking the ground. The A 1000 road north from Barnet leads to Hadley Green, and just north of this Barnet suburb the road forks to Kitts End, where the monument known as the High Stone stands. Warwick's advance from St Albans took him along the Kitts End road to the High Stone.

Hadley Green is on a plateau which stretches to Barnet, and just south of the High Stone it widens to almost 2,000 yards; on this ridge both armies took up their positions. The plateau, at 400 feet, is the highest ground between London and York. Warwick's line probably ran across Hadley Green and a little way to the north of Hadley church (the present church was built after the battle); it would have stretched from a point west of the A 1000 across to where the ground starts to fall away north of the road called Camlet Way – just above Monken Hadley Common. Edward's line was about 300 yards to the south of Warwick's; it overlapped Warwick's on the right and was itself overlapped on the left. It therefore stretched, on the right, to Monken Hadley Common.

The return of Edward IV to England, his landing at Ravenspur on 14 March 1471, and his march to London have already been recorded in outline (p. 124). The Earl of Warwick's position in the kingdom, and the manoeuvring of the rival forces during the month that followed Edward's landing, need to be looked at in rather more detail in order to set the stage for the Battle of Barnet (see also p. 125). The brief period of Lancastrian restoration, which lasted from October 1470 to April 1471, marked the apogee of Warwick's power. He had married his eldest daughter Isabella to the Duke of Clarence and, so he thought, won that somewhat slippery royal gentleman to his side; his younger daughter Anne was married to Edward Prince of Wales – a match that he hoped might gain him the confidence, if not the friendship, of Queen

151

Margaret and the Lancastrian lords, by most of whom he was still regarded with deep mistrust; and above all it was Warwick, not the worn and wearied Henry, that ruled the kingdom.

But Warwick sat uneasily in Westminster. He ruled without the aura of monarchy, and, added to this grave disadvantage, his undoubted popularity with the lower classes did not extend to the merchants who, with their capitalist guilds, controlled the trade of London. These men viewed with considerable disapproval Warwick's attempts to align himself with the King of France in opposition to the Duke of Burgundy, whose territories now provided them with their best markets. Moreover, Henry's queen proved most reluctant to respond to her husband's urgings to join him in London; she was not prepared to bring her son from the safety of France until she was satisfied that no skulduggery was afoot. Her constant procrastination may have suited Warwick personally, but he was aware that her presence in the capital, and more importantly that of her son, might bring about a change of heart and strengthen the Lancastrian cause in a way which Henry alone could never achieve.

Warwick was sure that Edward of York, whom he had served so long and of whose abilities as a soldier he was perfectly aware, would attempt to regain his kingdom. The army that Warwick had promised King Louis of France would never cross the Channel, for by February 1471 every man was needed to secure the country against invasion. Warwick had reason for confidence: he had made his dispositions wisely, and the ring of steel with which he girdled the country had few gaps. The north had always favoured the Lancastrians, and now the powerful Neville family buttressed their support; his brother John, Marquis of Montagu, had an army at Pontefract, and although the loyalty of the Earl of Northumberland (whose title had recently been restored to him by Edward) was suspect, it was not thought likely that he would join Edward. The Earl of Oxford and Lord Scrope of Bolton were in charge of the east coast; the Earl of Pembroke was in Wales; the Dukes of Clarence and Somerset* and Lord Devon were raising the south-west; the men of Kent always rallied to Warwick, and the Bastard of Fauconberg was off the south coast with a fleet.

*There is a sharp difference of opinion among historians (near contemporary to modern) as to whether Somerset fought at Barnet, or whether – like Devon – he was in the south-west until the arrival of Queen Margaret. The writer is of the opinion that although he may have gone to the coast, he had returned in time to command Warwick's centre at the battle.

Warwick himself remained in London until on the news of Edward's successful landing he left the capital in charge of Henry, aided by Warwick's brother George Neville, Chancellor and Archbishop of York, and hurried into the Midlands to raise more troops.

Edward, having found the East Anglian coast too strongly guarded, landed at Ravenspur with less than 2,000 men. At Nottingham, where he felt strong enough to declare himself king, he was joined by Sir Thomas Parre, Sir James Harrington, Sir William Stanley and Sir William Norris, all of whom brought men, and by the time he reached Leicester Edward had a force of some 4,000 troops, which probably equalled that commanded by Warwick. The latter was still expecting Clarence to join him, and Montagu – who had made no attempt to intercept Edward on his march south* – had been ordered to bring his army of perhaps 3,000 troops to join Warwick, who had meanwhile shut himself into Coventry. Here he refused battle, and he also had some scathing remarks to make about the Duke of Clarence who, after he had deserted his father-in-law and made his peace with his brother at a meeting of their two armies near Banbury, persuaded Edward to offer honourable terms to Warwick and his followers should they surrender.

The road to London was open, and Edward took it, leaving Warwick, who had disdained surrender, behind the walls of Coventry. He celebrated Palm Sunday at Daventry and was at St Albans for the night of 10 April. Warwick had sent urgent messages to his brother George Neville to hold London for up to three days, by which time he would arrive and hope to take Edward in the rear. Oxford, whose troops had had to run before Edward at Newark, and Montagu had now joined Warwick, whose combined force was probably slightly in excess of what Edward commanded, even after Clarence's accession. But Edward was not to be caught between two fires. George Neville, in an attempt to rally the Londoners' patriotism, paraded the wretched Henry through their streets; but the citizens, whose interests he had squandered and whose sacrifices he had ignored, were not impressed. There were many Yorkists in London; Edward's queen, in sanctuary at Westminster, had recently given birth to a son; and the City merchants had everything to gain from Edward. The

*It is difficult to understand Montagu's lapse. As a result Warwick suspected his brother's loyalty, but this suspicion was proved quite unfounded. Possibly he thought himself too weak to attack and was waiting for Northumberland to act. The latter's neutrality undoubtedly saved the Yorkist cause.

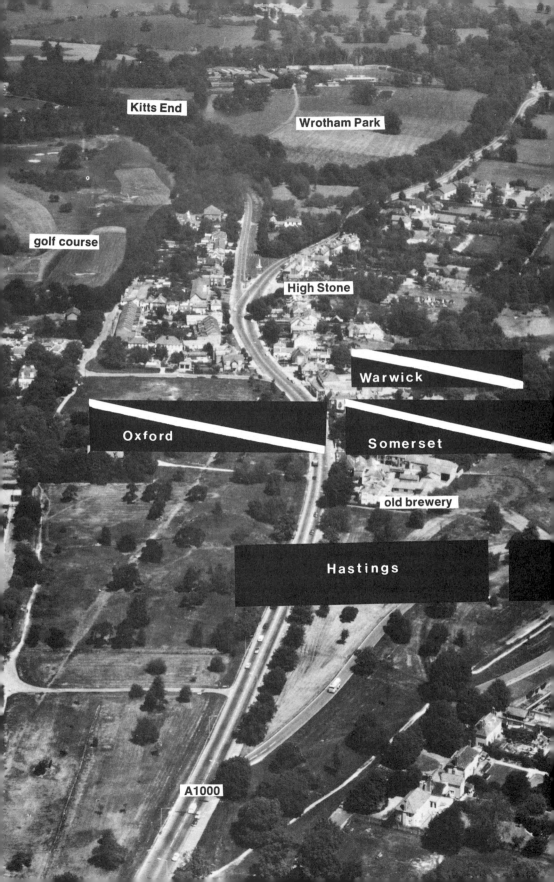

Kitts End

Wrotham Park

golf course

High Stone

Warwick

Oxford

Somerset

old brewery

Hastings

A1000

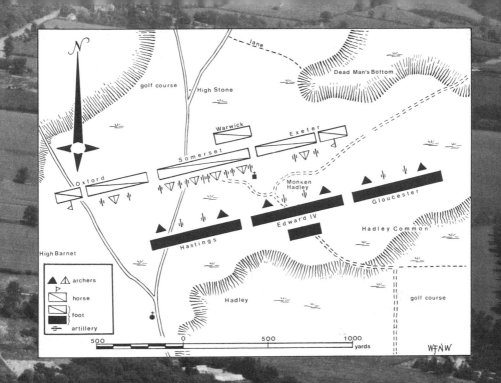

Exeter

Monken Hadley Church

Edward IV

Gloucester

eserve

Within the map:

N

golf course — High Stone — Jane — Dead Man's Bottom

Warwick — Exeter

Somerset

Oxford — Monken Hadley

Hastings — Edward IV — Gloucester

High Barnet — Hadley Common

Hadley — golf course

▲ △ archers
▷ horse
▬ foot
〜 artillery

500 — 0 — 500 — 1000 yards

WFNW

Tower was soon in Yorkist hands, and on 11 April his sympathizers opened Aldersgate and Edward entered his capital. The Chancellor had not been over-zealous in carrying out his brother's command, and in consequence was imprisoned only for a very short while.

Warwick does not appear to have learned that London was lost until he reached Dunstable on Good Friday 12 April. His progress had been slow, possibly because Edward had detached troops to hold him up, or perhaps because he was waiting for Somerset to join him. His plan to crush Edward against the City walls had failed. What action should he take now? The chroniclers bestow upon him a variety of intentions. The Yorkist author of *The arrivall of Edward IV* says that he hoped to surprise Edward off guard while celebrating the Easter festival in London – which scarcely flatters Warwick's intelligence. More likely are the suggestions that Warwick knew his man and knew that he would not just sit in London waiting to be attacked. Whether he was moving to block Edward's route to the Midlands via Ermine Street or whether Warwick was just waiting for Edward to attack him cannot be told, but we know that he advanced from Dunstable to St Albans on Good Friday, spent the night there and on Easter Saturday moved forward to within half a mile of Barnet, where, on learning that Edward had left London, he took up a position on Hadley Green – then called Gladmore Heath.

Edward needed no prompting to advance upon his enemy; he was never one to shirk a fight and he knew that only by destroying Warwick in open battle could he hope to retain the kingdom. He had been reunited with his wife and had seen his son for the first time on Thursday; Good Friday was spent in religious devotions; and by Saturday he was ready to march. Once more poor Henry was dragged up that northern road to be a helpless spectator of the quarrels that he had started but had long since ceased to influence. It was to be his last adventure.

Again we do not know the numbers that fought at Barnet. One chronicler puts the Lancastrian army alone at 30,000. This is almost certainly an unrealistic figure,* and if we say that Edward

*These high figures are often reached through a series of greatly
 exaggerated numbers relating to the various private armies that the
 magnates brought to the battlefield.

156

moved out of London at the head of 8,000 men to meet about 9 or 10,000 under Warwick we shall probably be nearer the truth.

Warwick had approached from St Albans by the only road existing at that time, which ran through South Mimms to Dancer's Hill and Kitts End; when he arrived at where the High Stone now stands he found himself on the plateau that stretches southward from Hadley Green to Barnet. In the vicinity of the Old Fold golf course's clubhouse the ridge becomes broad enough for him to deploy his army for about 800 yards on either side of the present A 1000 road – although in those days the road ran immediately to the east of the clubhouse – and here he had taken up a position on the afternoon of Saturday 13 April. His right battle was commanded by the Earl of Oxford, who was a very experienced soldier; it seems probable that he had Montagu with him,* for although fitted for independent command Warwick still did not entirely trust him. The centre was commanded by Somerset, and the left nominally by Warwick but with the Duke of Exeter in support. Warwick placed his horse on both flanks, and Somerset had the bulk of the archers in the centre. We get no information about any reserve; this was still not a regular feature of an order of battle, but nearly all the chroniclers make special mention of Edward's reserve. Almost certainly Warwick would not have remained on the left flank during the battle, and he may have been in personal command of a small reserve behind the centre.

Edward arrived at Barnet just as it was getting dark, and he soon cleared the place of Warwick's scouts. In spite of the darkness he wisely decided that his army should not camp in the village, but should take up a position close to the enemy ready for a dawn assault. It is no easy matter to deploy some 8,000 men for battle on unreconnoitred ground in the dark, and it is scarcely surprising that Edward failed to get exactly square to Warwick's line and came rather closer to the enemy than he intended. His right was commanded by his eighteen-year-old brother, Richard Duke of Gloucester; the centre battle he kept for himself, with Clarence under command – probably for the same reason as Warwick had put Montagu under surveillance; and Lord Hastings (who together with Lord Saye and Sele had landed with Edward) took charge of the left. Henry was probably stationed with the reserve, which would have been immediately in the rear of the centre battle.

The darkness of the night and Edward's miscalculation of

*Those who say that Somerset was not present at the battle give Montagu command of the centre.

distance saved his troops from a very unpleasant pommelling, for Warwick, who was superior in artillery – and apparently not short of ammunition – kept up a lively cannonade during the hours of darkness; but the missiles passed harmlessly over Edward's line, and his men were ordered to keep silence and show no fires.

The ground on which the two armies lay that Easter Eve 500 years ago even now holds a good deal of water, and at that time it and the surrounding countryside contained large areas of bog. Warm days and cold nights frequently produce thick mists from such ground, and so it was on the morning of the battle. As the light grew stronger and the darkness rolled away, the cold, stiff soldiers rose from the damp ground, reached for their arms and prepared for battle. In the blanket of fog that surrounded them even outlines could not be discerned, and the closeness of the rival forces was only apparent from the call of the trumpeters and the muffled sounds of armour being donned. At about 5 a.m. the order to advance banners was given, and both armies, high and proud in their bearing, bore down upon each other. This was to be a battle fought mainly on foot; Warwick himself, abandoning his usual custom of leading the first assault on horseback, sent his charger to the rear at the beginning, and throughout fought alongside his men on foot. But one chronicler describes Edward in the battle 'mounted on his white steed'.

The preliminary bombardment of whistling arrows and pounding cannon ball was of short duration, and no sooner had the two hosts, looming out of the murk, become entangled in hand-to-hand combat than it became apparent that Lord Oxford on Warwick's right, and Prince Richard on Edward's, had no enemy to their immediate front. Richard, to get to the Duke of Exeter, had to swing round and ascend a slight slope, but Oxford was on perfectly flat ground and bore down heavily on Lord Hastings's flank. Taken by surprise, Hastings' men seem to have crumbled at the first shock, for we hear nothing of resistance, but only of hasty, dis- organized flight. Oxford's men chased them into Barnet and out the other side. So far did these men run that soon they were spreading tidings in London of a Yorkist defeat.

Richard was not able to compensate for the loss of the Yorkist left by an equally impressive victory against Exeter. The Duke's men proved more stubborn, and Richard's task was more difficult. Somehow Exeter got his battle to face the exposed flank, and although sorely battered – he himself was soon to be struck down and left for dead – his troops did not break. In order to give Exeter some support Somerset's battle had to partially conform and both armies now veered round to face almost east and west. This change of front and the continuing mist saved Edward.

Barnet was a battle fought by the individual commanders, for in the fog the overall picture could not have been known to the opposing generals – especially not to Warwick, who we know fought on foot encased in heavy armour. Nevertheless, at this stage victory was in his grasp if only Oxford could return in time to take Edward in the rear. The Yorkist left had fled the field – although Edward may not have known this – the right was hard held by Exeter's men, and even giving ground; and in the centre, after three hours of desperate fighting with bill and halberd, Edward had thrown in his reserve and was still probably out-numbered. Oxford was the key to victory or defeat. The fates decided that it should be defeat.

It was something of a triumph that Oxford managed to rally any of his men, but somehow he rounded up 800; the rest were either lost in the fog or taking their share of plunder for what they had already done. He retraced his steps through Barnet and up the road that led to his old position, but by the time he got back, still groping his way through the thick mist, the two armies had changed position quite considerably. Oxford could hardly be expected to find Edward's column other than by sheer luck, nor could he be blamed, in the general obfuscation that now pervaded the field, for losing Warwick the battle. The first troops with whom his returning men came into contact were those of Somerset; as they came out of the fog some of Somerset's men mistook the de Vere standard of a radiant star for Edward's banner, which carried the device of a sun with rays, and Oxford's troops began to go down under a hail of arrows. The mistake was soon dis-covered, but worse was to follow. There had been much treachery throughout the Wars, and in this new Lancastrian army there were those whose complete loyalty to Henry had yet to be proved. Someone raised the cry of treason, and panic quickly spread. Soldiers understand defeat, and are often prepared to stand their ground and fight to the last even in a cause which they may not fully comprehend, but betrayal immediately saps morale. Oxford, convinced that the worst had occurred, rode off the field – and not only his men, but many of Somerset's followed him.

It was now around 9 a.m. and Edward's reserve had already been committed; Warwick strove valiantly to shore up his crumbl-ing line, but Edward gave him no respite. Both commanders realized that this was the crisis of the battle, and through the gradually thinning mist the extent of Warwick's disaster was plain to see. Montagu had stood firm, but had been killed – possibly by his own men – in coming to Warwick's assistance; Exeter was reported dead;* and Somerset, like Oxford, had disappeared in a northerly direction. What was left of the Lancastrian army had had enough, they would not rally to Warwick still standing defiant beneath the Bear and Ragged Staff. At last the scales of illusion fell from his eyes; he recognized defeat and turning from the fray lumbered off towards his horse. But he had left it too late. Impeded by his armour, and no doubt exhausted from hours of savage fighting – at forty-two he was not a young man – he never reached his horse, being cut down somewhere in the vicinity of where the High Stone now stands.

During this battle, which lasted between three and four hours, it seems that some 1,500 men were slain – and possibly more perished in the immediate pursuit across ground still called Dead Man's Bottom. As usual the figures given vary widely, but Sir John Paston, who fought with Warwick, is a fairly reliable witness and he admits to the loss of more than 1,000 Lancastrians. Even allowing for the fact that this was a battle in which Edward, angered by the number of men that had abandoned his cause for Warwick, withheld his edict that the common soldier should, as far as possible, be spared, the figure of 4,000 sometimes quoted is too high. Of those killed probably not more than 500 were Yorkists; but the victory was hard won, for Edward lost Lord Saye and Sele, Sir John Lisle, Sir Thomas Parre and no fewer than three members of the Bourchier family: Lord Cromwell, Viscount Bourchier, and Sir Humphrey Bourchier, a son of Lord Berners.

The death of Warwick, however, outweighed every other consideration. The story of this man enshrines all the chivalrous romanticism of the Middle Ages. He was not only immensely popular with the masses, but he made a deeper and more lasting impression on his own century than any other man who was not a prince of the blood. There are those, like King Edward, perhaps on account of the Second Battle of St Albans, ready to decry his military talents, but he was a soldier of considerable capacity and unquestioned courage. In many ways he was unlucky to lose his last battle: in its early stages he was let down by his brother and betrayed by his son-in-law, and later, had he waited only a few days, support coming in from the south would have enabled him to meet Edward with overwhelmingly superior numbers. But a victory for Warwick would have exposed England to further tribulation.

*He did in fact survive the battle.

160

CHAPTER 11

The Battle
of Tewkesbury

4 May 1471

*The site of the heaviest fighting is still open country, and indeed
has probably not changed very greatly in 500 years. It lies to the
west of the A 38(T) road from Gloucester, about half a mile south
of Tewkesbury Abbey. There are two principal vantage points:
the high ground where the road passes Stonehouse Farm (from
where Edward would first have seen the Lancastrian line), and
Tewkesbury Park. This latter eminence has only recently become
public property, having been bought by Tewkesbury Borough
Council for development as a golf course: it offers the best viewpoint,
even though from it the battlefield is partially obscured by trees.
The left of the Lancastrian line and (in the writer's opinion) the
right of the Yorkist is now covered by the densely populated area
around Crouch Court and Priors Park. Gupshill Manor, a black
and white half-timbered building on the A 38(T) road just south of
Tewkesbury, is now a public house; at the time of the battle the
road from Cheltenham ran immediately to the west of it, while the
one from Gloucester was further again to the west – they joined the
present road by Holme Hospital. The museum, in Barton Street,
has an interesting model of the battle.*

On the very day that Warwick died at Barnet (see p.125 or chapter
10 for a full account) the Queen, whose cause he had so unwisely
embraced, landed at Weymouth. She had with her, among others,
her son Edward; Lord Wenlock; John Beaufort, Somerset's
brother; Sir John Langstrother, Grand Prior of the Order of St John
of Jerusalem and a Sir John Fortescue.* From Weymouth the party
proceeded to Cerne Abbey, where they learned from the Duke of
Somerset the extent of the disaster at Barnet. Momentarily Margaret's great courage deserted her; she declared that she would

*If this was the same man as the Lancastrian Lord Chief Justice his
presence here must be considered very doubtful. That Sir John
Fortescue was attainted after Towton, but later pardoned by Edward
IV and retired to Ebrington in Gloucestershire.

161

return at once to France. But she was dissuaded by the optimism of her advisers and the eagerness of her son.

The Earl of Devon had joined the Queen with a considerable force; Somerset, who had left Barnet for the north with Oxford, but had turned back, had brought some troops with him; the Lancastrians still had a following in the north; Jasper Tudor commanded an army in Wales, and the Bastard of Fauconberg was off the Kent coast and preparing to assault London. With the advantage of hindsight we know that after Barnet and the death of Warwick the Lancastrian cause was adrift on a dark, tempestuous sea, but at the time it did not appear that way even to those who had fought on the losing side. Sir John Paston, who was slightly wounded at Barnet, assured his mother in a letter written only a few days before Tewkesbury that good tidings could soon be expected;* and this was not wishful thinking, but a confidence based upon the number of men that the Lancastrians could eventually gather under the nominal command of their queen and prince.

Edward received news of Margaret's arrival on Tuesday 16 April; this was only two days after Barnet, and as he must have been expecting her to come – for it was known that she was only waiting on a favourable wind – reports that he had already disbanded his whole army may not be absolutely correct, although he would certainly have needed to raise fresh levies. Windsor was chosen as a suitable rallying point, for it was the most strategic place from which to await information as to Margaret's intentions. It was a few days before Edward knew whether the Lancastrians meant to march on London, or in the first instance move northwards and join forces with Jasper Tudor. If she – or more probably the Duke of Somerset, for in the ten years since St Albans Margaret seems to have lost some of her fire – decided on a try for London, Edward at Windsor would bar the way; if she decided to march north then he would have made a start to head them off. Edward arrived at Windsor on 19 April, and by the time the feast of St George had been celebrated the Lancastrian intention had become fairly clear. The King broke camp on 24 April and marched, without undue haste, to Malmesbury, where he arrived on the first day of May.

Somerset, who was in command of the army, and Margaret's other advisers could not have hesitated very long in deciding to march north. Barnet had been lost through impatience; the lesson to be learned was the need to concentrate resources and attack with overwhelmingly superior numbers. The army as at present

*The Paston Letters, Vol.V, p.102.

162

constituted was sorely in need of money, cannon, powder and other supplies, and even its strength was insufficient for an independent assault upon London. To cross the Severn at Gloucester – a town which held many Lancastrian sympathizers – and join Jasper Tudor would have to be the first objective. If it was to be successfully achieved the minimum of delay was essential. Unfortunately, detours were necessary in order to collect supplies and reinforcements, and this put an intolerable strain on the Queen's army, which was required to march long distances over appalling tracks. From Cerne the army went to Exeter, where Sir John Arundel and Sir Hugh Courteney joined with a strong contingent of troops; after Exeter the route was via Taunton and Glastonbury to Bath. Here the Lancastrians resorted to artifice in sending out patrols and foragers to Salisbury and Yeovil. But Edward was not deceived; by now he had reached Cirencester and was perfectly aware that Margaret was not making for London, although he appears to have been in doubt as to what her immediate intention was.

The south-west had responded well in the matter of manpower, but the Lancastrians were still sadly deficient in artillery and other stores. It was therefore necessary to turn westward and enter the friendly city of Bristol, from where they procured some much needed ordnance, but at a cost in time that was to prove fatal. The Queen's army reached Bristol on 1 May, the same day as Edward arrived at Malmesbury. If he had guessed correctly that her intention was to cross the Severn at Gloucester he was nearer to that city than she was and could have cut her off. But Edward was clearly baffled, and the Lancastrians' next little strategem confused him still further.

The Queen and Somerset had no illusions as to their danger, and spending only one night in Bristol they made all haste for Gloucester, deciding to take the direct road along the plain through Berkeley. The commanders of the rival armies each knew the approximate position of their adversary, and so it was not difficult for the Lancastrians to anticipate Edward's line of march – assuming that his object was to bring them to battle. To gain time was essential; Somerset therefore decided to send his vanguard to take up a position on Sodbury Hill – some ten miles north-east of Bristol – as though to offer battle. The remainder of the army followed, but were ordered to break off to the left and head for Berkeley, leaving the vanguard to withdraw onto the main army, having, it was hoped, delayed the enemy. The ruse became more effective when half a dozen of the King's more eager quartermasters, who had ridden ahead of the army to procure the best billets for their masters, were captured in Chipping Sodbury. Now advancing more cautiously, it was noon on 2 May before the Yorkist army reached Sodbury Hill, only to find the position abandoned and no sign of any enemy.

Edward had been badly served by his scouts, but nevertheless the Lancastrians must be given great credit for a very clever piece of deception, for it is difficult to understand how they managed to vanish so completely, leaving Edward quite mystified as to their whereabouts. There was no choice for the King but to camp that night at Sodbury and await the reports of the patrols which had been sent out in every direction. In these hours of uncertainty only one sensible action illuminates an otherwise sombre picture; it was decided to dispatch messengers mounted on swift animals to warn Sir Richard Beauchamp, Governor of Gloucester, that he was likely to be attacked and that he must hold out until Edward's army could arrive. At last, at about 3 a.m., Edward received definite news that the Queen's army was on the road to Gloucester and already north of Berkeley. Two hours later the army broke camp and Edward led them, now in battle order, along the line of the Cotswolds towards Tewkesbury. The Lancastrians had stolen a march on him, but if Gloucester held they might still be kept from crossing the Severn.

Friday 3 May was a day of strenuous effort for both armies, testing to the uttermost the endurance of man and horse. The Lancastrian army, determined to hold onto their advantage, spent only six hours at Berkeley, being on the march again at midnight. They arrived before Gloucester at 10 a.m. to find the gates firmly closed against them; there was no time for argument with words or guns, because all knew that Edward was close at hand. As they struggled on to Tewkesbury the pace was beginning to tell. Sir Richard Beauchamp led a sortie from Gloucester and some precious artillery, laboriously bumping its way over appalling tracks, was captured. At last, in the late afternoon, the great abbey of Tewkesbury, standing above the little Swilgate brook and shaded by venerable trees, came into sight. Queen Margaret and her men had been on the march for sixteen hours and covered twenty-four miles.

A mile to the south of the abbey the river Severn can be forded at Lower Lode, but the crossing would have taken some time and the men had marched far enough. The decision to stand and fight was dictated more by exhaustion than by confidence in the outcome, but no one can deny that it was the right one. Somerset had the choice of ground and the position he adopted is generally thought to have been one just north of Gupshill Manor, with his left resting on the Swilgate brook and his right stretching to the low ground west of the main road. The writer does not agree that this was his position,

164

and as he is in a minority of two some space must be devoted to an explanation.

The principal authority for this battle is the author of *The arrivall of Edward IV in England* (the *Fleetwood Chronicle*) (see also p.156). The relevant passage runs: '. . . the same nyght they pight them in a fielde, in a close even at the townes ende; the towne, and the abbey, at theyr backs.' Now the Gupshill Manor position is three quarters of a mile from 'the townes ende'; this is certainly not conclusive evidence, for the author in saying 'at the townes ende' may be permitted some inaccuracy, but the position nearer the abbey appears to be a better one. The Lancastrian army is thought to have numbered 6,000 men (the Yorkists had about 3,500 archers and 1,500 cavalrymen) and so they would have required a frontage of around 1,000 yards. In the area between the cemetery and Priors Park the ridge is wide enough for the army to have been deployed without stretching to the brook, and invites a more difficult assault than the Gupshill position; a flank attack was most unlikely, and anyway the brook was no obstacle. But Tewkesbury Park (an area until recently inaccessible to visitors to the battlefield) may hold the key. 'There was a parke, and therein moche wood', near to which Edward sent 200 spearmen, and 'set them in a plomp [such a much nicer word than 'mass'!] nere a qwarter of a myle from the fielde'. This undoubtedly refers to Tewkesbury Park, and the position of these spearmen and their subsequent action seems to indicate that the Lancastrian line just overlapped the present Gloucester–Cheltenham road not very far south of Holme Hospital, and certainly no lower than the Crouch Court–Priors Park area. Neither this position nor the Gupshill one could control or protect the ford at Lower Lode.

Meanwhile, Edward's troops were in no better plight than the Lancastrians. The day was unusually hot for early May, and as the King 'toke his way thrwghe the champain contrye, called Cotteswolde' they could find no food for horses or men, and only one brook near Stroud from which to drink, and that was soon churned to mud by vehicle wheels. At the 'village called Chiltenham', which was reached about 5 p.m., Edward received information that his enemy were preparing to give battle. Pausing only to share out what few iron rations they had with them, the army was on the march again to Tredington; this village was only two miles from the enemy position and near enough to ensure that on the morrow the Lancastrians could not slip away. Edward's army had marched or ridden thirty-five miles in this long day; visitors to Tewkesbury Abbey who have seen the plate armour that was taken from the battlefield by the monks and nailed to the sacristy door will appreciate the immensity of this achievement.

The exact position of the Lancastrian line may be open to argument, but there is no doubt about their order of battle. The Duke of Somerset, who was in overall command, took the 'vaward', as the right-hand column was often called; Lord Wenlock, who had fought for the Lancastrians at St Albans and the Yorkists at Towton and who was finally to be found on the losing side, had command of the main battle, with the young Prince Edward by his side; and the Earl of Devon had the left or rearward wing. There was no reserve, and Queen Margaret had withdrawn either to the town or across the river to await events.

Early in the morning of Saturday 4 May Edward advanced from Tredington to the Cheltenham–Tewkesbury road, which then ran just to the west of Gupshill Manor. When he reached the ground now occupied by Stonehouse Farm the Lancastrian array would have become visible, although possibly not very clearly, for we are told that the ground contained many hedges, deep dykes and foul lanes – 'a ryght evill place to approache'. The King's order of battle must have been reversed at some stage, presumably because Hastings's performance at Barnet scarcely qualified him to oppose the most formidable Lancastrian commander. The chronicler clearly states that Prince Richard commanded the vaward, yet he took up a position on the left of the line with Somerset to his front; the King, who had Clarence with him, commanded the centre, and Lord Hastings had charge of the right wing. The Yorkists also had no reserve, but Edward sent 200 spearmen to protect his flank. These men were placed near to Tewkesbury Park; they may have been mounted, but spearmen are usually taken to mean foot soldiers, and the ground was totally unsuitable for cavalry.

The Yorkists prepared for battle some 350 yards from their enemy and Edward's first move was to bring a fairly heavy concentration of firepower on to Somerset's division. His artillery – in which arm he was considerably superior to the Lancastrians – could have raked the enemy from the battle line, but we are told that the archers formed a part of this preliminary bombardment, and so presumably both arms were somewhat advanced. Somerset had evidently reconnoitred the ground to his immediate front either the previous evening, or that morning before the battle, and when it became apparent that his men had had enough pounding he led most of them (leaving just a deceptive screen) along a partially concealed route to deliver a surprise flank attack. It seems to have been a sound tactical manoeuvre, and was almost certainly part of a coordinated plan whereby as soon as the Yorkist left had been struck Lord Wenlock would deliver a blow at the centre, and no doubt Devon also had orders to advance. It miscarried because the line of approach was slightly at fault, and the attack was completely unsupported.

When Somerset's men came into open ground they found themselves at the junction of the Yorkist left and centre battles; this was an unenviable position to be caught in, for although they undoubtedly took Edward off balance at first, their flank was exposed not only to Gloucester's troops, but to the 200 spearmen as well. This error of direction might have gone unpunished had Wenlock come down and engaged Edward; as it was, after some sharp skirmishing Edward began to roll Somerset's men back from whence they had come. Gloucester's troops do not appear to have played much part until the enemy were in retreat, but the spearmen seeing their opportunity attacked them in the flank. The chronicler indicates that after the initial shock Edward's division, helped by the spearmen, soon had Somerset's men on the run, in which case the spearmen must have been no more than 3–400 yards to the flank – assuming the chronicler was right, and that they were sent to watch the Tewkesbury Park area; they could scarcely have arrived in time had the fight taken place near Gupshill Manor.

Outnumbered and entirely unsupported, Somerset's vaward soon disintegrated and very likely suffered the heaviest casualties of the whole battle. Men fled in all directions, some forward to the safety of the park, others back towards the river, while still others struggled to regain the Lancastrian line. No matter which way they went they were cut down relentlessly. Somerset managed to get back to the ridge where, embittered by the knowledge of defeat, he is said to have dealt somewhat drastically with Lord Wenlock. Seldom if ever in the annals of war has there been a substantiated case of a commander-in-chief cleaving in the skull of a divisional commander for failing to support him, and it is unlikely, even allowing for the ferocity of the times and that Wenlock was a proven turncoat, that this in fact happened. Certainly Wenlock's helmet – if it really was his – which hangs in St Mary's Church, Luton, bears no evidence of such a dastardly act.

Unless Somerset withdrew from his fight before it was truly lost, it is possible that he never even saw Wenlock again, for as soon as

Overleaf: Battle of Tewkesbury with plan inset

167

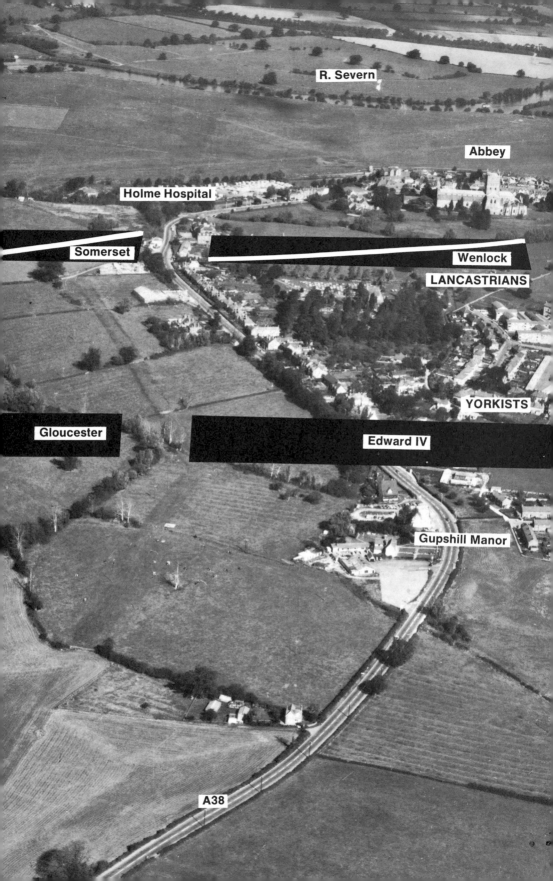

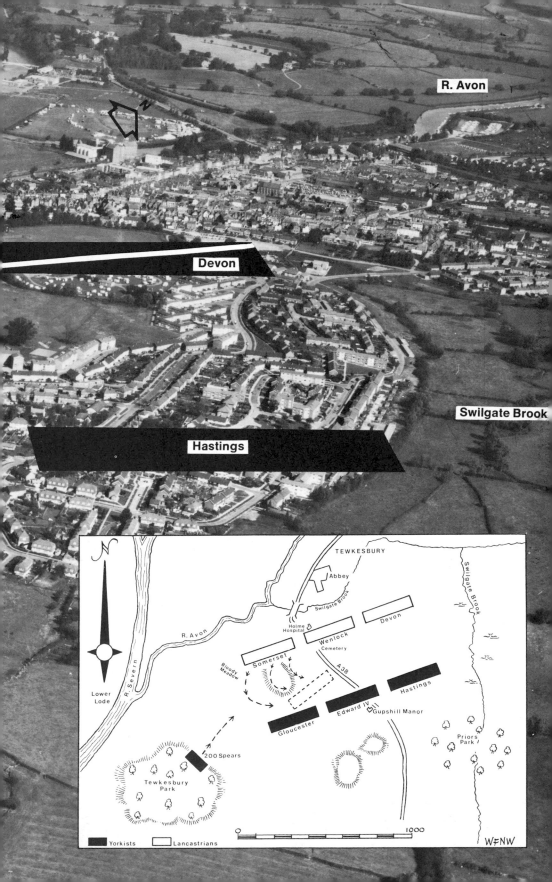

R. Avon

Devon

Swilgate Brook

Hastings

TEWKESBURY

Abbey

Swilgate Brook

Swilgate Brook

R. Avon

Holme Hospital

Wenlock

Devon

Cemetery

Somerset

A38

Bloody Meadow

Lower Lode

R. Severn

Gloucester

Edward IV

Gupshill Manor

Hastings

Priors Park

200 Spears

Tewkesbury Park

1000

WFNW

Yorkists   Lancastrians

the King had got Somerset's battle on the run he seems to have left the pursuit to Gloucester, while he and Lord Hastings advanced their troops up the gentle slope to engage the remainder of the Lancastrian army. We have no details of the short battle that ensued – other than the names of some, including Lord Wenlock, who were killed – but the Lancastrians must have been completely demoralized by the débâcle on their right, for they appear to have offered practically no resistance to an enemy almost certainly inferior in numbers and attacking uphill over difficult ground. Very soon the whole army was in retreat. As the Yorkists advanced, inexorably pressing back their enemy towards the town and the two rivers, they slashed and hacked at all in their path. Many were killed in a field still known (like the one at Towton) as Bloody Meadow, and others were drowned in the Avon or the Severn; a few escaped through the town and others took sanctuary in the abbey.

The chronicler Edward Hall says that 3,000 Lancastrians were slain – which would be about half their total force, and is almost certainly a considerable exaggeration. But perhaps between 1,500 and 2,000 died, for no quarter was given to those caught in these headlong pursuits. The Yorkist losses may have been less than 500. The fate of the Lancastrian principals is of some interest, because after years of ceaseless bloodletting the proud banners of Henry VI, Margaret of Anjou, Edward Prince of Wales, and the powerful Beauforts, so often in the past borne forward in splendid élan, were at Tewkesbury lowered to be seen no more on an English battlefield.

The most important casualty was Prince Edward, for with his death the legitimate descendants of Henry IV were almost extinct – within three weeks they would be. The story of his capture and subsequent murder can be disregarded; undoubtedly he was killed in the fighting, although probably while trying to make his way to the town during the rout. The commanders of the left and centre battles, Lords Devon and Wenlock, were killed (probably before the Lancastrians broke), as were John Beaufort Marquis of Dorset, Sir John and Sir Thomas Seymour and many other knights. What happened in the abbey is uncertain. The Duke of Somerset, Sir John Langstrother, Sir Thomas Tresham and other Lancastrians took sanctuary there, but it is said that the abbey did not possess a franchise as a sanctuary – at any rate not for those guilty of high treason. One story is that Edward and some armed men entered this great church, which even then enshrined centuries of a community's life and faith, and killed many men under its roof; another that Edward was persuaded to offer pardon to those who took sanctuary there. There may be some truth in both stories; but if Somerset, Langstrother, Tresham and other notables were offered pardon, their trial two days later before the Dukes of Gloucester and Norfolk, and subsequent execution, surely violated every canon of good faith.

There remains only to relate the fate of Henry VI and his queen. When Margaret learned of the defeat she and her ladies, among whom was Anne Neville, Prince Edward's wife, made all haste to leave the town. She is credited with having crossed the Severn by the Lower Lode ford and slept that night at Bushley. It seems scarcely possible that she could have done this, for mopping up was going on in Bloody Meadow and along the river bank for most of the day; it is much more likely that she had taken the precaution of crossing the river before the battle, and awaited the result in the house at Bushley known as Paynes Place. She was eventually captured – probably in the priory at Little Malvern – and brought before Edward at Coventry on 12 May. On 21 May this unhappy woman, whose fortunes had suffered so profound a decline and who had sullied and ruined herself in the interests of a weak husband and an untried son, was the object of great abuse and ribaldry as she rode in a litter through the streets of London behind the triumphant Edward. She remained his prisoner for four years until ransomed by King Louis for £50,000 on condition that she surrendered all her father's vast possessions. She died in April 1482.

The news of Edward's crushing victory had a salutary effect upon a people grown weary of war. For many years now the forges had roared almost night and day and the hammers had seldom ceased from fashioning implements of slaughter. It was time to call a halt. There were strong forces still arrayed against the King, but at Coventry he learned from the Earl of Northumberland that those in opposition in the north had laid down their arms, and by the time Edward was before the gates of London the troops that had assailed the city under the Bastard of Fauconberg had already realized the hopelessness of their cause, and had retired back to their Kentish homes.

The last act of the drama was performed amid the stern surroundings of the Tower of London. A few hours after Edward had made his formal entry into London the intelligent, highly sensitive Henry, called to a duty that in spite of many noble gifts he was totally unfitted to perform, passed into the corridors of history. Prince Richard of Gloucester was at hand at the time; what part, if any, he played in the crime will – as on a later occasion in the same place – never be known: but dark deeds sow their crop of dragons' teeth.

CHAPTER 12

Bosworth Field

22 August 1485

The battle was fought about two miles south of Market Bosworth (a small town some nine miles west of Leicester) on and around Ambion Hill, which lies between Sutton Cheney and Shenton. In September 1974 H.R.H. the Duke of Gloucester officially opened the Battle of Bosworth Centre, which the Leicestershire County Council have laid out in Ambion Hill Farm. This centre is open during the summer and autumn months all day at weekends and Bank Holidays, and week-day evenings. In the farmhouse there is an exhibition hall, model room and auditorium. There is a small admission fee to the Battlefield Centre and adjacent car park. There is no charge for visiting the battlefield, and public footpaths now exist enabling the visitor to view the site perfectly. There is a second car park at the disused Shenton railway station with an information point, and various picnic sites. One such is called King Richard's Field, stated categorically by the Centre as being the place where Richard died – but as the reader will see, the present writer considers this open to doubt.

The Battle of Bosworth has received much attention from historians on account of its important consequences; but the only contemporary record extant is the *Croyland Chronicle* and it has very little to say about the actual fight. Subsequent writers from the sixteenth century to modern times have had to do their best from this exiguous source, the few relics that have been found on or near the battlefield, and a careful examination of the ground. It is not surprising, therefore, to find a wide divergence of opinion as to exactly what happened. The main outline of the battle can be fairly easily reconstructed; the difficulty comes with details, such as the death of Richard and the positions taken up by the Stanley brothers.

But before recounting the battle it is necessary to examine the events that led up to it. Edward IV died on 9 April 1483, and left his crown and kingdom to his twelve-year-old son Edward, but fully aware of his wife's unpopularity – and more particularly of that of her Woodville relations – he had designated his brother Richard of Gloucester as protector during the young king's minority. When the King died his son was at Ludlow with his uncle Anthony Earl Rivers; Richard was in the north of England, and the Woodville faction had a slender control of the Council in London. Clearly they could not prevent the protectorship, but they hoped to establish a regency council to whom the Protector would be responsible. Towards the end of April the new king, accompanied by his uncle Rivers, his half-brother Sir Richard Grey, his chamberlain Sir Thomas Vaughan, and an escort of some 2,000 Welsh soldiers set out for London. Richard started south from Yorkshire at about the same time.

Richard III was not the wicked monster, distorted in body and mind, that the tendentious writings of Tudor historians would have us believe. It is true that he was below average height, and one shoulder was slightly higher than the other, but there is no reliable record of deformity. The impression of a cunning schemer is also suspect; it would seem that impetuosity, not guile, was the hallmark of his character. He was a sound commander and courageous fighter, who had served his brother loyally under arms in the north; moreover, in his short reign he proved himself to be in many ways an able and intelligent ruler. But he was a cold creature, who kept his own counsel and went his own way; he made some fearful blunders and when he most needed friends he found that friendship, for him, was but a veneer on the harsh canvas of hatred and suspicion.

He was also a typical product of his time in that he was intensely ambitious and, as his behaviour on the road to London shows, sufficiently ruthless to see that any obstacle to his ambition was swiftly removed. Lord Hastings, who at the time of Edward's death was one of Richard's principal supporters, had probably warned him that the Woodvilles had no intention of allowing him unfettered control. He therefore acted promptly in having the unsuspecting Rivers, Grey and Vaughan arrested when they went to meet him at Nottingham, and riding on to Stony Stratford he dismissed his nephew's Welsh escort, and with many protestations of loyalty accompanied the bewildered boy to his capital.

Edward V arrived in London on 4 May; his mother and other members of her family had sought sanctuary in Westminster Abbey on learning what had happened at Nottingham. Richard may not have had designs on the crown at this early stage, but he was determined to resist any opposition to his rule during the minority. To this end he set about securing the loyalty of a number of peers, chief among whom was the Duke of Buckingham, a lineal descendant of Edward III's fifth son and a man scarcely less ambitious than

Richard. Buckingham became the recipient of great riches and rewards, and for a time Protector and Duke worked closely together. Lord Hastings was their first victim. In spite of his intense dislike for many of the Woodvilles, jealousy of Buckingham had driven Hastings into their camp, and he had formed the foolish habit of holding, together with Lord Stanley and John Morton Bishop of Ely, a rival council to the Protector's. At a council meeting at the Tower on 13 June Richard suddenly had these three arrested, and Hastings was summarily executed on Tower Green. This was the Protector's first blunder, for it was one thing to execute Rivers (which he did twelve days later at Pontefract), but another to execute Hastings, who was of the old nobility and whose death would raise powerful antagonisms.

Three days later it became fairly clear that Richard was thinking in terms of the throne. He had probably realized that to rule unchallenged, which was what he intended doing, he would have to be king. He went with the Archbishop of Canterbury, and certain other nobles, to Westminster, where Queen Elizabeth was persuaded (the threat of force was clearly in the background) to surrender her second son, Richard Duke of York, from sanctuary. He joined his brother, who on Buckingham's suggestion had already been 'more comfortably lodged' in the Tower. Both boys were murdered there, probably in the autumn of 1483.

With the Princes safely in the Tower it now became necessary for Richard to justify his intended assumption of kingship. There was no great problem here. The old canard was raked up that Edward's marriage to Elizabeth Woodville was invalidated because he had been precontracted to Lady Eleanor Butler, and that it had been celebrated in an unconsecrated place; therefore Elizabeth's children were bastards. Clarence's offspring were even more easily accounted for, because since Edward had murdered their father in 1478 they could be conveniently excluded from the succession under their father's attainder. This doubtful reasoning did not entirely convince the citizens of London that Richard was therefore the true male Yorkist heir, but Buckingham worked so skilfully for Richard's cause that on 23 June he was able to head a deputation that waited on Richard at his riverside home of Baynard's Castle and swore allegiance to him as King Richard III. The new king was crowned amid the greatest splendour on 6 July.

In October 1483 Richard was faced with what could have been a most serious insurrection had he not got warning of it and struck before the insurgents were fully prepared. Buckingham, like Hastings before him, had suddenly veered over to the Woodvilles.

174

The exact cause of his discontent is uncertain, but it seems that the higher his fortune the higher rose his ambition, and that he thought he could plot a course for himself through devious channels to the throne. It is not his rebellion, nor its failure and his subsequent execution, that is of interest to the student of Bosworth Field, but the third member of the strange alliance.

The Woodvilles, presumably with Buckingham's knowledge and consent, had been in touch with Margaret Beaufort (now married to Lord Stanley) and through her had arranged for her exiled son Henry Tudor to invade England with troops supplied by the Duke of Brittany. On the successful conclusion of the enterprise Henry was to marry Elizabeth of York, and through this union it was hoped that the two great houses of Lancaster and York would be able to live in peace with one another. As is well known, this happy event was deferred for three years, but Henry did make an attempt – if a somewhat belated one – to honour his side of the bargain. He encountered a severe storm, and by the time he was off Poole only two of his fifteen ships were still with him, Buckingham was already dead and the insurrection in the West Country had been suppressed. Henry returned to Brittany; but he had at least shown that he was a force to be reckoned with, and in the months ahead many were comforted – and others disturbed – by the thought of an alternative ruler ready to cross the sea.

Richard was well aware of the insecurity of his position; at home, in spite of all his efforts towards good government, he had many enemies, and across the Channel exiled Lancastrians schemed to place Henry Tudor on the throne. The death of the Prince of Wales in April 1484 was a bitter blow; now without an heir, and with a wife who could bear no more children, he knew that Henry, with his intended bride, would gain many fresh supporters. An attempt that summer to bribe the Duke of Brittany's treasurer to have Henry kidnapped and delivered to Richard almost succeeded, but Henry was warned in time and escaped to Paris. There he was shortly joined by the Earl of Oxford, whose gaoler had obligingly released him from the fortress of Hammes, where he had been imprisoned since his unsuccessful attempt to invade England in 1474.

As 1484 gave way to 1485 King Richard was pursued and haunted by a profound feeling that the very air he breathed was charged with treason. It came almost as a relief to learn that the Lancastrian invasion, so long threatened, was now definitely planned for the summer of 1485. Until the recent treaty of friendship with Scotland, half England had been under arms against possible invasion on two fronts, but now there was something definite against

a knyght there was a Worthy man
a   That fro the tyme that he first began

Above: Woodcut of The Knight by Richard Pynson, from Chaucer's Canterbury Tales, in the British Museum. Below: 300 years of European helmets

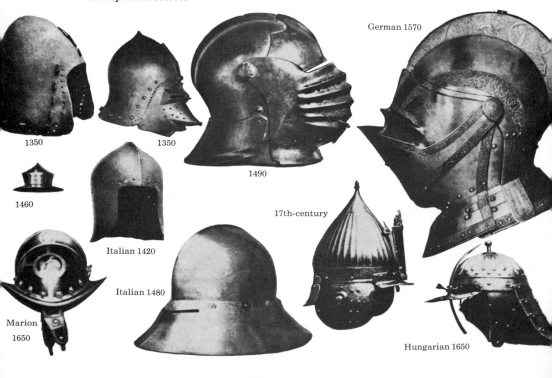

German 1570

1350

1350

1490

1460

17th-century

Italian 1420

Italian 1480

Marion 1650

Hungarian 1650

which to prepare. With the coming of the fighting season garrisons were strengthened and the commissioners of array were ordered to have their musters ready to march at a day's notice. No efforts were spared to portray through proclamations Henry Tudor's bastard descent on both sides of his family, and to remind Englishmen that he would be carried to their shores in French ships crowded with foreign soldiers. Richard took up residence in Nottingham Castle during June, from where he could be kept in constant communication with his lieutenants through his method of posting couriers at twenty-mile intervals along the principal highways.

Henry sailed from Harfleur on 1 August. His small fleet carried nearly 2,000 French mercenaries under Philibert de Chaundé, and with him sailed his uncle Jasper Tudor, Lord Oxford, the Bishop of Ely, Sir Edward Courtenay, Sir Edward Woodville and other knights, both Yorkist and Lancastrian, who had shared his exile. On 7 August the fleet entered Milford Haven and the troops disembarked at Dale. It is sometimes suggested that Henry would never have undertaken so rash an enterprise without first being assured that Lord Stanley, his brother Sir William, and Sir Gilbert Talbot (whose nephew, Lord Shrewsbury, was still a boy) would join him with their followers. In spite of the subsequent behaviour of these three there is no evidence for this, and it is more probable that Henry, although no warrior endowed with personal valour, had sufficient of the adventurer and gambler in his make-up to take his chance without specific guarantees.

Gradually the Welsh gentry rallied to his red dragon standard, the most notable being Rhys ap Thomas. As Henry moved through Cardigan to Montgomery, and from Newton to Welshpool, so his numbers increased – often at the expense of those whom Richard had relied upon to bar his way – and when he reached Shrewsbury Sir Gilbert Talbot joined him with 500 of Lord Shrewsbury's retainers. Neither Sir Walter Herbert in south Wales, nor Sir William Stanley in the north, had made any serious attempt to hinder the invader.

Richard was quickly aware of Henry's arrival, but the ease and rapidity with which the usurper marched through Wales not only angered but clearly also surprised him. In spite of the many preparations that had been going forward throughout the summer, by the time Henry was at Shrewsbury the King had still not mustered all his troops. There is a letter written about this time from the Duke of Norfolk to Sir John Paston desiring him to meet the Duke at Bury St Edmunds with the men he had promised the King, and

some lords from the south were still absent from the royalist camp.*
Lord Stanley had asked permission in July to return to his estates
in Lancashire. This had been granted with the proviso that he
should send his son Lord Strange as a hostage to Stanley's loyalty.
Now he was summoned to return, but made the feeble excuse that
he was suffering from the sweating sickness – there was an outbreak
of this dreaded disease at the time, but anyone who contracted it
usually had little chance to send apologies for absence. At about
the time Richard received Stanley's message Lord Strange was ap-
prehended trying to escape from Nottingham Castle; on being
questioned he implicated his uncle and Sir John Savage, but refused
to admit that his father had traitorous designs.

From Shrewsbury Henry marched to Stafford, where he had a
meeting with Sir William Stanley. Turning south-east from Stafford the rebel army advanced through Lichfield and Tamworth to
Atherstone. At either Lichfield or Tamworth Henry collected some
pieces of ordnance, which put a brake on the rapid progress his
army had been making hitherto. After their meeting at Stafford
Sir William Stanley's retainers had been marching parallel to
Henry's army, while Lord Stanley had been giving the impression
of falling back before the invader and was now south of Leicester.
On 20 August both the Stanleys met Henry at Atherstone, where
Henry probably had to be content with vague assurances from Lord
Stanley who would not at this stage have committed himself, for
his son was in the most unenviable position.

As soon as Richard's scurryers (mounted scouts) brought him
news that Henry was at Lichfield he realized that he could wait at
Nottingham for reinforcements no longer, because the rebels
might decide to take the road for London. Accordingly on 19
August the royalist army, with the King mounted on a great
white courser, left Nottingham for Leicester. Surrounded by
treachery and weighed down by doubts as he must have been,
Richard still held the advantage in numbers. Richard Brooke
cites Baker in his *Chronicles* as putting the King's army at 7,900
men; Norfolk with the vanguard had 1,200 bowmen, flanked with
200 cuirassiers under his son Lord Surrey; the King with the main-
guard had 1,000 billmen and 2,000 pikes, and Sir Thomas Brackenbury (which is wrong, for it was the Earl of Northumberland)
commanded the rearguard of 2,000 billmen with 1,500 horsemen on

*We do not know if Sir John, who was Sheriff of Norfolk, produced
these men on time. But the Pastons were a Lancastrian family, and a
year later Sir John was entrusted by Henry to seize the traitor Lord
Lovell.

178

the wings.* These figures are probably very near the truth. It is doubtful whether Henry could have mustered more than 5,000 men without the Stanleys.

On 21 August the two armies closed the gap between them. Henry marched east from Atherstone to a place called White Moors, which lies five miles from Atherstone up the Roman road through Fenny Drayton. Richard marched west from Leicester. We do not know the route he took; this would have depended on where he camped the night. The most probable site is the high ground immediately north-west of Sutton Cheney, which is the north-eastern end of a ridge that extends for about a mile in the direction of Shenton. Here the ridge, at 417 feet, reaches its highest point and would have given the King a commanding view over much of the surrounding country. If this was the place of his camp, Richard would have got there along the old road that ran through Kirby Mallory. Thus probably only two miles separated the camps and no doubt the scurryers of both armies reported back the respective positions.

The western end of Ambion Hill, which was a mile from Richard's camp, offers the best battle position in the neighbourhood. We can imagine that both commanders would have been anxious to secure this eminence; but Richard had the comparatively easy approach across a slight saddle and up the very gentle eastern slope of the hill, whereas Henry had at least one bog to circumvent, and a steep climb. The countryside has greatly changed since the time of the battle; what was then uncultivated open ground, with marshy land at the edges of the hill, is now well drained, productive grass and arable fields with a good many trees and hedges, and a large wood immediately to the south of the hill. The site of Richard's Well remains unchanged and is marked by a stone pyramid; it was in fact a spring and as the ground around it is still a little boggy in parts it is reasonable to assume that this, and the nearby Ambion Wood, was the area of marsh spoken of by the early writers. It may have extended to the south-west of the hill in the vicinity of the old railway line. The whole area was drained in the latter part of Elizabeth's reign.

Lead, stone and iron cannon balls of various weight have been dug up from time to time on what is now Glebe Farm; four were uncovered on the west slope of Ambion Hill just below the summit. We can thus be fairly sure that Richard's army did in fact occupy what would seem to be the obvious position stretching from the

*Richard Brooke, *Visits to Fields of Battle in England*, p.164.

crest of the hill back to the area of Ambion Hill Farm. We also get confirmation that Henry must have equipped himself with heavy cannon of the culverin type somewhere en route, for one of the balls weighed $14\frac{3}{4}$ pounds.

The position of the Stanley brothers before and during the battle is much more difficult to assess. After their meeting with Henry at Atherstone Lord Stanley is said to have drawn up his army to the south of the battlefield, the Dadlington area being the most popular among historians, while Sir William Stanley remained to the north at Nether Cotton. There is no evidence at all for either place (for we can discount Hutton's theory of fortified camps), nor for the number of men that the brothers had under command, but it seems probable that they were divided, one each side of the battle ground, and they certainly started the morning as observers and joined in when they saw how matters were going – Lord Stanley, in particular, was a trimmer *par excellence*. No matter where they spent the night of 21 August, they must have drawn close to the field on the 22nd, and perhaps Lord Stanley observed matters from the rising ground of Greenhill Farm – for he could have seen little from Dadlington – and Sir William would have had an excellent view of Ambion Hill from the high ground on the present Bosworth–Shenton road. They probably did not have more than 4,000 men under command between them.

The royalist camp was early astir on the morning of 22 August, and Norfolk set off for Ambion Hill soon after first light. The army probably marched and fought in column of battles, with the King commanding the main battle and marching behind Norfolk, while Northumberland brought up the rear. The men-at-arms would still be mounted during the advance, but on reaching the chosen position they would send their horses to the rear and prepare for battle on foot, clustered around their liege lord. Before he left camp Richard sent a final message to Lord Stanley to join him at once, or else Lord Strange would die; Stanley is said to have replied that he had other sons and that he would not join the King. This may be true, but Lord Strange certainly did not die.

Henry Tudor was not the experienced general that Richard was, and he seems to have underrated the need for speed. His chances of reaching the top of Ambion Hill first were always slender, but he made them no better by dallying in his overnight camp. Richard was almost in position before Henry had encountered his first obstacle – the bog. Considerable confusion has been thrown on the whole battle through the chronicler Hall's statement concerning the effect of the sun on the rival armies. Hall enlarged on the more

180

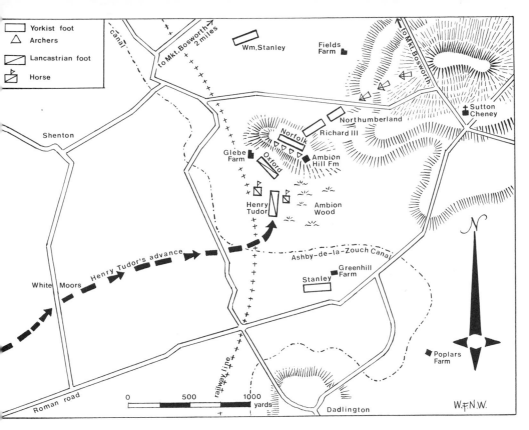

Key:
- Yorkist foot
- Archers
- Lancastrian foot
- Horse

to Mkt. Bosworth
2 miles

Wm. Stanley

Fields Farm

to Mkt. Bosworth

canal

Shenton

Northumberland

Richard III

Norfolk

Glebe Farm

Oxford

Ambion Hill Fm

Sutton Cheney

Henry Tudor

Ambion Wood

Henry Tudor's advance

Ashby-de-la-Zouch Canal

White Moors

Stanley

Greenhill Farm

railway line

Roman road

0   500   1000
yards

Dadlington

Poplars Farm

N

W.F.N.W.

Battle of Bosworth Field. Note Glebe Farm, below. In this area lead, stone and iron cannonballs have been found from time to time

old covert

Sutton Cheney

Fields Farm

Northumber- land

Richard III

Norfolk

Ambion Hill Farm

Richard's Well

Glebe Farm

Oxford

Ambion Wood

N

Henry Tudor

railway line (disused)

authentic account of Polydore Vergil and put the sun at one moment in the faces of the royalist army. This was never the case; but the rebel army, which had the sun right in their eyes at the commencement of their march, were temporarily relieved of this handicap when they had to swing north to avoid the marsh at the south and south-western edge of the hill. Henry also sent a message to Lord Stanley before leaving his camp; but the trimmer was still trimming (which makes his reported statement to Richard slightly suspect) and told Henry to make his own dispositions and that he would join him at the appropriate time.

Henry's advance to Ambion Hill would have been, like Richard's, in column of battles with the cavalry on the wings; Lord Oxford commanded the van, and Henry with Lord Pembroke marched at the head of the main battle. Having skirted the marsh, Oxford found himself at the foot of the hill somewhere in the vicinity of where Shenton railway station once stood. A few hundred yards above, the Duke of Norfolk's archers were watching and waiting. It was now that Richard missed what was probably a certain chance of victory. While the main battle of the rebel army was still edging round the marsh, Oxford deployed the vanguard into line with the archers to the front and the billmen close up behind; Sir Gilbert Talbot had command of the Shropshire levies on the right and Sir John Savage with the Welshmen formed up on the left. Oxford also ordered up the artillery. This was a cumbersome manoeuvre to perform with an enemy poised only a few hundred yards away on a hill above, but it was allowed to proceed unchallenged. The battle then commenced with Henry opening up a lively cannonade.

These preliminary bombardments with their accompanying arrow storm never did a great deal of damage, but were sufficiently irritating to encourage the leading ranks to close the gap and indulge in the more acceptable form of slaughter at close quarters. However, on this occasion there was a strange pause with the armies watching each other warily. Oxford, fearful of being encircled if he went forward before the main body had closed up behind him, gave strict orders that no man was to advance more than ten feet from his standard. At first the royalist troops suspected some trap in this seemingly unnatural hesitation, and there was a brief interlude before both armies advanced to the attack. The resulting clash must have taken place somewhere in the area of Glebe Farm.

The battle lasted for around two hours. For Richard it was a sorry tale of treachery and tribulation. As Norfolk's and Oxford's

182

men became locked in hand-to-hand combat and the leading ranks were shorn away under the steel flail of sword, pike and bill, they were hastily reinforced by men from the main columns. Henry was not a great warrior and seems to have played little part in directing the battle, but Richard, who lacked patience though not courage, was never far from the fighting, and probably placed his standard on the crest of Ambion Hill. Norfolk, a veteran of many fights, was the first important casualty – some say the victim of a personal confrontation with Oxford – and soon wide gaps began to appear in the array of both armies. After more than an hour the struggle still hung in equipoise, and all depended on two men watching from the sidelines and a third from even closer at hand.

We do not know what promises, if any, were made at Atherstone, but it seems almost certain that Sir William Stanley, a declared traitor who had allowed Henry unchallenged passage through north Wales, had guaranteed his intervention. Lord Stanley would not have committed himself so deeply to his stepson, and Northumberland, who had no desire to go the way of his father and grandfather, both of whom had been killed in earlier battles of this war, was clearly awaiting a lead from Stanley. It was not long in coming, but even before the Stanleys had launched their men against him, the King had been made aware that Northumberland's rearguard would not support him in his hour of need. Now it was all too clear to him how desperate the situation was.

The manner in which King Richard met his death, or the exact spot, will never be known. Only one thing is certain: he scorned every opportunity of safety through flight, and went down fighting in the best traditions of medieval chivalry. Long flowery speeches before the battle, and deeds of exceptional personal valour in the course of the fight, embroider many of the old chronicles. Sixteenth-century historians have woven a tale of combat between the personal adherents of Richard and those of Henry, and almost every succeeding writer has followed this pattern. They may be correct, but Colonel Burne* will have none of it and gives it as his opinion that the King died near the well now called after him, when attempting to ride down Lord Stanley. Such a theory has equal claims on our credence; but let the reader judge for himself.

Those who would have us believe that briefly the two principals met face to face in mortal combat say that at about the time Northumberland's defection became apparent information reached

*Battlefields of England, pp.146, 154.

Richard that Henry, although still well in the rear of the fight, had moved from the centre to the more exposed left flank. The King, accompanied only by his personal bodyguard – perhaps eighty men in all – immediately rode down the north-west slope of Ambion Hill and right across the front of Sir William Stanley's men, who were at that moment preparing to ride to Henry's aid. The proud Plantagenet and his few remaining loyal lords bore down upon those protecting the Welsh usurper. In the first few seconds of this conflict of truly majestic splendour Richard cut down Sir William Brandon, Henry's standardbearer, and then unhorsed Sir John Cheyney – a formidable warrior both in courage and poundage. For a few minutes it looked as though this sudden and unexpected onslaught would achieve its object; but just in time Henry's supporters, now supplemented by William Stanley's men, closed around their leader. The Red Dragon of Cadwallader fluttered again and the English king was dragged from his horse and hacked to death. Thus, according to the majority of writers, died the second and last King of England to be killed in battle. Like Harold before him, the victim of a man who had even less claim to the throne than he had.

Colonel Burne holds this account to be totally false. He suggests that on a hot August day the clouds of dust and steam of sweat thrown up by the battle would have made it impossible for Henry's position to be accurately located, and that anyway it would have been too far in the rear for a small body of horsemen to reach unchecked. He suggests that it is more probable that Richard rode round the left flank of his army (the south and south-west of Ambion Hill) in a frenzy of rage to be at the traitor Lord Stanley. Here undoubtedly he would have encountered the bog in which his horse may well have floundered. Hence Shakespeare's line, 'A horse, a horse, my kingdom for a horse', could well have historical fact. No replacement was forthcoming and the King died fighting on foot surrounded by enemies.

Perhaps there is some truth in both accounts. Certainly Henry's standardbearer was killed, and presumably he would never have been far from his lord. On the other hand the marsh and Richard's Well are firmly entrenched in the legend of the battle – and the story that Richard drank from the well before the battle is most unlikely.

With the King dead his followers had no reason, or wish, to prosecute the fight to the very end, and, with the exception of a few who had personal feuds to be settled, most of the royalist army either laid down their arms or abandoned them during flight

184

from the field. They appear to have dispersed in all directions, and the pursuit was a half-hearted affair extending no further than Dadlington to the south. A little way from here, on a hill still known as Crown Hill, Lord Stanley placed the golden circlet worn by Richard in the battle upon the new king's head. It had been found in a thorn bush, presumably hidden there by a looter intent on recovering it.

Most accounts of the battle agree on the casualty figures, and place the royalist army as losing somewhere around 1,000 men, and the victors not more than 200. These figures would indicate that although the pursuit may not have extended very far, at least in places it must have been rather bloody. A number of royalist leaders besides the King fell on this August day, the most important being the Duke of Norfolk, Lord Ferrers of Chartley, Sir Robert Brackenbury, Sir Robert Percy and Sir Richard Radcliffe. Norfolk's son Lord Surrey was captured and sent to the Tower, and Sir William Catesby was one of the few prisoners to be executed. Sir William Brandon was almost the only personage of note to be killed in the rebel army.

King Richard's body was stripped naked, slung over a horse and taken to Leicester in the wake of the victorious army. Here it was exposed to the public view for two days, and after this shameful treatment the last Plantagenet king was buried in the church of the Greyfriars.

The death of the Yorkist Richard and the triumph of the Lancastrian Henry was not the last fight in that sorrowful episode in our history known as the Wars of the Roses. Two years later the impostor Lambert Simnel was made the figurehead of a revolt in which the Earl of Lincoln, whom Richard had nominated as his heir, and Viscount Lovel, one of the late king's most loyal friends, played the principal parts. Henry was obliged to crush them at the Battle of Stoke on 16 June (see p. 190). Bosworth did, however, introduce another great dynasty into a world on the threshold of some of its most magnificent years. In the course of the next century a whole galaxy of dynasties produced some of their brightest luminaries: the Valois in Europe, the Osmanlis in Asia Minor, the Safavids in Persia, and the Mughals in India. The Tudors in England could justly claim their rightful place among these illustrious houses.

Principal Battles of The Wars of the Roses
In Chronological Order

1455: 22 May

First Battle of St Albans. When in March 1454 King Henry VI recovered from the long mental illness that had caused the Duke of York's first protectorate, it was obvious that war could not long be delayed (for the political background see chapter 7). The Duke of Somerset was released from the Tower and reinstated in the King's favour, whereas the Duke of York and his colleagues were dismissed from their offices and sent back to their estates, soon to be in peril of their lives. York summoned his friends to arms, and at the head of 3,000 men and accompanied by Lords Salisbury and Warwick he marched against the King in London. However, Henry left pro-Yorkist London for Leicester and, on learning that York was at Ware, set up his standard at St Albans. The King had with him the Dukes of Somerset and Buckingham, Lords Pembroke, Northumberland and Devon and about 2,000 men.

The Lancastrians attempted to hold the town behind two barriers in Hollywell and St Peter's Streets against Yorkist attacks from the east. Two frontal attacks made no headway, but Warwick infiltrated his troops through an unguarded part of the town's defences and spreading out took both barricades in the flank. The whole action lasted only half an hour and no more than 100 Lancastrians were killed; but the toll among their senior officers was very heavy. Somerset, Northumberland and Clifford were killed; Buckingham's son died of wounds and Buckingham himself was wounded.

1459: 23 September

Blore Heath. After four years of uneasy peace the King presided over a wasting realm. No parliament had been summoned for three years, the country was sadly divided and distressed. The Yorkists were armed, armies were marching across all England. Lord Audley had recently raised a Lancastrian army centred round Market Drayton, and the Queen—through whom the King ruled—sent him orders to intercept Lord Salisbury, who was marching from

Yorkshire to join the Duke of York at Ludlow. The two armies met head on two and a half miles east of Market Drayton at a place called Blore Heath. Salisbury, with 3,000 troops, was outnumbered by more than two to one, but could not avoid giving battle.

Audley took up a position just west of a little stream that crosses the Market Drayton–Newcastle-under-Lyme road, and Salisbury's men were drawn up about 150 yards east of the present Audley Cross, which marks the spot where Lord Audley fell. The Yorkist left rested upon the boggy edge of a wood, but their right was in the air, and Salisbury made a laager of his wagons to protect this flank. Whether Salisbury feigned retreat in order to draw Audley on is not certain, but the Lancastrian commander was definitely the one to attack. Two cavalry charges were repulsed, the first with heavy loss to the Lancastrians, and then they mounted an infantry attack up the hill to the Yorkist position. But this too failed; there was no support from the cavalry, Lord Audley had already fallen and 500 Lancastrians chose this moment to desert to the enemy. Salisbury's victory was complete and in the pursuit, which continued for two miles, the slaughter was very heavy. Possibly 2,000 Lancastrians perished in this battle, but less than 200 Yorkists fell.

1460: 10 July

Northampton. Immediately after Blore Heath the Yorkists were dispersed near Ludlow without a battle, owing to the treachery of a large part of their army. York himself retired to Ireland, Salisbury and Warwick to Calais. The Queen summoned a parliament and Henry gave his assent to a bill of attainder against all the principal Yorkist leaders. At the end of June the Calais exiles made a landing in Kent, seized Sandwich and gathering support entered London on 2 July. Here they were joined by almost all the Yorkist peers and their retainers. An army of some 30,000 was assembled, and leaving a part of it to blockade the Tower—held

by Lancastrians—the remainder under Lord Warwick set out to meet the King. The court had been in Coventry, but on learning of the Yorkist advance the King moved to Northampton, and here on 10 July, entrenched in a meadow just south of the town, Warwick found the Lancastrian army under the Duke of Buckingham.

The Duke had less men than Warwick, but his position was a strong one and his earthworks were lined with artillery. The first attack, on a three-battle front, was repulsed; it seemed that the position was too formidable a one for any frontal assault to succeed. Indeed, had it not been for the treachery of Lord Grey of Ruthen, holding the left of the Lancastrian line, Warwick might never have had the victory. But when Grey let in the Earl of March (York's son and later Edward IV) he quickly rolled up the Lancastrian line, allowing Warwick's attack in the centre to succeed. The casualties were not high, but as at St Albans many of the Lancastrian leaders (including Buckingham, Shrewsbury and Egremont) were killed. The King was captured and once more led back to London.

1460: 30 December

Wakefield. In the September after Northampton the Duke of York came to London, and although he failed to win the crown he obtained from Henry the right of succession for himself and his heirs on the King's death. But Queen Margaret, then in north Wales, was not prepared to disinherit her son and soon had a very large army mustering in the north. The Duke of York marched to meet her and with an army of between 5,000 and 6,000 men reached his castle at Sandal (just south of Wakefield) on Christmas Eve. A few days later the much larger Lancastrian host was upon him.

Although details of the Battle of Wakefield are scarce, it appears that York refused to await expected reinforcements and marched out of the castle to give battle. Leaving the castle by the south gate he had to swing round it to meet the Lancastrians, who were assembled between Sandal

England and Wales: Wars of The Roses battlefields

and Wakefield. Heavily outnumbered he found himself between the two arms of a pincer movement and his army was quickly defeated. The Duke himself was killed in the battle, together with many other prominent Yorkists.

1461: 2 February
Mortimer's Cross. Queen Margaret was not present at Wakefield, but she accompanied the Lancastrian army on its destructive march south to St Albans. Warwick arrived in London at the beginning of February. On learning of York's death he appears to have made no effort to get in touch with the Earl of March (now Edward Duke of York) who was then on the Welsh march. But Edward, although only nineteen years old, was already a capable soldier and in a battle at Mortimer's Cross (some four miles south of Wigmore) defeated a Lancastrian force under the Earls of Wiltshire and Pembroke.

We know nothing of the details of this battle, except that in the morning, through some freak atmospheric condition, three suns were said to be visible. Edward took this as a propitious omen and after his victory added the sun to his banner: the device that was to serve him so well at Barnet ten years later (see p. 159). The beaten army was pursued as far as Hereford (some sixteen miles to the south), and although the two commanders escaped ten important prisoners, including Pembroke's father Owen Tudor, were summarily executed in Hereford. Edward then marched to join Warwick, but arrived too late for the second Battle of St Albans.

1461: 17 February
Second Battle of St Albans. The Earl of Warwick left London on 12 February and reached St Albans that evening. He had under command an army variously estimated as between 9,000 and 30,000 men—the former figure being nearer the mark. Margaret had started her march from Yorkshire with some 30,000 men, but many had gone home with their loot; she probably brought 11–12,000 soldiers into the field at St Albans. Warwick covered a long front from St Albans to Nomansland Common with four unconnected defensive positions, and laid out a number of complicated defensive devices.

The Lancastrians opened their attack on Warwick's left position in St Albans itself, and met stiff resistance from his archers positioned round the watch tower and Eleanor Cross. It took them much of the morning before the street fighting was done with, and a swing to their left in order to engage Warwick's position on Bernard's Heath was possible. The main engagement was fought either here or on the high ground

above Sandridge a mile to the north. The wind was blowing a light snowfall into the Yorkists' faces, which greatly hindered their bowmanship; added to this their centre, under Warwick's brother, Lord Montagu, was hopelessly outnumbered and left to fight unaided for many hours. When Warwick eventually brought the right wing to their assistance a pre-arranged desertion by a large contingent of troops from Kent had the most demoralizing effect on the entire Yorkist army, which began to retreat. Although the line was temporarily stabilized by Warwick above Nomansland Common defeat was now inevitable. Warwick, whose generalship on the day had been sadly wanting, at least managed to leave the field at the head of 4,000 disciplined troops. For full details of this battle, see chapter 8.

1461: 29 March
Towton. After St Albans Henry was reunited with his queen, but he refused to let his army advance on London (a costly mistake), and instead the Lancastrians headed north again, plundering as they went. Meanwhile, Warwick acted swiftly and at the beginning of March had Edward proclaimed king in London. Edward fully realized that there could not be two kings in England, and on about 12 March he set out for the north. Lord Fauconberg had marched in advance and Warwick had been despatched to raise troops in the Midlands. Somewhere north of the Trent Edward assembled his large army of about 40,000 soldiers. A slight Yorkist reverse was suffered at Ferrybridge, where Lord Fitzwalter's troops were surprised and their commander killed in an attack led by Lord Clifford; but Clifford's force was soon caught and Clifford himself killed. The Yorkists then proceeded to the higher ground, where the Lancastrians were drawn up between the villages of Towton and Saxton.

The battle that was fought on this windswept plateau lasted for nearly the whole day. Rather more than 80,000 men took part and this time the snowstorm that set in favoured the Yorkists. The advantage seemed to go first to one side then to the other in this fiercely contested battle. About midday the Duke of Norfolk's troops arrived on the field and took position on the Yorkist right flank. With his numbers thus increased Edward was at last able to turn the Lancastrian left and gradually—still fighting desperately—they began to fall back, closely pressed by the Yorkists. Eventually discipline snapped and in the mad rush to cross the Cock Beck and gain the London road thousands of Lancastrians perished. The exact numbers of those who died on the

field of battle, or in the marshy fields of the beck, are not known; but there has been no greater slaughter in any battle fought on British soil. For a full account see chapter 9.

1464: 25 April
Hedgeley Moor. In the years 1462 and 1463 the Lancastrians were continually stirring up trouble in the north of England, with Queen Margaret travelling between Scotland and France attempting to gain assistance (sometimes successfully) for Henry's declining cause. But the Duke of Somerset and Sir Ralph Percy surrendered Bamburgh and Dunstanburgh Castles respectively on Christmas Eve 1462 in return for free pardons, and later Somerset swore allegiance to Edward and was rewarded with high office. Although these castles (and Alnwick as well) were later retaken by the Lancastrians they were soon isolated, and with Henry a wandering fugitive, Margaret driven overseas and the Scots ready to treat with Edward, there were hopes of a permanent peace. However, Margaret was working hard in Lorraine to organize a fresh conspiracy in the north of England, and Somerset quite suddenly betrayed the trust that Edward had shown him and raised the northern counties for Henry. Warwick marched north to subdue the rebellion, and Montagu was sent to the border to escort the Scottish commissioners to York to discuss a renewal of the peace treaty. His journey was not without excitement; on his way to Newcastle with a small escort he narrowly escaped an ambush laid for him by Somerset. A few days later, now with a larger force, he was attacked at Hedgeley Moor, some seven miles south of Wooler, by Somerset and Percy.

It is not likely that either side had many troops in the brief engagement that followed, and the opponents were probably fairly evenly matched, but when Sir Ralph Percy fell leading Somerset's van the Lancastrians appear to have lost heart and fled the field, leaving Montagu to proceed unimpeded.

1464: 15 May
Hexham. The Lancastrian position in the north, where lay their only remaining strength, was fast crumbling. The Scots had agreed to cease sheltering them, and their Northumbrian strongholds could not expect to withstand for long the heavy siege weapons that Edward was hurriedly assembling. But they could still put an army into the field, and Lord Montagu again set out from Newcastle to oppose it. He found Somerset's men drawn up in a meadow called the Linnels some three miles south east of Hexham on the banks of the Devil's Water.

It was a hopeless position from which to fight any sort of battle, the field being almost totally enclosed and too cramped to allow of free manoeuvre. The Lancastrian soldiers seem to have realized this, for many made off at the Yorkist approach without so much as discharging an arrow. It required no great feat of generalship to demolish those that stayed to fight. Montagu practically surrounded the meadow, and then made a frontal attack through the one opening at the east end. Those that were not killed in this attack were pressed across the river into West Dipton Wood and forced to surrender. Battle casualties were not great, but the executions that followed (including that of Somerset) were on a scale unparalleled even in these bloodthirsty times. Henry remained north of the Tyne during the fight and escaped to the Lake District, where he was among predominantly loyal subjects.

1464: June
Bamburgh Castle. After Hexham there remained to the Lancastrians only the three great castles of Bamburgh (opposite the Farne Islands), Dunstanburgh (some twelve miles farther down the coast) and Alnwick. These had already changed hands more than once, and now Warwick and Montagu (created Earl of Northumberland after Hexham), bringing with them Edward's massive siege pieces, set out to smother the last embers of Lancastrian resistance. Alnwick, on 23 June, and Dunstanburgh the next day yielded without resistance, but Bamburgh refused the summons. This castle was held by Sir Ralph Grey and he had been exempted from the general pardon. Soon the debris from the ramparts was being blasted into the sea, and resistance, which never stood a chance of succeeding, quickly collapsed.

The affair is of interest in being the first time that a battering train was used effectively in England. The King's great guns, 'London' and 'Newcastle' (made of iron) and 'Dijon' (a brass cannon), were supported by bombardels, and it was with some ease that they breached the walls, allowing Warwick to lead an assault that completed the work. Grey was seriously wounded, but this did not save him from being dragged before the High Constable, John Tiptoft Earl of Worcester, who had a reputation for recognizing no law but the axe.

1469: 26 July
Edgcote. After Hexham and the surrender of the Northumbrian castles it seemed as though the Lancastrian cause could never recover sufficiently to become a

serious threat to Edward IV. The Beauforts, the Tudor Earl of Pembroke, the Duke of Exeter—in fact almost all the Lancastrian leaders—were in exile, and in July 1465 Henry was caught on the borders of Yorkshire and Lancashire and sent to the Tower. But the Yorkist strength lay in the twin pillars of the King and Warwick. Between 1465 and 1469 the King, by a series of foolish and underhand acts, estranged Warwick, who from being his most loyal and useful adherent became his most embittered enemy.

The break between Warwick and Edward was the signal for a big revival of Lancastrian activity on both sides of the Channel. Jasper Tudor returned to Wales and here and elsewhere rising broke out; Warwick had crossed to Calais where he was joined by the King's brother Clarence, who married Warwick's daughter there. Warwick, having fermented a serious rebellion in the north of the country, then landed in Kent, where he raised a considerable army with which he marched on London. Edward, who was at Nottingham dealing with the Yorkshire rebellion, found himself between two hostile forces. He had some 15,000 men under arms with him, but the loyalty of many was suspect; however, his newly created Earls of Devon (Stafford) and Pembroke (Herbert) were marching to his assistance with 6,000 and 14,000 archers respectively. Meanwhile the northern rebels, under Sir John Conyers, had carried out a skilful march on Leicester and got between Edward and the Earls. The latter joined forces at Banbury, where Devon and Pembroke quarrelled. As a result, Devon drew off his men, leaving Pembroke with only 14,000 Welsh bowmen to face a vastly superior force under Conyers, and possibly Warwick's army, which was marching towards Towcester On 25 July the two forces were in contact and some skirmishing for position took place round three prominent features near Danes Moor. Danes Moor is situated about five and a half miles north-east of Banbury, some two miles east of Wardington, which is on the Banbury-Chipping Warden (B4036) road. On this day the northerners lost Sir Henry Neville, son of Lord Latimer.

On 26 July Pembroke's men were attacked in force, but through the efforts of their commander and his brother Sir Richard Herbert, held their own for some hours against superior numbers. Eventually, lured down from their hillside position into the valley, and betrayed by the vanguard of the King's army under Sir Geoffrey Gate, who arrived late on the scene and then joined the enemy, the Welshmen broke. One near contemporary

account puts their casualties as high as 4,000, but this is probably a considerable exaggeration. Pembroke and his brother were taken prisoner and summarily executed. The fractious Earl of Devon was captured a few days later and also executed. As a result of the battle Edward became Warwick's prisoner, but after keeping him at his Middleham castle for a while Warwick found it expedient to release him

1470: 12 March
Empingham. In early 1470 there was a rising in Lincolnshire; the rebels were led by Sir Robert Welles, and strongly supported by Warwick and Clarence in spite of their outward display of loyalty to the King. On learning of the rebellion Edward acted with commendable rapidity. Issuing commissions of array he soon had a powerful force with which he marched to Stamford. Sir Robert's father, Lord Welles, and Sir Thomas Dymock, the King's Champion, had been summoned to the King and admitted being implicated in the rebellion. At Stamford, when Sir Robert refused to disperse his men, both his father and Dymock were executed. Edward then proceeded against the rebels.

He found them in a field some five miles north-west of Stamford, just off the present A1 road. There was not even a skirmish; the rebels were so terrified by the few rounds fired by the King's artillery that they fled, hastily casting off their coats with the tell-tale colours of Welles, and giving to the place its name of Losecoat Field. Sir Robert Welles was captured and beheaded, but not before he had made a confession implicating Warwick and Clarence in the rebellion—a fact apparently not previously realized by the King.

1471: 14 April
Barnet. In October 1470 Warwick drove Edward out of England and reinstated Henry as king. Aided by money and ships supplied by his brother-in-law, the Duke of Burgundy, Edward returned in March 1471. Landing in Yorkshire he was soon able to assemble a small army and gather reinforcements as he marched south. Montagu in Yorkshire and Warwick in Coventry were successfully by-passed, while Clarence (unknown to Warwick) was preparing to return to his brother's camp. On 12 April King Edward entered London unopposed. He left again the next day to confront Warwick, who had marched through St Albans with a mixed Lancastrian and Yorkist force of about 9,000 men and taken up a position on Hadley Green, just north of Barnet. Edward, at the head of some 8,000 men, arrived at Barnet on the evening of 13 April, and in spite of the darkness advanced to

within a short distance of Warwick.

The battle started early the next morning in a thick ground mist. In the initial stages the Yorkist left (under Lord Hastings) was beaten from the field by the Earl of Oxford's battle, but Prince Richard of Gloucester (the future Richard III) had some success on Edward's right. The fight in the centre was sternly contested. Oxford, returning from the pursuit of Hasting's men, misjudged the position, and in the mist his banners with their star were mistaken for Edward's sun and he was attacked by men from Warwick's centre. Thinking treachery was afoot, Oxford and his followers rode off the field. The battle lasted between three and four hours and ended in a complete victory for Edward. The Earl of Warwick, who had fought on foot, was struck down trying to regain his horse. For full details see chapter 10.

1471: 4 May

Tewkesbury. On that Easter Sunday which saw Warwick's defeat and death at Barnet, Queen Margaret with her young son landed at Weymouth and was soon joined by many Lancastrian leaders with the remnants of their fighting men. The Duke of Somerset took command of the assembled army and, realizing the impossibility of fighting without further reinforcements of men and materials, decided to move towards Wales and join forces with Jasper Tudor, collecting military stores from Bristol on the way. Edward was at Windsor for the feast of St George and as soon as he learned of Somerset's intention he set out —on 24 April—for the West Country. There followed an exciting chase with the Queen's army trying to get across the Severn and Edward desperately anxious to bring her to battle. A little time was wasted in Bristol, Gloucester closed its gates to her and on arrival at Tewkesbury (3 May) the Lancastrians were too tired and too hard pressed to cross the Severn. Somerset decided—wisely, for he had the choice of ground—to stand and fight rather than risk a lengthy crossing with weary troops. He had about 6,000 men, which was rather more than Edward could put against him, and the Yorkists were in no better shape after their gruelling march than their opponents.

The next morning Edward opened the battle with a fairly heavy artillery bombardment, which induced Somerset to lead an attack on the junction of the Yorkist left and centre battles. The situation could have been dangerous for Edward, had Somerset's centre under Lord Wenlock supported him. As it was fighting alone and attacked on two sides, Somerset's men were driven back and the King advanced his battle to the attack. The Lancastrians, demoralized by the débâcle on their right, offered little resistance to Edward and soon the whole line broke. The slaughter during the retreat was heavy: perhaps 2,000 men perished in the battle and on the banks of the Severn. Queen Margaret made good her escape, but her son was killed and Somerset was taken from the sanctuary of the abbey and executed. The battle is fully described in chapter 11.

1485: 22 August

Bosworth. Edward IV died in 1483. His son was only twelve years old and so Edward designated his brother Richard as protector. Richard had Edward's two sons imprisoned in the Tower and himself proclaimed king. He had many enemies both at home and abroad, and on 7 August 1485 Henry Tudor landed near Milford Haven with about 2,000 French mercenaries and a handful of Lancastrian lords and knights. Gathering reinforcements as he advanced through Wales, Henry then marched via Shrewsbury, Stafford and Atherstone. Richard was at Nottingham, and moved from there to Leicester on 19 August, and by 21 August the two armies were in striking distance of each other two or three miles south of Market Bosworth. Richard's army (without the Stanley brothers) was not much short of 8,000 men, while Henry had only about 5,000. However, the loyalty of the Stanleys to Richard was very suspect, and during the battle both of them opted for Henry, bringing with them perhaps a total of 4,000 men.

The battle was fought on and around Ambion Hill, close to Sutton Cheney, and lasted for only two hours. Richard gained the best position, but failed to take advantage of it by attacking Henry's van under Lord Oxford while it was still deploying. In the event Oxford was allowed time to launch his attack and the Duke of Norfolk, commanding Richard's forward battle, was soon killed. For the first hour the fighting was evenly matched, but the battle was lost for Richard through treachery. Both the Stanleys deserted his cause, but even more damaging was the failure of the Earl of Northumberland to bring the rearguard into action when he saw which way the Stanleys were moving. The battle ended with the death of Richard, for his followers had no stomach for continuing the fight after their king had been slain. For a full account see chapter 12.

1487: 16 June

Stoke Field. The early years of Henry VII's reign were by no means carefree; his dynasty was beset by enemies in Britain and at the court of Burgundy; in the spring of 1487 a serious insurrection was launched from Ireland. An imposter called Lambert Simnel, made out to be Clarence's son, Edward Earl of Warwick (who at that time was actually a prisoner in the Tower), was sponsored by an Oxford priest and supported by the Earl of Lincoln, whom Richard had made his heir, and the ardent Yorkist Lord Lovel. Simnel was crowned King of England in Dublin on 24 May 1487, and on 4 June the boy 'king', accompanied by Lincoln and Lovel, landed near Furness in Lancashire and advanced through Yorkshire at the head of 1,500 German mercenaries (kindly supplied by his 'aunt' Margaret, Dowager Duchess of Burgundy). As they marched the rebels gathered reinforcements, although not nearly as many as Lincoln had hoped for. Henry was at Kenilworth, but calling up nearby levies he set off at once for Nottingham. By the time he arrived there (14 June) the rebels were at Southwell, some twelve miles to the north-east. According to the contemporary account of a herald, Henry moved to Radcliffe on 15 June, while the rebel army crossed the Trent by the ford below Fiskerton and took up a position on an open escarpment some 1,500 yards south of East Stoke. Here the King met them on the morning of the 16th as he was marching towards Newark. The rebels held the advantage in numbers (perhaps 9,000 to Henry's 6,000), but apart from the German mercenaries their soldiers were not well armed or trained.

The royalists advanced to the attack in three well spaced out divisions, the van being commanded by Lord Oxford. This division, being somewhat isolated, was severely punished and only saved from complete disaster by the arrival of the King's main battle. As the royalist divisions closed up the rebels were first held and then pushed back off the ridge. The fight lasted for more than three hours and was fiercely contested, the rebel army being well buttressed by the German contingent. Their commander Martin Schwartz and Lincoln were killed in battle; Lovel escaped by swimming the Trent and was never seen alive again, and Simnel was captured and put to work in the royal kitchens. The rebel soldiery were slaughtered by the thousand in a gully at the foot of the ridge and in the marshy riverain fields. They had, however, inflicted very heavy casualties on Henry's army—possibly as many as 2,000 men, most of whom were from the vanguard. By his victory at Stoke Henry secured the safety of the Tudor dynasty.

CHAPTER 13

Scotland and the Tudors

Flodden

9 September 1513

The battlefield of Flodden is one of the few in Great Britain that is still very much the same as it was at the time of the battle. No doubt the fields are better cultivated, the hedges are new and in places scrub woodland has given way to orderly plantations. But apart from a few farm buildings, a slightly enlarged village, a partial drainage of the bog and some new roads the site must have looked very much the same in 1513.

The actual battle took place immediately to the south of Branxton village, which is about three miles south-east of Coldstream and to the south of the main Morpeth–Coldstream road, the A 697, Ordnance Survey one-inch map, sheet 64. The ground over which the battle was fought, and the two Scottish positions prior to the battle, are on private property and can be visited only by permission of the owners. The exception to this is the monument erected on Pipers Hill, which can be reached by a public footpath. However, because of the undulating ground the visitor has no real need to leave the roads to view the field of battle. Just north of the village of Milfield a side road runs north-west to Branxton; about two miles along this road the ground rises steeply and the road cuts across the west end of Flodden Hill. The first Scottish position was on the high ground crossed by this road, from just to the west of it stretching eastwards almost to the main road. The road leads to Branxton Hill (which was the second position of the Scots), and from the top of this hill, near where a track leads to the farm, a good view can be obtained of the battlefield immediately to the north. An even better view of the English position (which was along the ridge where the monument stands) can be had from the fields directly to the north of the farmyard – although, of course, permission from the farmer would be necessary to walk through these.

James IV came to the throne in 1488 after the insurgent lords had defeated his father's troops in battle at Sauchieburn and, in open defiance of the young prince's orders, had murdered their king, who had taken refuge in a nearby mill. The new king was fifteen years old, of an age to be fully aware of the dark deed of shame through which he had ascended the throne. It was to cast a deep shadow across his path, and it is said that in penance for the rest of his life he went girt with an iron chain to which he added a fresh link every year. With the possible exception of Robert I, James IV was the best loved and most forward-looking king to sit on the Scottish throne. In the twenty-five years of his reign he developed the country's commerce, stabilized the currency, improved the navy and efficiently overhauled the administration of justice. These and other achievements more than offset his short-comings and occasional acts of folly.

A contemporary description of James at the time of his death, when he was about forty, tells us that he was of 'middle size and of a strong body and red hair – used to much exercise and of slender diet'. Undoubtedly, he was a man of good physique and pleasing appearance, for his attraction to and admiration for women is well known. Having been deeply in love with Margaret Drummond, whom he would have married had she not been poisoned along with her two sisters at breakfast one morning, he finally consented in 1502 to take Margaret Tudor as his bride. Margaret was an extremely passionate woman, who after her husband's death saw no reason to dissemble her passions. The ten years of their marriage were on the whole happy ones, although even she was unable to satisfy James's carnal lust, and his frequent, and usually fruitful, visits to mistresses were the source of constant complaint.

James's relations with his father-in-law were for the most part cordial. Before his marriage he had made one foolish mistake when he championed the cause of the impostor Perkin Warbeck, but for most of Henry VII's reign James strove, not without some success, to maintain peace in the dangerous and shifting quick-sands of European politics. He had raised Scotland to a position of eminence and often found himself holding the balance of power in the constantly changing alignments of the great European powers. James was always ready to stand by the 'Auld Alliance', but obdurately refused to be drawn into war by England, France, Spain or the papacy.

After Henry VII died in 1509, the English throne was occupied by a man of very different mettle. Henry VIII, with his rich inherit-ance, youthful exuberance and impetuosity, presented the Scottish king with an entirely different proposition from his more careful and cautious father-in-law. Nevertheless, for the first two years of Henry's reign the friendly relationship between England and

Right: Thomas Howard, Earl of Surrey by Holbein, in Windsor Castle.
Left: James IV, from drawing attributed to Jacques le Bourcq, in the library at Arras

Scotland was if anything strengthened. But by 1511 a tight ring of steel in the form of the Holy League was being drawn around France by the Papal States, Spain and Venice, and it was not long before the Emperor Maximilian and Henry VIII decided to join the League and complete the encirclement. During the next two years there were many sparks that might have started a conflagration between England and Scotland: fierce Border raids for which both countries could share the blame; semi-official naval hostilities in which James lost Andrew Barton, one of his best sea captains, and both countries lost valuable ships; Henry's refusal to hand over the Bastard John Heron, who had killed Sir Robert Ker, Warden of the Scottish Middle March; and, most hurtful to the Scottish queen, her brother's insistence on keeping her legacy of valuable jewellery. Throughout this time James did all in his power to avert war; but Henry was determined to invade France, and his principal concern was that James should not march in his absence. However, the 'Auld Alliance' was deep-rooted and in July 1512 James took the decisive step of renewing it.

Even so, when 1513 – the year that was to bring a cataract of

193

misfortune on Scotland – was ushered in England and Scotland were still exchanging civilities. Henry sent Doctor West to Scotland for the second time and James sent Lord Drummond to England; but West was quite unsuccessful in moving Queen Margaret to use her influence in favour of her native country, and as Drummond's offer of reconciliation was conditional upon Henry refraining from war with France it was treated with unconcealed contempt. More successful missions had been carried out by Louis XII's envoy de la Motte. This Frenchman combined in equal measure the talents of soldier, pirate and diplomat: on his way to Edinburgh he was perfectly capable of sinking a few English ships and bringing others captive to Leith. Such high-handed piracy was most satisfactory, but perhaps what endeared him even more to James was a consignment he brought him of wine, gunpowder and other warlike stores.

Meanwhile the French queen added her blandishments. Anne of Brittany begged James to advance as her true knight three feet into English soil and do battle in her honour; and just in case this fervid plea did not strike the chord of chivalrous romanticism in James it was reinforced with 14,000 French crowns and a ring of gold set with a turquoise from off her own finger. This and other legends surround the events leading up to Flodden. We do not know for certain whether Anne sent James her ring, nor do we know what truth there is in the sinister warnings James is said to have received first in the royal chapel at Linlithgow, and then from the market cross in Edinburgh, against undertaking the hazardous enterprise upon which he was then setting out.* What we do know is that by the summer of 1513 the French were in grave peril of destruction; James had agreed to advance into England should Henry invade France, and when in June the English king crossed the Channel at the head of a large army, James made preparations to honour his pledge to King Louis.

On 26 July he sent Lyon herald to Henry, who was encamped outside Thérouanne, with a message to this effect. Henry replied on 12 August in a letter containing a superb piece of Tudor hubris. Having castigated James for constantly breaking the treaty of perpetual peace and dishonourably waiting to attack until Henry was out of the country, he is at pains to show that such perfidious

*Robert Lindesay of Pitscottie in his *The Historie and Cronicles of Scotland*, Vol. I, is the principal source for these and other Flodden legends. Some are undoubtedly not true, but a turquoise ring later preserved in the College of Arms was said to have been removed from James's body after the battle.

behaviour comes as no surprise to him. 'We cannot maruayle, considering the auncient accustomable maners of your progenitours, which neuer kept lenger faythe and promise than pleased them.' He ended by assuring James that he had no intention of desisting from his attack on France.† The die was cast, war was now inevitable. But Henry had had no illusions that it would be otherwise, and before leaving England he had said to the Earl of Surrey, who was appointed Lord Lieutenant of the North, 'My Lord, I trust not the Scots, therefore I pray you be not negligent.'‡ Surrey, son of that Duke of Norfolk who had fought against Henry Tudor at Bosworth Field, was now an old man of seventy, but he was neither negligent, nor negligible, as the Scots were soon to discover.

Supporting the French king actively by an invasion of England was the second big mistake that James made in his relationship with the southern kingdom, and it was to cost him much more dearly than had his support for Perkin Warbeck. He never thought in terms of conquest, but he set himself the task of causing a diversion that he hoped would bring Henry hurrying back from France. James had no illusions as to the dangers and difficulties that lay ahead, and although he is alleged to have said that 'only millers and mass priests' were left in England, this statement is hardly borne out by the size of the army he assembled – or else he had a very healthy respect for 'Christ's Church militant here in earth'. He knew very well that Surrey would march against him with a formidable force; and the events of history should have warned him that Scottish attempts to stir up trouble in England had a nasty habit of rebounding on the Scots.

During the first fortnight of August the bulk of the Scottish army assembled near Edinburgh. It was the largest and best equipped army ever to leave Scotland until modern times, but it was a heterogeneous force, and it is a measure of the King's popularity throughout Scotland that he could command the loyalty and weld into one fighting machine men from the Highlands, Lowlands and Borders, who not so long ago comprised three different races. As usual the numbers have been wildly exaggerated, and modern historians are left to grope their way as best they can through a bewildering number of variations. It seems fairly certain that between crossing the border and the actual Battle of Flodden there was considerable desertion – many who were only there

†*Hall's Chronicle*, p.547.
‡ibid, p.555.

for the loot being anxious to get it safely home; it is also generally agreed that there was no great disparity between the strength of the two armies, and that the Scottish army may possibly have been the stronger. It may well be that 40,000 men crossed the border on 22 August, but that rather fewer than 30,000 remained to fight at Flodden. This number would have included a French contingent under Count d'Aussi; the French had what we would now call a military mission in Scotland, which was there partly to strengthen their ally's military effort, but also to teach them modern fighting methods and in particular the use of the continental long-handled pike and the two new pieces of artillery which they had recently given James.

Artillery was still a comparatively new arm, and although useful in siege warfare and for strengthening a defensive position the heavy cannon of those days (culverins, sakers and serpentines) was quite unsuited to any mobile form of warfare, and the Scots needed 400 oxen and twenty-eight packhorses to draw their guns and ammunition. James was very proud of his cannon, and rightly so, for the seventeen pieces of 'great ordnance' that he brought to Flodden Field (and left there) were far superior to anything the English could pit against them. But in the battle, in which artillery played only a minor part, it was the English guns that caused the most alarm.

Lord Home commanded the Borderers, and while the Scottish army was still mustering he opened the campaign with a large-scale mounted raid into Northumberland. It was entirely successful until on 13 August, as the force was returning laden with booty, they were surprised in an ambush near Milfield. Sir William Bulmer's archers took severe toll of the raiders and regained the plunder. This disaster, called by the Scots the Ill-Raid, was an inauspicious beginning, nor were the Borderers destined to redeem this failure in the forthcoming battle.

James crossed the Tweed at Coldstream on 22 August, and having reduced Wark Castle marched downstream to attack Norham. The Bishop of Durham, to whom Norham Castle belonged, considered this great fortress, perched on its inaccessible eyrie many feet above the Tweed, to be impregnable. The visitor today would be inclined to agree with him. But the combination of James's heavy cannon (which certainly proved their worth here) and the castle's inadequately supplied magazine forced the governor to beat the chamade after a siege of only six days. The river Till is a formidable obstacle and in 1513 it was bridged at Twizel, Etal and Ford and then not until Weetwood some ten miles further

196

upstream; it was therefore important for James to take Etal and Ford Castles. Etal was not properly fortified, and the owner of Ford, Sir William Heron, had been taken by the Scots as a hostage for his bastard brother John, who was still at large in England and was soon to join Lord Surrey's army. Lady Heron surrendered the castle in the hope that it would be spared. There are many entertaining stories of James's dalliance at Ford, and how he succumbed to the charms of the chatelaine, who, animated by a desire for vengeance, allowed herself to be seduced so that she could delay the advance of the Scottish army, and inform upon it to Lord Surrey. Alas, most of them are untrue. It is possible that James agreed to her asking Surrey to release two important Scotsmen taken in the Ill-Raid in exchange for her husband; but if so nothing came of it, and after two or three days at the castle James took his leave of Lady Heron and burned her castle down.

Meanwhile, Surrey had been assembling his army first at Newcastle and then at Alnwick, where he arrived on 3 September and where he was joined by his eldest son Thomas Howard, the Lord Admiral, who brought him about 1,000 armed men from off the fleet. England's main army was, of course, in France with Henry, and the one that Surrey had now raised consisted chiefly of a cross-section of northern society. The local lords, gentry, yeomen and peasants formed the backbone of the army. They were not professional soldiers, but they were well accustomed to bear arms, and in the days when archery practice was compulsory they were good bowmen.* Surrey also had his own 500 licensed retainers, who were more akin to professional soldiers, but of these only one was a man-at-arms (heavy cavalryman). The army, which probably totalled about 26,000 in all, was strong in archers and billmen, but weak in artillery and without heavy cavalry – Lord Dacre commanded a force of 'prickers', who were irregular horsemen recruited from the border, and for the approach march most of the infantry would have been mounted.

With the exception of Hastings the Battle of Flodden has evoked more interest and received more attention from historians than any other battle fought on English soil. In consequence we have a large number of accounts, almost all of which differ to a greater or lesser degree as to what were James's and Surrey's intentions before the battle, and as to exactly how the battle was fought. There are a number of contemporary, or near contemporary,

*It is interesting to note that Flodden was the last major battle in which the longbow was used.

sources that can be studied – some of which appear in the bibliography for this chapter – including what is purported to be Admiral Howard's official dispatch.† Other than this, and Lord Dacre's letters to Wolsey and Henry VIII, all accounts are secondhand – even the Bishop of Durham was not present at the actual battle – and much of what they say is slanted towards whichever side they favoured; there are few points upon which they are agreed.

At least one modern writer‡ bases his account on the assumption that James misappreciated Surrey's intention and, thinking he was marching into Scotland, gave the order to retire across the Border but was surprised before he could reach the Tweed. This is not the generally accepted view, and much must depend on what importance can be placed on the interesting – although by no means invariable – custom of those days of challenging one's opponent to battle and even naming the day and time at which the fight was to take place, in much the same way as we would arrange a football match. We tend to forget that warfare in the sixteenth century was a much more dignified – if equally unpleasant – affair than in modern times, and that the nobility usually set much store on chivalrous conduct.

On 4 September Surrey sent Rouge Croix to James, whose army was still encamped around Ford, to say that as James had invaded the realm, spoilt, burned and raided divers houses, and killed many people, he had come to give battle. Two days later James sent his herald Islay to accept the challenge, and Surrey replied that he would be bounden in £10,000 and good securities 'to gyve the sayde Kynge batayle by frydaye next at the furthest'.* Thomas Howard in his dispatch quotes James as saying 'he would abide him [Surrey] there till Friday at noon'. On arrival at Wooler Surrey was therefore indignant to learn that James had in the meanwhile taken up a very strong defensive position on Flodden Hill. On 7 September he wrote a letter to James reminding him of his agreement to give battle on Friday the 9th in his original position, and expressing surprise that 'it hath pleased you to chaunge your said promyse and putte your self into a grounde more like a fortresse or a campe . . .'. He suggested that James came down on the next day to the plain of Milfield.† James was

†Either Surrey delegated the task to his son, or else his own dispatch is no longer extant.
‡G. F. T. Leather, *New Light on Flodden*.
*Richard Faques, *The Trewe Encountre*.
†State Papers Scotland, Henry VIII, Vol. I, folio 17. P.R.O.

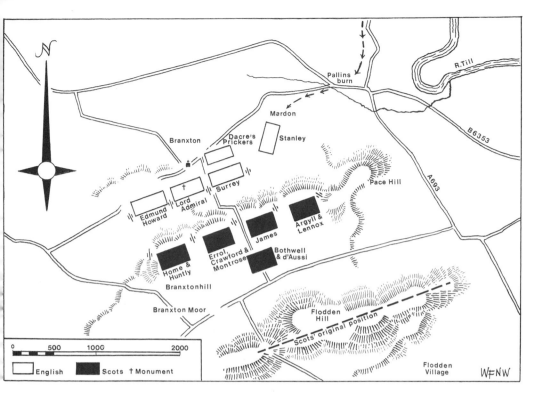

N

Pallins burn

R.Till

Mardon

B6353

Branxton

Dacre's Prickers

Stanley

A693

Surrey

Pace Hill

Edmund Howard

Lord Admiral

Argyll & Lennox

James

Home & Huntly

Errol, Crawford & Montrose

Bothwell & d'Aussi

Branxtonhill

Branxton Moor

Flodden Hill

Scots' original position

Flodden Village

WFNW

0   500   1000   2000

☐ English   ■ Scots   † Monument

Battle of Flodden. Aerial photograph shows the centre and western sectors of the field, which is virtually unchanged since the time of the battle

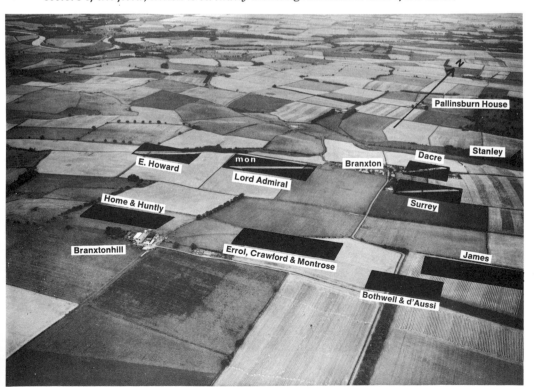

N

Pallinsburn House

E. Howard

m o n

Branxton

Dacre

Stanley

Lord Admiral

Surrey

Home & Huntly

Branxtonhill

Errol, Crawford & Montrose

James

Bothwell & d'Aussi

most indignant at this suggestion and he had one of his servants tell Surrey 'that it besemed not an erle, after that manner to handle a Kynge' and that he would use no sorcery, 'nor had no trust of any grounde'.‡ This uncharacteristic attitude of the Scots (who usually abandoned a strong position on the slightest pretext) presented Surrey with a grave problem. His offer to fight on what he considered to be fair ground on 8 September had been refused; he clearly couldn't assault James's well-nigh impregnable position; yet his duty was to defeat the Scots, and he almost certainly considered that the original pledge to give battle on 9 September, which had been agreed to by James, still held good. He decided to take a very daring but well calculated risk.

On 18 August 1513 Queen Catherine of Aragon had signed a pardon for the Bastard Heron,** and at around that time he, with a small party of outlaws, had joined Surrey's army. Here was a man who knew the countryside well and could help Surrey with his plan to march round James's flank and tempt him from off his strong position on Flodden Hill. On 8 September the English army crossed to the right bank of the Till by the Weetwood bridge and camped that night in the area just to the north of Barmoor Castle. It appears that, as was so often the case with a Tudor army, the commissariat was breaking down: food was short and the troops were reduced to drinking water. This latter may sound to us no great hardship, but drinking water was much more unpleasant then than it is now – a few years later Thomas Howard, by then Duke of Norfolk, was to lose nineteen men in one day from drinking puddle water.

It is generally agreed that Surrey advanced his army in two main columns, or battles, each with two wings. The column that would be on the right, or vaward, was commanded by the Lord Admiral, with his right wing under his younger brother Edmund Howard, and his left wing under a veteran knight, Sir Marmaduke Constable. Lord Surrey commanded the main battle, or 'rearward' in this advance, with his right wing under Lord Dacre (to whose horsemen had been added a contingent of Northumbrians), and his left wing under Sir Edward Stanley, whose soldiers were men from Cheshire – less a detachment which had been lent to Edmund Howard. Each wing was said to comprise 3,000 men (a suspiciously even number), and *The Trewe Encountre* tells us that Thomas Howard had 9,000 in his main body, while his father had 5,000.

‡*Hall's Chronicle*, p.560.
**Patent Roll 5 Henry VIII, pt.1, m.18, Roll No. 620.

200

We know that the vaward and the artillery crossed the Till by the Twizel bridge, but where Surrey put the remainder across will never be known. The object of Surrey's daring manoeuvre, in which he marched a half-starved army round the flank of the enemy to put himself and his army between that enemy and home, was principally to deceive James as to his intention in the hope that he would shift from his strong position. There is therefore no real reason why we cannot accept the wording of Howard's dispatch literally: 'The Lord Howard at 11 of the clock the said 9th day passed over the bridge of Twizel with the vaward and artillery and the said Earl [Surrey] following.'* However, most writers have elected to take 'following' as meaning at a later time and not following in Howard's footsteps. Surrey is therefore credited with crossing the Till at almost every bridge or ford between Twizel and Sandyford (about five miles upstream), and Stanley is often thought to have crossed still later and at a third place.

The flank march had probably taken the army through Duddo, and there was no doubt in the minds of Heron and Dacre, who knew the country, that Twizel was the only crossing place for the cannon – Etal was far too close and might have invited another Stirling Bridge. What then was the purpose in dividing the army, for even if it was not done in the face of the enemy it was always a grave risk? There were two possible reasons. The first was speed: for it would have taken a long time to pass 26,000 men and some cannon over the fairly narrow Twizel bridge, and the day was already well advanced. The second was that there was no need for the less heavily encumbered main body to use a bridge, and a shorter march was desirable. But surely a tried and competent commander such as Surrey would never have risked dividing his army widely for the saving of a few miles' marching. It seems probable therefore that if Surrey didn't actually follow his son over Twizel bridge he crossed by the ford at Castle Heaton, a mile downstream. There is also some reason for believing that Stanley's wing acted almost independently and crossed even later than Surrey.

Once across the Till there is further speculation as to the different routes that the columns took to get round behind the Scottish position. This is not a matter of great importance, except to note that when they arrived in the area of the Pallins' burn they

*The dispatch was written in old French and the exact wording is sometimes confusing. Some translations have 'following' as 'after'.

would have been confronted by a formidable bog, which was a quarter of a mile broad and stretched in an east–west direction for more than a mile.* There was a narrow bridge, or causeway, across its centre, but the guns had to be taken almost to Sandyford before they could get across. Undoubtedly the Lord Admiral's battle arrived at Branxton village first, but Surrey with the main battle could not have been too far away. To the south of Branxton village the ground rises very slightly, and it was as Thomas Howard was preparing to deploy along this ridge soon after three o'clock on a very unpleasant afternoon, with a southerly wind blowing sheets of rain into the faces of the English, that he observed the entire Scottish army drawn up on Branxton Hill, less than half a mile away.

Meanwhile, what had brought the Scottish host to Branxton Hill? It is not always that design is fulfilled in the planning of a battle, but Surrey's strategem and manoeuvre were soon to be successful. When the English army had headed across the Till for Barmoor, it was quickly lost to view from the Scottish position on Flodden Hill by the lie of the land and the scrub of the sparsely clad slopes; but James was not without information, for his scouts kept a constant vigil. The Scottish king's task was made no easier by the fact that in a loose-knit army such as he commanded it was necessary to make decisions in council. We know very little of these decisions, for most of those who made them never lived to tell the tale. But even if James was convinced that Surrey meant to honour his gage, some of the council were sure that he meant to invade Scotland. The old Earl of Angus (Bell-The-Cat as he was often called), with whom James had never been on the best of terms since they shared a mistress in Janet Kennedy, urged immediate retreat into Scotland, but this James refused, telling Angus he could go home – which the old man did, leaving his two sons to perish in the battle. With this option ruled out by James, he could either go forward into England and call Surrey's bluff, or stay where he was until he was quite sure exactly what the English were doing. He decided on the latter course.

Probably as a precautionary measure he moved part of his force to the eastern slope of Flodden Hill in case Surrey meant to attack him in the flank, and there is some evidence that the cannon were positioned to command the river – although the English army never came within effective range – but it was not until he knew for certain that Surrey was crossing the Till that he gave orders to

*Much of this area is still very boggy, and heavy agricultural machinery has been known to almost disappear in it.

202

move. Branxton Hill, which lay just a mile to the north, offered almost as strong a defensive position as the one he was then occupying, and as soon as Surrey's intention was clear James's obvious course was to deny this hill to the enemy. Accordingly at about midday the Scottish army about-faced (which meant a reversal in the original positions in the line) and marched towards Branxton Hill. The camp followers, in accordance with the Scottish custom, set fire to all the straw and rubbish. No doubt the smoke from this damp dross drifting in the southerly wind added to the murk and gloom of the afternoon, but it certainly could not, as is sometimes alleged, have obscured the Scottish advance – this was effectively done by the valley in between the two hills.

The Scottish army was in five columns, four up and one in reserve, and would have arrived in its new position somewhere around 2 p.m. The left comprised Lord Home and his Borderers, and the Earl of Huntly with his Highlanders; the second column was also divided and the commanders were the Earl of Errol, and the Earls of Crawford and Montrose (jointly); then came the King's column (said to have been the largest) with the Earls of Cassillis and Glencairn and Lords Herries and Maxwell as supporting commanders; the Earl of Bothwell's Lothians were initially in reserve and with them was Count d'Aussi and the French contingent; the extreme right of the line was held by the Highlanders under the Earls of Argyll and Lennox. We are told that a bow shot (probably about 200 yards) divided each column, and allowing room enough in the ranks for the long-handled pikes the line must have stretched for 2,000 yards, which is almost the full extent of the Branxton Hill feature. Robert Borthwick, the Scottish master gunner, had his cannon in position in time to fire a harmless salute to the English as the van crossed the Pallins' burn bog.

Thomas Howard was not a young man at the Battle of Flodden, but this was his first important command on land. He lived to a great age and to fight the Scots and French on many occasions; he was not a brilliant general, although he had his successes, and when later on he was constantly in receipt of armchair advice from Henry VIII in Whitehall he was inclined to grumble. But he can be excused on this occasion for taking the *Agnus Dei* from his neck and sending it with a frantic appeal to his father to close the gap quickly. On reaching the Pipers Hill area he would have been very conscious that his left flank was in the air, for Surrey was still some way behind him, and if James had decided to attack he could have seriously mauled the Lord Admiral and just conceivably defeated the two halves of the English army in detail.

The talisman had the desired effect on Surrey, who hastened to come into line with his two sons. As soon as he saw the Scots drawn up in four forward columns Surrey decided to conform, a manoeuvre that cannot have been too difficult to execute, but one that has never been satisfactorily explained. However, the result was Edmund Howard on the right, possibly with Lord Dacre's Northumbrians attached; the Lord Admiral next to him with Sir Marmaduke Constable; then Surrey, and the left and fourth column would have been Stanley's if in fact he had come up into line at this time, which seems very unlikely. There remain Lord Dacre's 'prickers': these Surrey kept under his own command and used as a mobile reserve. The fact that almost all accounts agree that the battle started with a cannonade is of interest in showing the immense exertions that must have been extorted from the English gun teams, who had to march round the bog and come into line in time to open the battle at about 4 p.m.

Very little damage was done by the artillery of either side in this opening phase, but the English bombardment had some effect on the morale of the Borderers, for there is no doubt that they descended the hill first, and this was probably due to a dislike of being shot at while standing still. With them came Huntly's Highlanders, and the whole column smashed into Edmund Howard's men with undiminished momentum, for the English right flank rested on flat ground. The fight in this sector of the line was very fierce and the Scots had much the best of it. The Cheshire contingent that had been taken from Stanley's command wasted no time in fleeing from the field, leaving dangerous gaps into which the Scots thrust their huge pikes. But the others stood their ground and offered a stubborn resistance. Sir William Fitzwilliam, Sir John Lawrence, Sir Wynchard Harbottle and Sir William Warcop were among the slain, and Sir Henry Grey and Sir Humphrey Lisle were captured. Edmund Howard was unhorsed at least twice, but managed to fight his way to his brother's column. The situation was finally restored when Surrey ordered Dacre's horsemen into action. There is a letter of Lord Dacre's extant in which he records that just as he was moving to Howard's assistance the Scottish cannon opened up and some of his men fled; nevertheless, he broke the back of the attack. Fortunately for the English, Home's Borderers then fell to looting, and neither his men nor Huntly's took any further part in the battle.

What caused James to order the rest of the Scottish army to abandon their strong position and fall upon the enemy we shall never know. Possibly he thought that Lords Home and Huntly, having so badly damaged the right wing of the English, would then turn upon the Lord Admiral's flank – as they should have done – and that now was the chance to roll up the enemy; or possibly once the left wing had gone into action there was no holding the remainder and the King had little choice. This would have been in keeping with Scottish impetuosity, but if so it is strange that the men on the right wing led by Lennox and Argyll kept their position; however, the ground they held is undulating and they might not have seen clearly what was happening on their left. Moreover, if – as seems probable – Stanley's men were not yet in position there would have been no enemy immediately to their front.

In any event the English line had little time to recover from the blow dealt to its right before the two centre columns of the Scottish army, with Lord Bothwell's men in close support of James, advanced upon them. The ground was wet and slippery; the descent from Branxton Hill was fairly steep; a deep ditch (then probably a boggy area) lay at the bottom of the hill, beyond which the ground rose somewhat to the main English position. Not an easy march at the best of times; but for men encased in heavy armour, carrying unwieldy eighteen-foot pikes and being raked by cannon fire, it must have seemed an eternity of time before, trampling over their fallen comrades, they got to grips with the foe. Had Lords Home and Huntly been able to rally their men for further efforts against the English right flank they would certainly have made it a tougher and more dangerous fight for Surrey, but the battle was won and lost in the Pipers Hill–Branxton Church area in the two hours or so in which the whole front joined in close and intensive action. And it was won and lost not so much through the quality of the men engaged – for with few exceptions those on both sides fought valiantly – but through the quality of the weapons.

The English cannon must have done some damage to the advancing Scots, but we are assured that in this main battle their arrows failed for the most part to pierce the Scottish armour. It was the long pike that cost the Scots the battle. This cumbersome weapon was first used by the Swiss as protection against cavalry, which arm they themselves did not possess; with well trained men maintaining the momentum of the heavy phalanx it could be a devastating tool of destruction. But Count d'Aussi had not had sufficient time in which to train the Scots, and anyway by the time they reached the English position the momentum of their attack was already failing. Once forced to fight at a standstill the English bill just chopped the pikes into useless pieces.

What exactly happened on the Scottish right will always remain something of a mystery. Certain facts are known. Argyll's and Lennox's Highlanders did not join in the mêlée on their left front: their battle with Sir Edward Stanley's column was almost a separate engagement; these men, like the clansmen and Borderers of the Scottish left, were not encumbered by heavy armour and were therefore more vulnerable to Stanley's arrows; and, lastly, we gather from most accounts that they did not put up much of a fight. Stanley's column arrived on the battlefield late; whether this was due to his having been purposely delayed as part of a deception plan in the early stages of Surrey's approach march, or to a serious bottleneck at the crossing of the Till, does not greatly matter. When he did arrive Stanley was quick to see where his duty lay – the unbroken Scottish column had to be engaged at once. The eastern end of the Branxton Hill ridge falls fairly steeply just south of Mardon village, before the ground rises again to Pace Hill, and up this slope Stanley's men scrambled – some accounts say the ground was so slippery that the men removed their boots. It seems that Stanley divided his force, keeping a number of men to engage the Highlanders from the front, while the bulk of his troops took them in the flank – if this was so it was one of the earliest examples of fire and movement. At all events the attack, pressed home fiercely, was entirely successful, and soon the Scots were in flight, leaving their gallant commanders and a few staunch supporters to die upon the field.

Stanley then reformed his column and came down the hill to administer the *coup de grace* to the Scottish centre, which had borne the brunt of the afternoon's work. King James, perhaps realizing that he could contribute little by way of generalship, was determined to lead his men in the forefront of the battle. His column was opposed to Surrey's, and he had in close support Bothwell and Count d'Aussi, while on his left the Earls of Crawford and Montrose were hotly engaged with the Lord Admiral's men. But this battle in the centre, and therefore the whole day, had been virtually decided before the effect of Stanley's troops could be felt. Most of the Scottish leaders, including the King, had been slain; daylight was closing in and the carnage of the field was already appalling. For two hours or more the combatants had been locked together in a grim and deadly struggle; in the flail and agony of destruction men had sunk to the ground in tangled heaps, and a proud army had ceased to exist.

That night the English slept on the field they had won. The next morning Lord Home, who had managed to rally some of his Borderers, appeared with them on the skyline, but a few rounds of

206

cannon fire warned them off, and there was little left to stop the half-starved English from enjoying the fruits of the richly provided Scottish camp. All through that day the grisly business of sorting out the dead went on. Many of them were so badly mutilated that they were unrecognizable – indeed only with difficulty could Lord Dacre, who knew him well, and Sir William Scot, his captured secretary, recognize the body of the Scottish king. Among the thousands – probably at least 5,000 – of Scotsmen who were killed were some two dozen earls and barons; James's bastard son by Marion Boyd, the 23-year-old Archbishop of St Andrews; the Bishops of Caithness and the Isles; two abbots and many knights. The chronicles of calamity have few precedents for the extinction in battle of almost a complete generation of a country's nobility. The estimate of English losses made immediately after the battle was as low as 400 men,* but the actual figure was almost certainly higher, and some prisoners were taken when a pursuing force got lost. Only a few men of rank were killed and they were mostly those who fell in the first engagement on the right of the line.

King James has been frequently criticized for losing a battle in which the advantages were all in his favour. He was not an experienced general, but it is difficult to see how he could have done any better, given the Scotsman's inherent desire to be always, and immediately, at the throats of the enemy. He certainly could not have defeated the English army in detail as they were crossing the Till, as is sometimes suggested, because time and space were against him; he might conceivably have done better had he attacked Thomas Howard before Surrey joined him, but his presumed intention of staying on the hill and letting Surrey, who for many reasons had to offer battle quickly, come at him, was a far better proposition. His only mistake, if mistake it can be called, was his failure to hold his men steady on Branxton Hill in the face of alarming, but not too damaging, cannon fire.

As for Surrey, he was an old man but as tough and hard as the sword he held in his hand. He had taken an appalling risk, but fortune had favoured him and he had tumbled and humbled the Scots, who were to cause no further serious trouble for almost thirty years. Howard heads rested lightly upon their shoulders during the Tudor era, the family fortunes rose and fell, but Flodden was definitely a Howard benefit. Edmund was knighted on the field; Thomas would soon become Lord Surrey; and in February 1514 the victor was reinstated in the family title of Duke of Norfolk.

*Letters and Papers of Henry VIII, Vol. I, 444.

CHAPTER 14

The Tudors in Scotland

Pinkie Cleuch

10 September 1547

The site of the battle was most probably in the cultivated ground half a mile south-east of Inveresk church (Ordnance Survey one-inch map, sheet 62), just to the south of the railway line – and perhaps a little to the west of the site marked on the one-inch map. There are two vantage points for viewing the ground. The castle on Fawside (or Falside) Hill was just behind the English position, and with the aid of glasses the visitor can get a good view of the battle area, but the Scottish position is now obscured by buildings. The best impression of their position is obtained from the golf course to the west of the river Esk and just off the B 6415 road. The Scottish centre occupied ground a few yards west of the clubhouse. The Inveresk eminence, which was an important tactical feature at the time of the battle, is now built over, but from it one can get down to the Esk and walk for some way along the bank. This walk gives one a further idea of a part of the Scottish position, but the town of Musselburgh now completely covers the left of their line.

After Surrey's victory at Flodden (see chapter 13) the road to Scotland seemed to lie open. But Henry, who was philandering in France having recently captured two comparatively unimportant towns, allowed the opportunity to pass and decided upon a policy of conciliation rather than one of total conquest. For the rest of his reign Scotland was always an elusive will-o'-the-wisp; no matter how ardently he wooed her – gently or roughly – he was forever chasing and never catching. If he was to succeed he had first to break the 'Auld Alliance' between Scotland and France, and when persuasion failed he resorted to force. His object was union – perhaps even suzerainty – and he hoped to achieve it through a mixture of treachery, marriage and, later, the reformed religion. His approach was often irritatingly arrogant, and for much of his reign the troops he kept on the border were occupied in oppressing a people who seemed to him as stubborn as they were remote.

Apart from the constant border raids, there were at least three more serious engagements during Henry's reign. In November 1542

208

the Scots invaded the west marches of England and bore down upon Sir Thomas Wharton, who advanced to meet them from Carlisle, with about 15,000 men. On the 24th of the month they suffered a defeat at Solway Moss which was almost as disastrous as Flodden; and although this time their king was not among the slain – indeed James V did not take part in the battle – he was so disheartened by the result that shortly afterwards he took to his bed in Falkirk Palace and died. In July 1543 a ray of sunlight illuminated the otherwise sombre Scottish scene when two treaties were signed at Greenwich, and it seemed as though the union of the two nations would be cemented with the marriage of Edward Tudor and Mary Stewart. But three months later the Regent (the Earl of Arran) was persuaded by that turbulent priest Cardinal Beaton to nullify these treaties. Henry was not the man to be trifled with in this manner, and in the spring of 1544 he sent Lord Hertford at the head of some 35,000 men on a punitive expedition to Edinburgh and Leith. In February 1545 the Scots at last succeeded in turning the tables on their oppressors. At Ancrum Moor they surprised and outmanoeuvred an English force of 3,000 men under Sir Ralph Evers. More than 1,000 Englishmen were taken or slain and among those who perished were Evers, Sir Brian Layton and Lord Ogle. However, it availed the Scots little, for Henry determined on a more terrible vengeance than in 1544 – and in Froude's pithy phrase, 'the heavy hand of Hertford was again laid on Scotland'.

Henry VIII died in January 1547 leaving an uneasy peace with Scotland that rested upon a collateral agreement in the Treaty of Campe with the French, which had been ratified amid much splendour at Hampton Court the previous August. Scotland was included in this treaty so long as she was prepared to honour the terms of the 1543 treaties signed at Greenwich – which, as we have seen, she was not. While Francis I was alive there was little likelihood of trouble from the French – he was old, ill and tired of fighting – but only a week or two after Lord Hertford (by now the Duke of Somerset) had been granted full powers as Protector of the Realm by the young King Edward VI's council Francis died. He was succeeded on 1 April 1547 by Henry II, who was no friend to England, and who was deeply influenced by the Queen Dowager of Scotland's powerful Guise family.

Broadly speaking the Protector attempted to pursue much the same line in foreign affairs as was being taken at the end of Henry's reign. For Scotland, union through the marriage of Mary and Edward was still the linchpin of the English coach of state, although Somerset was determined on a much more liberal policy for the Scots than that of total subjection envisaged by Henry. But the Scots, encouraged by the French king's enthusiasm for their cause (and no doubt unaware of his dangerous designs), made it clear that they had no intention of honouring any treaty that would bind their queen in marriage to the English king.

It is difficult to be certain when Somerset decided that it would be necessary to achieve his purpose by war, but by April 1547 warlike moves were afoot and preparations built up steadily throughout the summer, although Somerset never despaired of getting his way through conciliation. Apart from anything else, in the summer of 1547 a war with Scotland might easily have provoked one with France: Henry II was determined to regain Boulogne before the treaty date of 1554, and Lord Cobham was constantly reporting on the weakness of Calais. Measures to strengthen both these towns had been resented by the French, and although an attack on Calais by Henry might involve him with the Empire, Somerset could not be certain that Charles would stand by his commitment in respect of the 'Old Conquest' – as Calais was called – and a war on two fronts was a possibility. But the union of the two crowns in one empire was the keystone of Somerset's foreign policy, and if the Scots were too stubborn or too stupid to see the advantages that would accrue to them from this 'Godly and honourable a purpose', he considered it his duty to impose it by force. On no account should Henry II and French troops dominate Scotland.

Once having decided upon this policy, it was a pity that Somerset dithered in its execution. Well before June, when warlike activities were temporarily halted – presumably for further peace probes to be made – it must have been obvious that the Catholic, pro-French party had recovered most of the ground lost by the murder, in May 1546, of the Chancellor Cardinal Beaton, and were too far committed to France even to consider Somerset's proposals. At this time St Andrews Castle was still held by the Chancellor's murderers, now known as 'the Castilians'. From the original sixteen who had forced their way into the castle and murdered Beaton their number had grown to 120 – including John Knox – and although they had found the castle well supplied they were glad to be revictualled from time to time by an English ship. Arran had granted them a truce by which they retained the castle until absolution for the killing of Beaton could be received from Rome. This absolution eventually arrived containing the dubious clause *Remittimus irremissibile*, which did not satisfy the Castilians, and

Edward VI, by Holbein, in the Hanover Museum

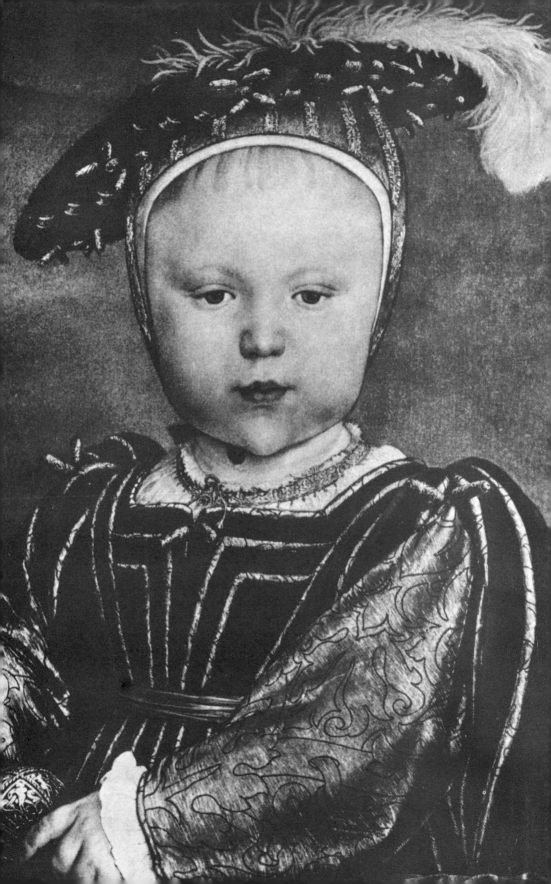

Arran again laid siege to the castle, but with the same irresolution as before – no doubt due to the fact that the Castilians held his son hostage. However, by the end of June the French had taken a hand; a fleet, under the redoubtable captain Leo Strozzi, the Prior of Capua, not only avoided the English ships but bombarded the castle for five days. On the last day of July, having been severely shaken by the naval guns, which had been disembarked and positioned on the abbey and St Salvetor's College, and now cut off by land and sea, the Castilians surrendered to Strozzi.

The key to successful union with Scotland would surely have been the reformed religion, and in apparently making no attempt to relieve St Andrews Somerset blocked the one avenue down which his proselytizing zeal might conceivably have brought him to success; for the capture and removal to France of the Castilians had gravely weakened the Scottish reformers, who if not too enthusiastic over union at least regarded Somerset favourably as a pillar of the Reformation.

Even as late as August the Protector could not bring himself to invade without one more attempt at conciliation. Cuthbert Tunstall, Bishop of Durham, and Sir Robert Bowes met the Scottish commissioners on the border with an offer to waive all outstanding differences between the two countries if the Scots would honour the marriage treaty. When this last attempt at a peaceful settlement failed the massive preparations which had been going forward throughout the summer for a campaign that was calculated to last a month were almost completed. Once more Scotland was to be seared by war, and the wretched inhabitants of that rugged Border country, whose life, based upon a primitive agriculture, was always a constant battle against nature, were yet again to see their homesteads burned about them by those terrible men who wore upon their tunics the fiery cross of St George.

Somerset's army mobilized at Newcastle at the end of August, and marching via Morpeth, Bamburgh and Berwick crossed the border on 1 September. It was not a large force, but it was well balanced. Most accounts put the total around 16,000 – 4,000 of which were cavalry, and there were 1,400 pioneers. A supporting arm of eighty cannon contained fifteen pieces of 'great ordnance', and there were 900 carts and many wagons. One account puts the total transport as high as 12,000 vehicles, but this is almost certainly excessive, for the army was in part supplied by the fleet, which sailed, under Lord Clinton, parallel to the advance. The cavalry arm, which was to play so important a part, and suffer the most casualties, in the forthcoming battle, comprised some 2,000 light horse under the veteran warrior Sir Francis Bryan; 500 horse from Boulogne, brought over by Lord Grey of Wilton, who was given the overall command of the cavalry; 200 mounted Spanish arquebusiers under that experienced mercenary Pedro de Gamboa; an Italian mercenary troop, under their captain Malatesta; and the Gentlemen Pensioners of the Royal Bodyguard.

By 5 September the army had reached Cockburnspath, a small place sixteen miles from the border where a spur of the Lammermuir Hills runs down to the sea. One of Somerset's numerous spies had brought intelligence that the Scots had been preparing defence works here and that the English might be brought to battle. It is a natural position from which to hold up an advancing enemy, and it had the advantage that the high cliffs and surrounding hills offered protection from the guns of the English fleet; but if Somerset's superior artillery could not have blasted the Scots from their hillside positions, their right flank could have been turned. To come so far forward would dangerously have lengthened their line of communication, and in the event of defeat disaster would have been even more total than in fact it was. Some trenches had been dug at Cockburnspath, but Arran had wisely chosen to hold a much stronger position.

Safely through the glen, Somerset indulged himself in his favourite sport of castle-burning. George Douglas's castle at Dunglass, whose small shabbily attired and equipped garrison was commanded by Lord Home's nephew, surrendered; but Lord Home's man at Thornton (Tom Trotter) and the captain of the Hamilton castle at Innerwick were not so obliging. It did not take the English pioneers very long to reduce these two small keeps, and by midday the army was passing Dunbar, whose garrison made an ineffectual hostile demonstration, for which they were not called to task. That night Somerset camped near the much stronger Douglas castle at Tantallon, but he must have decided that too much time would be lost in assaulting that stronghold, for the next day he retraced his steps and after marching through East Linton camped at Longniddry.

From Longniddry the army marched along the seashore and made camp on 8 September in the region of what is now the Prestongrange golf course. A little less than a mile to the south the ground rises steeply to Fawside and Carberry Hills, and Somerset drew the army out of the camp to occupy the forward slopes of these two features. His line would have been well extended, but not dangerously so, for he was not taking up a defensive position. Fawside Castle (which he invested and later burned) was above him and almost in the centre of his line but it was lightly held, and anyway those of his soldiers immediately in front of the castle were in dead ground. Somerset must have known by now that he was hopelessly outnumbered, and the purpose of this extended line may have been to give the Scots a false impression of his strength. There would seem to be little other reason for it, because from this commanding position he could see only too well that the choice before him was a frontal attack or withdrawal – and Somerset was not the man to come so far and turn back without a blow.

Arran had under his command about 25,000 men, and so in numbers he greatly exceeded the English army, but he was much weaker in cavalry (having probably no more than 1,500 lightly armed and mounted troops) and he was also inferior in artillery. Moreover, although the threat to the nation had temporarily closed their ranks, Arran could not be entirely sure of the loyalty of some of his subordinate commanders. He had displayed considerable tactical skill in the choice of his position. His left, under the Earl of Huntly, was protected by the sea, and he had thrown up an earthen wall in an attempt to give protection against the English naval guns; he also stationed the Earl of Argyll and his 3,000 Highland bowmen on this flank. The whole army was behind the Esk, and Huntly's division guarded the only bridge across that river. Arran himself commanded the centre, or main battle, which occupied the ground known as Edmonstone Edge that rose fairly steeply behind the high banks of the river. The Earl of Angus was in command of the vanguard on the right flank, and his southern flank was protected by an almost impassable bog; the cavalry, or what was left of it by the time of the battle, was also positioned on this flank.

When the English army reached Prestonpans the fleet was off Leith, and Somerset ordered Lord Clinton (presumably through a pinnace that kept in touch with the army) to stand his ships off Musselburgh and come ashore himself to confer. Clinton, who had seen the enemy position from behind their lines, was able to give Somerset information of a kind he could not otherwise have obtained. However, although the weather that September was reported to be not too good, it would have been clear enough for Somerset and his lieutenants (the Earl of Warwick, Lord Grey of Wilton and Lord Dacre) to get a detailed view of the enemy's front, for although Edmonstone Edge lay almost two miles from the English lines, the intervening country was flat and open to the river.

At this length of time we cannot be absolutely certain exactly where the Battle of Pinkie was fought, or of some other facts,

214

because what was then the deep, pastoral peace of partially cultivated fields, dotted with rough patches of gorse and broom, has
now been largely swallowed up by the bricks and mortar and noise
and bustle of busy Musselburgh. But Fawside Hill is much as it
used to be and so (now that most of the trees have been cut down) is
Carberry Hill; from these two vantage points, and from Musselburgh golf course across the river, it is still possible to develop
some sort of topographical sense, and it is not too difficult to put
oneself into Somerset's mind as he stood on Fawside Hill that
September day to confer with his admiral and his army lieutenants.*

Somerset was an experienced general, and more than that he
knew the men he was fighting. They held an impregnable position,
which he had to assault by a frontal attack with a force that was
vastly inferior numerically, although stronger in firepower. He
also knew that the sight of an English army on Scottish soil did remarkable things to the Scots – he was soon to have further proof of
this – and it must have crossed his mind that given sufficient provo-
cation Arran would find it difficult to restrain his men. But a wise
commander could not count on this, and Somerset had to plan his
assault. On his right front there was a hillock (a now almost in-
distinguishable feature in the town of Inveresk) on which stood –
and indeed its successor still stands – St Michael's Church; this
eminence commanded much of the enemy position and would
afford Somerset excellent opportunities for enfilade fire. Somerset
had to take possession of this hill, and with his inferior numbers he
would want to pack a punch on Arran's left, where even if the
bridge was held the river banks were not so high, and moreover the
fleet would bring cross-fire to bear on the enemy. This then was
the plan. Its execution was made more simple by the impetuosity of
the Scottish cavalry.

On the morning of 9 September the Scottish horsemen crossed the
river and carried out a series of manoeuvres in front of the English
lines, daring their enemy to come off the hillside and attack. At
first Somerset refused to be drawn, but he was prevailed upon by
Lord Grey to allow the heavy cavalry to sweep into action just at
the moment when Lord Home and his men were wheeling around
and therefore off balance. The engagement was short but fierce,

*The present writer, having spent a considerable amount of time
examining the site, studying the map in the Bodleian Library and
reading contemporary accounts of the battle, has drawn his own
conclusions. These do not agree in all respects with what are probably
the two best modern accounts of the battle, written by Sir Charles
Oman and Sir James Fergusson, but he is greatly indebted to these two
authors.

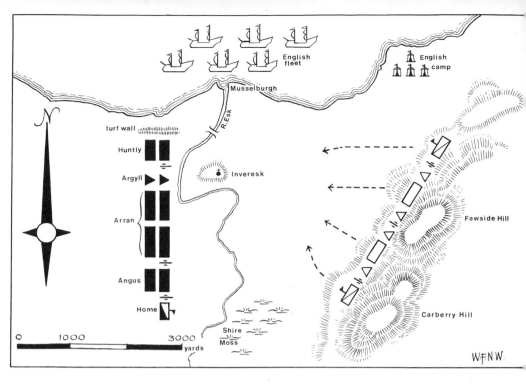

Top: Pinkie Cleuch—8 a.m. Below: Pinkie Cleuch about 10 a.m. The key
in the lower plan applies to both illustrations

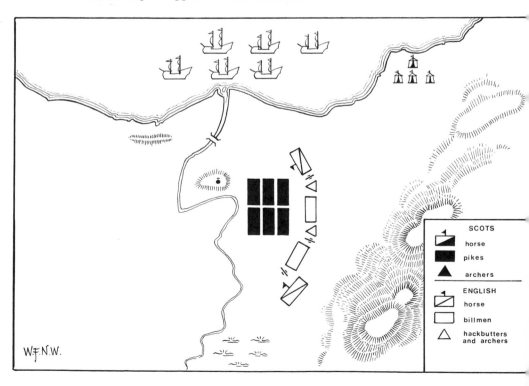

and although the Scots, now realizing that they had drawn too great a weight upon themselves, attempted to break off the fight, the English were in no mood to let them go. Before the remnants escaped to their own lines Arran's cavalry had been sadly mauled. Their commander Lord Home was injured when his horse fell during the retreat and his son, with one or two other gentlemen and two priests (Scottish clergy frequently figured in the roll of honour during these border wars), was made prisoner. Through this ill timed and quite pointless performance, Arran's cavalry was no longer a fighting force.

That same afternoon Somerset, now with little risk of being cut off, determined on a forward reconnaissance. Accompanied by his personal staff and a strong escort, he rode over the ground almost as far as the Inveresk hillock. As the party was returning they were startled by the sound of a trumpet behind them, and turning saw a trumpeter and herald, whose tabard bore the royal arms of Scotland. Somerset and Warwick halted to allow these two men to approach. The herald bore a message from Arran – who obviously hoped that Somerset might have been dismayed by the strength of the Scottish position – offering an exchange of prisoners, discussion of peace terms, and a safe conduct for the English to recross the border. Somerset refused the offer, and very properly rejected a challenge from Huntly that in the event of his not agreeing to Arran's terms the matter should be settled personally between Huntly and Somerset with twenty men apiece. Warwick, who did not bear the responsibilities of head of state, was eager to accept this challenge, but Somerset forbade him, and in dismissing the herald commanded him to tell Arran that 'we have been a good season in this country; and am here now but with a sober company, and they a great number: and if they would meet us in field, they shall be satisfied with fighting enough'.*

Another account is that Somerset offered to withdraw if Arran would stand by the terms of the matrimonial treaty, or at least guarantee Mary's continued presence in Scotland for another ten years without contracting her in marriage to a foreigner. This message might well have been sent, but now – as before – it would have been unacceptable to the Scottish leaders, and as such suppressed from the rank and file lest it weaken their resolve to fight.

About eight o'clock on the morning of Saturday 10 September – to be known in Scottish history as 'Black Saturday' – Somerset moved his men forward in the execution of his grand design. His

*E. Arber, *An English Garner: Tudor Tracts*, p.103.

*Pinkie Cleuch: Above: Scots' position west of River Esk at about 8 a.m.
Below: Scots' advance from their early morning position to battle line*

fifteen heavy pieces of ordnance were probably sakers, whose maximum effective range was about 1,630 paces, and so they would have to be brought for some distance across this open but rough ground, adding further difficulties to an operation that was necessarily somewhat unwieldy. Manoeuvring his force into a position from where it could deliver a strong thrust at Arran's left wing meant having to expose his own left flank, but now that the Scottish cavalry had been almost totally destroyed this was a calculated risk which he was justified in taking. Moreover, it probably had the desired effect of presenting the fiery Scots with a temptation they could not resist.

We should now pause to consider the generally accepted theory that the Scots thought that Somerset was hurrying across their front to make for his fleet and embarkation, and that it was in this belief that they abandoned their strong defensive position in order to defeat the English army before it could be safely embarked. If the relative positions of the opposing forces are marked on the map it is possible to gain the impression that almost the whole English army was sidestepping across the Scottish front; but a careful study on the ground quickly dispels this error. The left flank of the English would certainly have had to turn across Angus's front, but the advance of the remainder towards Inveresk church was

Pinkie Cleuch showing positions at height of battle

almost completely frontal, and only the stupidest Scot in Arran's and Huntly's divisions could have misconstrued this manoeuvre as a retreat on the ships – still less on the camp, which lay almost parallel to the original position on Fawside Hill. And yet it was Argyll's Highlanders who first crossed the Esk.

It seems far more likely that the Scots abandoned their battle-winning position for one of two reasons – probably a combination of both. They could not afford to let the English have possession of the Inveresk hill – hence the early manoeuvre of the Highlanders, who were quickly followed by Huntly's division; and the sight of an English army parading itself on their front may once again have impelled the Scots with a desire to rush with the frenzy of rage at the throat of every English antagonist. Angus was the one leader who could be forgiven for thinking that Somerset was withdrawing his army, but he was the only one who demurred at the order to advance across the river.

Once they had abandoned their position and crossed the river the Scottish army was lost, for it had little with which to match the English cavalry and artillery. Somerset was not slow to adapt his plan of battle to the new, and entirely beneficial, position with which he was now confronted. It was necessary to halt the Scottish advance, which once all the divisions were safely across the Esk had formed itself into a solid phalanx, from rolling him up before he could reorient his centre and right and bring up his artillery; and for this he used his superior cavalry arm. The Scots had adopted their traditional formation of schiltrons, but on this occasion more by accident than design. Once across the river the three wings converged to form one huge mass of pikemen, whose flanks were unprotected, because Argyll's Highlanders had left the battlefield after coming under fairly intensive fire from Clinton's guns while crossing the Esk, and on the other flank what was left of the cavalry remained detached from the battle. However, these sturdy infantrymen, with their leather-quilted jacks, steel helmets and huge pikes, kneeling or standing shoulder to shoulder, were perfectly capable of withstanding cavalry – although, of course, hopelessly vulnerable to artillery.

The fight, which probably took place just south of Pinkie House, where the railway line now crosses arable fields, was hard pounding from start to finish. Most of Somerset's cavalry was on his left wing, and at a time when the Scots, who had advanced from the river at a great pace, had momentarily halted, Lord Grey led his troops against Huntly's division, which was positioned at the north-east of the phalanx. The Scottish ranks were immovable.

220

The pikemen stood their ground, battered but defiant. When the first charge was thrown back Somerset ordered another, this time against Arran's troops, and once more the horsemen threw themselves upon that bristling wall of steel, only to recoil with their mounts jumping over heaps of corpses and groaning men. Sir Andrew Flammock, who carried the royal standard of England, was nearly taken; however, he emerged from the fray with the standard (less its staff) safely in his keeping. But the enemy had been halted and Somerset had had time to adjust his line and bring his artillery to bear upon the huge and unwieldy mass of Scottish foot. The cavalry had not charged in vain.

Once the guns were in position, the English superiority in this arm was soon to win the day. The sakers had a point-blank range of about 340 paces and the gunners could have asked for no easier or more satisfactory target. As they raked the solid mass of pikemen, the Scots could be seen quivering and writhing under the repeated volleys. Wedged tight, they could only stand and stare as the cannon pulverized the phalanx and cut swathes down which the dead and dying slowly sank to the ground. Now it was also the turn of the Spanish arquebusiers who, riding at full tilt along the flanks of the enemy, poured their fire with devastating effect into the mass of helpless pikemen. At this stage of the battle Somerset decided that the Scots were sufficiently battered for him to advance his infantry, and before their bowstrings could become dampened by the heavy rain that descended over the field his archers had sent a hail of arrows into the rapidly disintegrating Scottish schiltron.

Somerset, with Warwick beside him, had been carefully watching the growing discomfort of the Scots, and when this three-pronged assault of artillery, arquebusiers and archers had thrown the enemy completely off balance he ordered the cavalry to sweep down on them again. In the noise and tumult of this very confused close combat it is difficult to say which division of the Scots broke first. Contemporary accounts agree that Angus was the one commander to keep his head and realize the necessity of an orderly withdrawal out of artillery range, but whether Arran's centre had already broken, or whether seeing Angus's men fall back they lost heart and ran, is uncertain. Visibility had become poor during the rain storm and at one stage Huntly's men mistook Angus's men for English, which only added to the confusion of the hapless Scots. Small wonder, then, that when they saw the whirlwind of English cavalry descend upon them the Scots had had enough. The whole army broke and streamed across the rivers. Some made for Dalkeith, others went back through their camp towards Edinburgh, while yet others raced along the seashore for Leith.

Thus in a matter of hours the entire chivalry of Scotland was beaten. Retreat developed into rout; the English army had by now shaken off the bonds of discipline, and overtaking their ancient foe before they could reach sanctuary scythed them down in thousands. Figures vary, but in the few hours that it took Somerset and his officers to regain control the slaughter had been immense; and no doubt there were many of rank who might have been spared for ransom had they not been dressed like their men. Probably around 10,000 Scots perished on the fields surrounding Pinkie Cleuch that day.* The roll of honour was long and illustrious: Lords Elphinstone, Cathcart and Fleming, Sir James Gordon of Lochinvar, Sir Robert Douglas of Lochleven and many other gentlemen of note. Lord Huntly was unhorsed and soon taken, Lord Home had been wounded the day before and his son captured, Lord Hay of Yester, Sir John Wemyss and the Master of Sempill were also among the prisoners. Angus lay in a furrow and feigned death until the pursuit had passed him, when he found a horse and escaped. The English lost about 500 men, most of whom were from the heavy cavalry, and Edward Shelley, commander of the 'Bulleners' – as the Boulogne horse were called – was England's only important captain killed; Lord Grey had a pike wound in the mouth and many others were wounded, including Sir Thomas Darcy, and Pedro de Gamboa. For the next two days men and women would be searching among the carnage and the debris to remove for decent burial the mortal remains of those they had lost.

The road to Edinburgh, and beyond to Stirling if need be, lay open to the conqueror; but during the next week the English remained comparatively inactive in the area of Leith, which town was burned, as was Kinghorn on the other side of the Forth. It is very difficult to fathom Somerset's thinking at this time. He must have realized that one victory – conclusive as it was – could not by itself achieve its object. He had the Scots at his mercy, and had he acted swiftly he might have seized the young queen before she could be moved to the comparative safety of the island of Inchmahone. Such an action would have enraged the Scots, but Pinkie had done that already, and it would have completely checkmated French designs. Here was a war that probably should never have been started, but once embarked upon should have been pressed to its logical conclusion. As it was, Somerset hoped to control an embittered nation by the retention of a number of strongpoints, and

*Estimates made by Somerset and others present at the battle vary from 7,000 to 14,000, but most accounts fix the figure as around 10,000.

222

before he left the country – or very shortly afterwards – the English had taken and garrisoned Blackness, the islands of Inchcolm and Inchkeith controlling the Firth of Forth, Broughty Castle at the mouth of the Tay, Dundee, Haddington (whose garrison and defences he later greatly strengthened), and a number of border towns and castles.

At the end of 1547 Somerset had a firm grip on Scotland. Lord Grey had been put in command of the north with his centre on Berwick; he was also Warden of the East Marches, while Lord Wharton remained in charge of the west marches, from which he made frequent sallies into Annandale, doing a considerable amount of damage. Sir Andrew Dudley had command of that exposed and vulnerable outpost Broughty Castle, which the Scots very nearly took back in November, and from it he attempted to hold Dundee. Sir John Luttrell commanded the important island of Inchcolm.

But the year 1548 was one of mixed fortunes for the English cause in the north. Haddington, whose tactical importance was considerable, was to be besieged by a large Franco-Scottish force, and in July the French ambassador met the Scottish Estates in the abbey there – which lay just outside the besieged town – and informed them that Henry II had decided that Mary Queen of Scots should marry the Dauphin. Assent to this match was given 'unanimously', on the understanding that the Scots would retain their freedom, ancient laws and liberties, but there were those among the nobility – and in particular Arran – who thoroughly disliked the strengthening of the French bond. However, the Queen Dowager was now in the ascendant, and by 13 August the Scottish Queen was safely in France, and Somerset must have realized that all hopes of a marriage between her and Edward were gone.

Bibliography

Chapter 1: Norsemen
Chapter 2: Normans
Belloc, Hilaire, *William the Conqueror*,
  Peter Davies, 1933.
Bryant, Arthur, *The Story of England*,
  Collins, 1953.
Burne, A. H., *Battlefields of England*
  (ch. 2 only), Methuen, 1950.
Burne, A. H., *More Battlefields of England*
  (ch. 1 only), Methuen, 1952.
Complete Peerage, The, Vol. XII, Pt. I,
  St Catherine Press, 1953.
Compton, Piers, *Harold the King*,
  Robert Hale, 1961.
Churchill, Winston S., *A History of the
  English Speaking Peoples*, Vol. I,
  Cassell, 1956.
Douglas, D. C., *William the Conqueror*,
  Eyre and Spottiswoode, 1964.
Freeman, E. A., *The Norman Conquest*,
  Clarendon Press, 1869.
Fuller, J. F. C., *The Decisive Battles of the
  Western World*, Vol. I (ch. 2 only),
  Eyre and Spottiswoode, 1954.
George, H. B., *Battles of English History*,
  Methuen, 1895.
Lemmon, C. H., *The Field of Hastings*
  (ch. 2 only), Budd and Gillatt, 1957.
McGuffie, T. H., 'October 14th, 1066',
  History Today, Oct. 1966.
Muntz, Hope, *The Golden Warrior*,
  Chatto and Windus, 1948.
Oman, Charles, *A History of the Art of War
  in the Middle Ages*, Methuen, 2nd
  edition, 1924.
Ramsay, James, *The Foundations of
  England*, Vol. II, Swan Sonnenschein,
  1898.
Schofield, Guy, 'The Third Battle of 1066',
  History Today, Oct. 1966.
Spatz, W., *Die Schlacht von Hastings*, 1896.
Stenton, F. M., *Anglo-Saxon England*,
  Clarendon Press, 1943.
Stenton, F. M., *William the Conqueror
  and the Rule of the Normans*, Putnam,
  1908.

Primary Source
William of Poitiers, *Gesta Willelemi Ducis
  Normannorum et Regis Anglorum*,
  part translated in *English Historical
  Documents*, Vol. 2, Eyre and
  Spottiswoode, 1953.

Chapter 3: The Barons' War—Lewes
Chapter 4: The Barons' War—Evesham
Beamish, Tufton, *Battle Royal*, Muller,
  1965.
Bémont, Charles, *Simon de Montfort*,
  trans. E. F. Jacob, Clarendon Press, 1930.
Blaauw, William Henry, *The Barons' War*,
  Baxter, 1844.
Bryant, Arthur, *The Story of England*,
  Collins, 1953.
Burne, A. H. *Battlefields of England*
  (ch. 4 only), Methuen, 1950.
Burne, A. H., *More Battlefields of England*
  (ch. 3 only), Methuen, 1952.
Churchill, Winston S., *A History of the
  English Speaking Peoples*, Vol. I,
  Cassell, 1956.
Davis, H. W. C., *England under the
  Normans and Angevins*, Methuen, 1905.
Denholm-Young, N., *Collected Papers*,
  University of Wales Press, 1969.
Knowles, C. H., 'Simon de Montfort
  1265–1965', Historical Association
  Pamphlet 3409, 1965.
Labarge, Margaret (Mrs Margaret Wade),
  Simon de Montfort, Eyre and
  Spottiswoode, 1962.
Oman, Charles, *A History of the Art of War
  in the Middle Ages*, Methuen, 2nd
  edition, 1924.
Powicke, F. M., *King Henry III and the Lord
  Edward*, Vols. I and II, Clarendon
  Press, 1947.
Powicke, F. M., R. F. Treharne and
  C. H. Lemmon, *The Battle of Lewes:
  Essays*, Friends of Lewes Society, 1964.
Ramsay, James, *The Dawn of the
  Constitution, 1216–1307*, Swan
  Sonnenschein, 1908.
Stubbs, William, *Select Charters*, 9th
  edition revised by H. W. C. Davis,
  Clarendon Press, 1929.
Treharne, R. F., *The Baronial Plan of
  Reform 1258–1263*, Manchester University
  Press, 1932.
Treharne, R. F., 'The Personal Role of
  Simon de Montfort in the Period of
  Baronial Reform and Rebellion, 1258–
  1265', *Proceedings of the British
  Academy* XL, 1954.

Primary Sources
Chronicle by Monk of Lewes, MSS Cott.
  Tib. A.X.

Chronicle of John de Oxenede, MSS. Cott. Nero, D.II.

Chronicle of Lanercost Abbey, MSS. Harl. 2425.

Chronicle of William of Hemingford, MSS. Cott. Nero, D.II.

Chronicle of William of Knighton, MSS. Cott. Nero, D.II.

De Bellis Lewes et Evesham, MS. Cott. Claudius, D.VI (*Chronicle of William de Rishanger*).

Halliwell, J. O., ed., *Great Chronicles of St Albans*, being the chronicle of Matthew Paris extending to 1259 and William de Rishanger continued to 1322, Rolls Series, Vol. 28, 1863–76.

Holinshed's Chronicle, Vol. II, London, 1807.

Rymer, Thomas, *Foedera*, Vols. I and II, London, 1704–32.

Chapter 5: The Scottish Struggle for Independence—Stirling Bridge and Falkirk

Barrow, G. W. S., *Robert Bruce*, Eyre and Spottiswoode, 1965.

Brown, P. Hume, *History of Scotland*, Vol. I, Cambridge University Press, 1899.

Boutell, Charles, *Arms and Armour*, Reeves and Turner, 1874.

George, H. B., *Battles of English History*, Methuen, 1895.

Grimley, Gordon, *The Book of the Bow*, Putnam, 1958.

Mackenzie, Agnes Mure, *The Kingdom of Scotland*, Chambers, 1940.

Ramsay, James, *The Dawn of the Constitution, 1216–1307*, Swan Sonnenschein, 1908.

Primary Sources

Chronicle of Lanercost Abbey, MSS. Harl. 2425.

Chronicle of Walter of Guisborugh, also referred to as Walter of Hemingford.

Chronicle of William de Rishanger, MS. Cott. Claudius, D.VI.

Stubbs, William, ed. *Vita et Mars Edwardi Secundi*, Chronicles and Memorials of Great Britain and Ireland during the Middle Ages, London, 1883.

Chapter 6: The Scottish Struggle for Independence—Bannockburn

Barrow, G. W. S., *Robert Bruce*, Eyre and Spottiswoode, 1965.

Brown, P. Hume, *History of Scotland*, Vol. I, Cambridge University Press, 1899.

Boutell, Charles, *Arms and Armour*, Reeves and Turner, 1874.

Christison, General Sir Philip, Bt, and Iain Cameron Taylor, *Bannockburn: A Soldier's Appreciation of the Battle*, National Trust for Scotland, 1960.

George, H. B., *Battles of English History*, Methuen, 1895.

Linklater, Eric, *Robert the Bruce*, Peter Davies, 1934.

Mackenzie, Agnes Mure, *The Kingdom of Scotland*, Chambers, 1940.

Mackenzie, W. M., *The Battle of Bannockburn*, James MacLehose, 1913.

Maxwell, Sir Herbert, Bt, *Robert the Bruce*, Putnam, 1897.

Morris, John E., *Bannockburn*, Cambridge University Press, 1914.

Oman, Charles, *A History of the Art of War in the Middle Ages*, Methuen, 2nd edition, 1924.

Ramsay, James, *The Dawn of the Constitution, 1216–1307*, Swan Sonnenschein, 1908.

White, Robert, *A History of the Battle of Bannockburn*, Edinburgh, 1871.

Primary Sources

Barbour, John of Aberdeen, *The Bruce*, ed. J. Pinkerton, London, 1790.

Chronicle of Lanercost Abbey, MSS. Harl. 2425.

Chronicle of Walter of Guisborugh, also referred to as Walter of Hemingford.

Chronicle of William de Rishanger, MS. Cott. Claudius, D.VI.

Gray, Sir Thomas of Heton, *Scalacronica*, ed. J. Stevenson, Maitland Club, 1836.

Holinshed's Chronicle, Vol. II, London, 1807.

Vita et Mod Edwardi Secundi, Chronicles and Memorials of Great Britain and Ireland during the Middle Ages, London, 1883.

Chapter 7: The Wars of the Roses— A General Survey

Ashdown, Charles Henry, *British and Foreign Armies and Armour*, T. C. and E. C. Jack, 1909.

Boutell, Charles, *Arms and Armour*, Reeves and Turner, 1874.

Burne, A. H., *Battlefields of England*, Methuen, 1950.

Churchill, Winston S., *A History of the English Speaking Peoples*, Vol. I, Cassell, 1956.

Harriss, G. L., 'The Struggle for Calais: an Aspect of the Rivalry between Lancaster and York', *English Historical Review*, LXXV, 1960.

Kendall, P. M., *Warwick the Kingmaker*, Allen and Unwin, 1959.

Mowat, R. B., *The Wars of the Roses*, Crosby Lockwood, 1914.

Oman, Charles, *The Political History of England, 1377–1485*, Longmans, 1910.

Oman, Charles, *Warwick the Kingmaker*, Macmillan, 1905.

Ramsay, James, *Lancaster and York: 1399–1485*, Vol. II, Clarendon Press, 1892.

Scofield, Cora L., *The Life and Reign of Edward IV*, Vol. I, Longmans, 1923.
Wolffe, B. P., *Fifteenth Century England: 1399–1509* (the personal rule of Henry VI), Manchester University Press, 1972.
Young, Peter, and John Adair, *Hastings to Culloden*, G. Bell, 1964.

Primary Sources
Bruce, John, ed., *Historie of the arrivall of Edward IV in England*, Camden Society, 1838.
Gairdner, James, ed., *The Historical Collections of a Citizen of London in the Fifteenth Century*, Camden Society, 1876. (William Gregory, Mayor of London 1451–2, was author until 1452.)
Gairdner, James, ed., *The Paston Letters* A.D. *1422–1509*, 6 vols, Chatto and Windus, 1904.
Hall's Chronicle, London, 1809.
Whethamstede, John, *Registrum Abbatiae Johannis, Whethamstede*, 2 vols, ed. Henry T. Riley, Rolls Series, 1872.

Chapter 8: The Second Battle of St Albans
Ashdown, Charles Henry, *The Battles and Battlefields of St Albans*, Gibbs and Bamforth, 1913.
Burne, A. H., *Battlefields of England*, Methuen, 1950.
Kendall, P. M., *Warwick the Kingmaker*, Allen and Unwin, 1959.
Mowatt, R. B., *The Wars of the Roses*, Crosby Lockwood, 1914.
Oman, Charles, *Warwick the Kingmaker*, Macmillan, 1905.
Ramsay, James, *Lancaster and York: 1399–1485*, Vol. II, Clarendon Press, 1892.
Young, Peter, and John Adair, *Hastings to Culloden*, G. Bell, 1964.

Primary Sources
Gairdner, James, ed., *The Historical Collections of a Citizen of London in the Fifteenth Century*, Camden Society, 1876. (William Gregory, Mayor of London 1451–2, was author until 1452.)
Standing, Percy Cross, ed., *Memorials of Old Hertfordshire*, London, 1905.
Stow, John, *Annales*, London, 1615.
Waurin, Jehan de, *Anchiennes et Chroniques d'Engleterre*, Vols. II and III, ed. Mlle Dupont, Paris, 1859.
Whethamstede, John, *Registrum Abbatiae Johannis, Whethamstede*, 2 vols, ed. Henry T. Riley, Rolls Series, 1872.

Chapter 9: The Battle of Towton
Burne, A. H., *Battlefields of England*, Methuen, 1950.
Kendall, P. M., *Warwick the Kingmaker*, Allen and Unwin, 1959.

Markham, Sir Clement, 'The Battle of Towton', *Yorkshire Archaeological and Topographical Journal*, X, 1889.
Mowat, R. B., *The Wars of the Roses*, Crosby Lockwood, 1914.
Oman, Charles, *A History of the Art of War in the Middle Ages*, Vol. II, Methuen, 2nd edition, 1924.
Oman, Charles, *Warwick the Kingmaker*, Macmillan, 1905.
Peel, Frank, 'The Battle of Towton', paper read before the Heckmondwike Antiquarian Society in 1884.
Ramsay, James, *Lancaster and York: 1399–1485*, Vol. II, Clarendon Press, 1892.
Ransome, Cyril, 'The Battle of Towton', *English Historical Review*, IV, 1889.
Young, Peter, and John Adair, *Hastings to Culloden*, G. Bell, 1964.

Primary Sources
Ellis, Sir Henry, ed., *Three books of Polydore Vergil's English History, comprising the reigns of Henry VI, Edward IV and Richard III*, Camden Society, 1844.
Gairdner, James, ed., *The Historical Collections of a Citizen of London in the Fifteenth Century*, Camden Society, 1876. (William Gregory, Mayor of London 1451–2, was author until 1452.)
Gairdner, James, ed., *The Paston Letters* A.D. *1422–1509*, 6 vols, Chatto and Windus, 1904.
Hall's Chronicle, London, 1809.
Vergil, Polydore, *Anglicae Historiae*, Camden Society, 1884.
Whethamstede, John, *Registrum Abbatiae Johannis, Whethamstede*, 2 vols, ed. Henry T. Riley, Rolls Series, 1872.

Chapter 10: The Battle of Barnet
Burne, A. H., *Battlefields of England*, Methuen, 1950.
Cass, Frederick Charles, 'The Battle of Barnet', *Transactions of the London and Middlesex Archaeological Society*, 1890.
Honeybourne, M. B., 'Battle of Barnet', Barnet Press, 1971.
Kendall, P. M., *Warwick the Kingmaker*, Allen and Unwin, 1959.
Mowat, R. B., *The Wars of the Roses*, Crosby Lockwood, 1914.
Oman, Charles, *The Political History of England, 1377–1485*, Vol. II, Longmans, 1910.
Oman, Charles, *Warwick the Kingmaker*, Macmillan, 1905.
Ramsay, James, *Lancaster and York: 1399–1485*, Vol. II, Clarendon Press, 1892.

Primary Sources
Bruce, John, ed., *Historie of the arrivall of Edward IV in England*, Camden Society, 1838.

Chronicle of the Abbey of Croyland (third continuation), trans. from the Latin by Henry T. Riley, London, 1854.

Gairdner, James, ed., *The Paston Letters* A.D. *1422–1509*, 6 vols, Chatto and Windus, 1904.

Hall's Chronicle, London, 1809.

Holinshed's Chronicle, Vol. III, London, 1808.

Standing, Percy Cross, ed., *Memorials of Old Hertfordshire*, London, 1905.

Stow, John, *Annales*, 1614.

Chapter 11: The Battle of Tewkesbury

Burne, A. H., *Battlefields of England*, Methuen, 1950.

George, H. B., *Battles of English History*, Methuen, 1895.

Hammond, P. W., H. G. Shearring and G. Wheeler, 'The Battle of Tewkesbury', Tewkesbury Festival Committee, 1971.

Oman, Charles, *A History of the Art of War in the Middle Ages*, Vol. II, Methuen, 2nd edition, 1924.

Oman, Charles, *The Political History of England, 1377–1485*, Longmans, 1910.

Ramsay, James, *Lancaster and York: 1399–1485*, Vol. II, Clarendon Press, 1892.

Simons, Eric N., *The Reign of Edward IV*, Muller, 1966.

Young, Peter, and John Adair, *Hastings to Culloden*, G. Bell, 1964.

Primary Sources

Bruce, John, ed., *Historie of the arrivall of Edward IV in England*, Camden Society, 1838.

Gairdner, James, ed., *The Paston Letters* A.D. *1422–1509*, 6 vols, Chatto and Windus, 1904.

Hall's Chronicle, London, 1809.

Holinshed's Chronicle, Vol. III, London, 1808.

Chapter 12: Bosworth Field

Barrett, C. R. B., *Battles and Battlefields in England*, A.D. Innes, 1896.

Brooke, Richard, *Visits to Fields of Battle in England*, John Russell Smith, 1857.

Burne, A. H., *Battlefields of England*, Methuen, 1950.

Cheetham, Anthony, *The Life and Times of Richard III*, Weidenfeld and Nicolson, 1972.

Gairdner, James, 'The Battle of Bosworth', *Archaeologia*, LV, 1896.

Hutton, W., *The Battle of Bosworth Field*, London, 1813.

Markham, Sir Clement, *Richard III: His Life and Character*, Smith, Elder, 1906.

Oman, Charles, *The Political History of England, 1377–1485*, Vol. II, Longmans, 1910.

Ramsay, James, *Lancaster and York: 1399–1485*, Clarendon Press, 1892.

Young, Peter, and John Adair, *Hastings to Culloden*, G. Bell, 1964.

Primary Sources

Chronicle of the Abbey of Croyland (third continuation), trans. from the Latin by Henry T. Riley, London, 1854.

Ellis, Sir Henry, ed., *Three books of Polydore Vergil's English History, comprising the reigns of Henry VI, Edward IV and Richard III*, Camden Society, 1844.

Hall's Chronicle, London, 1809.

Chapter 13: Scotland and the Tudors—Flodden

Barnett, Correlli, *Britain and Her Army, 1509–1970*, Alan Lane, Penguin Press, 1970.

Barrett, C. R. B., *Battles and Battlefields in England*, A. D. Innes, 1896.

Brown, P. Hume, *History of Scotland*, Vol. I, Cambridge University Press, 1899.

Burne, A. H., *Battlefields of England*, Methuen, 1950.

Churchill, Winston S., *A History of the English Speaking Peoples*, Vol. II, Cassell, 1956.

Elliot, Fitzwilliam Elliot Andrew, *The Battle of Flodden and Raids of 1513*, Andrew Elliot, 1911.

George, H. B., *Battles of English History*, Methuen, 1895.

Leather, G. F. T., *New Light on Flodden*, Martins Printing Works, Berwick-upon-Tweed, 1937.

McEwan, Sir John of Marchmont, Bt, *The Battle of Flodden*, privately printed, 1962.

Mackenzie, Agnes Mure, *The Kingdom of Scotland*, Chambers, 1940.

Mackenzie, W. M., *The Secret of Flodden*, Grant and Murray, 1931.

Oman, Charles, *A History of the Art of War in the 16th Century*, Methuen, 1937.

Vickers, Kenneth H., *A History of Northumberland*, Vol. XI, Andrew W. Reid, 1922.

Primary Sources

Articles of Battle, or Gazette of the Battle of Flodden, as published in John Pinkerton, *History of Scotland*, Vol. II, p. 456, London, 1797.

Faques, Richard, 'The Trewe Encountre or Batayle lately don betwene Englande and Scotlande', taken from John Skelton, *A ballade of the Scottysshe Kynge*, London, 1882.

Hall's Chronicle, London, 1809.

Holinshed's Chronicle, Vol. II, London, 1807.

Letters and Papers of Henry VIII, Vol. I, Part II, arranged and catalogued by James Gairdner, H.M.S.O., 1905.

Lindesay, Robert of Pitscottie, *The Historie and Cronicles of Scotland*, Vol. I, ed. A. H. G. MacKay, William Blackwood, 1899.

Lindesay, Robert of Pitscottie, *The Cronicles of Scotland*, Vol. II, ed. J. G. Dalyell, Edinburgh, 1814.

Chapter 14: The Tudors in Scotland Pinkie Cleuch

Arber, E., *An English Garner: Tudor Tracts*, Constable, 1903.

Barnett, Correlli, *Britain and Her Army, 1509–1970*, Alan Lane, Penguin Press, 1970.

Brown, P. Hume, *Short History of Scotland*, Oliver and Boyd, 1955.

Dalyell, J. G., *Fragments of Scottish History*, 1798.

Fergusson, James, *The White Hind*, Faber, 1963.

Jordan, W. K., *Edward VI: The Young King*, Allen and Unwin, 1970.

Oman, Charles, *A History of the Art of War in the 16th Century*, Methuen, 1937.

Pollard, A. F., *England Under Protector Somerset*, Routledge and Kegan Paul, 1900.

Primary Sources
Hamilton Papers, The, Vol. II, B.M.
Murray, J. H., ed., *The Complaynte of Scotlande*, Early English Text Society, 1872–3.

List of books studied in connection with armour, weapons and uniforms

Ashdown, C. H., *British and Foreign Arms and Armour*, T. C. and E. C. Jack, 1909.

Collie, G. F., *Highland Dress*, King Penguin, 1948.

Ffoulkes, Charles, *Armour and Weapons*, Clarendon Press, 1909.

Hunter, Edmund, *Arms and Armour*, Wills and Hepworth, 1971.

Journals of the Society for Army Historical Research, 1921–73.

McClintock, H. F., *Old Irish and Highland Dress*, Dundalgan Press (W. Tempest), 2nd edition, 1950.

Martin, Paul, *Armour and Weapons*, H. Jenkins, 1968.

Norman, Vesey, *Arms and Armour*, Weidenfeld and Nicolson, 1964.

Tappan, E. M., *In Feudal Times*, Harrap, 1931.

Tylden, Major G., *Horses and Saddlery*, J. A. Allen, 1965.

Wilkinson, F., *Arms and Armour*, Ward Lock, 1965.

Index

229

Acknowledgements

By kind permission of the British Library Board: 11, 40, 76
Radio Times Hulton Picture Library: 40, endpapers
The Mansell Collection: 2, 18, 24, 36, 37, 40, 85, 109, 176, 209
Master and Fellows of Corpus Christi College, Cambridge: 11
Scottish National Portrait Gallery: 95
Town plan of Battle reproduced by courtesy of G. W. May Ltd.

Battles
In Britain
and their political background

Volume 2

1642–1746

A musketeer, from a seventeenth-century exercise manual for musketeers

Battles
In Britain
and their political background
Volume 2

1642–1746

William Seymour

Drawings, Maps and Battle Plans by W. F. N. Watson

BOOK CLUB ASSOCIATES
LONDON

By the same author
ORDEAL BY AMBITION
BATTLES IN BRITAIN, Volume I

To Jenny
Whose map-reading passeth all understanding.

Acknowledgements:
Cooper Bridgeman Library, 146: Editions R. Laffont, 59; Mary Evans
Picture Library, 18, 38 (top), 40, 47, 51, 57, 80, 85 (btm right). 100–1, 121,
140, 144 (top right), 161 (top right), 184 (top right); Mansell Collection,
endpapers, 2, 11, 12, 13, 38 (btm), 60, 72 (top), 85 (top left and right, and
btm left), 91, 111, 114 (top right), 117, 124–5, 128, 142 (top), 143, 158, 163,
175, 178, 183 (top left, and btm left and right), 184 (top left), 189 (btm),
202: National Portrait Gallery, 72 (btm), 114 (top left), 142 (btm), 144
(top left), 161 (top left), 183 (top right): Radio Times Hulton Picture
Library, 56, 139

William Seymour photographed the illustrations (copyright ©
Sidgwick and Jackson Ltd) on pp. 45 (btm), 62–3, 76–7, 94–5, 119 (btm),
133 (btm), 135 (btm), 152–3, 170–1, 193 (btm), 219 (btm)

W. F. N. Watson drew the maps, battle plans and drawings (copyright ©
Sidgwick and Jackson Ltd) on pp. 23, 25, 33, 45 (top), 61, 75, 93, 104, 105,
106, 107, 119 (top), 126, 133 (top), 135 (top), 137, 146 (top), 151, 169, 193
(top), 199, 207, 211, 213, 219 (top)

This edition published 1979 by Book Club Associates
by arrangement with Sidgwick and Jackson Limited

Copyright © 1975 William Seymour and Sidgwick and Jackson Limited

Design by Bob Burroughs

Picture research by Mary Walsh

Filmset by Typesetting Services Ltd, Glasgow
Printed in Great Britain by litho by
The Anchor Press Limited, Tiptree, Essex
This edition published 1976 by Sidgwick & Jackson Limited
1 Tavistock Chambers, Bloomsbury Way
London WC1A 2SG

Contents

Preface

In the introduction to the first volume of this work, which covered battles from Stamford Bridge (1066) to Pinkie Cleuch (1547), I stressed the point that our knowledge of the battles is far from precise: eyewitness, or contemporary, accounts are often at variance with each other, because they were not committed to paper until some time after the event. It is unwise to be dogmatic about battles that were fought hundreds of years ago. The historian's task, therefore, is to sift through the facts and where they are open to more than one interpretation, or the exact site of any battle cannot be certainly determined, to present them to the reader in a straightforward and easily understandable manner, so that he can have the enjoyment of walking the site and deciding for himself just how it happened, and in some cases where.

An excellent example of this that occurs in the present volume is the Battle of Cheriton (March 1644). Although in this case the sequence of events and many details of the fighting have been accurately chronicled, the actual positions of the contending armies have never been satisfactorily determined. I have accordingly treated the chapter on this battle somewhat differently, and devoted extra space in which to present the case for my own and other writers' ideas: for on the position of the battle line depends the site of the battle. The reader can then form his own opinion as to which position is correct.

In both volumes of the work I have eschewed the temptation to pursue the might-have-beens of history – to forecast the possible outcome of any battle had the losing side been the victors. There was not space for this fascinating, but usually fruitless, undertaking. However, a more practical exercise for those who have studied both volumes is to examine the reasons why the percentage of men killed to the total numbers engaged in battles during the hundred years between 1450 and 1547 was more than double that of the hundred years between 1642 and 1745, when increased knowledge had produced more destructive weapons. The difference cannot be entirely accounted for by the massive slaughter at Towton, for the percentage figure was nearly as great at Sedgemoor, nor were the victors noticeably more merciful in their treatment of the defeated foe during the Civil War and at Culloden: but possibly

TABLE OF BATTLES BY COUNTIES

England

			Chapter
Berkshire	First Battle of Newbury	1643	*3*
Hampshire	Cheriton	1644	*4*
Lancashire	Preston	1715	*10*
Leicestershire	Naseby	1645	*6*
Somerset	Sedgemoor	1685	*9*
Warwickshire	Edgehill	1642	*2*
Herefordshire and Worcestershire	Worcester	1651	*8*
North Yorkshire	Marston Moor	1644	*5*

Scotland

Aberdeenshire	Alford	1645	*7*
East Lothian	Dunbar	1650	*8*
	Prestonpans	1745	*11*
Inverness-shire	Culloden	1746	*11*
Nairn	Auldearn	1645	*7*
Perthshire	Sheriffmuir	1715	*10*
Ross and Cromarty	Glenshiel	1719	*10*
Stirlingshire	Falkirk	1746	*11*
	Kilsyth	1645	*7*

pursuits were better controlled and less barbarously conducted in the last hundred years of British battles.

In the two chapters on the Jacobite rebellions I am aware that in occasionally describing the supporters of the Old and Young Pretenders as 'rebels' I may incur the wrath of many Scots. Nevertheless, they were in rebellion against the legitimate government and this description, as an occasional variation from the constant use of the word 'Jacobite', seems permissible. Similarly the words 'English' and 'Scottish' are sometimes used to describe the rival armies. Technically this is wrong, and is only done for convenience and simplicity. The government forces included a number of Scots loyal to the crown, and latterly in the 'Forty-five campaign some Hessians. Prince Charles Edward's army contained Irish and French contingents and even some English Jacobites. Both armies claimed to be royalist, but in these chapters that designation is applied only to King George's troops.

To many of the people who so kindly helped me in the writing and preparation of the first volume I owe a further debt of gratitude for their continued assistance in this part of the work. I hope that they will forgive me if I do not mention them again individually; but there are others, not called upon earlier, but who were good enough to give me their time, encouragement and specialist knowledge in the preparation of this volume. Mr Charles Chenevix Trench, the Reverend J. W. S. Mansell and Colonel Angus Cameron have read through parts of the manuscript and given me the benefit of their advice, and Colonel Cameron also drove me across half Inverness to visit battlefields. Mr Bernard Bruce of Cauldhame was equally helpful in my endeavours to reconstruct the rather complicated Battle of Sheriffmuir. Mr Sharpe France, county archivist, Lancashire Record Office, supplied me with the plan of Preston, reproduced on page 189, and once again I am indebted to the director of Ordnance Survey for permission to base the battle maps on the Ordnance Survey sheets. To all of them I offer my grateful thanks.

William Seymour
Falconer's House
Crichel
Wimborne
Dorset

CHAPTER 1

The First Civil War

The Protagonists:
Their Arms, Armies and Armaments

*The First Civil War lasted from 1642 to 1646, and fighting took place
throughout much of England and Scotland, while in Ireland the
savage rebellion that broke out in October 1641 had considerable
influence on the war. It is not possible in a single short chapter to
recount the progress of the Civil War, in which there were more than
fifty battles, sieges and skirmishes of note, but its origins, and the
composition of the two armies that took part in it, have been traced
in outline. In subsequent chapters five of the principal battles in the
First, and one in the Third, Civil War will be dealt with in detail.
See pp. 32–6 for brief descriptions in chronological order of the more
important battles and sieges of the First Civil War.*

The origins of the Civil War stretch back to the end of the Tudor
era. It was not the Stuarts' fault that they inherited an economy
moving rapidly towards inflation, and an unfinished Reformation –
though Charles I, through his extravagance and obstinacy, certainly
exacerbated the situation. The eventual crisis that precipitated the
outbreak of hostilities was a political one: in essence Charles's
complete refusal to yield to his opponents in Parliament. But
basically it was a quarrel whose ingredients of recalcitrance,
religion and economics opened wide gulfs and chasms as the
unhappy reign unfolded. From 1629 for eleven years Charles ruled
without a parliament, and during that time many of his subjects
became increasingly discontented with government through a
council of courtiers who were often inept, sometimes corrupt, and
nearly always factious: a council presided over from time to time
by a monarch who had a high sense of God-given duty, which he
strove to perform conscientiously, if often misguidedly, and who
saw himself as the absolute arbiter over people and events in a
society where 'a subject and a sovereign are clean different things'.
   It is wrong to think that at the beginning of the seventeenth
century religious discontent was confined to Puritan strongholds
in East Anglia and certain other parts of the country. Calvinist
theology dominated the Church of England (even Whitgift, who

persecuted Puritan parsons for their failure to perform certain rituals, held Calvinist views), and although the doctrine of the Dutch theologian Arminius, with its leaning towards certain aspects of Roman Catholic ritual, was beginning to gain ground, in most country churches there was neither surplice nor church music, while the altar occupied a central position. Charles himself was a sincere Protestant, but he favoured a more elaborate ritual than most of his subjects. His appointment of William Laud, a convinced Arminian, to succeed George Abbot as Archbishop of Canterbury opened the way to a doctrinal split in the country.

Laud, and other high church prelates, found Charles anxious to believe that a return to the more elaborate ritual would meet with general satisfaction, and that dissent and criticism could be expected only from a small minority. Nothing could have been further from the truth, least of all in Scotland. Here, in 1638, the National Covenant was drafted as a protest against Laud's imposition of the new Prayer Book and the appointment of bishops and churchmen to civil posts, and the two Bishops' Wars were entirely religious in origin.

In England, although the bishops came in for much obloquy as the enforcers of Laudian measures and the religious problem generally was perhaps the most important underlying current of discontent, this was not the immediate cause of the Civil War. There were other equally grave problems, and among them the more earthy economics played their part. The value of money had been steadily falling since the days of Elizabeth, and Charles quite simply had not the means to finance his foolish and quite useless military adventures in France, the upkeep of an expensive court and an extravagant, although informed, taste in art and architecture. His determination to rule without Parliament presented fiscal problems that, inevitably, were eventually insoluble. Nevertheless, his enforcement of tonnage and poundage, a manipulation of the customs duties and an agreement with Spain to transport bullion in English ships for the payment of Spanish troops, enabled him to exist for a while without recourse to Parliament. The Spanish agreement was most unpopular with merchants and Protestants, for it favoured a nation openly hostile to countries with which the former did trade and for which the latter had religious sympathies. But it was the reintroduction of ship money that caused the greatest furore.

This tax had been imposed under Elizabeth as a levy on the coastal counties and sea ports for the benefit of the navy. As such it was a sound tax and not greatly resented. But when Charles

Above: John Pym, champion of the rights of Parliament against Charles I. Right: The Earl of Warwick, one of the foremost objectors to ship money. Below: The House of Commons in 1648

Cancellarij sedes

Left: Charles I in the House of Lords, from a contemporary print.
Above left: Charles I, after Lely. Above right: Archbishop Laud, his
controversial Archbishop of Canterbury. Below: Execution of Strafford
at the Tower on 12 May 1641

A Doctor VTher Lord Pri
te of Ireland;
B the Sherifes of London
C the Earle of Strafford
D his kindred and Friends

attempted to extend it to inland counties he had gone too far. Many of his subjects came out in open defiance against this imposition. Prominent among the objectors were the Earl of Warwick and Lord Saye and Sele, but the man who was to gain immortality through his contumely was an influential Buckinghamshire landowner called John Hampden. Hampden was one of many who refused to pay this tax, and the crown prosecuted him in 1637 to show reason why he should not pay twenty shillings levied on his lands. The case rumbled on for many weeks, first before the four barons of the Exchequer and then before the judges of the King's Bench and Common Pleas. In the end Hampden won his particular case on a technicality, but by a slender majority the judges upheld the legality of ship money. It was a hollow victory for the King and gained him nothing, for by 1640 resistance to the tax was almost nationwide.

His subjects' refusal to pay ship money was not in itself sufficiently damaging for Charles to have to terminate his personal rule. It needed the First Bishops' War* and the clear, cogent and closely reasoned arguments of his greatest servant, Thomas Wentworth, Earl of Strafford (whom he was so soon to sacrifice), before at last, in April 1640, a parliament was summoned. Wentworth, with considerable experience of successfully managing the Irish parliament, felt confident that he could manipulate the less turbulent members who would assemble at Westminster. But he was wrong. He found men in the Commons who were too strong for him, and who had come there determined to plunge Parliament into constitutional assertiveness. This was not at all what Charles wanted, and three weeks after it first met he dissolved the Short Parliament. No money was forthcoming to pay the reluctant levies now being raised to bring the dissident Scots to heel. The result of the Second Bishops' War was a foregone conclusion: Charles's largely untrained, ill disciplined and indifferently led force was no match for 20,000 Covenanters under tried military commanders such as Alexander Leslie and William Baillie. At Newburn (near

* In 1637 Charles I attempted to impose the new Prayer Book upon Scotland; this was bitterly opposed and led to the forming of the Covenanting party in Scotland. Matters went from bad to worse, and the Assembly, sitting without the bishops in defiance of Charles's command, ordered the abolition of episcopacy. There followed in 1639 and 1640 what became known as the Bishops' Wars. General Leslie had command of the Covenanting army and Montrose acted as his second-in-command. In the second battle at Newburn in August 1640 the Scots gained a very easy victory over the English, and the King had no alternative but to offer terms.

14

Newcastle) on 20 August 1640 the English were routed, and the Scots thereupon occupied the five northern counties of England, demanding payment of £850 a day until the occupation could be terminated by treaty.

It was very obvious, indeed it was a stipulation of the Treaty of Ripon, that another parliament must be called to raise money for the indemnity and to arrange terms for the withdrawal of the Scots. Accordingly, on 3 November 1640 what became known as the Long Parliament assembled. Civil war was far from anyone's thoughts when this parliament first met; nevertheless the atmosphere was tense, filled with the presage of storm. This time there could be no quick dissolution, for the Commons held the purse strings. There were at that time about 300 Members, mostly country squires and merchants, and they knew their position to be a strong one; nor could Charles expect overwhelming support in the Lords, for many who sat there were uneasy at his apparent disregard for what they considered their indefeasible privileges. Moreover, throughout both Houses there was a broad streak of Puritanism, dedicated men for whom no toil was too hard in pursuance of their high ideals.

Until his death at the end of 1643 the leader of the Lower House was John Pym. When the Long Parliament assembled he was fifty-seven years old, a widower and a man who lived entirely for his work. He stood out above all his colleagues, remarkable alike for his intellect, eloquence, cool judgement, administrative ability and leadership. He was supported by able men such as Lords Brooke, Mandeville, Saye, and Warwick; and in the Commons by Hampden, William Strode, Denzil Holles, Arthur Hesilrige and Harry Vane. But his was the guiding hand, he the chief architect of reform and revolt. Pym was no warmonger – he stood rather for peace, tolerance, justice and a freedom of the spirit – but the cataclysm of events and the stubbornness of Charles edged him towards the brink and beyond.

This is not the place to detail the actions of the Long Parliament, whose initial proceedings though drastic and mostly abhorrent to Charles gave promise of a settlement. It is only necessary to catalogue briefly some of the principal events that in spite of this early promise inevitably widened the gulf between king and people and eventually led, inexorably, to civil war.

Almost Parliament's first act was to set up a committee to deal with what they considered the misdemeanours of the Earl of Strafford. On 11 November Strafford was impeached, and he was brought to trial in March 1641. Unable to topple him through impeachment Parliament resorted to a bill of attainder and the

King found it necessary, in the interests of peace and the safety of his queen, to bow to the inevitable. At noon on 12 May this loyal and able statesman was beheaded. Strafford was but the first of the King's councillors and intimate circle to feel Parliament's displeasure; others had to flee the country to escape impeachment, and Archbishop Laud, who disdained flight, was eventually beheaded after a long imprisonment.

In January 1641 Parliament passed the Triennial Act, and later followed this up with a bill to ensure that it could not be dissolved without its own consent. Ship money had been declared an illegal tax in the previous December, and steps were taken to close the door on all non-parliamentary taxation. In July the prerogative courts were abolished, and by the time Parliament rose for a short recess the King, albeit reluctantly, had given his assent to most of the important measures that Pym had included in his programme. Only the religious question remained outstanding. On this the House was deeply divided and Pym was not anxious to precipitate action for the present.

It seemed to many that by resolute and dexterous management the most dangerous reefs had been avoided, and that the ship of state might now sail on into calmer waters. But in fact Charles had granted nothing that he did not intend to repudiate as soon as he could regain the initiative. And Pym – unlike most of his colleagues – knew this very well. Some signs of returning popularity gave Charles encouragement, and he still held two trumps; he retained the right to appoint his councillors, and he controlled the armed forces of the state. With a confidence that was characteristic, but scarcely justified, he proceeded to Scotland, where he hoped to gain a party among the Scottish nobles. While he was there an event occurred, the results of which were eventually to bring the country to civil war.

In October 1641 the Irish Roman Catholics revolted against the English and Scottish settlers. They greatly feared that the upsurge of Puritanism in England would bring still further repression and confiscation of land upon them. From north to south the flame of revolt quickly spread; the slaughter was appalling and mischievous rumours were afoot. It was given out (falsely) and widely believed that Charles was in sympathy with his Roman Catholic subjects and had given them licence for what they did. An army had to be raised immediately to quell the rebellion, but Pym's belief that the King could not be trusted with such an army prompted him to challenge one of the last of Charles's remaining prerogatives. On 8 November Parliament agreed to request the King that he should

16

appoint only those councillors and ministers approved by them. A fortnight later the Grand Remonstrance, the most damaging indictment that foe and faction could devise, passed the Commons by the narrowest of margins. Soon afterwards an earlier suggestion, made by a backbencher called Oliver Cromwell, to wrest control of the armed forces from the King, was taken up and embodied in the Militia Bill.

Parliament was no longer unanimous in its thinking; none of these measures was passed without a struggle. Gradually the two parties – Royalist and Parliamentarian, or pejoratively, Cavalier (cavaliero) and Roundhead – took shape. Nevertheless, war was still not inevitable, although in January Charles did his best to make it so. Accompanied by some 300 troopers he came to Westminster to arrest five Members of the Commons who were the ringleaders in a move to impeach the Queen. Warned of trouble the Members had escaped by river, leaving Charles looking remarkably foolish and his opponents greatly strengthened. On 10 January he and his queen slipped furtively out of London. When he next entered the capital it was as a prisoner on trial for his life.

From London to Hampton Court, from there to Windsor and then to York. For the country a period of agonizing suspense; for the Royalist faction a period of advice and counter-advice. The Queen and certain hotheads of the court were constantly advising the King to sever the last hopeful strands of peace; the moderates, who comprised Charles's few remaining friends in Parliament – men like Hyde and Lord Falkland – urged him to negotiate while it was still possible. The King seemed to accept their advice; he made many concessions in matters of church and state, and he even went some way towards a compromise over the question of the armed forces. But Pym was not fooled; he knew very well that these were delaying tactics. The King was taking steps to secure important ports; he was looking to the north for support, and to Ireland for an army. Meanwhile the Queen was to go overseas taking the crown jewels with which to buy foreign aid.

In March 1642 the Commons passed the Militia Bill as an ordinance; it was a step which virtually signified that sovereignty had passed to them. The country was sliding, with gathering momentum, towards civil war. In June Pym passed through a greatly reduced and now pliant Parliament nineteen propositions, which made religious as well as secular demands on the King. Charles had always stood uncompromisingly for the absolute rule of kings, defying any interference or advance of democracy; had he accepted

Costume of noblemen in
early seventeenth century

the nineteen propositions he would have become little better than
the puppet of Parliament. The choice before him was to surrender
or to fight. Charles chose to fight.

On 22 August 1642 King Charles unfurled his standard at Nottingham. The country moved into civil war with the utmost repugnance;
for much of its course both sides were looking for opportunities
to patch up the quarrel, although Charles and the extreme
Royalists were never prepared to give an inch of what they
regarded as hallowed ground. Almost to the very end the Parliamentarians persisted in the myth that they were not fighting the
King; it was the same story as 200 years earlier in the Wars of the
Roses: one reason, so they said, that they took up arms was to
free the King from his 'evil councillors'.

The population in England and Wales at this time was about
four and a half million, with perhaps another million in Scotland
and Ireland. This was not a class war, for the ruling class was
split down the middle on the issue, but it is possible to see certain
sections of the population adhering to one or other party. The
Stuarts had created the majority of the 125 peerages then in
existence, so it is not surprising to find more than twice the number
of peers in the Royalist camp as in the Parliamentarian. The

18

merchants, on the other hand, tended to side with the Parliamentarians. The landed gentry, who formed the largest part of the ruling class, were about evenly divided, and to some extent they influenced the lower classes, for they could raise their tenantry in support of the side they favoured. Labourers, craftsmen and artisans, not owning loose allegiance to any overlord, seemed mostly to favour Parliament. It can be seen, therefore, that both sides had an almost equal pool from which to draw volunteers; but what little military talent there was available at the outbreak of hostilities was mainly Royalist, for in their ranks were the most soldiers of fortune with experience of war on the continent.

If the parties were more or less equal in the availability of manpower, Parliament held the advantage geographically, in that their support came mostly from the rich eastern and south-eastern counties and they held London. Royalist strongholds were in Wales, most of the north – other than certain parts of the West Riding and Lancashire – the western Midlands, and the south-west. Parliament was operating on interior lines, and the longer the conflict went on the greater advantage would accrue to them.

In 1642 there was no standing army as such. The defence of the kingdom rested in the first instance with the navy, and in the event of invasion there were fortress garrisons and the county militia, known as the trained bands. The navy, which was soon to be put in charge of the capable Earl of Warwick, was small but efficient; the conditions of service had been so bad under the King that when hostilities broke out most of the officers and men sided with Parliament. This was a great loss for Charles, for it meant that the important Parliamentarian ports could be supplied by the fleet. It made it extremely difficult for Charles to obtain foreign aid even if such could be arranged, and the very fact that the navy was hostile to the Royalist cause made foreign countries wary of proffering the much desired help.

The militia, or trained bands, were mostly infantrymen – musketeers and pikemen. They came directly under the lieutenant of the county and were officered by local gentry. The name 'trained bands' indicated that the men were available for training rather than that they had been trained, and with the notable exception of those from London and Cornwall they were almost entirely untrained. The London men were easily the best organized and equipped; they almost alone could be persuaded to fight outside their own county boundaries, and their well drilled and trained regiments, comprising some 8,000 men, were a formidable ready-made force for Parliament. In addition the Honourable Artillery

Company sent out a number of competent officers to the Parliamentarians (and a few to the Royalists) trained in their New Artillery Garden.

It was important for both sides, particularly the Royalists who were deprived of the Tower's large arsenal, to take possession of the major ports and garrison towns in order to obtain their ordnance. Charles's attempt to gain Hull in July had been thwarted by the navy, and when hostilities broke out Colonel Goring, Governor of Portsmouth, found himself blockaded by the fleet and attacked by land. He surrendered the port and escaped to Holland to join the Queen. Dover Castle was seized from the Royalists and both Plymouth and Bristol declared for Parliament. The latter was taken by the Royalists in July 1643 and proved an invaluable source of supply for the successful Royalist army in the south-west. In spite of these serious losses Charles secured many of the county trained bands' magazines, and early victories brought him a rich haul in warlike stores. Up and down the country the King's commission of array was read in the principal towns with varying results – sometimes being greeted with enthusiasm, sometimes in silence and at other times resulting in hostile clashes. Wherever Charles found the trained bands unwilling to march with him he disarmed them and used their magazines for equipping his volunteers.

The build-up of the armies in the first instance was from volunteers, and both sides had a ready supply. But the majority of those enlisting were without military experience, and very undisciplined; nor could they be officered by men of experience. In August the King received a welcome addition to his handful of men with battle experience when his nephews the Princes Rupert and Maurice joined him from Holland with some men, arms and ammunition, having overcome a number of adventures at sea. The King also had a possible reservoir of trained men from Ireland, and some battle-hardened officers from the English regiments in Dutch service managed to reach him. But getting troops to England with the navy hostile was a continuing problem, and in the first years, while both armies were gaining experience, it was a very amateurish war.

For at least two months prior to the outbreak of hostilities the Royalists had been actively recruiting, and Members of Parliament had left Westminster in good time to stir up support for their cause, but by 22 August Charles was still without an army, having scarcely more than 800 horse and 300 foot. However, at the beginning of September volunteers began to come in from Yorkshire and other counties. A small amount of artillery was also acquired. On 13 September the King left Nottingham and made for Shrewsbury, where some 6,000 infantrymen and 1,500 dragoons were said to be assembling, with whom he intended to secure Chester in order to safeguard communications with Ireland.

Money was an even greater problem for Charles than it was for Parliament, but, apart from the invaluable financial assistance rendered by the Prince of Orange, there were those at home most generously disposed. Many of the landed gentry either came themselves or sent their sons with a horse and arms, and usually money to support them; some of the wealthier magnates, such as the Marquis of Worcester, were even more generous and subscribed huge sums to the cause, or raised and maintained quite large bodies of armed men. These scions of patrician England both led and filled the ranks of Charles's cavalry. Their greatest asset was derived from the hunting field, which had given them 'an eye for a country' and the courage to cross it at speed. It had also given them better horses and a higher standard of horsemanship than their enemy. Oliver Cromwell, probably the most proficient of Parliament's soldiers, soon saw the need to improve the standard of his own troopers to fit them to 'encounter gentlemen who have courage, honour and resolution in them'.

Both parties thought that a single battle would decide all. The

Cuirassier ('Lobster'), wearing close helmet and three-quarter armour of laminated plates. Dragoon in burgonet and breast-and-back over buffcoat, snaphance musket, powder flask and bullet pouch slung at right side. Each man carries two pistols in saddle holsters

King foresaw a return to London at the head of a victorious army and the chance to start afresh with a new parliament of a more friendly shade. The Parliamentarians, equally sure of victory in the field, would bring the King back to his capital to sit in state carefully and tightly trammelled. By the middle of October Charles felt himself ready to put his cause to the hazard and march on London. As he rode across England his army gathered strength. At Bridgnorth there was a warm welcome and more recruits, and at Wolverhampton further levies from Wales joined his standard. By now he had mustered 13,000 men: fair material, but unfortunately insufficiently armed.

Meanwhile, Parliament had raised and equipped an army formidable in numbers if not in professional skill, which was marching towards the King under the command of the Earl of Essex. The London trained bands formed an important nucleus, but by and large Parliament raised its men in the same way as the King – volunteers from those areas under its influence – and its cavalry leaders were men of much the same stamp as the Royalists, many of them being armigerous (men entitled to bear heraldic arms). John Hampden armed his tenantry and turned them out in dark green, while Oliver Cromwell recruited a troop of horse* comprised of Huntingdonshire volunteers. Lords Brooke, Bedford, Mandeville (later Manchester), Stamford, Robartes, and Saye and Sele, Sir Arthur Hesilrige (with his fully mailed troop of 'Lobsters'), Denzil Holles and many such others all raised men and commanded one of the nineteen regiments of foot, or seventy-five troops of horse, which with five troops of dragoons made up the bulk of Essex's army. By 10 September Essex had brought this army as far as Northampton. A steady stream of raw recruits kept trickling in, so that soon he had under command some 20,000 men. But even before the first major engagement at Edgehill (see p. 32 or chapter 2 for full details) this number had somehow dwindled to no more than 13,000–14,000.

Both armies experienced great difficulty in keeping up their numbers. Pay was usually in arrears and men, who with a few notable exceptions were only interested in the money and the loot, were inclined to drift away when neither was forthcoming and the fighting had receded from their own neighbourhood. There was also a certain amount of wastage in unnecessary garrisoning of towns, castles and even houses. Nor was there any sensible system

* In Essex's army the cavalry was at first raised in single troops of about sixty to eighty men, but the strength of the infantry regiment was the same as that in the Royalist army—1,200 men.

Pikeman and infantry officer. The officer carries a half-pike. Both armies had basically similar arms and accoutrements

23

of recruiting losses; the King relied mainly on commissioning officers to form new regiments and in consequence there were many regiments hopelessly under strength. In spite of this problem, and apart from the need, by both sides, to have resort to impressment by 1643, there was little change in the composition, equipment and strength of the armies until in 1644 Parliament gained the support of an 18,000-strong Scottish army.

Parliament made more positive attempts to strengthen morale and discipline in the early stages of the war than did the Royalists. They tried to overcome the difficulty of getting men to serve outside their counties by forming associations of counties, such as the Western Association which comprised troops from Bristol, Gloucester and neighbouring areas. But this military grouping by districts was only really successful in the Eastern Association, and that because Cromwell provided the necessary drive and energy. The lack of discipline and the harm this did was apparent to most commanders, but only Cromwell seems to have taken real measures to combat it in the period before the New Model was formed. In raising his regiment he tried to select men who 'made some conscience of what they did', and his insistence on the observation of Christian principles was accompanied by strict, not to say severe, discipline. Such steps as these went some way to offset the undoubted advantage of better officers possessed by the Royalist army, at any rate during the first part of the war.

It is only possible to give the bare outline of the arms and equipment in use at this time; to the student of war fuller details are available in books by such eminent authors as J. W. Fortescue, C. H. Firth, H. C. B. Rogers, A. H. Burne and Peter Young (see bibliography for this chapter). The Royalist cavalry from the beginning of the war (and the Parliamentarian soon afterwards) was organized in regiments of six or more troops, the troop being commanded by a captain with a lieutenant and cornet under him. There were occasional slight variations in the cavalryman's arms: basically he carried a pair of pistols and a sword, but in Essex's original army there were some cavalrymen carrying carbines, and Cromwell's first troop was described as consisting of arquebusiers. Again at the beginning of the war there were a few regiments of cuirassiers, but these soon disappeared (with the exception of Hesilrige's 'Lobsters'), because apart from their being cumbersome there were too few horses suitable for mounting them. The more usual defensive armour was a light headpiece known as a pot, and back and breast plates worn over a buff leather coat.

Gustavus Adolphus was responsible for recent changes in

Musketeer with 48-inch barrelled matchlock and rest, and sleeveless
buffcoat and bandolier with wooden bottles containing charges of
powder. Cavalry trooper in lobster-tailed pot, with breast-and-back over
apron-skirted buffcoat. Vambrace or bridle gauntlet on bridle arm

25

cavalry tactics, but formations and use of cavalry in England in 1642 mostly followed the old continental pattern, for those officers with experience had fought mainly in the Dutch and German armies. Cavalry was drawn up six ranks deep (usually on the wings) and advancing at a trot would discharge their pistols by ranks until the opposition had been sufficiently battered to allow them to close in with the sword. But Prince Rupert, who had served under Gustavus Adolphus, soon changed these tactics in the Royalist army, and advancing only three ranks deep at a fast trot, or even gallop, thrust in with the sword and only then used the pistol. Cromwell, too, quickly adopted these more mobile tactics. Such were the cavalry tactics in theory, but a cavalryman is a more difficult article to train than an infantryman, and in practice matters were often very different.

Dragoons were mounted infantry and rode an inferior type of horse. They were armed with sword and carbine and in battle were usually used in support of cavalry, but on account of their mobility they were sometimes sent forward to hold key points such as bridges. Loosely organized according to the tactical situation, they almost always fought on foot, one in every ten men remaining in the rear with the horses.

The infantry regiment of 1,200 men was organized into ten companies, but certainly in the Royalist army this was very much a paper strength and formation. Before the end of 1642 many of Charles's regiments had only one or two companies, although Parliament's practice was to amalgamate weak regiments to maintain the full strength where possible. Each company had a captain, subaltern and ensign with usually three sergeants, of whom two were in charge of the musketeers and one the pikemen – there being at the beginning of the war two musketeers to every pikeman.

The pikemen, who were still considered the élite of the infantry even though the increase in musketeers was giving this arm more effective bite, carried a pike that was in theory eighteen feet long, but invariably shortened by the men to about sixteen feet. The pikemen also carried a cutting sword; it was not of much value and General Monck was of the opinion that a rapier-type weapon would have been better. Pike drill was fairly complicated, but when properly executed was most effective. There were many instances in the Civil War when the fortune of the day was decided 'at the push-of-pike'. The pikemen usually formed the centre of the line, and would fall in six deep with the musketeers on their flanks. They were severely handicapped by their defensive armour:

an iron helmet and back and breast plates – known as a corslet – were most unpleasant in the warm weather and at all times restricted mobility.

Musketeers were armed with the matchlock (with the exception of the small artillery guard, who usually carried an early flintlock), which was a cumbersome, inaccurate weapon that fired a heavy bullet of about an ounce for a distance of up to 400 yards, although there was no hope of accuracy above 100 yards and not much at that range. They usually marched carrying twelve cartridges apiece, and the rate of fire was so slow, owing to the reloading problem, that even fighting six ranks deep the leading rank, who after discharging their muskets retired to the rear, only just had time to reload before coming to the front again to continue the 'rolling fire'. The burning match, a two-foot piece of impregnated cord that the musketeer had to carry, made his role a hazardous one, for it was not unknown for a spark to explode all the charges in a man's bandolier. The matchlock was very prone to misfire, most unreliable in wet weather and could completely eliminate surprise in any night attack. The musketeer also carried a sword, but preferred to use his musket butt for close quarter fighting. He was more mobile than the pikeman, but much more vulnerable to cavalry.

The Earl of Essex seems to have placed much reliance on the role of artillery, not only for siege purposes but also in the field. Having the benefit of the London and Hull arsenals he was able to start the war with a well provisioned ordnance and artillery train, whereas it took the King some time to gain parity. Nevertheless, although the principal armies on both sides had many cannon, their chief value was in siege warfare, and in most of the set-piece battles one does not find them playing a very prominent or decisive part. The rate of fire, even with light cannon, was very slow, and sometimes as many as eight horses were needed to drag the guns over the bad roads, while teams of oxen were required to haul the heavy siege pieces – the exception to such slothful progress being the light guns of the Royalist army mounted on carriages with their gunners riding; these were the forerunners of horse artillery and another innovation borrowed from Gustavus Adolphus.

The culverin, a five-inch calibre gun firing a fifteen-pound shot, although not the heaviest type of siege gun was the one principally used: the demi-culverin (nine-pounder) was a dual purpose cannon, used occasionally as a siege gun, but also in the field as heavy artillery. The field guns were generally drakes, a collective name for the lighter calibre sakers, minions, falcons, falconets and robinets. Range was seldom a problem, for armies were usually drawn up for battle well within the range of even the lightest cannon, and for siege purposes the gunners liked to open fire just outside musket range. A gun crew normally consisted of three men, and, although the heavy artillery was organized in batteries and came directly under the officer commanding the artillery train, pairs of the lighter field pieces were allotted to regiments and took up positions in the front line.

It is a fallacy to imagine that until the New Model Army was dressed in red coats, differing only in the colour of their facings according to regiment, the two armies were without uniforms or uniformity. It is true that officers and sergeants might be permitted to wear what they chose, but an attempt was usually made to clothe the private soldiers in some form of standard dress. Nevertheless, colonels of regiments dressed their men as they thought fit, and in consequence there was often a kaleidoscope of colours – red, purple, green, grey and blue. In due course a few regiments could be distinguished by the colour of their coats. Hampden's men in green have already been mentioned, the Earl of Newcastle dressed his in white, Prince Rupert favoured blue, Colonel Montagu preferred red faced with white, and Lord Manchester green faced with red; but surely the sartorial prize must have gone to Lord Brooke, who had his men in purple.

However, although one colour (such as red in the regiments of the Eastern Association) might predominate, there was no easy means of telling friend from foe and often the two sides wore distinguishing scarves of orange and red, or even simpler emblems. Sir Thomas Fairfax, having had his cavalry worsted at Marston Moor, rode to safety through the enemy lines merely by removing the white handkerchief, which was the Parliamentarian token for that day, from his hat (see p. 98). The term 'Roundhead' probably originated from the cropped heads of the apprentices who championed the Parliamentarian cause before hostilities began, when the name was first used. It seems that at the beginning of the war some Parliamentarian officers lived up to their soubriquet by wearing their hair short, but soon shoulder-length hair styles were the fashion in both armies.

The New Model Army warrants a special mention, for although it should not be allowed to eclipse the fine record of many of the other armies that took part in the struggle it was the precursor of our regular army and the first successful attempt to weld together an efficient fighting machine. When it first took the field in May

1645 it was only one of many Parliamentarian armies and smaller formations – at this time, with the Scots, Parliament had about 70,000 troops on its pay roll. The First Civil War was now drawing to its close and one has, therefore, to look further ahead to see the New Model as an instrument of ultimate victory.

The need for a properly organized, disciplined and permanent force was first brought to the attention of Parliament by General Waller in June 1644, but the composition of the New Model underwent some paper changes and a good deal of delay at the hands of the Committee of Both Kingdoms. It was eventually decided that its total of 22,000 other ranks was to be derived from eleven regiments of horse, each of 600 men, twelve infantry regiments of 1,200 men each and 1,000 dragoons. Unfortunately the list of artillery for the New Model, which was reported to the House of Commons on 19 April 1645, was not printed in the Journals, but the army was provided with a formidable train of artillery and we know that the field guns were principally demi-culverins and sakers. The cavalry were well mounted on medium-weight horses of fifteen hands or just over, and were all volunteers. The infantry, however, were a scratch lot to start with. It was found impossible to make up their numbers even with pressed men and Royalist prisoners of war, and when they first took the field they were 4,000 short of establishment, although within a month or two their numbers had been made good, but with untrained recruits.

The question as to who was to command this new élite force caused some argument between the two Houses. The Lords were inclined to favour Essex or Manchester, but the Commons pressed the case strongly for Sir Thomas Fairfax, against whom there could be no complaint on military or other grounds. He was a professional soldier who had distinguished himself in the field, and he had taken no part in politics and so did not come under the ban imposed by the Self-denying Ordinance. This ordinance disallowed a member of either House to execute any office or command, military or civil.

There was at the time of the ordinance some dissatisfaction with the military leadership, and in December 1644 Oliver Cromwell and one or two others conceived this measure as a means of removing the incompetent Manchester, and even Essex, from their commands. The Lords at first threw the ordinance out, but the Commons won the day with their nominee and Sir Thomas Fairfax was appointed commander-in-chief on 21 January, with Philip Skippon as major-general of the foot and chief of staff. The post of lieutenant-general of the horse was not immediately filled; Cromwell was the obvious choice, but there were difficulties on account of the Self-Denying Ordinance, which the Lords eventually passed in April. However, Parliament could always make exceptions to its own decrees and Cromwell's continuing success in the field, and his own conviction that the Almighty would be seriously displeased if he resigned his command, seemed reasons enough to give him a series of extensions from the ensnaring coils of the ordinance, although his official position in the New Model was not confirmed until 10 June.

The problem of leadership was not confined to the New Model. Throughout the First Civil War there was on both sides a constant obfuscation of command. This was due largely to jealousy and petty squabbling, while the Parliamentarian generals were also confounded by committees. We have said that in its early stages this was an amateurish war; nevertheless in due course it produced commanding generals of some repute. Men like Montrose, Hopton and Newcastle for the King, and Lord Essex, Thomas Fairfax and William Waller for Parliament at times handled their armies with rare distinction, nor were there lacking men of competence, skill and daring among those who held lower rank: Oliver Cromwell, Philip Skippon, Marmaduke Langdale, Prince Maurice, Lords Astley, Digby and Byron, Sir Bevil Grenvile and William Balfour, to name but a few. Some of these men (and others like them), pre-eminent for their leadership and high capacities, were never touched by envy's brush, but unfortunately there were those who often became slaves to self-interest and faction, which at best manifested itself in a preference for local over national patriotism and at worst in insensate jealousy and damaging intrigue.

Many of the King's troubles in this respect emanated from his nephew Prince Rupert, who stands in a class by himself. Young, impulsive, brave and very sure of himself, he was inclined to treat with contempt Charles's older advisers and commanders. He quickly antagonized the first two Royalist commanders-in-chief (Lord Lindsey, killed at Edgehill, and the septuagenarian Lord Forth) by insisting on complete independence as general of the horse; he had little use for Lord Wilmot, and Lord Digby – among others – was jealous of his closeness to the King. A brilliant cavalry leader and a master of siege-craft, it was perhaps a mistake to make him commander-in-chief, for although completely tireless in the performance of exacting duties he lacked many of the qualities necessary for a successful commander of an army. Moreover, he had replaced the popular Forth, who although not outstanding had made no overt blunders and, unlike Rupert, had few enemies at court. The mercurial George Goring replaced Wilmot as general of the horse in August 1644. An ambitious, unscrupulous and somewhat dissolute man, he shared Rupert's audacity, powers of endurance and quick insight, but beyond that the two men had nothing in common and were the worst of friends. The King's generals must have tried his patience very sorely; yet he seldom made reproaches or uttered lamentations.

The divisions within the Parliamentarian army in some ways went deeper than those that Charles had to contend with, for they involved affairs of conscience. There were the inevitable petty quarrels and personal slights: Lord Essex and Sir William Waller disliked each other intensely, and Lord Manchester and Oliver Cromwell gravely mistrusted each other. There were also accusations of incompetence and cowardice, resulting on one occasion in Lord Saye's son Nat Fiennes being sentenced to death. But more disruptive than these was the dissension on the fate of the King, and more particularly on religion. The strong Anglican and Presbyterian element throughout Parliament and its army found its dogmas vitiated by the Independents, as the various sectaries of the old Separatists were now collectively called. These people, chief among whom was Cromwell, held differing political as well as religious views which deeply disturbed their more orthodox colleagues and put an almost unbearable strain on the Scottish alliance.

The Parliamentarian commanders were also a prey to the objurgations of controlling committees. Both sides set up county committees for the purpose of maintaining their armies in a particular county, but the higher command in the Royalist army was not fettered by frequent armchair operational advice from a collection of civilians. That the conduct of Parliament's war should have been in the hands of a committee is understandable, but commanders in the field can never give of their best when they know that they are constantly in danger of interference from a remote controlling authority. The Committee of Safety was succeeded by the Council of War, which in turn gave way to the Committee of Both Kingdoms when Scotland entered the war. To these committees Parliament delegated operational responsibility, until on 9 June 1645 Fairfax was informed that they were 'leaving it wholly to you who are upon the spot to do what by the advice of your council of war you shall judge most conducive to the public interest'. Thus, with future operations properly confined within the narrow ambit of personal command, Fairfax could prepare the way for a decisive punch and death grip.

Principal Battles and Engagements of the
First Civil War
in Chronological Order

1642: 23 September
Powick Bridge. The first engagement of the Civil War was a cavalry skirmish south of Worcester in the meadows surrounding Powick Bridge. Prince Rupert, while covering Sir John Byron's intended withdrawal from Worcester, defeated an advanced cavalry force of Lord Essex's main army under Nathaniel Fiennes.

1642: 23 October
Edgehill. The first major battle of the Civil War. The two armies were fairly evenly matched numerically with around 14,500 men apiece. The Earl of Essex commanded the Parliamentarian army, but although the King was present at the battle, and took an active part, he had delegated command of the Royalist army to the Earl of Lindsey, who was superseded by the Earl of Forth just before the battle began. The two armies were drawn up for battle shortly after midday, the Roundheads some two miles south of Kineton and the Royalists just north of Radway. Prince Rupert commanding the Royalist cavalry on the right wing and Lord Wilmot on the left were entirely successful in their first charge, but the fight in the centre was most stubbornly contested. The Royalist centre was gradually pressed back almost to its start line, and after three hours' hard fighting both armies had had enough. Victory in the field went to neither side, but the King had forced Essex to withdraw, leaving the road to London open. For full details of this battle see chapter 16.

1642: 12 and 13 November
Brentford and Turnham Green. On the morning of 12 November Prince Rupert attacked Denzil Holles's regiment under cover of a morning mist, and after a sharp engagement drove it back into Brentford. The battle in Brentford against Holles's regiment and that commanded by Lord Brooke was short and sharp and resulted in the Royalists gaining possession of the town. But on the following day King Charles found his way to London barred at Turnham Green by a large Parliamentarian army, which included the City trained bands. Charles felt unable to take on this large force with an army greatly weakened by cold and hunger. He withdrew to Reading and the threat to London was removed.

1642: 6 December
Tadcaster. Lord Newcastle, having won a victory at Pierce Bridge on 1 December, and now in command of all the Royalist forces in the north, attacked and defeated Lord Fairfax at Tadcaster. The victory was important, for it drove a wedge into the Parliamentarian defence of Yorkshire. This victory, however, was somewhat offset when Sir Thomas Fairfax (Lord Fairfax's son) captured Bradford, Leeds and Wakefield from Sir William Savile in January 1643, which successes forced Newcastle to fall back upon York.

1643: 19 January
Bradock Down. Sir Ralph Hopton and Sir Bevil Grenvile fell back with the Royalist army across the Tamar into Cornwall before Parliamentarian troops commanded by the Earl of Stamford. Once in Cornwall the Royalists were heavily reinforced by the Cornish trained bands and at Bradock Down, near Liskeard, Hopton and Grenvile utterly defeated Stamford and took more than 1,000 prisoners together with a number of guns and some ammunition.

1643: 2 and 4 March
Lichfield. The battle here, in which the Royalists lost the city, was a comparatively minor one, but in it Lord Brooke was killed while in command of the Parliamentarian forces. His death was a considerable blow to Parliament – there had even been talk of his succeeding Essex as commander-in-chief.

1643: 19 March
Hopton Heath. This successful Royalist skirmish, some two miles from Stafford, was part of the King's plan to regain Lichfield. It is chiefly notable because in the hour of victory the Royalist commander, the Earl of Northampton, was killed. As a sequel to this fight the King sent Prince Rupert to the Midlands where he took and sacked Birmingham on 3 April, and after a stiff resistance he gained Lichfield Close and Cathedral on 21 April.

1643: 16 May
Stratton. Following James Chudleigh's minor success against Sir Ralph Hopton at Sourton Down in Devon on 25 April, Lord Stamford decided to carry the war into Cornwall, for he had more than

double the amount of men under Hopton's command. He took up a nearly impregnable position near Stratton in the extreme north-west of Cornwall. Hopton advanced from Launceston to meet him, and the assault was entrusted to Sir Bevil Grenvile, who was familiar with every inch of the countryside. The battle was fiercely contested before the Cornishmen, sweeping up the hill in a four-pronged attack, put the enemy to flight, killing 300 men and capturing a further 1,500 including Chudleigh.

1643: 18 June
Chalgrove Field. Rupert, acting upon information from the turncoat Colonel Hurry, marched from Oxford on 17 June in an attempt to intercept a valuable treasure convoy and to deter Essex from his intended blockade of Oxford. He narrowly missed the convoy, but surprised some sleeping enemy troops in the village of Chinnor. While falling back on Oxford he was overtaken by the Roundheads commanded by Sir Philip Stapleton and John Hampden. Rupert, with considerable superiority of numbers, and having cleverly forced his enemy to fight at a disadvantage, routed them with his cavalry. John Hampden received a wound in the shoulder from which he died six days later.

1643: 30 June
Adwalton Moor. Lord Fairfax and his son Sir Thomas, realizing that they could not withstand a long siege in Bradford, marched out to give battle to Lord Newcastle's army, which although numerous comprised for the most part untrained peasants armed only with scythes. However, Newcastle did have 4,000 properly armed soldiers and this was sufficient to defeat the Roundheads decisively. The Fairfaxes retreated to Hull, and with Bradford captured other towns quickly fell, and soon the whole of the West Riding was in Royalist hands.

1643: 5 July
Lansdown. Lord Stamford's defeat at Stratton enabled Hopton to leave Cornwall and join forces with Prince Maurice and Lord Hertford. After an inconclusive affair against General Waller's army at Chewton Mendip on 12 June, both armies manoeuvred for position around Bath. Eventually

Marston
Moor ✕
✕ Tadcaster
✕ Adwalton   Hull ●
   Moor

Winceby ✕

Rowton Heath ✕   ✕ Nantwich   ✕ Newark

✕ Hopton Heath
✕ Lichfield

✕ Naseby

Powick Bridge ✕   ✕ Edgehill
                  ✕ Cropredy Bridge

● Oxford
✕ Chalgrove Field

● Bristol   ✕ Aldbourne Chase   ✕ Brentford
Lansdown ✕   ✕ Newbury
          ✕ Roundway   ♦ Basing House
            Down

✕ Langport   ✕ Cheriton

✕ Torrington
✕ Stratton   ● Sherborne
              Castle
     Exeter ●

Lostwithiel ✕   ✕ Bradock
                 Down

WFNW

Waller gained the commanding Lansdown Hill, and on 5 July Hopton's Cornishmen, again led by Sir Bevil Grenvile, forced their way against stiff opposition, which included well sited artillery, to close in hand-to-hand battle. The position was gained at heavy cost. The cavalry losses were extremely heavy, and worse still Sir Bevil Grenvile fell in the hour of victory.

1643: 13 July
Roundway Down. Waller had been defeated at Lansdown, but not destroyed. The Royalists were tired and short of supplies, particularly powder. They were further disheartened when, on the day after the battle, their general was seriously injured by the explosion of almost their last ammunition wagon. The army conveyed the wounded Hopton first to Chippenham then to Devises, where Waller laid siege to the town. The Royalist position was hopeless, and surrender would have been inevitable had not Prince Maurice brought cavalry relief from Oxford under Lord Wilmot. Waller withdrew his cavalry from the outskirts of Devizes to meet this threat on the chalk hill a mile above the town called Roundway Down. Here his cavalry, including Hesilrige's formidable 'Lobsters', was utterly defeated and scattered. The abandoned infantry soon surrendered. It was a total disaster for the Roundheads, who lost more than 1,500 men and all their cannon, ammunition and baggage.

1643: 23–6 July
Siege of Bristol. After the defeat at Roundway Down Waller withdrew towards London leaving the way clear for Rupert to join forces with the western army, and together, on 23 July, they laid siege to the important city of Bristol. On 26 July an assault from the Somerset side by Cornish troops was repulsed with heavy loss, but Rupert managed to slip in a posse of troops on the Gloucestershire side. Before the situation became completely desperate the governor, Nathaniel Fiennes, surrendered. He was later sentenced to death for incompetence (but not cowardice), which sentence was remitted. The capture of this city was an important prize for the Royalists.

1643: 28 August–4 September
Surrender of West Country towns. Sir John Digby's minor victory at Torrington against local levies won the towns of Barnstaple and Bideford for the Royalists at the end of August, and on Warwick's failure to relieve Exeter from the sea the city surrendered to Prince Maurice on 4 September.

1643: 18 September
Aldbourne Chase. On 26 August Lord Essex at the head of some 15,000 men marched from Hounslow to relieve Gloucester. Having attained his objective he so confused the King, who commanded the Royalist army, by skilful manoeuvring that he had reached Cricklade before the Royalists started in pursuit. Prince

Rupert at the head of a flying column came up with Essex's army – dangerously extended – at Aldbourne Chase, which lies between Chiseldon and Aldbourne. The action that followed was inconclusive, but it had the effect of slowing down the Roundhead army and allowing the Royalists to get to Newbury ahead of them. For fuller details see chapter 17.

1643: 20 September
First Battle of Newbury. Advancing from Wantage on 19 September Essex found Newbury already in the hands of the Royalist army. The way back to London was effectively barred, and to get there Essex would have to give battle. The First Battle of Newbury was fought to the west of the town round the area of Wash Common, Enborne Heath and Skinner's Green, the fighting being heaviest at Round Hill, Wash Farm and Enborne Heath, although the opposing lines extended almost to the river Kennet. It was a confused battle in which artillery played its most important part in all the Civil War battles. The cavalry fight on the southern flank was a fierce affair in which the Royalists came off best, but their infantry fought poorly. As at Edgehill there was no clear-cut victory, but the Royalists, finding themselves short of powder, left the field during the night. For full details see chapter 17.

1643: 11 October
Winceby. This was a small cavalry engagement between a Royalist force commanded by Sir John Henderson, Governor of Newark, and Oliver Cromwell, in which Cromwell (whose horse was shot under him during the scuffle), helped by Sir Thomas Fairfax, put the Royalists to flight. Many were killed in the flight, and others drowned in the waters of the fens.

1643: 11 and 12 October
Siege of Hull. On the same day as Cromwell's victory at Winceby the garrison of Hull, which was under the command of Lord Fairfax, made a sortie against Lord Newcastle's besieging force and drove them from many of their strongpoints, capturing some cannon. On the next day Newcastle raised the siege, and on 20 October Lincoln surrendered to Lord Manchester.

1644: 25 January
Nantwich. Lord Byron in Cheshire had been reinforced by Royalist contingents arriving from Ireland and with these he hoped to clear the county for the King. He laid siege to Nantwich, the only important town in Cheshire still held by Parliament, but on 25 January Sir William Brereton, whose troops had recently been joined by those under Sir Thomas Fairfax, attacked Byron's besieging army, which had been divided on either side of the river Weaver. Byron was forced to fight against superior numbers on ground very disadvantageous to cavalry. Defeat was made certain when troops from the Nantwich garrison sallied forth and took him in the rear. Byron and most of the cavalry

escaped, but more than 1,000 prisoners were taken, including Colonel George Monck. Many of these prisoners enrolled themselves under Parliament.

1644: 22 March
Relief of Newark. The Royalist commander at Newark was Sir Richard Byron (Lord Byron's brother). The town was of extreme importance to the Royalists as a link between their forces in the north and south. Sir John Meldrum together with Lord Willoughby had laid siege to the town and the King ordered Prince Rupert to march to its relief. Rupert outmanoeuvred Meldrum and on 22 March he surrendered, being forced to leave his siege artillery and a large quantity of muskets and pikes to the victors. It was a very important Royalist success.

1644: 29 March
Cheriton. This was the first decisive major victory that the Parliamentarian army achieved, and it had important consequences. It was fought between General Waller, commanding a Roundhead army of some 10,000 men, and Lords Forth and Hopton with a numerically inferior force of not above 6,000 troops. Cheriton is east of Winchester and close to Alresford, which town the Royalists managed to gain before the battle. Waller's army encamped for the night of 28 March in the fields below Hinton Ampner and the battle was fought to the north of their encampment and immediately to the west of Cheriton Wood, which played an important part in the early stages. There is some dispute as to the exact positions held by the two armies, and the details of this battle together with an account of the battle will be found in chapter 18.

1644: 29 June
Cropredy Bridge. In this inconclusive engagement north of Banbury, Charles, commanding an army of at least 9,000, which included 4,000 cavalry, was attacked by an army inferior in numbers commanded by General Waller, who had the assistance of Major-General Browne. The armies had been marching parallel to each other on either side of the river Cherwell, until Charles, thinking to intercept a force coming to the aid of Waller, pushed forward with his leading troops, creating a dangerous gap between the forward and rear elements of his army. Waller, seizing his opportunity, forced a crossing of the river at Cropredy Bridge, putting 1,500 horse, 1,000 foot and eleven guns onto the east bank, and marched north with the bulk of this force to attack the King's forward element. Lord Cleveland hurrying up with cavalry from the rear had little difficulty in defeating the small force left by Waller to guard the bridge. Waller then found himself trapped between the two halves of the King's army and only with difficulty did he regain the bridge and cross to safety. Casualties were not heavy on either side, but Waller lost all of his eleven guns and a number of standards.

1644: 2 July
Marston Moor. By the beginning of June the Marquis of Newcastle's army was tightly beleaguered in York. Prince Rupert had the King's permission to march to its relief, an operation which he executed with considerable skill. He then decided, although his instructions were not specific on this point, to give battle to the combined Parliamentarian and Scottish army that had been besieging the city. Accordingly, on the morning of 2 July he moved his army to the west of York and occupied ground to the north of the Long Marston–Tockwith road, where later in the day he was joined by Lord Newcastle's troops. The allied army deployed for battle on the high ground south of the road. No action took place during the day, but the allied commanders decided to attack in the evening. The battle, which was fought partly in a thunderstorm and partly under a harvest moon, resulted in a Royalist defeat, and the north was lost to the King. Full details in chapter 19.

1644: 1 September
Tippermuir. This brief fight was Montrose's first success for Charles in Scotland. In command of about 3,000 men, most of them poorly armed and with no cavalry, he defeated a force of 7,000 under Lord Elcho three miles west of Perth.

1644: 2 September
Lostwithiel. Lord Essex, commander-in-chief of the Parliamentarian army, advanced into Cornwall on 26 July at the head of about 10,000 men. The King, with some 16,000 troops, came after him and was at Liskeard by 2 August. Essex had taken up a defensive position a little way north of Lostwithiel with his headquarters in that town, and he sent 1,000 foot down to Fowey to hold the port. During August the King was joined by Sir Richard Grenville with 1,800 foot and 600 horse and on the 26th he sent Lord Goring (who had joined him shortly after Marston Moor) on a wide flanking movement to seize St Blaisey and the port of Par. Essex, realizing he could not now expect reinforcements either by land or sea, hoped to avoid battle against a numerically superior force and managed to evacuate Sir William Balfour and 2,000 cavalry along the unguarded Lostwithiel–Liskeard road. The foot fell back towards Fowey, and being pressed took up a position on a line from Tywardreath to Castle Dore where they were attacked in their centre and on their left flank by the troops from St Blaisey. The situation quickly became hopeless, and Essex abandoned the army and took boat for Plymouth leaving General Skippon to surrender. More than 6,000 men laid down their arms upon generous terms, and the Royalists took forty guns and a large quantity of small arms.

1644: 13 September
Aberdeen. Although Montrose had a better equipped army than the one that fought at Tippermuir, his cavalry only numbered forty-four horse and he was inferior by about 1,000 men to the Covenanters under Lord Burleigh, who were drawn up to meet his advance in a strong position on a hillside south-west of the city. Burleigh attacked the flanks of the Royalist army with his cavalry, but on both wings they were beaten back in disarray. The Covenanters' centre was then charged by Montrose's Irish brigade, whose determined advance proved too much for Burleigh's men. Montrose had now seriously disabled two of the three Covenanter armies.

1644: 27 October
Second Battle of Newbury. In the course of his march back from Cornwall to Oxford, Charles found the way barred by a large Parliamentarian army in the neighbourhood of Newbury. He took up a position north of the town covering the strongpoints Speen, Donnington and Shaw House. In the absence of Essex, Manchester commanded the Roundhead army and had about 19,000 men as against 12,000 Royalists. The Roundhead plan was a daring one involving a wide flanking march of some fifteen miles by Waller with 12,000 men round the front of the Royalists to come in on their left flank at Speen; Manchester was to hold the enemy in play in front of Shaw House. The flank march carried out on 26–7 October was entirely successful and Waller gained some measure of surprise. Fighting on the Royalists' left flank (under Prince Maurice) was severe and Speen was lost, but Waller failed to break through, and Manchester's attack, which did not go in until 4 p.m. on the 26th, also made little progress. In the gathering darkness the battle ended indecisively. Charles considered his position untenable, and early the next day withdrew to Oxford.

1645: 2 February
Inverlochy. Montrose, returning from the harrying of Clan Campbell, was nearly trapped in the Great Glen between Lord Seaforth's army of 5,000 in his front and 3,000 embittered Argylls under Duncan Campbell in his rear. Being unable to fight his way out with only 1,500 men, Montrose decided to double back by a circuitous route and surprise the Campbells at Inverlochy. In bitter weather and without much food or any warmth Montrose marched his men along the steep, treacherous ledges beneath the mountain peaks. And at dawn, from the shadow of Ben Nevis, his men fell upon the astounded Campbells encamped around Inverlochy Castle. Argyll at once took to flight, but Duncan Campbell put up what resistance he could. However, the furious charge of Montrose's and Alasdair Macdonald's men proved too much for the Campbells and the fight was soon over. Duncan Campbell fought bravely and was killed together with some 1,500 of the clan. Montrose lost only a handful of men but among them a valued friend in Sir Thomas Ogilvy.

1645: 9 May
Auldearn. Colonel Hurry, commanding the Covenanting army, attempted to lure Montrose into country that was known to be unfriendly to him, and there give battle in circumstances favourable to himself. He accordingly fell back in front of Montrose from Elgin almost to Nairn, and then suddenly turned upon his pursuer hoping to gain surprise. Surprise was not achieved, although Montrose had little time in which to take up a suitable defensive position. He occupied the high ground just north of the village of Auldearn with a small force of some 500 men under Alasdair Macdonald, and kept the main body of his troops on the reverse slope of the ridge running to the south of the village. Hurry made the mistake that Montrose hoped he would of attacking Macdonald with his entire force, which left his right flank open to attack from the Royalists' main line of battle. Macdonald's men were nearly worsted in a very fierce battle for the hill, but the Gordons, who formed the main part of Montrose's troops on the reverse slope, smashed the Covenanters' flank and allowed Macdonald to rally his Irishmen and complete the defeat of the Covenanters. For a fuller account of this battle see chapter 7.

1645: 14 June
Naseby. This was the last major battle of the First Civil War. The defeat of the Royalist army under the King and Prince Rupert by the New Model Army under Sir Thomas Fairfax virtually destroyed the King's military machine. The battle was fought over the undulating ground immediately north of Naseby. Fairfax with more than 13,000 men, including 6,500 cavalry under Oliver Cromwell and Henry Ireton, was opposed by only some 7,500 Royalists. Prince Rupert on the Royalist right wing met with initial success, but the King's cavalry on the left was defeated by Cromwell. In the centre the Royalist infantry fought with great determination and bravery, but after three hours' hard slogging were eventually overpowered by weight of numbers and captured almost to a man. The battle is discussed in chapter 20.

1645: 2 July
Alford. It was now the turn of Montrose to draw the Covenanters away from a strong position into an area where he thought he had better prospects of offering battle successfully. He drew the Covenanting General Baillie southwards from Strathbogie, and prepared to meet him on high ground south of the river Don at a point about a mile to the west of the present town of Alford. Both armies were almost equal in infantry, but Baillie had superiority in cavalry. He was, however, at a disadvantage in having to ford the river before bringing his men to the attack, and Lord Gordon, on Montrose's right, gave him little chance to regroup after crossing the Don. In a fierce fight with troops under Lord Balcarres, Gordon succeeded in driving Baillie's cavalry off the field, and then turned on the Covenanting centre. At the same time Lord

Aboyne and Colonel O'Kean advanced against the enemy. Montrose gained the victory, but in the pursuit Lord Gordon, his great friend and able lieutenant, was killed. For a fuller account of this battle see chapter 7.

1645: 10 July
Langport. After the Roundhead victory at Naseby, Leicester surrendered and Parliament urged Fairfax to march to the relief of Taunton. This town had long been a tiresome thorn in the King's western side: the garrison under its intrepid commander Robert Blake had resisted three sieges. On 4 July Lord Goring raised the siege for the last time and fell back towards Bridgwater, taking up a strong position in difficult, waterlogged ground near Langport. Goring was outnumbered, and a feint towards Taunton, intended to confuse Fairfax's army, was only partly successful. Fairfax attacked Goring's main position with 1,500 musketeers, backed up by elements of two cavalry regiments and a strong infantry reserve. At first Goring's men fought desperately in the marshy fields bordering the rivers Yeo and Parret, but they were broken and routed. Cromwell's troops, which had not been engaged, joined in the pursuit. About 2,000 prisoners were taken, and others, less fortunate, fell prey to the clubmen. Goring's army, virtually the King's last hope, was destroyed.

1645: 15 August
Kilsyth. Not long after Montrose's victory at Alford he received news of King Charles's defeat at Naseby and he clearly saw the need to cross the border and go to the King's aid. By the middle of August Montrose had under his command his largest army since he first commenced operations, but Baillie was still capable of putting into the field a greater force, and he was not prepared to let Montrose slip away. The two armies met in some meadows a mile north-east of Kilsyth. At that time these meadows formed a basin of what is now a reservoir, and Baillie occupied a commanding position on the high ground which gave him a considerable advantage. However, the Covenanting Committee, which usually accompanied the army in the field, ordered Baillie to carry out a dangerous flank march in full view of the enemy so as to prevent any possibility of Montrose's army escaping from what they confidently considered was a well set trap. The result was disastrous, because before long Baillie was to find his army cut in two. There was, however, a fierce fight on Montrose's left flank, which had become threatened by the advance portion of Baillie's army. The situation here was brought under control by the veteran Lord Airlie and the Ogilvys, while Alasdair Macdonald, as impetuous as ever, had brought a seemingly unwise attack on Baillie's hilltop position to a successful conclusion. Baillie's defeat was absolute and his infantry almost annihilated. Montrose was, for the time being, master of Scotland. For a fuller account see chapter 7.

1645: 15 August
Capture of Sherborne Castle. Once the castle walls had been breached by a mine, the Royalist garrison under Sir Lewis Dyves was unable to hold out. The siege is notable for the action of the Dorset clubmen. These local peasants came out in strength to meet Cromwell on Hambledon Hill, and, although principally interested in the defence of their properties, they were, in Dorset, in league with the Royalists during the siege of Sherborne.

1645: 23 August and 11 September
Capture of Bristol. With Sherborne Castle taken the way was open for Fairfax to reduce the most important stronghold still left to the Royalists, Bristol. Prince Rupert commanded between 1,500 and 2,000 men in this city but the defences were weak in places and there was a plague epidemic raging. Summoned to surrender on 4 September Prince Rupert prevaricated for some days until on the 10th Fairfax lost patience and mounted an attack. The garrison around Prior's Hill Fort resisted strongly, but was ultimately overborne and slaughtered. Unable to stem Fairfax's cavalry, who had gained entrance where the walls were virtually down, Rupert, on being again offered terms, surrendered the city on 11 September.

1645: 13 September
Philiphaugh. Montrose, the recent victor of Kilsyth and many other battles, now found himself with a pathetically small army of 500 Irish infantry and perhaps 1,000 mounted gentlemen – there were no other ranks among his cavalry. David Leslie, on receiving information of the weak state of the Royalist army, carried out a remarkably swift march to take Montrose's men by surprise as they were camped just below Selkirk. Attacking through the morning mist with some 4,000 horse the result was never in doubt. Montrose and most of the cavalry made good their escape, but only about fifty Irishmen received quarter.

1645: 24 September
Rowton Heath. A cavalry battle fought in difficult cavalry country two miles south-east of Chester between Sir Marmaduke Langdale (Royalist) and Major-General Sydenham Poyntz. Poyntz was forced to attack and was at first worsted, but obtaining infantry support from Colonel Michael Jones, who was besieging Chester, he eventually chased the Northern Horse off the battlefield. This defeat, together with an unsuccessful sally under Lord Lichfield (who was killed) by the Chester garrison, virtually sealed the fate of the city. Charles marched out of it the next day with 2,400 horse: Lord Byron surrendered the city on 3 February 1646.

1645: 14 October
The sack of Basing House. Basing House, the home of the Catholic Marquis of Winchester, stood athwart the London–Winchester road and occupied a position of great strategic importance. It had been held for the Royalists throughout the Civil War, and on 11 October it refused Cromwell's summons to surrender. The heavy guns soon made irreparable breeches in the walls and at 6 a.m. on the morning of the 14th the defenders were totally unable to repel the storming parties. The destruction of life and property that followed was exacerbated by sectarian idealogy. The house was looted and completely destroyed. More than 100 people were killed.

1646: 16 February
Torrington. Lord Hopton, with a force of 5,000, most of which were cavalry, did what he could to hold this Devon town. When patrol action flared up unintentionally after dark, Fairfax decided to mount a full-scale attack. After a brief struggle some of Hopton's cavalry, fighting in narrow streets unsupported by infantry, broke, and he would have been unable to hold the town even if his entire stock of powder – stored in the church – had not blown up. The engagement is chiefly notable as being virtually the last in the First Civil War in which there was organized fighting.

1646
End of war. The loss of Torrington left the way open to the west: Launceston and Bodmin were quickly occupied: Exeter surrendered on 13 April and Barnstaple and Dunster Castle a week later. Lord Astley's 3,000 men, confronted at Stow-on-the-Wold (21 March) by Roundheads under Brereton and John Birch, showed no wish to fight. Charles gave himself up to the Scots at the beginning of May. Newark surrendered on 6 May, and when Oxford hauled down the flag on 24 June the First Civil War had ended.

CHAPTER 2

Edgehill

23 October 1642

Virtually the entire battlefield is now Ministry of Defence land and being a high security area no admission is possible for the general public, although those with a special purpose or interest can apply for a pass from the headquarters of the C.A.D Kineton. However, an excellent panoramic view of the field of battle can be obtained from Edgehill itself – especially if the visitor has binoculars.

Edgehill is about seven miles north-west of Banbury off the A422, and is the long ridge that connects that road with the Kineton–Knowle End road (B4086). Just opposite the Castle Inn is a car park; a public footpath leads through the wood to fields immediately above Radway Grange, and from here there is an uninterrupted view to Kineton and beyond. The main fight took place south of Thistle Farm, over what was then much less wooded country. Thistle Farm is now used by the army and Battle Farm has disappeared. There are two monuments; one on the Kineton road, which is sometimes said to mark the left of the Parliamentarian line before the battle, but is almost certainly too far to the north-west for this; and the other by the copse known as Graveground Coppice, where many of the dead were buried – but that one is in M.O.D. territory. Local tradition has it that the King had his standard at the tower on Edgehill before the Royalist army began their descent of the hill, in a field at the junction of the Westcote Farm–Kineton–Radway track at the beginning of the fight, and probably near Battleton Holt when it was captured. Prince Rupert's charge took place immediately to the left of the Kineton road and parallel to it.

After King Charles had raised his standard at Nottingham (see p. 18) and determined to regain his former authority through what he hoped would be one decisive trial of strength, neither side was in a hurry to put the issue to the test. The King's army was at first too weak to undertake successfully any military enterprise, and Essex did not march out of London until almost three weeks after Charles had laid down the gage.

Clearly Essex's main task was to ensure that he put his army between London and the King. This he failed to do, and he is often blamed for being slow, indecisive and a poor strategist. Some of

Left: Robert Devereux,
Earl of Essex, first
commander of the
Parliamentarian army
Below: Charles I on the
eve of the Battle of
Edgehill

these labels stick, although he was lamentably served by his intelligence, not having definite news of the King's advance on London until six days after Charles had left Shrewsbury on 12 October. Furthermore, after Essex left London he dissipated his force quite considerably, leaving garrisons at important places such as Worcester, Hereford and Banbury. It is easy with hindsight to see that had he concentrated his army in the Warwick area he would have outnumbered the Royalists and possibly won a decisive victory, and that by holding on to Worcester for too long he allowed Charles to slip by him. But so long as the Royalists were recruiting on the Welsh marches Essex probably considered it important to keep the south and west Midlands protected.

Whatever his reasons for holding too far to the west, Essex, on reaching Kineton on the night of 22 October, with an incomplete army and artillery train, found that the King had stolen a march on him. Charles spent the night of 21 October at Southam and marched to Edgcote the next day. He had, therefore, a clear run to London. However, during the night of the 22nd information concerning the whereabouts of the Roundhead army came in from Prince Rupert's patrols, and the King decided to take his nephew's advice and postpone the intended attack on Banbury in favour of giving Essex battle. Accordingly the army was ordered to occupy Edgehill.

Owing to their wide overnight dispersion it was gone midday before the Royalist assembly was complete. We are told that it was a bright, cold morning, and as the King's men looked down from their commanding height there stretched before them a flat but beautiful landscape, a scene of pastoral peace with tiny farmsteads, lush meadows and hedges aflame with scarlet hips. But if the King's men had leisure to enjoy this enchanting view, his generals were more concerned with the advance of the Parliamentarian army more than a mile below them.

Throughout all the preliminaries to this battle Essex's staff work, and particularly his intelligence, seems to have been consistently bad. He had a spy in the King's camp and yet it was not until he was on his way to worship in Kineton church (probably about 8 a.m.) that he learned of the Royalist army's change of plan, and that they were assembling only three miles away. The Roundheads' billets, like those of the Royalists, were very widely dispersed, and no arrangements had been made for the army to concentrate early on that Sunday morning. Essex did not, therefore, have his army deployed for battle some two miles south of Kineton until almost the same time as the Royalist assembly was

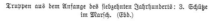

Truppen aus dem Anfange des siebzehnten Jahrhunderts: 3. Schütze im Marsch. (Ebd.)

Truppen aus dem Anfange des siebzehnten Jahrhunderts: 2. Schütze Pulver ins Rohr schüttend. (Ebd.)

Arquebusier marching and holding his arquebus (left) and loading his arquebus (right)

complete on Edgehill. Both armies now remained motionless, both poised for battle but neither anxious to strike the first blow. Essex was clearly not prepared to attack uphill, so if Charles wished to engage he would have to come down to the plain. The Royalist army began the steep descent about 1 p.m.

Although Essex fought at Edgehill with an incomplete army, he was certainly not inferior in numbers, and it seems that the two armies were fairly well matched numerically with around 14,500 men each. Royalist morale was high, for exactly a month before Prince Rupert had gained the better of an untidy skirmish at Powick Bridge, just south of Worcester. Both parties had been taken unawares, but Rupert's speed of action and élan won the fight. The Cavaliers had the satisfaction of seeing 1,000 Roundhead horse and dragoons put to ignominious flight.

However, this boost for morale was somewhat offset by dissensions among the higher command that came to a head while the army was preparing to deploy for battle. Charles was, of course, the titular head of the army, but he had delegated command to the Earl of Lindsey, and Prince Rupert had been given the independent command of the cavalry – a fact that had annoyed Lindsey. While the army was at Shrewsbury it had been joined by a much abler soldier than Lindsey who, like Rupert, had fought under Gustavus Adolphus: this was the Scottish veteran Patrick Ruthven,

Earl of Forth. He now supported Rupert in advising the King to deploy for battle after the Swedish fashion, rather than the Dutch, which was what Lindsey favoured. The Swedish brigade formation, with two forward wings, a withdrawn centre and an advance element of musketeers, was much more flexible than the Dutch, but needed experienced men if it was to work effectively. In the circumstances Lindsey was probably right to advocate the simpler Dutch formation (and in fact the result was a sort of compromise), but the King overruled him, whereupon he resigned his command and put himself at the head of his own regiment. Lord Forth succeeded him as commander-in-chief.

Prince Rupert retained his independent cavalry command and was himself on the right of the Royalist line, having under his immediate command a squadron of the Lifeguard and four regiments of uneven strength – perhaps a total of 1,700 men. The cavalry on the left was under Lord Wilmot, who had five regiments comprising 755 men in the first line and 300 in the second.* The Royalist foot, consisting of five brigades, was drawn up with three brigades forward and two in the second line. The strength of the brigades was uneven and their armament even more so. The brigade commanders were Charles Gerard, Richard Feilding, Henry Wentworth, John Belasyse, and Sir Nicholas Byron. Most of the brigades had three regiments – Feilding's had five – and the total foot was probably no more than 11,000. The infantry was not up to strength in musketeers, and there were a good many men fighting only with the most elementary weapons. There were some 1,000 dragoons operating in advance of the cavalry, and the army had fourteen light cannon and six heavy pieces. The siting of the artillery must be speculation, for there is little reliable contemporary evidence. Probably most, if not all, of the light pieces were allotted to the brigades and placed between the forward regiments, while the heavy demi-cannon and culverins were sited well in the rear and certainly at one time were firing from the lower slopes of Edgehill, having been brought down the steepest part with the utmost difficulty. As the battle proceeded they were probably hauled up the road towards Battleton Holt.

* These and some other figures for the two armies engaged at Edgehill are taken from Brigadier Peter Young's *Edgehill 1642*. He admits that his calculations are only approximate, in the absence of official strength returns, but after studying the various suggestions put forward by historians past and present it seems to the writer that Brigadier Young's figures—the result of deep research—are probably as near correct as we shall get.

The Royalist army was deployed for battle just north of Radway with the right wing on – or possibly a little beyond – the Kineton–Knowle End road and its left in the vicinity of Brixfield Farm. Certain familiar features of the battlefield were not present in 1642. Edgehill had hardly any trees on it: Radway church stood a little to the south of the present one; The Oaks and the two spinneys, Graveground Coppice and Battleton Holt, were not there. But the country, particularly in front of the Royalist left, was enclosed by a network of hedges – which was probably the reason for Lord Wilmot's being allotted the larger body of dragoons.

It cannot be said with certainty exactly where Lord Essex deployed his men for battle; in most contemporary accounts the landmarks are hazy and features exaggerated. Sir James Ramsey, another veteran with Swedish experience, was in command of the left wing, and he has left a fairly detailed account of his tactical dispositions. There is also a report written directly after the battle and signed by four brigade commanders, which tells us that the left wing had to be considerably extended, because the wind was much to the Royalists' advantage. From neither can it be determined exactly where the left wing rested, but probably on the Kineton–Knowle End road near Radway Ground, with the line running through the southern end of Graveground Coppice to a little way beyond The Oaks.

Lord Essex, who favoured the Dutch formation and tactics, had three brigades each of around 4,000 men; that commanded by Charles Essex was on Ramsey's right and slightly in the rear, and it had four regiments in line; Sir John Meldrum's brigade was on Charles Essex's right with three regiments in line and one in the rear; and the third brigade, commanded by Thomas Ballard, was behind Essex's in support of the left wing, and some of his musketeers were interspersed between Ramsey's horse, and also placed *en potence* on the extreme left. There is some difficulty over the position of the remaining horse. Lord Feilding had his regiment on the right of Meldrum's brigade and perhaps all the 700 Parliamentarian dragoons were on the extreme right. It is probable that Balfour's and Stapleton's regiments were placed in the rear of Meldrum's brigade to strengthen that part of the line which was weakest in infantry. In all there were forty-two troops of horse totalling about 2,200 men, around 12,000 infantrymen, 700 dragoons and an artillery train of which we have few details, but in numbers of guns it exceeded the King's.

The fight at Edgehill falls into four fairly well defined phases. A brief preliminary, and virtually harmless, cannonade; the Royalist cavalry advance, which was successful on both flanks; the main battle in which two Roundhead cavalry regiments mauled the Royalist infantry so badly as to prevent what looked like being a decisive victory; and a state of utter exhaustion with the Royalists back more or less on their starting line and the Roundheads unable to do more than leave them there.

Possibly to tempt Charles down the hill – and if so it succeeded admirably – we know from a statement by Edmund Ludlow that Essex opened the fight by ordering his gunners to fire into the enemy, and they laid their aim at what appeared to be the King's entourage. The ball fell short and the place is known to this day as Bullet Hill. But a slightly more intensive, although equally ineffective, artillery duel took place when both armies were deployed for battle. Its immediate result was to make Prince Rupert, always eager to be at the throat of his adversary, decide it was time to charge Sir James Ramsey's force, which was awaiting him up the Kineton road.

Rupert, for all his impulsiveness, found time to ride round his troops instructing their commanders to keep close order and to use their swords only, until such time as they had penetrated the enemy lines. What he failed to do – and it is difficult to blame Lord Forth for this, for Rupert had an independent command – was to provide for a proper cavalry reserve other than the small band of fifty Pensioners. This omission was to cost the Royalists dear. We have a picture of a well controlled, steady advance at a pace no faster than a trot. The dragoons, under Colonel James Usher, had already done good work in chasing the enemy musketeers from hedge and ditch; nevertheless, this splendid array of cavalry, riding almost knee to knee, was assailed by cannon fire and the rattle of intense musketry – most of which did little harm.

On nearing the enemy the pace would have been increased; and for Ramsey's men, most of whom had had no previous experience of warfare, to the terrifying spectacle of this concentrated charge was to be added the consternation of treachery. It seems that Rupert may have known that a gentleman, with the singularly inappropriate name of Sir Faithfull Fortescue, was planning to lead his troop over to the Royalists at the moment of attack. This he did, but in their haste to perform this act of treachery some of the men failed to remove their orange scarves, and about eighteen of the troop were killed by their new allies. Their desertion, coupled with the lines of Rupert's horse bearing down upon them in irresistible strength, was too much for Ramsey's men who, with few exceptions, turned away from the flailing swords and firing pistols and made all speed for Kineton, hotly pursued by the victorious Cavaliers. Nor was Prince Rupert able to check more than a very small portion of them; this was finally achieved by John Hampden's force, whom they met on the Warwick road north of Kineton. Thus almost the entire right wing of the Royalist army vanished from the battle.

It was much the same story on the left flank, but here the opposition was less numerous and through the efforts of one or two determined officers not all of the men went plundering in Kineton. Lord Wilmot's advance was almost simultaneous to that of Prince Rupert, but he had more difficult country to cross. The dragoons to his front, under Sir Arthur Aston, had done as good if not better work than that done by Usher's men on the right, and Wilmot had only Lord Feilding's cavalry and Sir William Fairfax's infantry regiments to deal with. It is possible that had these two regiments made any show at all, the two cavalry regiments under Balfour and Stapleton would have come to their assistance; but Wilmot's men went through Feilding's regiment as a cutter through corn, and Fairfax's soldiers did not stay to argue the toss. However, Sir Charles Lucas, Lord Grandison and one or two others managed to rally some of the triumphant Cavaliers before they had gone too far, and brought them back to take a further part in the battle. In both these charges – particularly Rupert's – the Roundheads almost certainly suffered considerable casualties, for although plunder may have been the victors' principal aim we can be sure that there were those among them unmoved by the process of death and mutilation.

Sergeant-Major-General Sir Jacob Astley, possibly the most experienced soldier of them all, had command of the Royalist foot. His well known prayer, 'O Lord, Thou knowest how busy I must be this day. If I forget Thee, do not Thou forget me', followed by his exhortation, 'March on, boys', set the infantry in motion about the same time as the two cavalry brigades began their charge. The advance proceeded at a steady pace, for regiments six deep in the ranks cannot be hurried and still keep station. The attack was to be launched with all five brigades in line, and as they marched Gerard's and Byron's brigades moved forward into the gaps between the three originally deployed in the front line. It must have seemed to the Roundhead infantry watching this long wall of red, blue and buff, their steel glinting in the October sun, that nothing could stop the onslaught. Already their left wing was in disarray, for when Ramsey's men broke the horse had stampeded through Denzil Holles's regiment, and bravely as Holles struggled

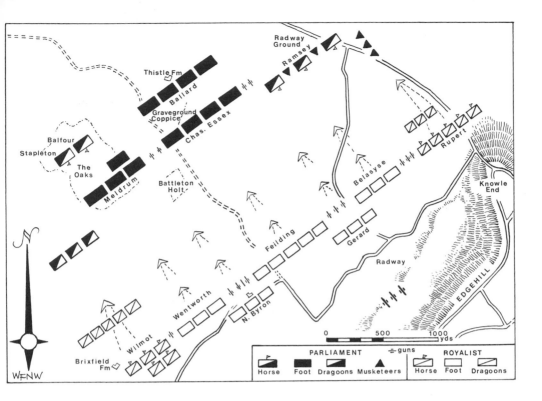

Above: Battle of Edgehill: the armies deployed at the start
Below: Battle of Edgehill

to maintain some semblance of control, only with difficulty did he prevail upon three companies to stand. Worse still, Charles Essex's brigade had left the field without firing a shot; Rupert's whirlwind to their left and the sight of the Royalist columns to their front had quite overcome their courage. What was there to prevent the utter destruction of Parliament's army? The answer lay in two not very large cavalry regiments.

Amid the smoke and carnage of an ever-shifting infantry battle it is not easy for the participants to know exactly what is happening on their immediate front, let alone along the rest of the line. In consequence we get a number of somewhat confusing personal accounts from which to piece together what probably happened on that October day almost 350 years ago. We can be fairly sure that Stapleton's and Balfour's regiments (Stapleton on the right) had formed up behind Sir John Meldrum's brigade, and that there must have been a good many gaps in the Parliamentarian line, for out of twelve regiments and forty-two troops of cavalry there were now only seven regiments and fifteen troops left on the field. It seems, therefore, that the cavalry had no need to ride round the flank to attack, but that they could easily have passed through the infantry to meet the advancing Royalists in a frontal charge.

This they almost certainly did, even though some accounts say that the whole Royalist line had come to push-of-pike before any cavalry engagement, because Wentworth's brigade, which was on the left of the Royalist line, was not attacked by the cavalry and could scarcely have been bypassed. Stapleton rode at Sir Nicholas Byron's brigade and after stubborn fighting was repulsed, or at any rate held, by the courage of the pikemen; but Balfour had complete success against Richard Feilding's brigade, and scattering two regiments he carved his way to the battery of heavy guns and cut their traces. On his way back he was fired upon by his own artillery. Fortunately the guns were manned by Stapleton's cavalrymen, as the gunners had fled, so the damage was slight. At this stage of the battle the King, seeing the discomfiture of his centre, sent the young princes (the future Charles II and Duke of York) back to Edgehill and himself rode forward to encourage his infantry, exposing himself for a time to considerable danger.

At the time of Balfour's return to the fighting line, Byron's brigade – now with one flank in the air – had been mauled but was still defiant; on his left Wentworth's regiments were virtually unscathed, but at the right of the Royalist line the brigades under Belasyse and Gerard were being hard pressed by Ballard. Lord Essex, who had been fighting in the forefront of the battle, pike

Prince Rupert's charge at Edgehill, after which almost the entire
Royalist right wing vanished from the battle

in hand, now ordered Lord Robartes's and Sir William Constable's regiments of foot to join Balfour and Stapleton in a combined attack upon Byron. The fighting here was some of the fiercest of the whole battle, for in Byron's brigade were the Lifeguard and Lindsey's regiment, the pride of the Royalist infantry. But fighting at push-of-pike to their front, and taken in the flank and rear by the cavalry, the brigade gradually gave ground. Sir Edmund Verney, who carried the Banner Royal, was killed and the standard snatched from his dying grasp (it was recovered that evening by the courage of Captain – later Sir John – Smith), while Lord Lindsey was mortally wounded and his son, Lord Willoughby d'Eresby, who went to his assistance, was captured.

It is difficult to know how Wentworth's brigade was employed at this time, for its three regiments would seem to have had only one opposed to it. Out of Meldrum's brigade two regiments were fighting with the cavalry against Byron, and Sir William Fairfax's men had fled the field some time previously, so presumably only Sir John's own regiment was opposing Wentworth. It was as well, for this brigade retiring in good order enabled the guns (which Balfour had been unable to spike) to open up with case shot, and with the help of the returning cavalry this stabilized the Royalist line during its withdrawal. While all this was going on Colonel Lucas led the 200 troopers whom he had managed to hold back from the pursuit on the left against Essex's rear. This could have been serious for the Roundheads had Lucas's men not got side-tracked into capturing the colours of those formations that had already decided to make for Kineton. Nevertheless they were able to add to the confusion that was now becoming general over the entire field.

The battle had started about 3 p.m. and only darkness was to put an end to it. In the failing light the cavalry began to return – and there were those who felt sure that had the horse been able to deliver a further charge at this crucial stage the Royalists would have won a decisive victory. It is impossible to say; but clearly neither men nor horses were in a fit state to charge, even had darkness not intervened. We cannot blame Rupert for failing to halt his troops once committed, for it is an almost impossible task; but had Sir John Byron's men on the right and Lord Digby's on the left been kept in reserve the story of the Civil War might have been quite different and many battles left unfought. As it was, all that the cavalry was capable of doing was to shore up the infantry line as, fighting every yard of the way and somehow still in possession of their guns, whose traces Balfour had cut, the

Royalists fell back pivoting on their right flank to a line parallel to, and almost on, the present link road running from Radway to the Kineton road.

Both armies had had enough; it was for most of the men their first taste of battle, and after three hours of hard slogging they were utterly exhausted. The night was cold, food and fuel were short, and the armies sought what comfort they could. The morning of 24 October found the Royalists back on Edgehill, and the Roundheads, who had retired in the night towards Kineton, now reformed below the hill. Lord Essex had received considerable reinforcements: John Hampden had arrived with two infantry regiments, and a cavalry regiment and some guns had also joined him. The King had received no reinforcements, but his cavalry – unlike Essex's – was virtually intact. Neither side seemed anxious to resume the contest, and Charles sent Clarenceaux King at Arms to offer pardon to all those rebels who would lay down their arms. The herald received short shrift, and as he was blindfolded for most of the time that he was in the enemy lines he had little of use to report to the King on his return. Later that day Charles ordered his men back to their billets around Edgcote, and Essex took his men to Kineton and then on to Warwick.

Many attempts have been made to assess the casualties in this battle, but the true figure will never be known. As is so often the case, both sides put out unrealistic claims of enemy losses, while playing down their own. Although accurate strength returns are not available there is plenty of evidence to show that many regiments were sadly depleted as a result of the battle, but a good proportion of these may have been runaways who never returned to the colours. The Royalist cavalry suffered only a handful of casualties, and no doubt the Parliamentarian horse that fled were swift enough to avoid much bloodshed, but the large numbers of infantrymen who broke on their left wing may not have been so fortunate. Undoubtedly the heaviest battle casualties took place in the fighting around Byron's and Feilding's brigades, and here the Royalists probably came off worst. They certainly lost more men of note, but not necessarily of senior rank. To hazard a figure could be misleading, but if forced to do so from the unreliable evidence available one must stop at 2,000 killed altogether and perhaps as many again severely wounded. Lord Bernard Stuart's letter of 28 October 1642 says of the Royalists, 'What is killed and run away I think is about 2,500 and that is the most'. This figure, which excludes the wounded, is probably too high, and anyway deserters would account for the greater part of it. The Roundheads must have lost more men through desertion and may have suffered heavier casualties than the Royalists.

It is often said that the first major engagement of the Civil War was a drawn battle. As far as the actual fighting on the afternoon of 23 October went this assessment is fairly true, but the victory went to the King. Essex, in spite of the considerable reinforcements he had received, evidently considered his army too badly mauled to achieve the object for which Edgehill was fought, and in going off to Warwick he left the road to London open. Moreover, his withdrawal seems to have been a somewhat disorderly affair, for on the morning of the 25th Prince Rupert fell upon the rearguard and captured or destroyed a considerable amount of ammunition and other valuable stores. It was, too, the Royalists and not the Roundheads who gained the most important trophies from the field – seven cannon, two of them much needed twelve-pounders. How and when this happened is not entirely clear. Sir Edward Sydenham, writing to Ralph Verney, says, 'My Lord of Essex is retired in great disorder to Warwick, for the next morning he suffered his cannon to be taken away within muskett shott of his armie, and never offired to hinder them'. It is possible that Rupert grabbed them along with his other prizes that Tuesday morning.

To say that the King had won the battle is no hyperbole. Urged by many to remove himself far from the battlefield, he not only disregarded this pusillanimous advice but insisted on his army holding the field the next day. Essex refused the challenge and marched away. Had Charles shown the same resolution in the days that followed he could have won the campaign and probably the war. There were two possible ways in which he might have saved his country the agony of a prolonged civil war: by annihilating Essex's army at Edgehill, or by holding it at bay and getting to London first. His nephew's haste contributed to the failure of the first, and his own tardiness to the second of these possibilities.

Banbury was taken on 27 October and the King entered Oxford two days later, where he stayed for a few days before arriving at Reading on 4 November. His caution may have been due in part to not knowing exactly where Essex's army was, but he must have known that he had the advantage of distance, which could be – and in fact was – soon lost. Prince Rupert's idea of a flying column of some 3,000 men to reach London hard on the news of Edgehill might conceivably have succeeded, but the Londoners were busy putting their defences in order and there were 8,000 of the London trained bands in arms. Meanwhile Parliament put out peace feelers, which the King probably never intended to take seriously, although he received the commissioners while postponing any decision on one pretext or another. Windsor Castle had defied Prince Rupert's summons to surrender on 7 November, and Essex, now safely back in London, had been ordered to take the field again – but not to precipitate any action.

Charles was at Colnbrook on 11 November and still outwardly considering the possibility of a settlement, when with typical double thinking he decided he would obtain better terms from a frightened Parliament, and ordered Rupert to attack Essex's troops in Brentford. Advancing under cover of a dawn mist on 12 November, the Prince eventually overwhelmed the two regiments in the town (Holles's and Lord Brooke's), killing or capturing almost the entire force. The Cavaliers then proceeded to sack the town. It was a victory that availed them nothing, for Parliament and the Londoners were now thoroughly roused and troops poured out of London. At Turnham Green the King found the way to his capital blocked by 24,000 men. He fell back before this formidable host, leaving Brentford to be retaken, and entered Kingston.

A bold stroke south of the river might yet have gained the victory; but Charles, perhaps sensing that he had missed his opportunity, withdrew to Reading, which town he re-entered on 19 November. The Edgehill campaign was over, and the King, as a free man, would never again come so close to London.

Prince Rupert at the siege of Bristol. The city surrendered on 26 July 1643

CHAPTER 3

The First Battle of Newbury

20 September 1643

The battle was fought a little over a mile to the south-west of the town. Leaving Newbury on the Andover road (A343), the visitor should fork right at The Gun public house (three-quarters of a mile out of Newbury, opposite the Falkland memorial) and go down Essex Road. The site of the battle is not an easy one to pick out, for except for the roads, which do in fact surround the battlefield, it cannot be viewed from any public access. The south part of the battlefield, which saw much of the heaviest fighting, is now almost completely covered by a recently built housing estate. The rest of the ground is still fairly open – in fact at the northern end more open than at the time of the battle – but it is all in private ownership.

The fighting took place in three principal areas. Wash Common and Enborne Heath, which are now built over to a great extent, but still have some traces of heath; the centre in the area of Skinner's Green and what is now called Round Hill; and the flat northern part stretching from Skinner's Green almost to the river Kennet. These latter portions of the field can be seen very well from a track running across Wash Farm, but permission to walk along it must be sought from the farmer. Wash Farm is on the corner of Essex Road and the road leading off it towards Round Hill, exactly on the division of two one-inch Ordnance Survey maps (sheets 158 and 168) – which does not make the visitor's task any easier!

For the first nine months of 1643 the Royalists had on balance much the better of the conflict. This was particularly so in the south-west, where by September it seemed that only the destruction of Essex's army was needed for total victory. In this task the King failed, and never again was he to hold such an overall advantage.

The opportunity occurred when Essex marched to the relief of Gloucester. The annihilation of General Waller's army at Roundway Down (see p. 34) made it possible for Prince Rupert to assault and capture Bristol on 25 July (see p. 34). Weymouth, Portland and Dorchester surrendered to Prince Maurice and Lord Carnarvon in August (although they failed against Lyme and Poole) and at the beginning of September Exeter also surrendered to Prince Maurice. This left Gloucester remarkably isolated: it was in fact the only garrison still held by Parliament between the Bristol Channel and Manchester.

Charles has often been criticized for ordering the Oxford army to march against Gloucester, rather than combining with the army in the south-west in a bid for London. But given the situation prevailing at the time, especially in the north, where Newcastle's (Royalist) army was meeting with many difficulties, the decision to clean up Gloucester – thereby gaining control of the Severn valley and opening up the road to South Wales – was probably a wise one. The refusal of Colonel Massey, Governor of Gloucester, to surrender the city when Charles summoned it on 10 August, and his very determined resistance thereafter, came as something of a surprise to the Royalists, and brought fresh hope to a dispirited Parliament. The losses at the assault on Bristol had been very heavy, and the King was in no mood to repeat them, so he had occupied the heights above the city, and although lacking proper siege material had felt confident that he could reduce the small garrison of 1,500 men before any relief could reach them.

Meanwhile, the threat to this important outpost was causing grave anxiety to the Parliamentarian leaders in London. It was originally decided by Parliament that Sir William Waller would command the army designated to relieve Gloucester, but Lord Essex, as commander-in-chief of the Parliamentarian forces, decided to take personal command. On 24 August he reviewed a large assembly of troops on Hounslow Heath – business in London was virtually at a standstill to enable the London trained bands and auxiliaries to muster at full strength – and on 26 August he set out on what must have seemed a fairly desperate venture. At Brackley Heath the army was reinforced by a strong artillery and horse contingent, bringing Essex's total force up to about 15,000 men, of which 4,000 were cavalry. As he marched through Bicester to Chipping Norton and Stow-on-the-Wold, Prince Rupert and Lord Wilmot hung about his flanks, but caused him little trouble, and by 5 September Essex was in sight of Gloucester.

Frantic attempts to induce Massey, whose powder was down to three barrels, to beat the chamade failed. Charles, not wanting to fight Essex with an unsubdued garrison at his back, raised the siege and made off to Sudeley Castle. Essex, his first task accomplished, entered Gloucester in something of a triumph on 8 September. He now had to get his army back to London. His recent march, much of it through enemy-held country, had been a remarkable feat, and he was about to display further skill in some complicated manoeuvring which completely baffled the Royalists, whose primary purpose was to bring him to battle on the most favourable terms.

Leaving much of his heavy ordnance and powder in Gloucester, Essex set out for Tewkesbury on 10 September, and the next day Charles, so as not to lose touch, moved ten miles north to Evesham. Throughout this campaign Essex displayed strategical skill and a sense of calm and power that was well above his average, and now through a series of feints he had the Royalist intelligence thinking that he meant to strike north for Worcester, or even enter Warwickshire, whereas he had all along determined to regain London by the road running south of Oxford. On the night of 15 September he led his army out of Tewkesbury, and before the King had realized what he was up to he had surprised some 200 Royalist soldiers in their beds in Cirencester, had captured a badly needed supply train and was on his way to Cricklade.

When Charles discovered that he had been given the slip he set off in pursuit, and sent Rupert in advance with rather more than 3,000 troops to intercept the enemy. The Prince, displaying his usual energy, was at Faringdon by the time Essex was leaving Swindon, and striking south he caught up with the Roundhead army between Chiseldon and Aldbourne. Although Essex was marching across Aldbourne Chase with his army dangerously strung out, the opportunity to defeat the various sections in detail with a comparatively small cavalry force was probably never there, although Sir John Byron states that it was missed. Colonel Hurry, at the head of 1,000 men, had been detached to attack the column in the rear, while Rupert fell upon the flank. Hurry's attack caused considerable confusion among the five regiments of horse that comprised Essex's rearguard, but Sir Philip Stapleton in command of the van had time to draw back onto the main body, and Prince Rupert's charges were repulsed. Nevertheless, the action had the important effect of forcing Essex to put the river Kennet between him and the Royalist army and preventing his getting further than Hungerford on the night of 18 September.

The Royalists camped that night at Wantage, so Essex still had the shorter distance to go to Newbury, where his half-starved army would have obtained welcome rations from that Roundhead stronghold. But the resolution he had displayed hitherto seemed now to desert him, or else he sadly misjudged the dynamism of the King's nephew. The next day he continued somewhat leisurely

54

on his way, and the advance party sent to arrange billets in Newbury was rudely handled by Prince Rupert's cavalry, who had ridden into the town a few hours ahead of the main Royalist army. Essex, who was apprised of this unpleasant situation as he trudged the miry road out of Kintbury, had no alternative but to halt his army for the night in the rain-soaked fields lying between the rivers Kennet and Enborne.

The King now clearly held the advantage. He had placed his army between the Roundheads and London; he had acquired the food supplies destined for his enemy; and although he was short of powder this was expected to arrive from Oxford at any time. He therefore led his men out of Newbury to the west on the evening of the 19th, so as to be ready to meet Essex on the morrow. His main camp was on the flat ground north and east of Skinner's Green, but cavalry patrols were sent to occupy the ridge east of Wash Farm. There is some reason to believe that Prince Rupert advised against attacking until such time as the ammunition supply had been assured.* Apart from the fact that such advice would have been quite out of character, it does not make much military sense. The King's objective was to beat the Roundheads before they could regain London, and conditions could scarcely have been more unfavourable for Essex – indeed, as we shall see, he himself had little alternative but to fight. Behind the King Waller commanded an army 4,000 strong and Charles was not to know how little inclined Waller was to help Essex. It seems, therefore, that the council of war's decision that evening to seize the vantage points in readiness to attack the next day, and defeat Essex before Waller could come to his relief, was a wise one. Unfortunately, it was imperfectly executed.

And what were Essex's thoughts? Having undertaken this hazardous enterprise in preference to a subordinate he disliked, he could not afford to fail. There is a Royalist letter extant† in which the writer says that the Royalists expected the enemy to withdraw during the night, and no doubt Essex would have liked to go on his way unmolested. But to attempt to slip past to the south of the Royalist army would have been fraught with danger.

---

* Eliot Warburton, *Prince Rupert's Diary*, Vol. II, p. 292. In the Wiltshire Country Record Office there are three manuscripts, from which Warburton has drawn his work. They form a near-contemporary series of notes intended to form the basis of a biography of Rupert. Their precise origin is not known, but Colonel Thomas Benett, Rupert's secretary, may have been their author. They are certainly not a diary written by Prince Rupert.

† *Thomason Tracts*, E.69.

The ground was low-lying and difficult to move over, and his flank and rear would have been constantly exposed to attack. No, the road to London lay straight ahead through the enemy; and furthermore it lay along the ridge and plateau that jutted out as a broad finger between the two river valleys. Essex had been dilatory out of Hungerford; the lesson had been learned and he determined to have the high ground before first light on the morning of 20 September.

The First Battle of Newbury was a most confused affair, and as so much of the battlefield is now built over the visitor is bound to find it difficult to follow even the most lucid account. There are numerous documents and letters written by participants of both sides, but they are disconnected and usually view the fight from a narrow personal angle. Moreover, their site descriptions are often dangerously vague. From these we can build up some sort of picture, but it is impossible to be certain as to exactly how the battle was fought. We cannot even be sure of the numbers engaged, although it is known that the Cavaliers were considerably superior in horse, but the overall figure may have been much the same as at Edgehill and the armies almost equal at around 14,000. Essex may have had 10,000 foot to 4,000 horse and the King only 8,000 foot but 6,000 horse. Both armies appear to have had about the same number of guns (twenty), and at least six of them were heavy cannon.

The King took personal command at this battle with Lord Forth acting as chief of staff. Prince Rupert, Lords Carnarvon and Wilmot, Sir John Byron and Charles Gerard commanded cavalry brigades, while Sir Jacob Astley was again in command of the infantry and had under him, as brigade commanders, Sir Nicholas Byron, Sir William Vavasour, Sir Gilbert Gerard and John Belasyse. The Roundhead infantry consisted of four brigades each of three regiments and the London trained bands, who were not brigaded and at first formed the reserve. The cavalry was divided into two wings; Sir Philip Stapleton commanded on the right and John Middleton on the left. For some reason, possibly because he did not think his brigade commanders up to the task, Essex took command of the army's right wing (a foolish involvement for the commander-in-chief), while Sergeant-Major-General Skippon commanded the left wing and reserves. The Roundhead guns were under Sir John Merrick, who used them with considerable skill.

On the evening of the 19th the two armies were encamped almost opposite each other on the low ground south of the Kintbury road, along which the Roundheads had marched. Essex had left his baggage wagons in the area of Hamstead Park, and in the early hours of the morning he deployed his men for battle. Before he did so he issued – presumably through his brigade commanders – what would later be called an order of the day; he warned the men that the struggle would be a stern one and that the enemy held

Left: Cavaliers and Roundheads, from 'A dialogue or parley between Prince Rupert's poodle and Tobie's dog Peper', 1642

Right: Military costume, *c.* 1645

all the advantages of terrain. The troops needed no reminder of their present desperate plight and they were soon to show, as others after them would do, that when times are difficult Englishmen become determined, and when they are desperate they become indomitable.

The important ground lay to the south of the two army encampments. The Royalists had already sent a cavalry patrol as far as Wash Common and had brought up some guns, but through a carelessness that was to prove extremely costly they failed to take any steps to occupy the feature of tactical importance that became known as Round Hill. The southern part of what was to become the battlefield (Wash Common and Enborne Heath) was fairly open and good cavalry country, but to the west of this plateau the ground was much more broken, and narrow, steep-banked lanes ran down from the spurs intersecting the flat ground, which was covered by enclosures and the occasional copse. Essex extended his line to where Bigg's Cottage still stands,* just south of Boame's Farm, and before first light pushed his right onto Enborne Heath. General Skippon had orders to occupy Round Hill before dawn, and the guns, which had difficulty in traversing the very broken country, were brought up to the Crockham Heath area near where the London trained bands were at first positioned.

These manoeuvres by the Roundheads to seize the high ground were carried out unopposed, and when dawn broke the Royalist commanders were distressed to find that their position was overlooked by the enemy, who far from disappearing in the night had now imposed themselves upon ground from which it was vital to dislodge them. At the same time the Roundheads realized that they had paid too much attention to the right flank, and that the Royalists had a big concentration of troops opposite their baggage train. Skippon at once deployed men to cover this valley. A part of Lord Robartes's brigade and the Red Auxiliary regiment occupied the Skinner's Green area, and a contingent under Major Fortescue reached to and beyond the Kintbury–Newbury road.

The fortunes of the day would be decided on the Round Hill spur and the edge of the plateau between that hill and Wash Farm and immediately to the west of the farm. The Roundheads needed the high ground if their artillery was to be of value and, as we have seen, they had by first light a precarious footing on part of it. The task of dislodging them fell chiefly to Sir John Byron's cavalry

---

* It is possible that Essex spent a part of the night 19–20 September in this cottage, in spite of its position on the extreme right of his line, which makes it an unlikely place for his headquarters.

58

brigade and his uncle Sir Nicholas's infantry brigade. Sir John has left a graphic account of this part of the battle, in which he starts by deploring the negligence that made the assault on Round Hill necessary. In the pearly softness of a September dawn he received his orders to support the foot with his own and Sir Thomas Aston's regiments of horse. The fight began at about 7 a.m. and the leading infantry (Colonel Lisle's regiment) were soon in trouble assaulting over difficult country a hill held by determined men supported by two light cannon. Sir Nicholas threw more regiments into the attack, but they too got bogged down and called for cavalry support.

The infantry had attacked the hill from the east. Sir John assures us that this was not cavalry country, and he rode forward to reconnoitre before committing his regiments. Even now one would think twice about assaulting this hill with cavalry, but then the fields surrounding it were smaller and more thickly fenced. In obtaining a lodgement on Round Hill Sir John and his men displayed great courage and skill. He seems to have attacked from the low ground to the north-east of the hill close to Skinner's Green. Here he found the enemy infantry screened by a high hedge with a gap only wide enough for one horse to pass through at a time. While he was giving orders for it to be widened his horse was shot in the throat and he had to seek a fresh one; during his absence Lord Falkland, Charles's Secretary of State, 'more gal-

Siege warfare, from a seventeenth-century treatise on military regulations

Try your match. | Guard your pan. | Present.

Give Fire. | Come up to your Musket. | Return your match.

Take up your rest. | Blow of your loose Powder and cast about your Musket. | Trail your rest & open your charg

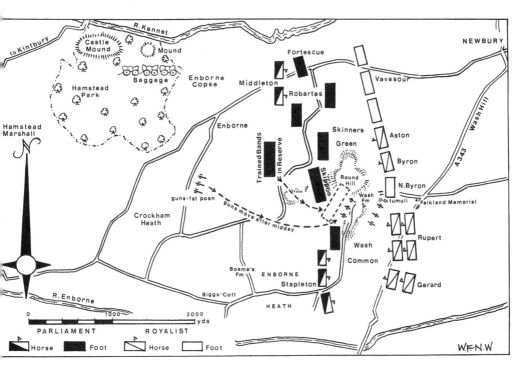

Left: Plate from a seventeenth-century exercise manual for musketeers, showing various different positions
Above: First Battle of Newbury
Overleaf: First Battle of Newbury

lantly than advisedly' spurred his horse through the gap and was killed instantly. As soon as the hedge had been flattened Byron's men galloped through and into a hail of musket balls and case shot from the two drakes. The punishment they received was too severe to be withstood, and amid a tangle of flailing hooves and rearing horses the order to withdraw was carried out.

Throughout this battle it is impossible to be certain of the timing, because most narratives disregard such details. We know that action along the whole line began at about 7 a.m. and that sporadic firing was still going on as late as 10 p.m., although as might be expected the main fighting stopped at nightfall; we also know from a contemporary account that 'the fight was at its hottest at 4 p.m.'. It must have been well into the morning therefore before this cavalry attack took place, and some time must have elapsed while Byron rallied his men for another charge, during which the Roundheads removed their cannon to the rear. This second attack

N

Robartes

Middleton

Trained Bands

Skippon

Essex

Enborne Heath

Fortescue

Vavasour

Round Hill

Byron

Tumuli

Wash Hill

N. Byron

Rupert

Gerard

Stapleton

carried out by Sir John's and Sir Thomas Aston's regiments drove the Parliamentarians back from the summit of the hill until they had their backs to another high hedge. Here the fight became more stubborn, and once again the cavalry were unable to make headway against the flying shot and bristling pikes. Another pause in the battle while Skippon altered his position to hold Skinner's Green Lane, and then a third cavalry charge completely routed the enemy, who were only saved from total disaster by the thickness of the hedges, the steepness of the banks and the fact that Skippon had also brought up the four London regiments he still had in reserve. The cavalry suffered heavy casualties in these assaults, but they did a magnificent job.

It was probably about midday when Sir John Byron finally withdrew his brigade from the Round Hill area, leaving what he had captured to be held by the infantry. And now the main battle switched to the Wash ridge and the high ground to the south and east. Fighting had been heavy on this plateau for many hours and was to continue, in one form or another, with the utmost ferocity for the rest of the day. Some say the King had meant to stay on the defensive here, but it was good cavalry ground and Prince Rupert, who revelled in the intensity of risk, was never one to stay inactive: he led three full-blooded charges mainly against Sir Philip Stapleton's cavalry wing. Charge and counter-charge, cut and thrust, with the fortune of war going first to one side then to the other. Stapleton's men beat Rupert's first charge right back onto their main body. A second charge fared little better, for the Roundheads had been able to deploy more troops; but in the third charge Stapleton found himself outnumbered and assailed from front and flank and his men were gradually pressed back to the edge of the heath, although those Cavaliers who followed into the lanes were mercilessly dealt with. The Royalists had lost three standards and the Roundheads two, the ground was a mass of bodies, but Stapleton's cavalry had been driven off to play no further part in the battle. It was now the turn of the Roundhead infantry, who by their courage, cohesion and pertinacity were to gain the chief honours of the day.

Lord Essex's first biographer (Robert Codrington, writing in 1646) tells us that the Lord-General was everywhere encouraging his men, and that when Rupert's horse had broken through Stapleton's regiments he rallied them and 'with undaunted courage stormed with them up the hill'. This no doubt was most admirable, but hardly the duty of a commander-in-chief, and clearly it was Skippon who master-minded much of the battle. Having retained a footing on a sizable slice of the Round Hill–Wash Farm ridge, he brought up his cannon to engage the Royalist artillery, which had been doing considerable damage firing from the vicinity of the tumuli on Wash Common. He advanced the London trained bands to hold the mouth of Skinner's Green Lane, and in response to an appeal from Essex he sent his commander the Red Auxiliaries, having already sent the Blue to strengthen Fortescue, who was being pressed on the left flank.

Once Skippon had stabilized the Roundhead centre and got the heavy cannon into the firing line, matters improved considerably. The Royalist guns, which had been giving the Red Regiment of the London trained bands a considerable hammering, were now switched to engage in what was probably the fiercest and most sustained artillery duel of the whole war. The Blue Regiment had been placed on the right of the Red and it too had had to withstand some pounding, and this regiment also bore the brunt of a further charge from Prince Rupert's cavalry. Through it all, we are told, the Londoners 'stood undaunted like a grove of pines in a day of winde and tempest, they only moved their heads or Armes, but kept their footing sure, unless by an improvement of honour they advanced forward to pursue their advantage on their Enemies'. Had the Royalist infantry behaved with the same spirit, the King would most likely have won the battle, but with the exception of Nicholas Byron's brigade they appear to have been, if not cowardly, certainly spineless.

The fighting continued, often sharp and bitter, to around seven at night – and sporadically thereafter. The men must have been desperately weary, for at some time all had been committed, and most of them time and again. It was a very confused fight and there were incidents whose place and timing are not easily pinpointed. The Roundhead paper *Mercurius Civicus* in its account of the battle states that the Royalists 'wheeled about a great body of Horse, and a little below the hill fell upon the rear of our army, which occasioned us to withdraw a part of our army from off the hill to assist those which were engaged'. Some of these cavalrymen, or others shortly afterwards, had stuck green branchlets in their hats, which was the Parliamentarian emblem for that day, but the ruse was quickly detected. The hill in question must have been Round Hill, but the timing in the day's events of this particular mêlée is uncertain.

Little has been said about the fighting on the northern part of the field. It was never so vital as in the centre, or on the southern plateau, where both sides were endeavouring to turn the other's flank; but it was at times hotly contested and we have seen that Fortescue had to be reinforced, for little stood between him and the baggage wagons at Hamstead Park. On this flank too there was a curious incident mentioned in Lord Digby's account of the battle, but never fully explained. During the afternoon a party of Roundhead troops (presumably either from Middleton's cavalry or Fortescue's infantry) attempted to seize a ford over the Kennet in the Guyer's Field area, but were driven back by Sir William Vavasour's men. It is difficult to understand what they hoped to attain – unless they had had enough and were making for home.

As darkness enveloped the bloodstained field the fighting dwindled to desultory fire and the occasional skirmish among stragglers. Both sides were weary beyond measure. The Roundheads had on balance fought the better of the two, but the King's army still lay intact between them and Newbury – it might be said between them and starvation. Essex's men settled down for a few hours' rest, ready to break through, or die in the attempt, on the morrow. But in Charles's camp there were the usual arguments and dissension. Lord Henry Percy, who commanded the artillery, reported that they had used eighty barrels of powder (sixty more than had been used at Edgehill) and had less than half a day's supply left – the expected barrels from Oxford having still not arrived. In spite of this Prince Rupert (who, it will be remembered, is reported as not having wanted to engage in the first instance) and Sir John Byron were for holding their ground. At the council of war they were overruled and the King, who with Lord Forth must take ultimate responsibility for the decision, ordered a withdrawal into Newbury for what remained of that night, and then on to Oxford.

Of the two principal antagonists Essex was the most deserving of the victor's crown. When on the next day – slightly puzzled – he fired at where the enemy should be, he found them gone. He had achieved his object: the road to London lay open before him. Charles is usually blamed for making a disastrous decision. But who can be certain that he was not right? He had suffered heavy casualties, especially among his leaders; a tough, desperate army was prepared to fling itself at him, and his guns were incapable of firing for more than a few hours. The greatest loss he suffered in this battle was perhaps in the death of one man – Lord Falkland. This nobleman appears to have sought death deliberately, because his spirit was broken by the sad state into which his country had lapsed. Had he lived his wise counsel and his overriding desire for a peaceful settlement might have influenced the King. Lord Digby, who replaced him as Secretary of State, was an altogether smaller man.

Besides Lord Falkland, Lord Carnarvon had been killed returning from one of the cavalry charges on the plateau, and Lord Sunderland had also fallen, together with many much valued senior officers. The Parliamentarians lost far fewer men of note – only six colonels compared with eleven Royalists. Any attempt to assess the total killed could be misleading. There are accounts of the numbers of dead seen on the field the next day, but in each instance some sixty cartloads had already been taken off for burial. From the little contemporary information available one might get an overall figure of 3,500 at the most, and possibly the Royalists were just the heaviest losers.

Essex, still uncertain as to his enemy's whereabouts, was careful to keep south of the Kennet in the early stages of his march to London. He took the route through Greenham Common, Brimpton and Aldermaston. In a narrow lane between Aldermaston and Padworth the column was attacked by a party of Royalist cavalry and musketeers. Before he left Newbury Prince Rupert is alleged to have said that 'although the Roundheads were marching unto Reading they would make calves of many of them before they came unto the Veale [Theale]'. And it seems almost certain that he commanded this raiding party, although Lords Northampton and Wilmot and Colonel Hurry are sometimes mentioned in this capacity. Essex's rear was brought up by Sir Philip Stapleton's cavalry, then came a forlorn hope of 600 musketeers and after them the London trained bands. Stapleton's men, who had received considerable punishment the day before, panicked and stampeded through the infantry; for a short while the situation looked ugly for the Roundheads, but once again they were saved by their infantry, who lined the hedges and poured such effective volleys into the Royalist force that they were beaten off with the loss of more than 100 men.

Essex continued his march through 'the Veale' into Reading, and on 28 September he and his weary, but triumphant, men entered London to bask resplendent in the City's gratitude. Essex had achieved all that he had set out to do, and for this campaign (despite his occasional lapses into the role of regimental commander) he richly deserved his colleagues' encomium. He had halted the Royalist tide of success, he had put London still further from the King's reach and, at least for the time being, he had shown himself to be the linchpin of the Parliamentarian chariot of war.

CHAPTER 4

Cheriton

29 March 1644

*Until quite recently there was little or no dispute as to the site of
this battle; but in 1973 a full-length account of the campaign was
written in which the author disagreed with the generally accepted
position of the battlefield.* The present writer, having spent many
hours walking round the whole area, and having closely studied
the contemporary letters and papers, is not convinced that the
evidence contained in them justifies this new siting. That is not to
say that the more usual siting is absolutely correct, and indeed this
account is a slight variation.*

*In any event the whole area is easily viewed from public footpaths
and tracks. It is generally assumed that the battle took place to the
east of Cheriton (Cheriton is two and a half miles south of New
Alresford) between that village and Cheriton Wood, perhaps a little
to the south of the crossed swords on the Ordnance Survey one-inch
map, sheet 168. The small by-road running east from Cheriton goes
through the battlefield, and by walking along the lane running north
and south of the road (which passes immediately to the west of
Cheriton Wood), and the footpath which connects that lane with
another running parallel to it nearer Cheriton, the visitor gets an
excellent view of the ground. The battlefield has not greatly changed
in the last 300 years, except that the slopes of the two ridges, which
encompass the site in the form of a horseshoe, were much more
enclosed in 1644.*

*John Adair thinks the Royalists occupied the southernmost ridge
of the horseshoe (running south-west from Cheriton Wood) and that
the Roundheads were positioned in the area of Hinton Ampner, the
battle taking place in the low ground just north of the A272 Winchester–Bramdean road. This site can be viewed from the same tracks.*

The Battle of Cheriton had important consequences, but as a fight
it quickly developed into an untidy, muddled mêlée. It is not easily
pieced together from the confused contemporary accounts, and
most descriptions suffer from an over-simplification, or go to the
other extreme of plunging the reader into an impenetrable tangle

---

* John Adair, *Cheriton 1644*. See also his biography of Sir William
   Waller.

of detail. Perhaps the most fascinating task for the student of military history is to decide from the slender evidence available not how it was fought, for that in outline is moderately simple, but where it was fought. For that reason this chapter has been treated somewhat differently from others. The usual run-up to the battle is followed by only a brief account of the actual fight, and then space is devoted to trying to solve the riddle of the battlefield.

During the six autumn and winter months that separated the Battles of Newbury and Cheriton both sides achieved successes and suffered setbacks in approximately equal proportion. Prince Maurice made little progress in the south-west; Sir John (now Lord) Byron was sent north to form a new army in Cheshire, with which he caused Sir William Brereton some trouble before being decisively beaten when attempting to take Nantwich in January 1644 (see p. 34); two months later Prince Rupert won a resounding victory against Sir John Meldrum's force that was besieging Newark (see p. 34); in the south Arundel Castle changed hands twice; and on 13 December General Waller won a fiercely contested fight for Alton.

By the end of 1643 it had become obvious that the contestants were fairly evenly matched and that neither side could expect a swift or easy victory. Charles could brood over wasted opportunities, and the Roundheads had yet to win a victory of strategical importance. But in January 1644 there came the first great turning point of the war. On the 19th of that month a Scottish army numbering some 20,000 well trained troops crossed the Tweed to range itself on the side of Parliament. With the ending of the Irish war the previous autumn the King had obtained some of the Duke of Ormonde's English regiments, but neither in quality nor quantity could these match the Scottish invaders. It was not difficult to see how the fortunes of Parliament could now improve through the succeeding months.

However, no one could accuse the Royalists of losing the initiative through idleness. As soon as the army was back at Oxford after the Battle of Newbury the council of war set about making new plans that would once more point the way to London. While the Oxford army was to be principally employed in containing Essex north of the Thames, a new western army was to be raised and placed under the command of Lord Hopton* with a directive

* The day after defeating Waller at the Battle of Lansdown (see pp. 32–4) in July 1643 Sir Ralph Hopton (as he was then) received serious wounds when a powder barrel blew up close to him. He was probably not completely fit again when assuming command of this army.

to clear Dorset, Hampshire and Wiltshire of the enemy. His adversary was Sir William Waller, who was in command of the Southeastern Association. Here then were two great generals once again in opposition, who in happier times had fought on the continent as comrades in arms.

In this campaign Lord Hopton, no longer in command of his valiant Cornishmen, for whom his raw Hampshire levies and contingents out of Ireland were poor substitutes, proved no match for Waller. It is true that he was usually outnumbered and he was further handicapped by a lack of confidence at Oxford. He was anxious to make a start in Dorset and Wiltshire, where he could quickly have cleaned up the remaining Parliamentarian garrisons, but the King ordered him to support Sir William Ogle at Winchester, and then he was lured further east. Arundel Castle surrendered to him early in December 1643, but this strong fortress was poorly provisioned and its garrison contained an element of treachery, so that after only a fortnight's siege Waller retook it on 6 January. Three weeks earlier the Cavalier losses in the fight at Alton had been unpleasantly severe, so it was a decidedly chastened Hopton who fell back on Winchester thankful that the chilling voice of winter and the snow-covered ground kept Waller at a respectable distance.

Early in March Charles sent Hopton some sorely needed reinforcements – cavalry, infantry and four guns. His army now totalled about 6,000 men, of which 2,500 were cavalry, but with them came the Earl of Forth, which could be taken as a further mark of the King's lack of confidence in Hopton, for Forth being senior was to take command. Forth's position in the Royalist army was that of commander-in-chief under the King, who had actually assumed command at Newbury, relegating Forth to chief of staff. He was a man of immense experience and courage, but he was old, deaf and more fond of the bottle than it was of him, with the result that he suffered considerably from gout. He was obviously aware of his inadequacy as a commander in the field, for only with difficulty could Hopton prevail upon him to act in that capacity, and even then much of the campaign and battle was conducted by Hopton.

The Parliamentarian plan made that February was that Waller should open the spring campaign by taking Basing House, which dominated the London–Winchester road, and then advance on Winchester. When Charles had reinforced Hopton with 800 cavalry, Lord Essex had sent Waller 2,000 under Sir William Balfour, his best cavalry commander; Waller was therefore immeasurably

stronger in this vital arm. The garrison of the strategically important Basing House was under command of the owner's brother
Lord Charles Paulet, and there was reason to believe that he was
prepared to betray his trust. However, before the opportunity
presented itself he was himself betrayed. Sir Richard Grenvile,*
a soldier of considerable experience, had offered his sword to
Parliament on being captured soon after his arrival from Ireland,
and had been made a Lieutenant-general. This wild and unreliable
turncoat was totally unsuited to the mournful rigours of a Puritan
host, and he soon made his way to Oxford with a great deal of valuable information, including the plans for Waller. Paulet was
arrested, and Waller decided to bypass Basing House and march
straight for the Royalist army at Winchester.

The approach marches of both armies to the battle area are not
easily understood from contemporary accounts. For example,
Lord Hopton and Colonel Slingsby give different dates for leaving
Winchester, and Waller's London brigade under Major-General
Browne seem to have done an extraordinary manoeuvre if the
place called 'Trafford' is really Twyford as is generally assumed.
The certain facts are that Waller advanced from Midhurst to camp
in the area West Meon, Westbury, Warnford, where he skirmished
with what was probably a Royalist reconnaissance force, for
Hopton's main army does not appear to have come so far east.
On the 28th Waller sent Balfour to secure the important town of
Alresford,† but Hopton, correctly divining his intention, beat him
to it by the narrowest of margins. When he saw that the attempt
had failed Waller halted his army in and around Hinton Ampner,
a small village three miles south of Alresford.

The Royalist army bivouacked the night of the 27th on Tichborne
Down. The next day there was some skirmishing in the area that
was to become the battlefield. Waller had hoped to occupy the
ridge immediately above his encampment, which was the southern
part of a prominent horseshoe-shaped ridge whose toe encompasses
Cheriton Wood and whose heels point westwards towards Cheriton
village, but in this he was unsuccessful: Hopton, who had advanced
his main army to occupy the northern ridge, had by the evening
of the 28th established an outpost under Colonel Lisle on the
southern ridge. It is probable that Waller's attempt to take the
ridge was not seriously pressed, because a decision to fight had not

* The story of 'Skellum' Grenvile is delightfully told in Daphne du
  Maurier's book, *The King's General in the West*.
† At that time the London–Winchester road ran through Old Alresford
  and Bighton.

Ralph, Lord Hopton, appointed commander of the new Royalist western army

Sir William Waller, commander of the Parliamentarian army at the Battle of Cheriton

been definitely agreed upon. The Committee of Both Kingdoms had expressly ordered Waller not to engage the enemy 'except upon advantage', and there were those in authority advocating withdrawal. This was craven counsel, because for once, with an army of 10,000 men, of which 3,500 were horse, and an artillery train of sixteen cannon, they were very much stronger than their adversaries.

However, Sir William Waller was not the sort of man to pay much heed to committee decisions, and it seems that during the night he overruled the plan to withdraw – although he may have had some difficulty, for Lisle reported hearing the rumbling movement of wagons in the early hours. Certainly when dawn broke through a thick mist on the morning of the 29th the Roundhead army was preparing for battle. Under cover of the mist Waller sent 1,000 musketeers under Colonel Walter Leighton to occupy Cheriton Wood. Waller was renowned for his expert tactical eye; he was quick to perceive the important features of any battlefield, and on the previous evening he had decided that Cheriton Wood held the key to the ground over which the battle would be fought, for the possessor of the wood had a covered approach along either of the two ridges, and could therefore mount an attack without being forced into a frontal approach up the thickly enclosed slopes.

The sun was already beginning to disperse the mist before Hopton discovered what was afoot. He had ridden from the higher northern slope of the horseshoe across the valley and up to Colonel Lisle's outpost, when firing on his left told him that the enemy, far from retreating, were now in the wood. Lisle's position had become untenable and he was withdrawn; a few minutes later it was occupied by the main body of Roundheads. Hopton had as good a tactical eye as Waller, and fully realized the importance of Cheriton Wood. It is possible that he may have been deterred from occupying it earlier by Lisle's report that the enemy were withdrawing, but he wasted no time in trying to regain the initiative.

Lord Forth, whose gout was troubling him, had spent the night in Alresford, but as soon as he got Hopton's report he hastened to the battlefield. The contemporary account, as published in the *Bellum Civile,* indicates that Forth ordered Hopton to bring the Royalist army forward – possibly to the reverse slope of a lower and shorter ridge west from Cheriton Wood almost exactly half-way between the two arms of the horseshoe – 'and, seeing the posture the enemy was in, [he] commanded the Lord Hopton to draw the whole army and cannon up to him to that ground . . . And placing the foote and horse that the Earl of Brainford [Forth] brought with him on the right whing, himselfe with his owne foote and horse drew to the left, which was over against the woody ground that the enemy had newly possest.' It is not generally accepted that this intermediate ridge was the one occupied by the Royalists during the battle, but there are indications that it could have been. Certainly it seems from the above account that the army advanced from the north ridge, and although Hopton in his account of the battle does not specifically mention that Waller occupied the south ridge on Lisle's withdrawal, it would seem to have offered him the best possible position. The centre ridge was 'over against the woody ground' and is high enough to give protection to troops on the reverse slope.*

As soon as the army had come up Hopton ordered Colonel Appleyard with 1,000 musketeers to clear the wood. But as these troops breasted the ridge they came under intensive musket fire – perhaps from the enemy position on the ridge, but certainly from those in the wood – and Hopton decided to reinforce their attack by a flanking movement with one 'division' of commanded musketeers under Lieutenant-Colonel Edward Hopton. This double assault was quickly successful, for these particular Londoners (the White and Yellow Regiments) were undisciplined and inclined to be mutinous, and they were driven headlong from the wood. Hopton was now anxious to mount a strong attack on the enemy's vulnerable right flank, which could have been done under cover of the wood, but the more cautious Forth preferred to stand on the defensive and allow the enemy to attack him, if they did not in fact lose heart after their recent reverse and withdraw. It is impossible to guess what the outcome of a flank attack by Hopton on a somewhat shaken enemy would have been, but probably it offered the best chance of success for any army outnumbered by almost two to one.

Hopton is said to have accepted this decision of Forth's with good grace, but on riding back to consult with his chief he was alarmed to find that the right of the line was already engaged. It must have been about 11 a.m. when the young gallant Sir Henry Bard, probably disregarding orders and certainly acting 'with more youthfull courage then souldierlike discretion', launched his regiment down the slope and into the arena entirely unsupported. Sir Arthur Heselrige's 'Lobsters' quickly cut off his retreat and

* The same report states that Hopton took advantage of the ground 'and drew all his horse and foote in order on the side of the hill that was from the enemy'.

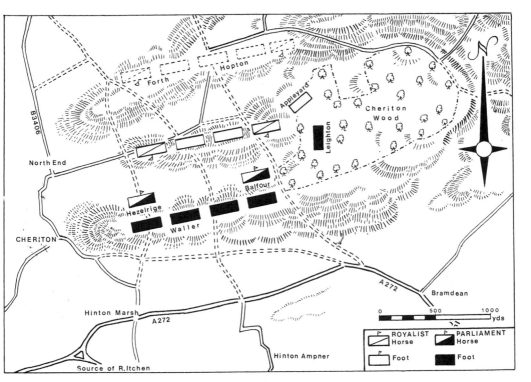

Above and overleaf: Battle of Cheriton

within a short space of time his whole regiment was either taken
or killed – Bard himself lost an arm and was captured.

After this fateful beginning the whole affair from the Royalist
side seems to have got out of hand. The spectacle was tragic as
regiment after regiment rode down the narrow bridleways into the
battle-scarred arena merely to be chopped before they could deploy.
Royalist accounts of the battle endeavour to show that all was not
confusion and that Lord Forth operated to some form of plan, but
in truth there was little direction from on high. By early afternoon
the infantry had joined the cavalry and the tangled mass of fighting
men swirled around in a shapeless pattern.

There were many individual acts of heroism, and the bearing of
the proud Cavaliers as they rode into battle was magnificent, but
cruel losses were suffered among the senior officers. Lord John
Stuart, lieutenant-general of the Horse, and Sir John Smith,
sergeant-major-general of Hopton's army, were both killed in the
last forlorn effort, when Lord Forth ordered Sir Edward Stowell's
brigade to charge. By that time all the cavalry save Sir Humphrey
Bennet's regiment were committed, and the Royalist right flank
had virtually collapsed. Even so there were musketeers still lining
the hedges and keeping the Roundhead cavalry, often led in person

75

Alresford

Royalists' original line

Hopton

Waller

Hinton Ampner

by Sir William Waller, at some sort of distance. According to Colonel Slingsby it was the initiative of an officer on the Round-head left wing that finally decided the issue, when he led his regiment in a sweeping hook against the fast crumbling Royalist right. But probably by about 4 p.m. the weight of numbers was telling and the whole line had become enveloped in a Roundhead pincer movement.

Lord Hopton conducted a masterly withdrawal in the face of this overwhelming disaster. The action fought by Stowell's brigade had given him valuable time, and the Queen's Regiment, which contained some Frenchmen, including its commander Captain Raoul Fleury, staged a most important and courageous delaying action, in which Fleury lost a foot. According to the Royalist paper *Mercurius Aulicus,* Colonel Richard Neville's regiment also covered the retreat, which was certainly not the uncontrolled rout described by the Roundhead Elias Archer. This cavalry screen enabled Forth and Hopton to get the bulk of the army with its guns back to Tichborne Down. Here the Cavaliers appeared to be contemplating a further stand, but when the Roundheads brought their cannon into action a few rounds sufficed and the retreat continued – although not before Hopton had withdrawn to safety all but two of his cannon.

On Hopton's advice the main army made for Basing House. Alresford was fired by the retreating soldiers, but only about five houses were burned, and if we are to believe Captain Harley many of the incendiaries (who seem to have been mostly Irish) were slain before they could get clear of the town. The Royalist army reached Basing House that night, and were soon back at Oxford. Winchester city – but not the castle – surrendered to Waller on 30 March, and before long he was in control of all Hampshire.

Even more so than in most Civil War battles it is difficult to assess the casualties at Cheriton. Harley put the Roundheads' loss at about sixty and the Royalists' at 300. There are other estimates (almost certainly exaggerated) of between 900 and 1,400 respectively. It seems to be agreed that no more than 800 Royalist horse out of some 2,500 rallied on Tichborne Down – but, of course, many had made off in other directions. We know that the Royalists lost two generals and five colonels killed, and Lord Forth (whose conduct throughout the retreat was most courageous), General Stowell and many other officers were wounded, so their total losses during a long afternoon of hand-to-hand grapple were almost certainly in excess of 300.

The Parliamentarian victory at Cheriton had most important

consequences. To begin with it was the first decisive major victory they had won: there had been minor successes and Essex had successfully barred the King from London, but here was defeat, naked and brutal, for a Royalist army that had sought battle. Morale rose and sank in the respective forces accordingly – and not only in the Roundhead army did morale rise, for the result of the battle gave a boost to the war party in Parliament. The King was at least temporarily forced onto the defensive, and could no longer expect to gain control of the south-east. The Royalists had been humbled, but were some way from being broken. Nevertheless, Lord Clarendon and Sir Edward Walker were justified in their appreciation of the results of Cheriton when the former said that the battle had 'altered the whole scheme of the King's counsels', and the latter that it 'marked a watershed in the war'.

Any attempt to retrace our ancestors' fights, to release the springs of historical imagination, requires that we should stand on the site and walk the ground on which the battle was fought. Our guide to the right place usually comes from the various maps, contemporary accounts, burial grounds, relics and, sometimes, local tradition. In the case of the Battle of Cheriton there is no contemporary map or plan extant, and in trying to locate the exact site of the battle it is first necessary to assume that the wood, which is the key to the whole question, is Cheriton Wood – in spite of the fact that this large, rather straggly wood is described by Captain Harley as 'a little wood on the top of that hill with a fense about it'. There are then certain facts from contemporary accounts that seem to be fairly well established, for they figure in most of them. They are:

1 During the skirmishing on the day previous to the battle Waller hoped to gain a foothold on the southern ridge of the horseshoe, but was unable to do so, and the day ended with Colonel Lisle on that ridge.
2 The Roundhead army encamped on the night of 28 March in Lamborough Fields just north of Hinton Ampner. Waller himself stayed with Lady Stukeley at Hinton Ampner House.
3 The Roundheads debated the advisability of withdrawing, but eventually decided to give battle.
4 In the early hours of the morning Waller sent Colonel Leighton up to Cheriton Wood, about 800 yards to his right front.
5 At about 7.30 a.m., when the mist had cleared, Hopton discovered the Londoners in Cheriton Wood. He immediately sent word to Forth, who rode out from Alresford.

6 When Forth arrived, which could not have been much before 8.45 a.m., he ordered Hopton to draw the whole army forward. They took up a position on a reverse slope, 'within muskett shott' of the enemy, which must mean within 400 yards.

7 The Londoners were evicted from Cheriton Wood and withdrew in disorder onto the main body.

8 Hopton asked permission to turn their flank, 'finding that he had from thence [i.e. Cheriton Wood] a faire way to fall upon

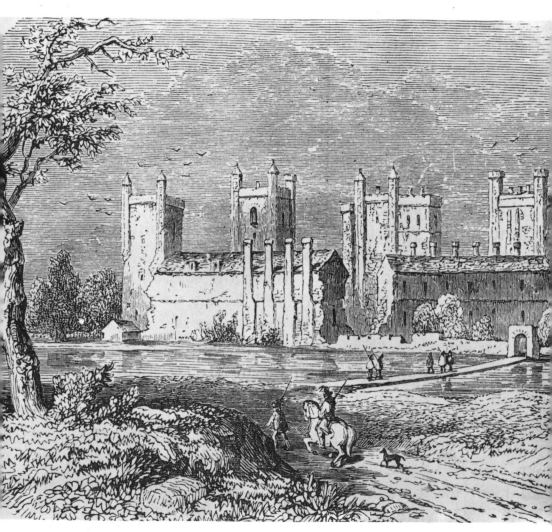

Basing House, which fell to Parliament on 14 October 1645. The house was looted and over 100 people killed in the sack that followed

the flancke of their whole army'. 'Faire' here meaning 'easy'. Permission was refused and the battle began with the impetuous action of Sir Henry Bard.

9 Harley states that when the enemy [i.e. the Royalists] had the wood the Roundheads, 'not to be outdared by their horse . . . drewe downe all our horse into a heathe, which stood betwixt the two hills where they did fight, but under favour of the enemy's ordinanse, the hills being one from another not a whole culvering shott'. He was presumably referring to a demi-culverin, which firing 'at utmost random' had a maximum range of 2,000 paces, but was not effective much above 400 paces.

10 Again in Harley's account there is mention of a village on the Roundhead left, which the Royalists obtained during the fight and set alight.

This is virtually all we have to go on, for what few battle relics have been found do not help us to determine the site, and the only known burial ground in the vicinity is not a Civil War one. It must be remembered that many contemporary accounts were written some time after the battle, when memories may have become confused; they are often contradictory and almost always biased. The student of the battle, viewing the ground from every angle, has carefully to consider these few facts and, working on what the late Colonel Burne called 'inherent military probability', decide for himself the location of the battlefield.

The fourth fact in the above list seems to be important. Why did Waller send a force of 1,000 musketeers into Cheriton Wood, 800 yards to his front? If he had intended to occupy the Hinton Ampner range there would seem to have been little point in sending a small force 800 yards or more ahead of the main line to be defeated in detail. Surely the reason for occupying this strategic position was to prevent the enemy from doing so, and Leighton's task was to advance ahead of the main army and threaten Lisle's troops. In this he succeeded, for Lisle must have been withdrawn before Forth appeared upon the scene.

The sixth fact gives the range from the top of the reverse slope. If Hopton had advanced as far as the south ridge of the horseshoe the enemy would have been firing from Cheriton Wood into his left flank at almost point-blank range; the reverse slope must have been to the north of this main ridge. The intermediary ridge favoured by the present writer is 650 yards from the south ridge and about 250 from what is now the edge of the wood.

Having evicted the enemy from Cheriton Wood Hopton saw that he could fall upon the flank of their main position without much difficulty. Had this been on the Hinton Ampner ridge (the position described in John Adair's *Cheriton 1644*) it would have involved Hopton in a longish ride across the open valley, whereas from the top of the wood he had an almost perfect covered approach.

Harley's statement that the hills were not a whole culverin shot apart does not rule out the generally accepted positions of the two horseshoe ridges, for these are about 1,700 yards from each other. The Hinton Ampner–south ridge positions would be around 1,400 yards apart, but the intermediary ridge is only 650 yards from the south ridge, which would seem to be too close for that description to fit. Harley's village is a more difficult problem, and seems to point to the Hinton Ampner valley, where Hinton Marsh definitely existed, although Little London (a mere cluster of houses) probably sprang up later and received the name as a result of the battle. There could not have been a village in the horseshoe, unless Cheriton had outlying cottages in those days.

Turning to local tradition, there is the site (still marked on some maps) of Gunners' Castle. This is just beyond the north-east end of Cheriton Wood, and seems an extraordinary place to site a battery of guns, wherever the battle was fought. It is said that ghosts haunt the Hinton Ampner valley, but more important local evidence comes from a farmer with seventy years' experience of the valley, who told the writer that even now with modern drainage the fields are often waterlogged in parts at the end of March. No contemporary account mentions water, or heavy ground for cavalry to manoeuvre on. The valley where the battle was fought is referred to as a heath – a description unlikely to fit ground that contains the headwaters of the Itchen.

John Adair's site is preferable to the one hitherto generally accepted (the two ridges of the horseshoe); but somehow it doesn't seem quite right and there are too many serious snags for the present writer to be entirely satisfied. Admittedly the site here suggested of the south ridge (Parliamentarian) and the intermediate ridge (Royalist) is too cramped for comfort, but this might have been the cause of the confused dog-fight into which the battle developed and it is an arena scarcely, if at all, smaller than that of Marston Moor, in which larger armies were involved. There is also the question of Cheriton Wood. If it was the same shape and size (and this seems doubtful) as it is now, both the generally accepted site and the one I myself favour have the difficulty of Hopton's left wing, which would have been partly masked by the south-west end of the wood. Nevertheless, it seems to be the site that fits in best with the few important known facts.

CHAPTER 5

Marston Moor

2 July 1644

The Battle of Marston Moor was fought on ground immediately to the north of the Tockwith–Long Marston road, these villages forming respectively the flanks of the opposing lines. Long Marston is situated about five miles west of York on the B1224 road leading to Wetherby. The Tockwith road runs north-west from the crossroads in Long Marston, and the obelisk commemorating the battle stands on the north side of the road about one mile from Long Marston (Ordnance Survey one-inch map, sheet 97).

Easily the best view of the battlefield is obtained from the high ground to the south of the road in the vicinity of Cromwell Plump. The ground rises gently from the road to this feature, which is crowned by a few trees. However, there is no track to it, and during the summer months the ground is likely to be under corn and permission could not be obtained to walk it until after harvest. But the visitor can walk up Moor Lane (which runs almost due north from the obelisk) and in just over 400 yards, where there is now a pond, the line of the great ditch can be faintly traced. The lane continues for another half-mile until it comes to a cross-lanes. By taking the left of the four lanes and continuing to its end the visitor arrives at what was White Syke Close, where Lord Newcastle's Whitecoats made their last stand – and where they were mostly buried. The site is probably just to the south of the lane's end. This walk takes one round that part of the battlefield where some of the fiercest fighting took place.

The year 1644 began badly for the Royalist forces in the north when the Earl of Leven, at the head of a large Scottish army, marched across the border on 19 January in support of the Parliamentarian cause. On the 25th of the month Sir Thomas Fairfax inflicted a crushing defeat on Lord Byron's troops, who were besieging Nantwich, capturing seventy-two officers and 1,500 men, of whom more than half subsequently joined the Parliamentarian army (see p. 34). Indeed, the Fairfaxes proved irresistible in the early months of the year: Sir Thomas cleared the West Riding of Yorkshire, and then with his father took Selby on 11 April, making another large haul of prisoners.

The Marquess of Newcastle, with a totally inadequate army, could do nothing but fall back before the Scottish invasion and was in Durham when Selby fell. Finding himself squeezed between the Scots and the triumphant Fairfaxes, he retired on York. By 22 April the Scots and the Fairfaxes had joined forces and York, that aristocrat among cities with its massive walls, enchanting medieval houses and narrow streets, prepared itself for a long siege. At first the city was only partially invested and Newcastle was able to occupy the suburbs; but on 6 May Lord Manchester at the head of the Eastern Association's army took Lincoln, and by 2 June he had arrived before York to join the investing force. Constant attacks made the outlying areas of the city untenable, so Newcastle destroyed the bridges over the rivers, withdrew to the centre and played out time as best he could with spurious offers to treat, but fighting pugnaciously to repulse any enemy attempt to breach the walls.

After his success before Newark in March (see p. 34) Prince Rupert had retired to Shrewsbury to build up his army. From here he was summoned to Oxford and was in consultation with the King between 25 April and 5 May. Rupert held firmly to the view that York must be relieved as soon as possible, and he put forward a plan based on maintaining the strengths of the garrisons around Oxford with a striking force sufficient to occupy Essex and Waller, while Prince Maurice made an all-out effort in the west and Rupert himself concentrated on the relief of York. But the dust had scarcely settled on the hoofmarks of Rupert's horse before those in conclave with the King set about altering his plan, with nearly fatal consequences to the King's 'Oxford Army'.

However, Rupert remained constant to that part of his plan which allowed for the relief of York. With only 6,000 foot and 2,000 horse he had not the strength to engage the formidable host of some 27,000 men now before the city, so on 16 May he marched from Shrewsbury to win Lancashire and gain recruits. His progress was mainly one of triumph, although his successes were not gained without some loss, and the captured towns and garrisons suffered the barbarities usually inescapable when men are engaged in ruthless internecine quarrel. Such losses as there were were made good by the acquisition of the Lancashire regiments and troops brought in by Lord Derby, whose countess had put up such a gallant resistance to the Roundheads at Lathom House. Moreover, on 1 June Rupert was joined by Lord Goring and Sir Charles Lucas at the head of 5,000 cavalry and 800 infantry. Lord Newcastle

Alexander Leslie (above left), who as the Earl of Leven led a large Scottish army across the border on 19 January 1644 in support of Parliament. The Marquess of Newcastle, who had been created a duke by the time this portrait (above right) was painted, Prince Maurice of Nassau (below left) and Lord Goring (below right) were all Royalist commanders

had sent these troops to him, for cavalry were more of a hindrance than a help in a closely beleaguered city.

While at Liverpool Rupert received a letter from Sir Thomas Glemham, Governor of York, outlining the critical situation of the besieged. There was no time to lose and now, at the head of 7,000 horse and probably as many foot, he set out across the Pennines, marching via Skipton, Denton, Otley and Knaresborough, which town he reached on 30 June. He had wisely spent three days at Skipton resting, reorganizing and training his new recruits for the coming battle.

The generals commanding the allied army (Scots and Parliamentarians) were determined to maintain the pressure on York and had firmly resisted messages from the Committee of Both Kingdoms that they should detach a force to intercept Rupert in Lancashire. However, when information reached them that the Prince was at Knaresborough with an army of 18,000 men – for it was wrongly assumed that he had been joined by Sir Robert Clavering with 3,000 men – their task was clearly to prevent this relief force from getting into York. Accordingly on the morning of 1 July they raised the siege and marched to Long Marston in order to bar the Knaresborough–York approaches.

This was a wise move, for the allied commanders had learned that the expected reinforcements under the Earl of Denbigh and Sir John Meldrum could not be with them for a few days, and thinking Rupert to have more men than he had they felt unable to detach a part of their army to deal with him. Rupert's military reputation was now at its height. The story of his exploits in the field had become a heroic apologue of skill and daring. From his next manoeuvre the legend could only gain strength. The direct route to York was barred by a superior force, so the Prince having thrown out a cavalry screen to deceive the allied army on Marston Moor, struck north and marched via Boroughbridge, where he crossed the Ure, then to Thornton Bridge and over the Swale, through the district known as Galtres Forest and down to Overton, a small village on the Ouse opposite Poppleton. Here he scattered an outpost of Manchester's dragoons and seized the bridge of boats that they were guarding. In the course of a long day Rupert had marched his men twenty-seven miles. That evening York was relieved.

Exactly what happened in the Royalist camp on the evening of 1 July is no longer known. Lord Goring certainly rode into York to report to Newcastle, his military chief, but Rupert for reasons of protocol may have remained with his troops on the outskirts of the city. Late as was the hour, and tired though they would have been, a cavalry reconnaissance force would almost certainly have ridden out that evening to observe the enemy, for Rupert was determined on battle. Newcastle, and his veteran chief of staff General King (recently made Lord Eythin), were for waiting. It seemed to be the more sensible course: the allied army outnumbered them by about 8,000 men, all of whom were presumably in better shape than Rupert's 14,000, who had just completed a strenuous march, and the York garrison of some 4,000 foot which had undergone the rigours of a long siege.

Reinforcements were expected under Clavering, and possibly Montrose; and more importantly, Newcastle thought – with some reason – there were cracks in the allied army which might soon become a cleavage. A case could also be made for the commander-in-chief spending a day or two integrating his and Newcastle's armies. But caution seldom played much part in Rupert's reasoning: he firmly believed that in war courage and resolution cast aside all veils and disguises and became the only arbiters of success.

Although Newcastle probably did not meet Rupert on the evening of 1 July, he sent him a letter which ended with the words: '. . . neither can I resolve anything since I am made of nothing but thankfulness and obedience to Your Highness's commands.' These courtier sentiments were taken at their face value by Rupert, who sent peremptory instructions for Newcastle to join him with his army at dawn the next day. However, it was not until 9 a.m. on 2 July that the two men met. Only then did Newcastle and Eythin inform the Prince of their reasons for not wishing to fight. By this time Rupert's army was getting into position on Marston Moor, and the matter was closed when Rupert told Newcastle about a letter (which he did not show him) that he had received from the King ordering him to fight.

This letter, which Rupert was to carry with him for the rest of his life, was written from Worcestershire on 14 June when the King's fortunes were at a low ebb. The relevant passages were, 'If York be lost I shall esteem *my crown little less*'; and again, '*But if* York be relieved, and *you beat the rebels' army* of both kingdoms, which are before it; then (*but otherwise not*)* I may possibly make shift (upon the defensive) to spin out time until you come to assist me. Wherefore I *command and conjure you,* by the duty and affection I know you bear me, that all new enterprises laid aside, you immediately march, according to your first inten-

* Inserted by Lord Wilmot.

tion, with all your force to the relief of York.' Crystal-clear orders that at all costs York must be relieved, but no direct mandate to engage the enemy in battle afterwards. However, Lord Colepeper appears to have known Rupert better than his uncle did, for on learning that the letter had been sent he exclaimed to the King, 'before God you are undpne, for upon this peremptory order he will fight, whatever comes on't'.

Meanwhile, there was some disagreement in the allied camp between the English and Scottish commanders. The English favoured giving battle at once, but the Scots – curiously more cautious, for their plan would have led them further from home – favoured withdrawing to prevent Rupert breaking through to the south, which seemed to be his most likely course. They won their point, and in the early hours of 2 July the army marched for Selby led by the Scottish infantry. The cavalry rearguard was not clear of the high ground south of the Long Marston–Tockwith road before Rupert's army commenced deploying to the north of the road. The head of the allied army was now within a mile of Tad-caster and the whole force was dangerously strung out along several miles of a narrow road. Fairfax at once sent messengers to recall the foot and artillery, for it was obvious that Rupert intended to give battle.

It is arguable that Rupert now missed his best opportunity of gaining a victory. For several hours the allied army, striving to regain the open ground and deploy for battle, was hopelessly vulnerable. The man who had been prepared to throw caution overboard a little while earlier now seemed content to wait upon events and hazard all on a set-piece battle for which he appeared to hold no advantage. But this is to look at only one side of the coin: Rupert had his problems. He was outnumbered anyway, and unless victory was certain – and in battle there is no such thing as certain victory – it would have been most inexpedient to attack without Newcastle's army; his own troops were not yet fully concentrated; and he himself probably did not arrive at Long Marston before the middle of the morning, by which time the chances of success had sensibly diminished. Knowing the man as we do one cannot help thinking that had it been possible to gather up his army for a quick swoop he would have done so. Admittedly Rupert was not a good commander-in-chief, but he never lacked the offensive spirit.

It was about 4 p.m. on a sultry afternoon, with the first thunder clouds gathering in the distance, before the whole of the allied army was back between the villages of Tockwith and Long Marston and in some sort of formation. An hour or so earlier they had established their artillery on the high ground south of the road and fired one or two rounds of defiance at the enemy, causing the loss of one Cavalier officer. But this cannonade and any skirmish there may have been on the Tockwith flank was of short duration.

The allied army was originally drawn up on the slope that descends gently from the low ridge on which stands the feature now known as Cromwell Plump – the command post of the allied generals. Immediately in front of the army was a field of rye and then came the Long Marston–Tockwith road (known as Marston Lane), which although then little more than a trackway followed the same line as the present road. North of the road the land was probably cultivated for about 400 yards up to the deep ditch that originally connected Atterwith Dyke (which used to run east of Atterwith Lane) with the Syke Bek that runs through Tockwith. The ditch had a hedge on most of its southern side and was partly filled in at its western extremity. Beyond the ditch the ground was at that time open moorland, and except for a number of gorse bushes that offered some protection to the Royalist left there was little cover between the ditch and Wilstrop Wood – which may have been larger in 1644. The only exception to this was Moor Lane, which runs north of the road from the site of the obelisk and was much as it is now, flanked by a hedge and shallow ditch.

The Royalist order of battle, numbers and dispositions were fairly accurately assessed and plotted on a plan (now in the British Museum) made at the time by Sir Bernard de Gomme. He gave a total of 11,000 foot and 6,500 horse, which may not have included officers, and if anything errs on the low side. Rupert probably commanded 18,000 men, which included 7,000 horse and an artillery train variously estimated as between sixteen and twenty-five guns. The strength of the allied army is less easily computed. Major-General Sir James Lumsden, who fought with the Scots army, has left a plan of the battle and an estimated strength of just over 21,000 men, which included 8,000 horse. Brigadier Peter Young, whose research on the battle has been more thorough than that of any other modern writer, does not dismiss this figure but thinks it may be too cautious. In his admirable book, *Marston Moor 1644,* he agrees with the generally accepted figure of 27,000 plus for the allied army assembled before York after Manchester had arrived, but the disparity between this number and Lumsden's figures for the battle is not precisely accounted for.* The total

* Pp. 68, 106 and 109.

was probably nearer 27,000 than 22,000, and the allies may have had a few more cannon than the Royalists – but little use was made of artillery in this battle.

Both armies drew up for battle in the conventional style of the time with their cavalry on the flanks and infantry in the centre. The Royalist right was under Lord Byron, who had Sir John Hurry, major-general of Rupert's horse, with him.* It comprised 2,600 horse and 500 musketeers interposed between the cavalry, and was drawn up in two lines, with one regiment of 200 horse under Colonel Tuke positioned in the right rear of the leading right cavalry regiment to prevent that flank being turned. The cavalry on the left was under Lord Goring, with Sir Charles Lucas to assist him. This wing too was drawn up in two main lines and again the flank was 'refused', this time by Sir Francis Carnaby's regiment. Goring would have ridden in the front line leaving his second-in-command with Sir Richard Dacre's brigade, which comprised the second line. This wing had about 2,000 horse and, like the right wing, 500 musketeers.

The infantry in the centre, probably under the overall command of Lord Eythin, was drawn up in three lines with the regiments six ranks deep, pikemen in the centre and musketeers on the flank. Their right front was somewhat advanced as a brigade under Colonel Napier had been placed to cover the gap between the centre and Byron's horse on the right. Sir William Blakiston's small cavalry brigade, probably no more than 800 strong, reinforced the infantry, taking position between the second and third lines. Newcastle's famous Whitecoats did not arrive on the field until the middle of the afternoon, and no doubt for this reason were placed on the right of the second and third lines under Sir Francis Mackworth. The centre comprised some 10,000 infantry and Blakiston's cavalry. Behind the infantry Rupert took personal charge of a small reserve of about 700 horse. The guns were mostly interspersed among the main body of the infantry, but four drakes were placed forward on the line of the ditch. The Royalist line stretched from about the Syke Bek in the west to just beyond Atterwith Lane in the east. The main position was some 200 yards north of the ditch, but the ditch and the hedge bordering Moor Lane were lined with musketeers. The men in the ditch had been

* Sir John Hurry had deserted from the Parliamentarian army in July 1643, but was back with them a few months after Marston Moor. He turned his coat yet again in 1646, was taken in the north of Scotland during Montrose's ill-fated expedition and, like Montrose, was executed in Edinburgh.

Right: Prince Rupert

given the unenviable task – even for a forlorn hope – of checking the advancing troops before withdrawing onto the main body.

The allied army was drawn up in something of a hurry and nationalist niceties had to be sacrificed to expediency, with the result that brigades were strangely intermingled. The cavalry and dragoons of Lord Fairfax's army, with the first line under his son Sir Thomas, were on the right opposite to Lord Goring. These troops, like the rest of the allied army, were drawn up in three lines, and like the Royalist cavalry were supported by musketeers. Oliver Cromwell, who was Lord Manchester's lieutenant-general of horse, commanded the first line of cavalry on the left wing. There were three Scottish regiments of horse (whose mounts were not comparable to those of the English) placed on each wing, and Sir David Leslie commanded those on the left. On the extreme left wing were 500 dragoons under Colonel Hugh Fraser. It is probable that the allied artillery was concentrated in the rear of the left wing.

The infantry in the centre were organized in fourteen brigades. In the first and third lines the English and Scots were intermixed: General Baillie commanded the Scots and General Crawford the English (part of Manchester's army) in the first line; General Lumsden's Scots occupied the second line; and according to a report submitted after the battle by the Parliamentarian generals, Lord Fairfax (he and Lord Manchester may have commanded their own brigades) had his foot on the right of the third line next to the cavalry. The same report* speaks of two Scots brigades in reserve. The cavalry wings each contained rather more than 5,000 troops, and with the reserve the centre may have had as many as 15,000 men. Lord Leven was in command of the centre, and Cromwell and Thomas Fairfax took charge of their respective wings.

When, at about 4 p.m., Lord Eythin eventually made his appearance at Long Marston it is alleged that he brought onto the field 3,000 of Newcastle's troops, most of whom were disgruntled over arrears of pay, and some of whom were slightly inebriated from plundering the abandoned allied camp before York. If this is true they soon forgot their troubles, for of all those who fought at Marston Moor none stood their ground so bravely as these men. It is to be feared that the most disgruntled man among them was Eythin himself – a veteran of many battles, but a commander with no spark of genius, and a man with a chip on his shoulder so far

* *A Full Relation of the Late Victory*. But Lumsden's plan shows Fairfax's men on the left and only one brigade in reserve.

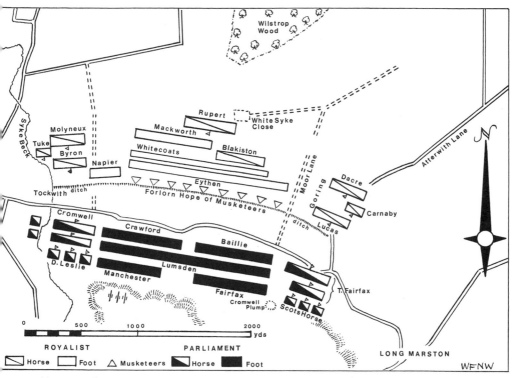

Above and overleaf: Battle of Marston Moor

as Rupert was concerned, dating from a continental battle sixteen years earlier. On being shown the dispositions he was not only disapproving but positively rude to Rupert, declaring that the army had been drawn up too close to the enemy. However, he told the Prince – who had probably already decided not to attack until the morrow – it was too late to make any alteration. By this time the allied army, which on their return from Tadcaster had been hastily deployed on the slope of the high ground south of the road, had advanced to a position perhaps only 250 yards from the ditch. This was necessary because from the area of the road most of the ditch is in dead ground, and is the position that seems to fit Scout-master-General Lion Watson's report.*

Rupert appears to have discounted the possibility of the enemy attacking that evening, as it was very unusual in those days for an army to attack with less than four hours of daylight (although Newcastle was not so sure), and having decided to await the dawn for his own attack he allowed the men – in modern parlance –

* *A More Exact Relation of the Late Battell.*

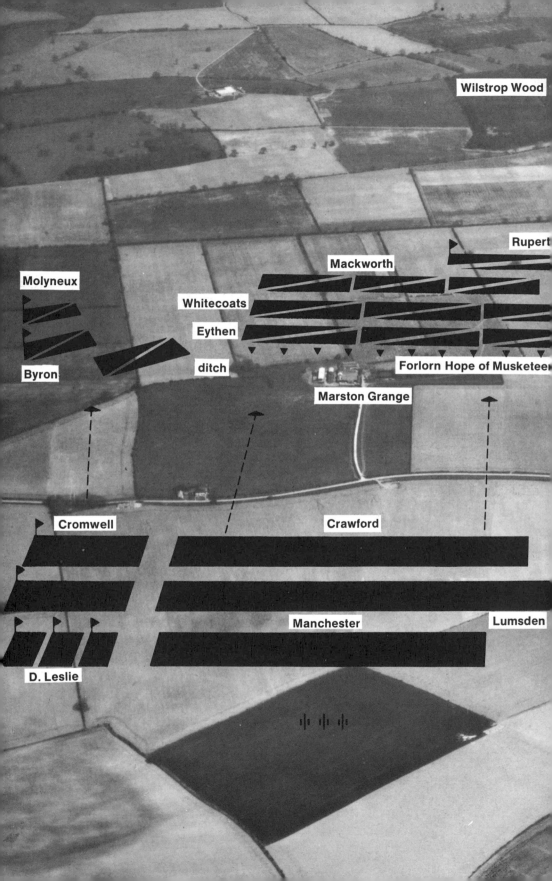

Wilstrop Wood

Rupert

Mackworth

Molyneux

Whitecoats

Eythen

Byron

ditch

Forlorn Hope of Musketeers

Marston Grange

Cromwell

Crawford

Manchester

Lumsden

D. Leslie

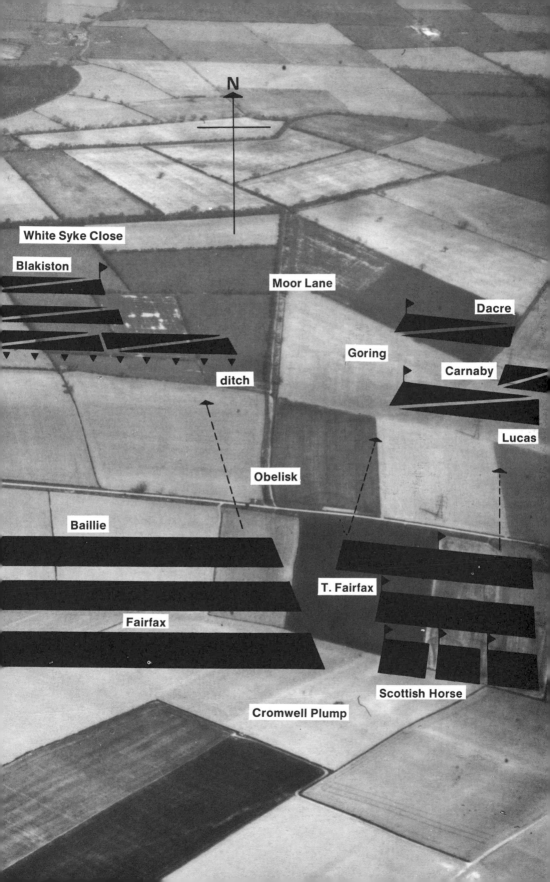

N

White Syke Close

Blakiston

Moor Lane

Dacre

Goring

ditch

Carnaby

Lucas

Obelisk

Baillie

T. Fairfax

Fairfax

Scottish Horse

Cromwell Plump

to stand down. He himself rode off to get his supper and Lord Newcastle retired to his coach for a smoke. This was surely a most unwise move on the part of a commander-in-chief, with the enemy almost rubbing noses with his forward troops and still nearly three hours of daylight left. Lord Leven seized his opportunity. At about 7 p.m., as the first few heavy drops of thundery rain began to fall, the unsuspecting Royalists looked up from their suppers to see the allied army bearing down upon them.

The clash of arms was almost simultaneous along the whole front, but the battle may be more easily understood if the account is split into the three sectors of the line. That on the allied left, where Cromwell and Leslie engaged first Byron's cavalry and then the reserve under Rupert, eventually driving them from the field; the cavalry fight on the Long Marston flank, where, although Fairfax himself won through, Goring routed the majority of his cavalry; and in the centre, where the infantry of both sides remained sternly embattled through the dusk and under a harvest moon, until the Whitecoats, forced back by Cromwell's triumphant cavalry, surrendered the ground only with their dead bodies. Thus a simple outline of a somewhat complicated battle.

As Colonel Fraser's dragoons began their task of clearing the hedge and ditch on Cromwell's immediate front the rain became heavy, and lightning from glowering clouds accompanied by peals of thunder replaced the noise of cannon as a backcloth to the battle. Cromwell owed his initial success, certainly in part, to the good work of Fraser's men and those of Crawford, whose infantry drove in Napier's advanced brigade, but also perhaps to the impetuosity of Lord Byron. It seems that instead of allowing Cromwell's troopers to pass over the difficult terrain of the ditch and then attacking them at a disadvantage, Byron adopted the normal cavalry tactics of immediate advance, which lost him the benefit of the musketeers that Rupert had given him. Be that as it may, he was beaten back, although his second line in some hard fighting – during which Cromwell received a flesh wound in the neck – temporarily stemmed the onslaught.

Prince Rupert, whom we have noted was eating his supper in the rear of the army when the battle began, lost no time in getting to horse and joining the reserve cavalry. It would not have been long before he realized the difficulties that Byron was in – though Goring on his left was making some headway against Fairfax. No doubt the proper place for Rupert was in control of the whole battle at his command post, while another led the reserve into battle, but when it came to action Rupert was never one for self-restraint. Moreover the chance to have a tilt at Old Ironsides, as he was to call Cromwell, was too good to be missed. Hence Rupert himself galloped off to the right at the head of Widdrington's brigade and his Lifeguard.

Almost certainly Rupert's wish to join battle with Cromwell was fulfilled: although the latter may have retired to Tockwith to have his wound dressed while David Leslie took command of that wing, the struggle there lasted for well over an hour and before the end Cromwell was undoubtedly back. This was no fast-moving cavalry action, but a battle of attrition with men hacking and thrusting at each other's limbs with their swords. Gradually the Royalist cavalry gave ground, until first one regiment and then another bent and finally broke before the storm. Lord Newcastle, upon the scene somewhat later than Rupert, tried in vain to check the headlong flight of horsemen towards and beyond Wilstrop Wood. And amid all this mayhem Prince Rupert, evidently horseless, contrived to escape capture by hiding in a bean field until the tide of battle had passed him by.

On the Royalist left flank matters fared somewhat better. The ground between Sir Thomas Fairfax's and Lord Goring's cavalry was not the neatly cultivated fields which now stretch east of Moor Lane to and beyond Atterwith Lane, but rough, wet ground liberally sprinkled with tough gorse bushes. The allied ranks advancing to the charge through this difficult country necessarily became somewhat disorganized, and Fairfax tells us that Goring's musketeers inflicted a number of casualties. This is understandable, but what is not so easy to believe is Captain Stewart's account in *A Full Relation* in which he tells us that Fairfax could only cross the ditch by advancing up Moor Lane and that his men, as they debouched in threes and fours, suffered the most heavily from Royalist musketeers. Undoubtedly the musketeers lining the ditch took some toll, but probably the Scots infantry on the cavalry's left suffered the most casualties. In fact there was little opposition until the ditch had been crossed, but thereafter the trouble began and only Fairfax, at the head of 400 men, achieved a breakthrough. His troops routed a small portion of Goring's cavalry and pursued them for at least two miles.

Goring, ably seconded by Lucas, in a hard fight that can be described in seconds but probably lasted the better part of an hour, eventually pushed back Fairfax's second line under Lambert and third under Eglinton, and pursued them through and beyond the Parliamentarian baggage lines. Some of the allied regiments (almost certainly Sir Hugh Bethell's was one) panicked and in doing so rode down the Scottish infantry on their immediate left, which added to the confusion. Fairfax reckoned that in the cavalry fight on this wing the allies had as many casualties 'as in the whole army besides'. Certainly his own family and that of the Montgomerys suffered severely.

Eyewitness accounts of this part of the battle are sparse, so it is difficult to be sure of the role played by individual regiments. But it seems that while some of Goring's first line were pursuing the enemy towards Tadcaster (thereby giving rise prematurely to rumours of a Royalist victory) others were plundering the baggage wagons, and some time elapsed before Goring could collect them up. Meanwhile Sir Charles Lucas had still to drive Eglinton's and Balgonie's Scottish horse from the field – and they fought most stubbornly – before setting upon the now unprotected flank of the Scottish infantry and causing grave damage. Fairfax, unable to rally his 400 men, returned from the pursuit almost alone to find most of his command gone and himself inextricably involved in the mêlée. Taking off his white Parliamentarian emblem he rode through the Royalist ranks, unscathed save for a sword slash in the face received during the charge, to join Lord Manchester's triumphant cavalry under Cromwell.

In the centre the infantry fight was as stubbornly contested and every bit as confused as it was on both cavalry wings. Crawford, as already mentioned, met with almost immediate success on the allied left centre, but elsewhere matters did not go so well for the Parliamentarians. Lord Newcastle, together with his brother Lord Charles Cavendish, fought with great valour (killing three men with his page's half-leaden sword) at the head of Sir Thomas Metham's troop of gentlemen volunteers. At the same time, and possibly with the help of Metham's troop, Blakiston's cavalry drove a wedge right through the middle of the allied line, routing Lord Fairfax's foot and a Scots brigade, whom they chased up the ridge south of the road. Lumsden did what he could to plug the gap, but prisoners had been taken and men killed as far as the third line, and the Scots generally had received a tremendous pounding, having been assailed from in front by Newcastle's Whitecoats and charged in the flank by Lucas's cavalry.

Incredibly, it was at this grave crisis in the battle, when the allied infantry appeared to be crumbling irretrievably, that all three allied commanders left the field. Lord Leven scarcely drew rein until he reached Leeds; Lord Fairfax made for his castle at Cawood, where finding no fires or candles he wisely went to bed; but Lord Manchester, more courageously, retired only a short distance and soon re-entered the fray to lead his men to ultimate victory. Total disaster was averted by the stout-hearted resistance of Lord Lindsay's and Lord Maitland's regiments – the latter commanded by Lieutenant-Colonel Pitscottie. Lining their musketeers with pikemen, they withstood three cavalry charges and held their ground while many around them fled, finally unhorsing Sir Charles Lucas and taking him prisoner. Generals Baillie and Lumsden never tired in their efforts to present some semblance of order among the allied infantry, but as the daylight departed and the thunder clouds dispersed to reveal a harvest moon the scene was one of the utmost confusion. Some men were in headlong flight, others managed to preserve their existence by the narrowest margins and chances. Arthur Trevor, arriving on the field at this time with dispatches for Rupert from the Duke of Ormonde, later commented, 'The runaways on both sides were so many, so breathless, so speechless, and so full of fears, that I should not have taken them for men, but by their motion which still served them very well.'

Such was the situation as the battle entered upon its closing stage. Both sides were without their commander-in-chief; the Royalist cavalry had been worsted on their right flank, but Goring had managed to rally many of his men on the left and was now occupying the position held by Sir Thomas Fairfax before the fighting began; in the centre the Royalist infantry was virtually intact. But the threat posed to their right flank would shortly develop into a thrust at the heart. In the brief lull before the final trial of strength, neither side could be confident that victory would crown its efforts.

Scoutmaster Watson (Parliamentarian) tells us that the battle was over and the field clear of the enemy by 9 p.m., but almost certainly he got his timing wrong, and anyway Royalist cavalry under Sir Philip Monckton remained on the field until midnight. The numbers engaged at the Battle of Marston Moor were larger than in any other battle fought on British soil with the exception of Towton, and although events moved with remarkable rapidity the various actions described above could not have been accomplished in much less than two hours. It is more likely that it was ten o'clock before the fighting ended under a moon that threw long shadows of horsemen across the carnage of the field, presenting to those onlookers who had come for the entertainment a strangely ethereal scene.

By the time Sir Thomas Fairfax had made his way through the enemy lines to the allied left wing Cromwell and Leslie had disposed of the Royalist cavalry and Prince Rupert. Fairfax, although fighting his first major battle, had given proof in smaller affairs that he was a most competent captain, and it was probably at his bidding that Cromwell's cavalry rode round between the embattled troops and Wilstrop Wood to come in on the left of the Royalist line. Fairfax would have seen enough of the battle in his wanderings to realize how precarious the allied position was, and he had sufficient tactical sense to grasp that if Goring's cavalry could be routed as Rupert's had been seeming defeat might be turned into victory.

The cavalry on the Long Marston flank were in exact reverse to their original positions; that is to say, Goring's men were coming down the slope from the area of Cromwell Plump, while Fairfax and Cromwell occupied the ground formerly held by Goring. There were other Royalist cavalrymen milling around the battle area, but with Lucas and Porter (Goring's major-general) captured and Sir John Hurry riding hell-for-leather for York there was only Sir Philip Monckton left to round them up, and this proved beyond

him. Goring's men were, therefore, hopelessly outnumbered and after a short, sharp fight, in which Sir Richard Dacre was mortally wounded, they were driven from the battlefield. The allied cavalry, which had been kept superbly under control, were then free to charge the rear of the by now hard-pressed Royalist infantry.

Lord Manchester was no general, but he was a good fighting soldier, who after a momentary lapse had returned to the field to lead his men, together with the thrusting Crawford, against Newcastle's Whitecoats and Major-General Tillier's and Colonel Broughton's Greencoats, who still stood unbroken and defiant. The weight of the attack, coming in as it did on the right of the Royalist infantry, had the effect of swinging the whole line round so that the axis of advance was west to east instead of south to north. The fighting here was the most stubborn of the whole battle, as the Royalists saw victory eluding them. Some contemporary accounts speak of the Greencoats (probably under Tillier, who was

The Battle of Marston Moor

captured) being the last troops to withstand the double onslaught of infantry and cavalry, but it is generally agreed that this honour rightly belongs to the Whitecoats, of whom it was said, 'they brought their winding sheets about them into the field'.

The pressure on the Royalist infantry became intolerable when the hammer of Cromwell and Fairfax began to pound on the anvil of Manchester and Crawford; nor were Baillie's and Lumsden's Scots standing idle, for recovering from wounds inflicted by Lucas's cavalry they now joined the pack for the kill. At the northernmost edge of the battlefield there was a field, partially enclosed by ditches, called White Syke Close. Pressed slowly back by the weight of the triple attack upon them, and now almost alone of the Royalist army still capable of fighting, it was said to be in this enclosure that the last glorious phase of the battle took place. Having caused considerable casualties to the Parliamentarian cavalry and foot before running out of ammunition, these Whitecoats disdained surrender and fought furiously with butt and pike, holding all at bay, until at last Colonel Fraser's dragoons pierced an opening through their ranks. The dam once broken, torrents of steel poured in. Then came the butchery, cruel and merciless.

It was said at the time that out of almost 3,000 men who took part in this last desperate stand, all but thirty lay dead on the field. But records of officer survivors known to have fought at Marston Moor indicate that the casualties in White Syke Close may not have been quite so great. Nevertheless, seldom in the annals of the British infantry have there been more indomitable soldiers than those amazing Whitecoats, who came grudgingly to the battle yet remained upon the field until the very end.

As with almost all these battles the casualties cannot be accurately assessed. The usual computation made by Parliamentarian scribes is between 3,000 and 4,000 Royalists killed and 1,500 made prisoner. Their own losses are often put as low as 300. Perhaps about 3,000 Royalists perished in fight or flight, but the losses in the allied army must have been more than 300. Fairfax's cavalry alone probably lost that amount or more, and in the early stages, and again at the end, both the Scottish and the English infantry took considerable punishment. It would seem more realistic to put the allied losses at approaching 1,500. The Royalists lost their entire artillery train, a great quantity of arms, powder and baggage, and enough colours 'to make surplices for all the cathedrals in England, were they white'.

The retreat in the dark towards York was an appalling shambles.

Only Lord Eythin appears to have made any attempt to rally some men in order to stave off pursuit, which continued with much bloodshed to within two miles of the city. The governor very wisely would admit only those troops known to have been part of the garrison. Even so the narrow streets were cluttered with the debris of battle – men suffering from terrible injuries, seared, wearied and in some cases dying. Prince Rupert, having lost his horse and his white poodle 'Boy', had remained hidden until dark and arrived in the city at about the same time as Newcastle, who had abandoned his coach in which were papers of some value to the enemy. The next morning, to the obvious distress of the inhabitants, Rupert gathered up the remains of his army and made off for Lancashire in the vain hope that fresh successes might retrieve the disaster of the battle. Newcastle, who had spent much money and effort in King Charles's cause, seems to have lost heart completely. He and Lord Eythin, abandoning Sir Thomas Glemham and York to their fate, made for Scarborough and took ship to Hamburg.

Among the generals the principal heroes of the battle were undoubtedly Thomas Fairfax and Oliver Cromwell. Rupert's stock suffered a severe setback. The legend of invincibility was gone; the victor of so many battles had lost the north for the King. As commander-in-chief he was the natural scapegoat and it must be admitted that after his brilliant manoeuvre to relieve York his performance as a commander was disappointing, although some allowance should be made for the froward Newcastle and Eythin. It has been truly said that the Royalists lost Marston Moor not so much through the prowess of their enemy as through their own mistakes.

Sir Thomas Glemham surrendered York on 16 July: with Newcastle's army demolished and Rupert's army away in the north he had no chance. Rupert had positive orders to save York, and yet he left it to its fate. But given the circumstances prevailing at the time it could never have held out for very long; it was better that he and his cavalry should be spared for other battles. After the fall of York the allied army split up. The Scots became preoccupied with Montrose in their own country, and Fairfax set about reducing the Royalist garrisons in Yorkshire. Manchester, with the Eastern Association's army, did practically nothing until the Second Battle of Newbury almost four months later (see p. 35), a contributory factor in the ever-widening breach between him and his more famous lieutenant-general of horse, Oliver Cromwell.

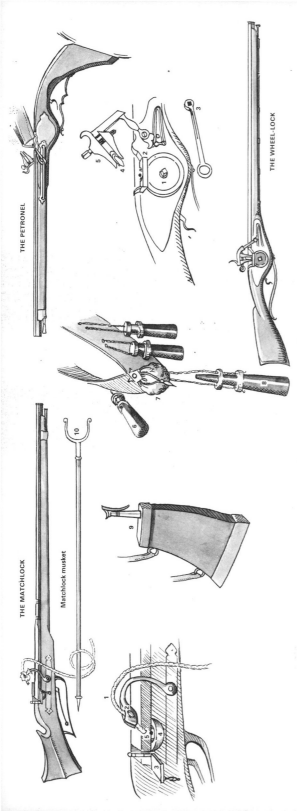

THE PETRONEL

THE WHEEL-LOCK

THE MATCHLOCK

Matchlock musket

Arquebus or matchlock musket

The matchlock musket or arquebus (like 'hackbut', derived from hakenbüchse) was in use from the end of the 15th century. It was the musketeer's weapon throughout the Civil War and was borne by at least one regiment at Sedgemoor in 1685. The slow match (1) of cord soaked in saltpetre is held in the serpentine (2). The pan-cover (3) being rotated outwards, the pan (4) is uncovered. When the trigger is pulled the serpentine carries the lighted match to the pan, igniting the priming powder there, which in turn, via the touch-hole (5), fires the charge. Charges of powder were made up and carried in wooden bottles (6) ('twelve apostles', usually eight in front and four behind) suspended by cords from a bandolier which also bore a bullet-pouch (7) and a larger wooden bottle of fine-grained priming powder (8). Additional powder was carried in a powder horn or flask (9). Because of the length of the matchlock and its weight of up to 20 lbs, a forked rest (10) was used as a support

The wheel-lock

The wheel-lock musket and carbine were much used by officers and mounted troops throughout the Civil War. A wheel (1), the upper edge of which protruded up through the bottom of the priming-pan (2), was turned with a key or wind-ing spanner (3) against the pressure of a strong V-spring until it engaged with a sear, which cocked the mechanism. When released by pres-sure on the trigger, the wheel spun sharply back, grating its serrated rim against a piece of iron pyrites (4) held against it in the pan by the lowered cock or doghead (5). The sparks thus produced fired the priming and thence the charge

The petronel

The petronel (French: poitrine) was a very large pistol or short carbine, with a sharply down-curving butt which was held against the chest rather than the shoulder, hence the name. Used by horsemen, it was supported by a shoulder-sling attached to the top or side so that it could be held in the aim and fired with only one hand, leaving the bridle-hand free

SCOTTISH SWORDS AND OTHER BASKET-HILTS

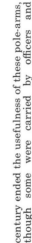

'Claideamh mor'—great sword (claymore)

Dragoon sword
Civil War

17th - 18th C
basket-hilted
Scottish broadsword
or claymore

Italian schiavona

POLE-ARMS

Spontoon
17th - 18th C

Sergeant's
halberd
1700 - 1799

Pike
14th -17th C

Lochaber axe
17th -18th C. Scottish

Voulge
16th-17th C

Pole-arms

Pole-arms continued in use during the 17th century. Companies of pikemen with 18-foot-long pikes, halberds and similar weapons not only protected the musketeers during the lengthy process of reloading, but also advanced to the attack 'at push of pike'. Improved muskets and the advent of the bayonet in the early 18th century ended the usefulness of these pole-arms, though some were carried by officers and sergeants for another 100 years as a mark of rank

Scottish swords and other basket-hilts

The claymore (claidheamh mor—great sword) was properly the 6-foot-long two-handed broadsword of the 14th-16th century Scots. The single-handed basket-hilted broadsword of the 17th-18th centuries, often called a claymore, may have been developed from the Italian Sciavona. The basket-hilt was usually lined with leather (the liner), and this type of broadsword was also much used in England, especially by cavalry and dragoons

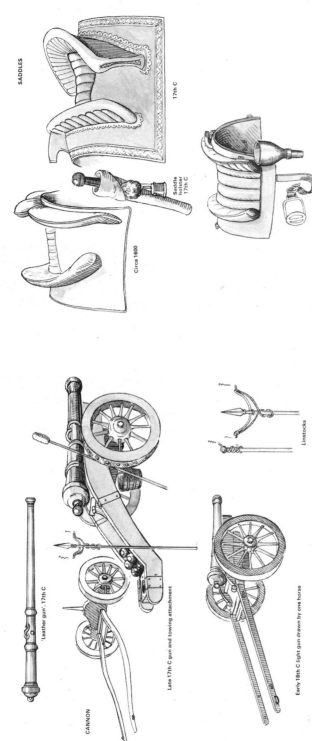

SADDLES

17th C

Saddle holster 17th C

Circa 1600

18th C saddle and furniture

CANNON

'Leather gun' 17th C

Late 17th C gun and towing attachment

Linstocks

Early 18th C light gun drawn by one horse

Cannon

Originally made of welded iron bars, cannon barrels were later cast, first of brass and then, from the mid-16th century, normally of iron. By the 17th century muzzle-loading cannon had assumed more or less the form they were to retain until the introduction of quick-firing breech-loaders in comparatively modern times, though a variation was the 'leather gun' of the Civil War, a lightweight, easily manoeuvrable copper or brass barrel bound with leather, on a light carriage. Cannon were fired by means of a slow match fastened to a portfire or linstock. According to their size and shot-weight pieces of ordnance received distinctive names such as cannon royal, firing a 48 lb shot and needing a team of up to twenty draught horses in tandem: the culverin 18 lb shot, with a team of nine horses: demi-culverin, 9 lb shot: falcon, 6 lb, and saker 5¼ lb

Saddles

By the 17th century saddles were beginning to assume a shape more familiar to modern eyes, though still retaining higher cantle and pommel until the 18th century, and still keeping a raised and padded front plate, presumably for comfort and support rather than for protection

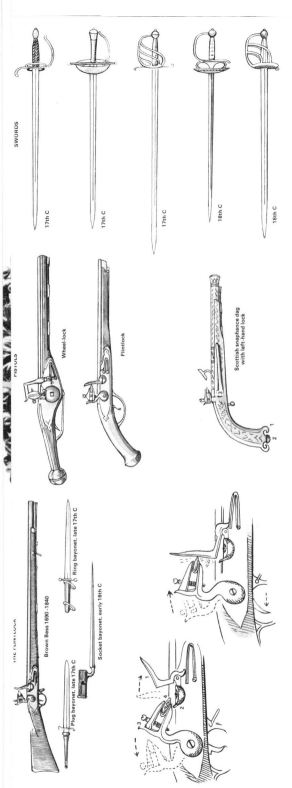

17th C

17th C

17th C

18th C

18th C

Wheel-lock

Flintlock

Scottish snaphance dag
with left-hand lock

THE FLINTLOCK

Brown Bess 1690-1840

Plug bayonet, late 17th C

Socket bayonet, early 18th C

Ring bayonet, late 17th C

The flintlock
The flintlock musket, known as Brown Bess, was in use from 1690 until 1840. When it had been muzzle-loaded with powder and ball from a paper-wrapped cartridge, the top of which had to be bitten off, the frizzen (1) was raised to uncover the pan (2) for priming, and then lowered again, and the cock (3) holding the flint (4) was drawn back. When the trigger was pressed, the cock fell, and the flint scraped hard against the frizzen. This produced sparks and at the same time forced back the spring-loaded frizzen, thus allowing the sparks to ignite the priming powder in the uncovered pan, which via the touch-hole fired the charge in the breech. The snap-hance lock was a late 16th–early 17th century fore-runner of the flintlock. It worked

on the same principle except that pan-cover and frizzen were separate, so that the pan-cover had to be opened before the frizzen was lowered into the firing position

Pistols
The invention of the wheel-lock made pistols a practical proposition and thus provided a fire-arm suitable for use by horsemen, which the matchlock certainly cannot have been. Scottish pistols or 'dags', snap-hance or flintlock, were made with all-metal stocks. They were often supplied as a pair, one with a right-hand lock, the other with a left. The butt, at first fish-tailed, was by the 18th century the so-called 'ramshorn' butt (1) with a ball (2) screwed into the base. This held a pin, the pricker, used to clean out the touch-hole. The dag usually had a ball-type trigger and no trigger-guard, and was fitted with a long belt-hook (3) along the plate, being worn suspended by this hook from a shoulder belt

Swords
The trend towards swords suited for thrusting as well as cutting continued during the 17th and 18th centuries. The increasing popularity of fencing at about the beginning of the 17th century led to the development of swords and rapiers more and more devoted to the thrust, with hilts of which the loops, bars, shell-guards and cups added to the quillons are too varied to be enumer-ated. Military swords retained greater weight than did dress rapiers, and cavalry swords still had weight and edge for effective cutting

Henry Ireton (left) and Thomas
Fairfax (right) were two of
Parliament's leading generals

Harrison and Colonel Ireton, was always in touch. Indeed, Ireton
came upon a rearguard left at Naseby and captured these unsuspecting men as they were at supper. The King had intended
spending the night at Lubenham, but when news reached him of
Ireton's coup he hastened to Market Harborough for a midnight
conference with Rupert and others of his council. All were agreed
that a further withdrawal with the enemy cavalry hard on their
heels would take on the aspect of a flight, which would be demoralizing and dangerous. Rupert was therefore ordered to draw
up the army early on the morning of the 14th along the commanding high ground that runs from East Farndon towards Great
Oxendon. This ridge, rather less than two miles south of Harborough, was an excellent defensive position, and there is reason
for thinking that Lord Astley, who commanded the infantry, was
anxious to await the enemy there. But later developments caused
Prince Rupert to take the offensive.

There is very little argument about the course the Battle of
Naseby took: it has been well documented, and on the whole it

was a fairly straightforward fight which lasted for about three hours. The same cannot be said about the initial manoeuvring for position. Contemporary accounts are apt to be confusing, and although the final dispositions of both armies are known with some accuracy the question of how they arrived at them and whether the Roundheads conformed to the Royalists (as is generally thought) or vice versa (as the present writer thinks) is not easily solved.

The early part of June had been very wet, but the morning of the 14th dawned bright and sunny with a north-west wind. Visibility was good and from their first position the Royalists would have had a view uninterrupted by trees and woods (which is no longer the case) to the higher Naseby ridge some four miles to the south. The ground between these two prominent ridges is very undulating and at that time was almost completely open. The shallow dales could hold water – even in summer – for there were many springs and the river Welland rises close to Naseby. In a letter written two days after the battle the writer describes the ground as 'some ploughed, some champion', and a 1630 map clearly shows strips of cultivated land leading from the Royalists' final position towards the low ground known as Broad Moor. The same map also indicates that at that time there was only one road worthy of the name in the area: the one leading from Naseby village past the present New House Farm to Kelmarsh.

Fairfax left Guilsborough in the early hours of the morning of Saturday 14 June, and by sunrise the whole army would have been established on the Naseby ridge, probably in the area of the road junction north of the obelisk on the present Clipston road. Fairfax could not be certain at this time that the Royalists would stand and fight, so the army may have advanced below the ridge. But it is more likely that at about 8 a.m. Fairfax and Cromwell, with a suitable escort, rode forward to reconnoitre the ground for the most suitable position. On either side of the Clipston road the ground slopes steeply from point 631, and even now the fields in that bottom hold water. Cromwell quickly realized that to attack with cavalry over such a rough, waterlogged area would be a hazardous operation such as might determine the Royalists to refuse battle. Turning to Fairfax, and pointing to the high ground a little way to the west of where they were, he said, 'Let us, I beseech you, draw back to yonder hill, which will encourage the enemy to charge us, which they cannot do in that place without absolute ruin.' Fairfax saw the wisdom of this and the army marched to its left.

The position eventually taken up by Fairfax stretched from the area of Red Hill Farm in the west to beyond where Paisnell Spinney now stands. From Streeter's engraving in Joshua Sprigge's *Anglia Rediviva** we have a pretty accurate plan of the Roundhead order of battle, although his positioning of some of the Royalist regiments is slightly suspect. Just before the battle, Cromwell had persuaded Fairfax to make Ireton commissary-general, or second-in-command of the cavalry, and he had charge of the cavalry on the left wing. On this wing the horse was formed up in two lines; each regiment had two 'divisions' (squadrons as we would call them) and each squadron three troops drawn up in line and in three ranks. The infantry in the centre was under Sergeant-Major-General Skippon and drawn up with five regiments forward and three in the second line. On the right Cromwell's cavalry was not only cramped for room, but had difficult ground in front of it; he drew it up in three lines, with two squadrons in the third line and Colonel Rossiter's 400 horse, who only arrived from Lincolnshire just before the battle began, squeezed in between the first and second lines.

The total strength of the army was about 13,500 men, the cavalry numbering 6,500, the infantry 6,000 and Colonel Okey's dragoons 1,000. There is a tendency to give this formidable force a frontage of only one mile, but without going into details as to how much room is needed in the ranks it is difficult to see how an army with a large cavalry component, and musketeers needing at least four feet, could do with less than 2,500 yards. To get even this their left must have rested on a very thick boundary hedgerow (part of which still stands) called Sulby Hedges, and indeed we are told that this was so, although it would have meant the left of Ireton's cavalry being off the hill on flat ground. It would also have meant that Okey's dragoons, whom Cromwell ordered to line the hedges, must have been firing into the right of the Royalist cavalry at almost point-blank range – yet it is not apparent that they did great damage.

At about 7.30 a.m., while the Royalist army was still on the East Farndon ridge, Rupert had sent his scoutmaster forward to discover the enemy's position. For some reason that is not easy to understand, even allowing for the undulating ground, this man returned with completely negative information, and so Rupert decided to go himself. He had reached the neighbourhood of Clipston when he saw the enemy's army at about the time they were

* Sprigge was Fairfax's chaplain at the time of the battle.

116

Sergeant-Major-General
Skippon, commander,
Parliamentarian
infantry, at the
Battle of Naseby

beginning their march to the Red Hill position. He was too experienced an officer to think that they were withdrawing, but he
realized that there was a chance to attack them while they were
unbalanced. Sending a galloper back to the King, requesting that
the army should be brought forward at once, he rode on to reconnoitre a position. This he found on a ridge known as Dust Hill,
which is now bisected by the Sibbertoft–Naseby road at point 555.

When the army arrived he drew it up with its right in the area
of the present Prince Rupert's Farm and its left at the eastern edge
of what is now Long Hold Spinney. The Royalists were outnumbered by nearly two to one. Clarendon gives a total of 7,400
with only 2,500 infantry, although other accounts indicate that
there were slightly more infantry and about 4,500 cavalry. If the
foregoing suggestion of events and their timings is agreed, then it
would seem that Rupert was doing his best to conform – with a
very thin line – to the Parliamentarian position, and although he
might have liked to get to windward of the enemy the Sulby
Hedges prevented this. Even though the King was in the field it
seems clear that Rupert had the overall command, and it would
have been better had he let his brother Prince Maurice lead the
right wing of the cavalry instead of doing so himself. The left

wing was under Sir Marmaduke Langdale, who had 1,600 not entirely reliable cavalrymen, while Rupert had more than 2,000. Lord Astley commanded the infantry and Streeter's plan shows three brigades (those of Sir Bernard Astley, Lord Bard* and Sir George Lisle) forward, and Colonel Howard's horse behind in support. A reserve of about 1,300 men consisted of the King's Lifeguard under the Earl of Lindsey, Prince Rupert's infantry regiment and – according to Clarendon – the King's Horseguards under Lord Bernard Stuart.

Shortly before the Royalist army advanced to the attack – which was a little after ten o'clock – Fairfax had withdrawn his entire army, less a forlorn hope of 300 musketeers, to the reverse slope of the ridge. He probably did this to ease the pre-battle tension of his many raw recruits, for he advanced the whole line into the forward position again as the enemy were almost at the attack – which in itself was no mean feat. Presumably what few light cannon he had remained forward, because we learn that they fired one totally ineffectual round at the advancing Royalists and that that was the only part played by artillery in the battle.

The Royalist line advanced at a steady pace, with the cavalry of the right wing slightly in advance, but battle was joined almost simultaneously along the whole front. Rupert's cavalry were caught in Okey's cross-fire, which probably accounted for their quickening pace, but except for Okey's own rather confused account in a letter to a friend in London we do not hear of many empty saddles. It seems that on this wing the cavalry of both sides halted for a short space of time when within a few hundred yards of each other. Ireton may still have been organizing his squadrons as they came forward, and Rupert, who halted first, may have wanted to give his horses a breather before the charge which he now initiated. The two right-hand squadrons of Ireton's broke the Royalists to their immediate front, but the centre squadron failed to press its charge and on the extreme left the Roundhead horse was – in less than half an hour – put to flight.

Both commanders now committed understandable errors. Prince Rupert, at the head of his triumphant 'divisions', pursued the fleeing enemy up to their baggage train, which was a little way to the south-west of Naseby. Ireton, whose fault was even more forgivable, saw that the infantry brigade on his immediate right was in peril and so turned his two squadrons inwards instead of

* Sir Henry Bard was not in fact made a peer until a month after Naseby.

118

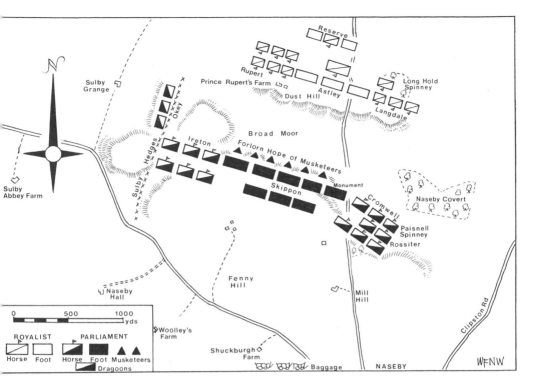

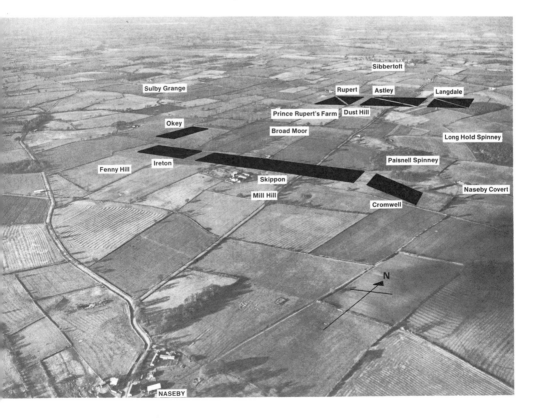

Above and below: Battle of Naseby

attending to the cavalry battle. The result was disastrous: his troops were badly mauled and he himself received two nasty wounds and was, for a short time, a prisoner. Soon most – but not quite all – of Ireton's cavalry were out of the battle.

The Royalist infantry in the centre, although heavily out-numbered, soon showed the value of battle experience. As the Roundheads came over their hill only a short distance separated them from the enemy. There was time for just one volley before the opposing ranks clashed and the battle became one of musket butts and push-of-pike. On the Parliamentarian right Fairfax's regiment held (they do not appear to have had much opposition), but on the left Skippon's regiment, commanded by Lieutenant-Colonel Francis who was killed, and even the more experienced troops under Colonels Montague and Pickering, were pushed back up the hill by the determined onslaught of the Royalist foot, led by that stout-hearted veteran Jacob Astley. Soon the Parliamen-tarian front line was in complete disorder, with colours fallen and officers striving in vain to rally their retreating men, who were scrambling to the comparative safety of the reserve lines.

We are told that the main fight in the centre lasted a good hour, and it was probably about half-way through it that Fairfax, returning from the extreme right of the line, saw the sorry state of his centre, for by now Ireton's intervention would have failed – probably worsted by Colonel Howard's supporting horse. Fairfax reacted swiftly. He and Skippon brought up the reserve and it was while the latter was leading Colonel Pride's men into the battle again that a musket ball pierced his armour and passed through his side. Fairfax, himself without a helmet, which had been lost in the cavalry action on the right, begged Skippon to retire, but the tough old soldier replied that 'he would not stir so long as a man should stand'. With the reserves committed the battle in the centre still remained in the balance. The Royalist troops strove magnificently against odds that were too great. Had it been a purely infantry encounter they might still have prevailed, but with Rupert still away on their right Colonel Okey saw his chance, and mounting his dragoons he thundered into battle against the right-hand ranks. At the same time a worse fate beset those on the left, for Oliver Cromwell, with several squadrons of his well disciplined cavalry, wheeled in to pulverize that flank.

Cromwell was enabled to do this because his cavalry on the Roundhead right had met with complete success. The ground on this flank presented problems for cavalry: the slope was steeper here and the hillside was dotted with gorse bushes, and there was

Defeat of Charles I at Naseby

also a fair-sized rabbit warren to be negotiated. Any idea that Cromwell's men swooped down on Langdale's Northern Horse in a whirlwind attack can be dismissed. Apart from the fact that a large part of Cromwell's 3,500 horsemen were well disciplined veterans – some belonging to his own Eastern Association – this fight had of necessity to be a much more controlled affair than the one on the other flank. Langdale was a brave and capable commander, and although the Northern Horse had recently been showing signs of disaffection they fought now with commendable courage. Nor is the criticism that Langdale failed to take advantage of the broken ground to scatter the Roundheads as they were descending the hill in loose formation valid, for the ground presented difficulties that were even greater for Langdale than for Cromwell. The plain fact is that the Royalists were hopelessly outnumbered – by more than two to one – and Cromwell was able to turn their flank with his right 'divisions'.

It was Whalley, on Cromwell's left, whose squadrons were the first to engage. Both sides discharged their pistols at virtually point-blank range and then fell to it with their swords. Soon the action had become general along the whole wing, with Rossiter's men in the fairly early stages starting to turn Langdale's flank. The two Royalist squadrons opposing Whalley were the first to break, but not until they had given a good account of themselves, and in less than an hour the whole of the Northern Horse was pouring back to behind their starting line. Sir Edward Walker tells us that 'four of the Rebel Bodies in close and good order' followed this defeated wing. The very nature of this controlled fight would have enabled Cromwell to keep a firm grasp on his squadrons, and he probably detached his first line to pursue the enemy with the limited objective of ensuring that they could not reform. Had Rupert been able to do something similar on the other wing he could scarcely have won the battle, but he might have saved his infantry from total surrender. But his attack was a much faster-moving and less well controlled affair.

At some stage in the battle, and it seems to have been as Langdale's men were streaming past him, the King took personal command of the reserves and advanced in an attempt to stabilize the line and aid his hard-pressed infantry. But the Earl of Carnwath is said to have seized his bridle exclaiming 'Will you go upon your death?', and prevented him from implementing this noble impulse. Then it was, Walker says, that the meaningless command 'March to the right hand' rang out, which was taken to mean 'everyone to shift for himself', and the reserves 'turned about and ran on the spur almost a quarter of a mile, and there the word being given to make a stand we did so, though the Body could never be rallied'.

Meanwhile, the wretched infantry were left on their own. Besides Cromwell's thrust on their left and Okey's on their right, some of Ireton's men had rallied and were in their rear. One brigade won the ungrudging admiration of its opponents by its stubborn resistance to every form of attack. Eventually it was practically ridden and trodden down when Fairfax brought up his own regiment of foot, which was still quite fresh having been only on the fringe of the battle, and led a concerted attack in conjunction with his Lifeguard under Captain Charles Doyley. It is probable that the heaviest infantry casualties were suffered by this brigade in the last minutes of the battle. Most of the other regiments laid down their arms and formed the greater part of the huge haul of prisoners – not very far short of 5,000 men in all.

While all this was happening Rupert was gradually gathering up what men he could to return to his duty on the field of battle. He had been rudely repulsed by the guard on the baggage train.

122

The commander had at first mistaken him for Fairfax, for both generals were wearing the same red headdress, called a *montero,* but on realizing his error he greeted him and his men with a hail of shot. Rupert's return to the battlefield was too late to be of any assistance to the .Royalist infantry, and in any event his horses were by now in no state to endure another fight over heavy ground. He therefore rode back to where the King and the reserves – most of whom had never been committed, but would have been had Rupert remained in overall command of the battle – were making that half-hearted stand mentioned by Sir Edward Walker.

Here, briefly, they faced the New Model, hastily reformed for a final thrust to victory. It was never made, for in spite of all that the officers could do what was left of the Royalist troops had had enough. One volley from Colonel Okey's dragoons and the field was deserted. This time the pursuit, although for the most part under control, was not limited as to distance and, attended by considerable slaughter, it continued for twelve miles, until at Great Glen, just short of Leicester, Lord Bernard Stuart with the King's Lifeguard managed to check it.

It does not appear that the Roundheads lost much more than 150 men, but the Royalist casualties are harder to assess. Contemporary accounts are confused and contradictory, but probably about 400 soldiers were killed in battle, and Langdale's cavalry may have lost as many as 300 in the pursuit. There was a most unpleasant incident when, unknown to Fairfax, some of his more licentious soldiery got among the Royalists' mobile brothel. These whores, 'who were full of money and rich apparell', were thought to be Irish, but were most probably Welsh. At least 100 were massacred and many more had their faces slashed, or noses slit, which was the unpleasant treatment meted out to such women in those days.

Virtually the entire Royalist commissariat fell to the victors: 200 carriages and sumpter-wagons, forty barrels of powder, a good quantity of much needed cheese and biscuit, the entire artillery train, 8,000 arms and a rich haul of colours. But more damaging by far than all of these was the King's cabinet, in which were his private papers that included copies of the most damning correspondence between himself and the Queen, outlining his plans for bringing over Irish papists and his efforts to secure foreign mercenaries and money from continental princes. As was to be expected, Parliament wasted little time in publishing these papers.

The King paused for a short while in Leicester and then rode on to spend the night in Ashby-de-la-Zouch. He displayed his usual calm in the wake of defeat and even then his unbounded optimism could not be suppressed. When Gerard's Welsh levies eventually joined him he had the makings of a fresh infantry force and he still had about 4,000 horse, and Goring's army was intact in the south-west. But in July Goring was brought to battle at Langport in Somerset by the powerful combination of Fairfax and Cromwell, and decisively beaten (see p. 36). The First Civil War was to linger on for another year until the capitulation of Oxford in June 1646, but it was the clamant disaster of Naseby that sounded the death knell of the King's military machine.

'When did you last see your father?' Painting by W. F. Yeames. The battles have all been fought and the hunt for the surviving Royalists is on

Cromwell, in his letter to the Speaker written on the same day as the battle, says that it lasted for three hours and was for much of the time 'very doubtfull'. This was perhaps a pardonable half-truth. The issue in the centre could for a short time be said to have been in some doubt, but the Parliamentarians were never in real danger of total defeat. Heavily outnumbered, outgeneralled and with the advantage only of a better infantry arm, Charles could have had little hope of victory. Battle should have been avoided until Goring had been hanged and Hopton had marched his army to the King. This is perhaps too simple a solution which does less than justice to a man who, until he became unstable, unprincipled and dissolute, had displayed considerable courage and powers of leadership. Nevertheless, it is difficult to avoid the conclusion that Goring lost the King his last chance.

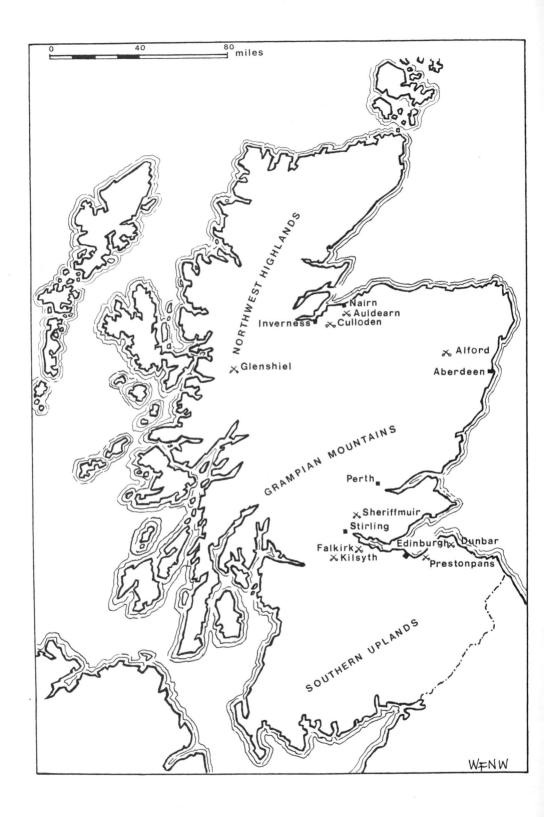

0   40   80 miles

NORTHWEST HIGHLANDS

Nairn
Auldearn
Inverness   Culloden

Glenshiel

Alford
Aberdeen

GRAMPIAN MOUNTAINS

Perth

Sheriffmuir
Stirling
Falkirk   Edinburgh   Dunbar
Kilsyth   Prestonpans

SOUTHERN UPLANDS

WFNW

CHAPTER 7

Montrose's Battles
Auldearn, Alford and Kilsyth

9 May 1645, 2 July 1645 and 15 August 1645

Of the three battlefields the most rewarding, from the visitor's point of view, is Auldearn. This small town lies just over two miles south-east of Nairn on the A96 road. The National Trust for Scotland have put an excellent plan and description of the battle at a view-point (Boath Dovecot) just to the west of the church. From here it is possible to see almost the whole of the battlefield and follow its course from the narrative. The church stands on the site of the 1645 one, but then the village consisted of just a few houses running north and south along the ridge due south of the church.

Alford (pronounced Arfud) is some thirty miles north-west of Aberdeen. At the time of the battle the village was a mile to the west of the present town, and the local inhabitants will point out the site of the church, smithy and shoeshop, which stood on the hill where now there are only farmsteads at a tiny place called Ardgathen. Looking north from this hill (with Gallowhill just in the left rear) the visitor gets an excellent view of the battlefield.

Kilsyth lies about fifteen miles north-east of Glasgow on the A803 road. The fields in which Montrose had his camp have now been flooded for a reservoir, but the west end of the reservoir can be reached by a very rough track that leads off the A803 road just by the entrance to the public park half a mile east of Kilsyth. From this end of the reservoir an excellent view of the battlefield, with the hill (near Banton) up which Macdonald attacked, can be obtained. The ridge immediately north of the reservoir is the one that Baillie was trying to reach so as to outflank Montrose.

No account of the Civil War, however brief, would be complete without mention of at any rate three of the battles in the remarkable series of victories gained, against great odds, by James Graham, fifth Earl and first Marquess of Montrose. Auldearn, Alford and Kilsyth were not large-scale affairs, but the first two were tactical gems. History has endowed Montrose with an aura of romantic heroism, for he was a much adored and courageous leader, a poet and a patriot, but he combined these qualities with

James Graham,
Marquess of Montrose,
the man who almost
succeeded in gaining
Scotland for the King

political foresight, and he was also a superb guerilla leader, who
at times displayed a military genius far in advance of most of his
contemporaries.

Montrose was born in 1612 and started his military career in
1638 in the Covenanter army commanded by Alexander Leslie –
later Earl of Leven – that tough veteran of the Thirty Years' War,
who commanded the Scots' army at Marston Moor (see p. 35 or
chapter 5 for a full account). During the next four years he made
a big reputation for himself, but soon became disillusioned with
the Covenanters. In signing the Covenant Montrose did not feel
that he was joining in an act of rebellion, but that the Covenanters
offered the best chance of redressing the grievances of the Scottish
nation without coming into conflict with the constitutional
authority of the crown. But what had started as an honest attempt
to resolve a religious problem became the means whereby a small,
self-appointed authority could gain political ascendancy in Scotland in opposition not only to episcopacy and the Prayer Book,
but also to the King. The man who stood at the head of this cabal
of diehard Presbyterians was Archibald Campbell, Earl of Argyll.
He and his cronies, while outwardly supporting the original aims
of the Covenant, were using them to gain sovereign control of
Scotland.

Argyll was a most unpleasant man, cowardly, cruel, dishonourable in his dealings and entirely without compassion. Nevertheless he was a shrewd and capable politician, and full of cunning. He was jealous of Montrose's popularity with the people, and annoyed when he became the leader of a moderate party that in 1639 drew up a Bond in which they asseverated their loyalty to King as well as Covenant. By the time King Charles unfurled his standard at Nottingham in 1642, Montrose was ready to break with the Covenanters. His soul flamed within him as he watched the ugly turn that events were taking in Scotland; but on the few occasions that he attempted to warn Charles of the dangers that were impending he was most coolly received. The King preferred to rely on the insidious advice of the Marquess of Hamilton, who in a court bedevilled by cabals of favourites was the interpreter of Scottish affairs.

It was not until the autumn of 1643 that Charles realized the extent to which he was being duped, and belatedly turned to Montrose as the man upon whom he could best count not only to counsel but to act. After he had been sent from Oxford to gain Scotland for the King there were to be disappointments and hardships before the tide began to turn in Montrose's favour. The Earl of Antrim had been sent to Ireland to raise his Macdonalds and land them on the west coast of Scotland by 1 April 1644, and Lord Newcastle was ordered to provide Montrose with cavalry. But Leven's army was well into England, which prevented Newcastle from sparing any troops, and when Montrose crossed the border at the head of 1,300 militiamen from Cumberland and Northumberland there was no sign of the Irishmen. He waited some days at Dumfries – during which time his English levies started to desert – before withdrawing into England, where he routed the Covenanter garrison at Morpeth and took the town. But he arrived too late to assist Prince Rupert at Marston Moor, and after that disaster was prevailed upon to hand over his small force to the Prince.

Many commanders bereft of all troops would have returned to headquarters, but failure never affected the buoyancy of Montrose's courage. The knight errant side of his character drove him on to pursue glory irrespective of reward. He determined to 'invade' Scotland with just two companions: Colonel Sibbald, who was later to abandon the Royalist cause, and William Rollo. Travelling in disguise, with Montrose posing as the two gentlemen's groom, these three journeyed to Tullybelton on the edge of the Highlands, where news was received that the Macdonalds (only about 1,100 of them) had arrived at last under Alasdair Macdonald, a man of action and a warrior of huge stature and great strength. Montrose ordered them to meet him at Blair Atholl. When he arrived there he found the men of Atholl on the point of fighting the strangers from Ireland, but the immense personal force of Montrose soon had the two parties agreeing to become allies against the enemies of the King. Now Montrose had the nucleus of an army. It comprised scarcely 2,000 men, ill equipped with primitive weapons and short of ammunition, but it justified the unfurling of the royal standard. On 28 August 1644 the precious piece of silk that had been so carefully concealed in Montrose's saddlebag was raised above his little force amid a fanfare of trumpets.

There followed small battles or engagements at Tippermuir, Aberdeen, Inverlochy (see p. 35 for accounts of these three battles) and Dundee. These were conducted with great skill and élan. Always fighting with inferior numbers to his enemy, Montrose time and again would snatch victory from seemingly certain defeat, or lead his men safely out of the most cunningly set trap. His name became a legend in the Highlands, and although he constantly found himself at the head of only a few hundred soldiers – for the clansmen invariably made for home when they had garnered sufficient loot – men were proud to serve with him, for he never asked them to do what he himself could not do better. In spite of difficulties, desertions and inadequate support from those he had relied on, by the spring of 1645 Montrose had the King's enemies in Scotland thoroughly demoralized.

In April of that year Montrose had under command 2,000 infantry, and when Lord Gordon and many of his clan had at last joined the Royalist army (the Marquess of Huntly was never reconciled to Montrose after an unfortunate affair right at the beginning of the campaign) he could muster some 250 cavalrymen. The Covenanter commander in the north was that Colonel Hurry whom we saw fighting for the Royalists at Marston Moor. He was determined to defeat Montrose and put to shame those less fortunate commanders – Argyll, Elcho, Balfour of Burleigh, and Baillie – who had tried and failed. He decided that his best chance of doing this was to lure Montrose into a part of the country where he had no friends; he therefore adopted the tactics of reculer pour mieux sauter and kept falling back in front of Montrose from Elgin nearly to Nairn. Close to Auldearn he turned upon his pursuer, hoping to surprise him by a night march. But as he advanced some of his men discharged their muskets to clear them of damp powder, and Montrose's sentries being on the alert heard them. Montrose had little time in which to make his dispositions, but he made them with boldness and skill.

The village of Auldearn then comprised just a few cottages that ran north and south along a low ridge. On the western slope of the ridge, which stretched down towards a burn, were the cottage gardens and outbuildings, and below them rough scrub extending to boggy land near the burn; this bog and a small hill protected the ridge from the south. Montrose placed his Irishmen, under Alasdair Macdonald, just to the north of the village, and the bulk of his troops to the south of the cottages, where they were hidden from view by the hill, and on the reverse slope of the ridge. He had no centre, save for a few men whom he placed among the cottages with orders to keep up a steady fire to give the impression that the village was strongly held. Macdonald was given the royal standard, and Montrose hoped that Hurry would attack him in mistake for the main body. Montrose would then fall upon the Covenanters' flank.

On the morning of 9 May Hurry marched headlong into the trap, but the plan nearly miscarried through the fiery impetuosity of Macdonald. He had been given too few troops with which to guard the standard – only 500 out of Montrose's total of 2,250 – and Hurry could put against him 3,500 foot and 400 horse. Never one to stand on the defensive, Macdonald probably thought that his best chance in the circumstances was to rush down the hill and attack Hurry as his men struggled through the marshy burn. It was a gallant gesture in the face of huge odds, but it nearly lost Montrose the battle. As the Macdonalds, badly mauled by Hurry's leading regiments (Lawers's, Lothian's and Buchanan's), tried to regain the high ground, Alasdair could be seen swinging his great broadsword and slicing off heads like artichokes from their stalks, but it was the coolness of Montrose that won the day. From his viewpoint he could see all too well how badly the battle was going. Turning to Lord Gordon and his men behind the ridge he loudly exclaimed, 'Why are we lingering here, my dear lord, when our friend Macdonald is driving the enemy before him? Shall all the glory of the day be his?'

The Gordons needed no further spur. They charged as cavalry should, no longer being so weak in numbers as to need supporting fire, but with sword in hand and with all the dash and fury of Cromwell's Ironsides. They rode straight at the Covenanters' flank and soon scattered their cavalry under Major Drummond, who crumpled into their own infantry. Confusion was made worse when Montrose and the rest of the Gordons followed in support, and Macdonald once more rallied his Irishmen. Isolated pockets of Hurry's army fought bravely, and he himself was almost the last to leave the field, but the victory was complete, and the slaughter savage. It is estimated that between 2,000 and 3,000 Covenanters perished in the battle and the rout, and large quantities of ammunition, money and stores were captured.

Auldearn successfully disposed of Hurry's army, but General William Baillie – the recently appointed commander in Scotland – and Lord Lindsay of the Byres were still in the field, each with a sizable army, and Montrose needed time before taking on another battle. He consequently avoided a fight with Baillie by one of those fascinating games of hide and seek in the hills at which he and his tough Highlanders were so adept, but having given Baillie the slip he felt strong enough to attack Lindsay in Atholl. However, before he could do so a messenger arrived from Huntly recalling his clan. Lord Gordon refused to obey the summons, but Montrose forbade him to put pressure on his clansmen as he wished to do. With the departure of the Gordons Montrose lost his cavalry arm, and he could not offer battle until he had built up his strength. Accordingly Alasdair Macdonald and Lord Gordon were sent off to recruit, while Montrose spent the time prowling round the skirts of his enemy. He found Baillie too firmly entrenched in Strathbogie, so he drew him southwards and lured him into unfavourable ground at Alford on the south bank of the Don.

Lord Gordon had managed to persuade about 200 Gordon troopers to join, or rejoin, the army, but Alasdair Macdonald was still away, which was a matter of considerable comfort to the Covenanters. Nevertheless, when Baillie saw Montrose's position he was loath to attack, but his every movement was subject to approval by the Committee of the Estates, and they ordered him to proceed. The upper reaches of the Don were a more formidable obstacle in those days, but near the present town of Alford there was a ford. It is difficult now to be quite certain of the exact location of this ford, but it was probably at, or close to, the present Bridge of Alford. Montrose had drawn his army up on the Gallowhill ridge overlooking the ford and the marshy ground surrounding it. The cavalry was divided and placed on the flanks, with Lord Gordon commanding on the right and Lord Aboyne on the left. Nathaniel Gordon commanded the infantry on the right and Colonel O'Kean (Macdonald's second-in-command, whose name is sometimes spelt O'Cahan) that on the left; in the centre John Drummond of Balloch and Macdonnell of Glengarry commanded

132

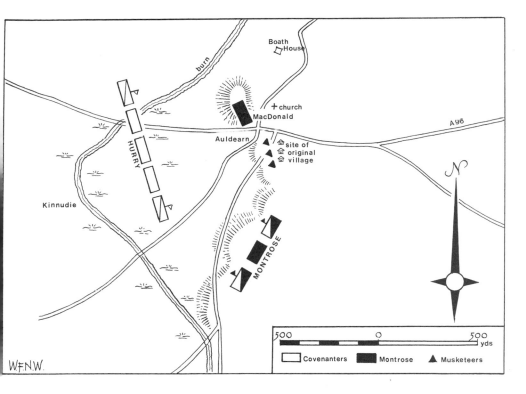

Above and below: Battle of Auldearn

the Highlanders and the Master of Napier was behind the hill with the reserve.* Both armies were almost equal in infantry with about 1,800, but Baillie had twice as many horse as Montrose.

The battle began on the Royalist right. No sooner were the Covenanters over the river than Lord Gordon was upon them with his handful of cavalry. As at Auldearn his shock tactics paid off, but not quite to the same extent. In Lord Balcarres he had a stout opponent, and a fierce cavalry fight ensued until Nathaniel Gordon came to his kinsman's rescue. He instructed his infantry not to fire at random among friend and foe, but to concentrate on hamstringing the enemy's horses. This completed the discomfiture of Baillie's cavalry, who were soon off the field, leaving the Gordons to turn against his centre. For much of the time that the right wing was so hotly engaged Aboyne and O'Kean remained motionless, but as soon as they saw the enemy left begin to crumble they advanced to the attack, and before long Baillie found both his flanks enveloped and Glengarry coming down the hill at his centre. Defeat was now certain, and when Napier appeared over the brow of the hill it became a rout. The Covenanter losses were not far short of those they suffered at Auldearn, while Montrose lost comparatively few officers and men considering the tough fighting on his right. But in the pursuit Lord Gordon was killed by a stray bullet. The death of this one man turned the victory sour: the Royalist army had lost a capable and courageous leader, and Montrose a devoted and irreplaceable friend.

Alford was fought on 2 July 1645, a little over a fortnight after the Royalist disaster at Naseby (see p. 35 or chapter 6 for a full account). Montrose realized that if he was to save the King he must cross the border, but before he could do this he needed to collect a sizable army. This took time, and while he was waiting for his 'recruiting sergeants' to do their work he baited Baillie by fleeting appearances in the neighbourhood of Perth. By the beginning of August Montrose had collected the largest army that he had yet commanded. Lord Aboyne (Huntly's second son) brought in 200 horse and 120 mounted infantry, Alasdair Macdonald and his Irishmen were back again, and the chiefs of Glengarry, Clanranald, the Macleans and the Atholl Stewarts were present with a

* Mark Napier in his *Memoirs of Montrose* (Vol. II, p. 527) puts a completely different construction on both Montrose's and Baillie's positions immediately before the battle. But having carefully examined the ground the writer agrees broadly with most other accounts. The site cannot be fixed with absolute certainty without knowledge of the exact spot where Baillie forded the Don, and this can no longer be established.

134

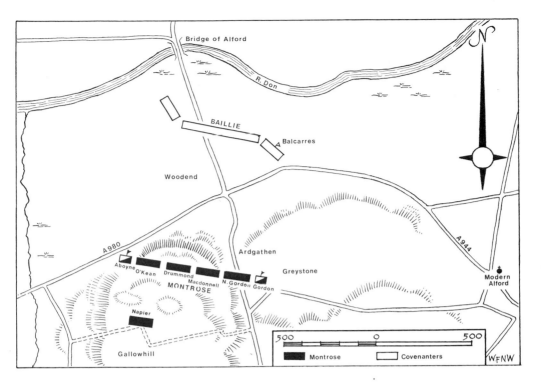

Above and below: Battle of Alford

good following. In all Montrose probably mustered around 4,400 infantrymen and 500 cavalrymen. Against this the Covenanters, when they had been joined by the Fife levies, numbered 6,000 infantry and 800 horse, but their new recruits were a raw, ill disciplined lot.

On about 10 August Montrose moved south. Slipping past Perth, he made for Stirling and crossed the Forth two miles upstream. Baillie, as was to be expected, came in hot pursuit. Montrose knew that Hamilton's brother, the Earl of Lanark, was marching towards Baillie with substantial reinforcements, and he decided to offer the latter battle before the two forces joined. By the night of the 14th the rival armies were within three miles of each other, but Baillie was anxious to wait for Lanark before attacking. However, he still had the incompetent committee round his neck, and they not only insisted on his attacking but actually altered his dispositions and plan of attack.

Montrose halted his army in some meadows a mile north-east of Kilsyth. These low-lying fields formed as it were a basin, and on the rim to the east Baillie drew up his men. He had what seemed a commanding position with a rough, rugged slope between him and Montrose; within this stern amphitheatre Montrose was soon to fight his most savage battle and gain his most decisive victory.

The fifteenth of August gave promise of being a scorching hot day, and Montrose, partly for comfort and partly to aid recognition, ordered his men to fight in their shirts. This strange sight seemed to goad Argyll and his committee colleagues into more damaging indiscretions than usual. They were firmly convinced that they had Montrose in a trap, and their only anxiety was that he might try to escape to the north. With this in mind they overruled Baillie's insistent objections and ordered him to carry out a flank march in full view (for it never occurred to anyone to use the cover of the hill) and almost within musket shot of their formidable foe. The result was soon a shambles – but not all of it on the Covenanters' side.

Montrose had sent some men forward to occupy a number of buildings on the lower slopes of the hill, and one of Baillie's officers could not resist the temptation to charge these men. This in its turn was too much for Alasdair Macdonald, who without orders launched the Macleans and the Macdonalds against these troops. The clansmen raced up the hill after their retreating foe and a fierce fight ensued on the hilltop. The Covenanter army was cut in two, for Baillie's advance guard had almost reached the height to Montrose's left. The Gordon foot and horse attempted

136

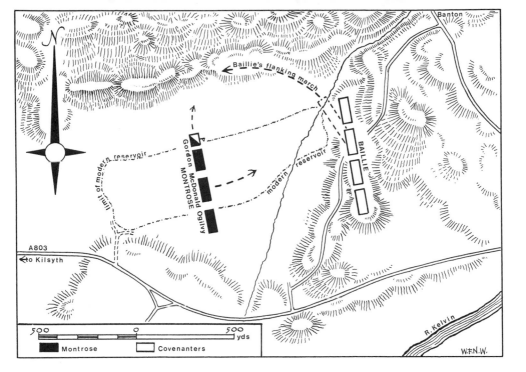

Battle of Kilsyth

to break this dangerous threat to their flank, but were out-numbered and before long in grave peril. Montrose dispatched Lord Airlie and the Ogilvys to redeem the situation, and this gallant man, now in his sixtieth year, led his troops with such spirit that even before Nathaniel Gordon reinforced him with more cavalry the battle on that flank was won. Macdonald's private war, undertaken at considerable risk, was also paying off, and Baillie turned in desperation to his reserve – the Fife levies. But he turned in vain: these gentlemen, seeing how matters stood, had wisely decamped towards their homes.

The day for Baillie was well and truly lost. When Montrose was trailing his coat round Methven Wood a few days before the battle, some female camp followers of the Irishmen had been captured and butchered; now no one could stop these men from taking their revenge on the defeated army. The well mounted senior officers made good their escape, as did most of the cavalry, but it is said that of the 6,000 infantrymen who saw the sun rise that August day, scarcely 100 were alive to see its going down.

In the short space of eleven months Montrose had defeated an enemy superior in numbers on six different occasions. He was now the master of Scotland. No Covenanter army remained in the country to oppose him; Argyll had fled to Berwick, and many other leaders were in exile. The principal cities made their humble submission, and vied with each other in their endeavours to please the victor. Royalist prisoners were liberated, but no revenge was permitted; both in Glasgow and Edinburgh the troops were kept strictly in hand. Undoubtedly this was the principal cause of Alasdair Macdonald – knighted by Montrose after Kilsyth – taking most of his Irishmen off to plunder Campbell country. These were halcyon days; but there was to be another battle, exile, return, capture (some say betrayal) and execution before the story of the Great Marquess was over.

At Philiphaugh on 13 September 1645 Montrose suffered his first major defeat at the hands of David Leslie, a much younger and possibly more able general than his kinsman Alexander, under whom he had fought at Marston Moor. As usual Montrose was short of men: the Earls of Home and Roxburgh had allowed themselves to be captured, and on the very eve of the battle the Earl of Traquair, who had almost certainly sent word to Leslie on the whereabouts and weakness of the Royalist force, ordered his son Lord Linton to march his men out of Montrose's camp. Nevertheless Montrose was taken unawares, even to the extent of being at breakfast some way from his army when Leslie approached through the morning mist. Heavily outnumbered, at first without their commander, and not drawn up for battle, their defeat was a foregone conclusion. Montrose fought furiously, but the odds were too great. He wanted to die on the field, but his officers persuaded him to escape. His troops surrendered on promise of quarter from Leslie, which promise was overruled by the Committee of the Estates, and a hideous slaughter ensued. The days of success were over; dark clouds loomed large on the horizon.

For the next few months Montrose strove, with only limited success, to build up another army, but little could be accomplished that winter beyond a minor success at Callander and some guerilla warfare on Speyside. However, by the spring of 1646 matters were beginning to go his way again, when quite suddenly he was faced with what was probably the bitterest moment of his life. On 31 May Montrose received a letter from his king ordering him to disband his army and leave the country. At the beginning of that month Charles had escaped from Oxford in disguise and sought refuge with the Covenanter army, who at once made it clear that he was to be little better than a prisoner. Almost their first demand upon the King was that he should issue this vindictive order.

Four years later, and in the service of a new king, Montrose landed once more in his beloved Scotland. There crossed in April

Charles I imprisoned in Carisbrook Castle, from a broadsheet of 1648

1650 from the Orkneys to Caithness a curiously mixed assortment of men: 500 Danes, 1,000 Orcadians, and a small cavalry arm of fifty gentlemen – all soldiers of fortune and many of them officers who had served with Montrose in the past. No one knew better than Montrose what a desperate, even forlorn, venture it was: Charles II was not such a weak man as his father, but he was young, ill advised and determined to regain his crown. He did not deliberately send Montrose to his death, but if there was a chance of success through double dealing it had to be taken. If Montrose could successfully dominate Scotland and allow Charles to break the promise he had made to the Covenanters, well and good; but if he could only come to Scotland on Covenanter terms then Montrose might have to be sacrificed. It was a piece of duplicity not uncharacteristic of the Stuarts.

The expedition, which might have succeeded beyond all expectations had Montrose gained a foothold in the Highlands, where many thousands would have joined him, was dogged by ill fortune from the start. Before Charles's last letter ordering him to lay down his arms ever reached Montrose, his small force had been brought to battle at Carbisdale at the head of the Kyle of Sutherland and utterly routed. Montrose, who was wounded several times

The execution of Montrose in Edinburgh in 1650

in the battle, was again prevailed upon to escape. After days of wandering across tracts of barren land, often draped in wetting mist from bog and river, he was captured on 30 April and taken to the castle of Ardvreck on the banks of Loch Assynt. Here the laird of Assynt, Neil Macleod, delivered him to the Covenanters.

On 5 May Montrose left Ardvreck for the long journey to Edinburgh. He was led through towns and villages mounted on a Highland pony, his feet fastened under its belly, suffering from his wounds and an incipient fever, with a herald proclaiming him traitor. Such foolish, cruel treatment miscarried in its purpose, for where there was meant to be hostility his courage and dignity drew forth pity and admiration. And so it was at the journey's end. He was met at the watergate of Edinburgh, where the grisly sentence of hanging, drawing and quartering was pronounced. Then, with arms pinioned, they transferred him to the hangman's cart and paraded him through streets lined by a wild mob specially worked upon to jeer and throw filth at their fallen foe. But his cool, resolute, almost debonair bearing conquered their steely hearts. They looked up at him not in anger, as his tormentors had hoped, but in the silence of sorrow and respect, for in every way Montrose was a man uplifted above the crowd.

140

CHAPTER 8

Charles II's Civil War

1650–51

The best way to view the sites over which the Battle of Worcester was fought is to approach the town from the south, starting at Upton-upon-Severn. Here eighteen gallant Parliamentarians held out in the church against 300 Royalists. The present A440 and A4021 roads north from Upton follow roughly the course taken by General Fleetwood's troops after they had won the fight at Upton, and at Powick the church tower still has the bullet marks of the brief encounter there. At Powick Bridge one gets some idea of the battle for the river crossing, but the area is now very built over and one cannot quite see the confluence of the rivers Teme and Severn from the new bridge.

Almost the only viewpoint worthwhile in Worcester itself is the cathedral tower, which Charles himself climbed to see how the outlying battle went. The verger will unlock the door leading to the steps. But it is a long, steep climb not to be recommended for the elderly unless they are absolutely fit. Once up at the top a perfect view can be obtained, and the various tactical features, such as Red Hill, Perry Wood, Fort Royal and the confluence of the rivers, can be picked out easily by those who have made themselves familiar with the course of the battle and possess a copy of, or have memorized, the plan of the city as it was in 1651.

The Commandery, which is situated in Sidbury just west of Fort Royal Hill, is open to the public and is of interest in itself, for it is still very much as it was at the time of the battle. It was in this building that the Duke of Hamilton died of his wounds a few days after the battle. It leads straight onto the site of Fort Royal – now an open grassed mound.

When Charles I was executed in January 1649 his son was almost immediately proclaimed Charles II by the Scots. But it took them eighteen months to get him to Scotland on the terms that they exacted. Eventually, by an agreement signed at Breda on 1 May and reaffirmed by oath on board ship just before he landed in Scotland on 23 June, Charles agreed to take the Covenant, to embrace Presbytery himself, to enforce it upon his English subjects

FAC-SIMILE OF THE WARRANT FOR THE EXECUTION OF CHARLES I.
A.D. 1648.

At the high Co^{rt} of Justice for the tryinge and iudgeinge of Charles
Steuart Kinge of England Ianuary xxixth Anno Dm 1648. /

Whereas Charles Steuart Kinge of England is and standeth convicted attaynted and condemned of High Treason
and other high Crymes And Sentence vppon Saturday last was pronounced against him by this Co^{rt} to be putt to death by the
severinge of his head from his body Of wch Sentence execution yet remayneth to be done These are therfore to will and
require you to see the said sentence executed In the open Streete before Whitehall vppon the morrowe being the Thirtieth ... day of
this instant moneth of Ianuary Betweene the houres of Tenn in the morninge and five in the afternoone of the same ——
day wth full effect And for soe doing this shall be yor sufficient warrant And these are to require All Officers and Souldiers
and other the good people of this Nation of England to be assistinge vnto you in this service Given vnder o^r hands and
Seales

Right: Charles II, after Lely

142

and to root out episcopacy. In order to gain a crown he was prepared to dissemble, as Henry IV of France had done some fifty years earlier when he observed, 'Paris is worth a mass'. It was a piece of hypocrisy practised more by the Presbyterians than by the King, for they well knew that they were imposing upon Charles a condition that he could not in full sincerity accept.

The Council of State in London had realized some time before Charles arrived in Scotland that it would have to send an army north to bring the Scots to heel. Thomas Fairfax was still nominally commander-in-chief of the English army, but he was not found willing to conduct what would obviously be a strenuous campaign. Oliver Cromwell had been home only a few weeks from excoriating the Irish Catholics, and was the natural choice to succeed Fairfax. He set off for Scotland on 28 June and crossed the border on 22 July at the head of just over 16,000 men. He had with him Generals Lambert, Whalley and Fleetwood and his army was well disciplined, well trained and homogeneous – almost everything that his opponents were not.

In June 1650 the army in Scotland was less than 6,000 men, and it became necessary to levy a large number of troops very quickly.

Broadsheet of 1651 satirizing the tough conditions laid before Charles II by the Scots before they would support his cause

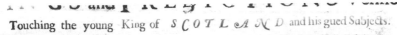

General George Monck (left), one of the leading Parliamentarian generals, played an important part at the Battle of Dunbar, where the Scots army of David Leslie (right) suffered a crushing defeat

When the two armies eventually met in battle the Scots under David Leslie had some 22,000 men, while the English army had been reduced by sickness to less than 12,000. However, the advantage of superior numbers was sadly offset by the quality of both the officers and the men that Leslie had to command. Power rested firmly with the Kirk and many of the Scottish Cavaliers, especially those who had been engaged in the disastrous Battle of Preston in 1648, were excluded from further command, preferment being on religious rather than military merit. For this and other reasons very few Highlanders were among the newly raised raw levies.

During August Leslie was content to avoid battle and watch the English army suffer the hardships of a particularly wet Scottish summer without tents and short of rations. At the beginning of September Cromwell, who had fallen back on Dunbar, was becoming desperate: to return across the border would be difficult and demoralizing, while to stay to face the winter with a rapidly diminishing army seemed likely to be disastrous. Leslie, who had been hustling the English along the coastal road in a march that closely resembled a retreat, took up a position on 2 September above the sick and weary English on a feature called Doon Hill at the very edge of the Lammermuir hills. Here he was virtually unassailable, and he sent a force to block the road to England at the Cockburnspath defile. He must have thought that he had brought Cromwell to the brink of catastrophe. But the English were out of artillery range, and had a fleet behind them; to crush them Leslie had to come down from the heights and give battle on the low ground – albeit with a superiority of nearly two to one.

On 3 September 1650, between the dead hour of 4 a.m., when a waning moon was just piercing the clearing rain clouds, and two hours later when a rising sun was warming the darkly purple hills, Oliver Cromwell won what was undoubtedly his greatest victory. Leslie, some say advised by an ever-watchful Committee of Estates, but more likely himself anxious to have done with the business, had left his hillside position on the previous evening. Cromwell and Lambert saw their opportunity and General Monck, with perhaps more experience than either of them, concurred in their plan. In essence this was to be a frontal attack, supported by artillery, under Lambert and Fleetwood, who would engage the Scottish line from across the ravine that protected them, while Cromwell would lead three of his best foot regiments and one of horse over the Brox Burn lower down and to the right of the Scottish position, and come in on their very restricted flank.

With such stealth was the attack mounted that the Scottish host was caught not fully prepared for battle. Nevertheless, they fought with determination and for some while their long pikes kept the English centre at bay; nor did Cromwell's flank attack make immediate headway. However, it was on this cramped right wing that the battle was won: after desperate work at push-of-pike, the English horse came through the infantry in one further furious clash which sent the Scottish cavalry scattering among their foot. Their army was soon hopelessly wedged between the ravine and the steep hills; great numbers were now a hindrance and merely fodder for darting pikes and flailing swords. It is said that 3,000 perished and as many as 10,000 were made prisoner. It was indeed a disaster of the greatest magnitude.

This crushing defeat inflicted upon the Kirk's army at Dunbar was no disappointment to Charles and the Royalist faction, who saw that the Kirk must needs turn to them if a new and more efficient force was to take the field. Stirling was the key to the Highlands, for the only serviceable road to the north crossed the Forth there. If Stirling could be held Cromwell could do what he liked in the south, but an army from the Royalist north could be assembled. As it happened Cromwell could not do exactly as he liked, for although Edinburgh yielded the governor of the castle continued defiant, and the English had to weaken their army still further by leaving garrison and siege troops in Edinburgh.

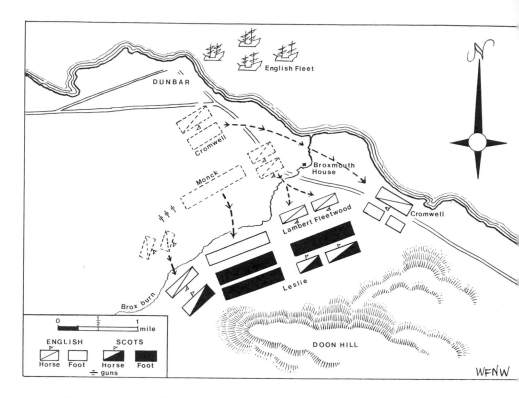

Above: Battle of Dunbar
Below: Cromwell at Dunbar – undoubtedly his greatest victory

During the autumn and winter months, while the Scots were building up a strong defensive position in and around Stirling, Cromwell marched and counter-marched between Edinburgh, Linlithgow and Glasgow without achieving very much. On 24 December the garrison of Edinburgh Castle surrendered upon honourable terms, but even with this obstacle removed Cromwell was not able to attempt anything against Stirling, and in February he became seriously ill. Meanwhile, Charles's personal position had sensibly improved. It is true that an attempt to break away from Argyll's steely clutches in October had been foiled, but as the latter became more and more dependent on the Royalists he was forced to treat Charles with greater respect. On 1 January 1651 Charles was crowned at Scone and made nominal commander-in-chief of the new army. Leslie, who was his second-in-command, retained operational control: Middleton was made lieutenant-general of the horse and Massey (who had defended Gloucester so stoutly for the Roundheads in the First Civil War) now had command of Charles's English contingent.

Cromwell's illness, watched with considerable anxiety by the Council of State and with pleasurable anticipation by the Royalists, lingered on throughout the spring of 1651, and it was not until June that he seemed to shake it off. By then changes in the command of the English forces had been made. Fleetwood was back in England organizing troops needed to meet any Royalist advance into the country: Harrison was in Cumberland with about 5,000 men: Lambert was in command of the horse in Scotland: Richard Deane (now a general but soon to be employed at sea as an admiral with Blake) had charge of the infantry, and Monck was also in Scotland with Cromwell. The problem was how to shift Leslie from his inexpugnable position around Stirling onto ground more favourable to the smaller English army.

For most of the summer Leslie relied upon Fabian tactics, and although at times he advanced to Torwood and showed signs of offering battle he would not allow himself to be caught at a disadvantage again, and Cromwell had to be content with the occasional skirmish. To turn his right flank by crossing the Forth in its upper reaches would be useless, but if Cromwell could cut off his supplies from Fife by crossing the Forth in the Queensferry area the Scots would be forced to shift from their commanding position and either give battle or head for England. Cromwell was well aware that they were likely to take advantage of a moderately clear run into England and for this he was well prepared (having summoned Harrison to Linlithgow for consultation on this very contingency), and indeed desirous of it. Accordingly on 17 July Colonel Overton crossed the Forth with a force of less than 2,000 men. Fortunately Lambert felt sure that Cromwell had underestimated the numbers necessary to ensure success, and he took personal command of a further 2,500 troops. It was as well, for on learning of this threat to his left flank and supply line Leslie sent Sir John Browne with 4,000 men to drive the English back across the Forth. In a short, sharp battle near Inverkeithing Lambert smashed the Scots, killing some say as many as 2,000 and taking their commander prisoner.

On learning of Browne's defeat Leslie determined to march his whole army against Lambert, but Cromwell was too close to him. The Scots were only a few miles beyond Stirling before Leslie realized the danger, and quickly swinging back on his tracks just regained his former position in time, for Cromwell and Deane had already reached Bannockburn. Still unable to force an issue with Leslie, Cromwell now transferred the bulk of his army across the Forth at Queensferry, leaving only a few regiments to keep watch on the enemy at Stirling. On 24 July the English had got the island of Inchgarvie and on the 29th Burntisland. Cromwell then marched on Perth, which surrendered to him on 2 August.

We do not know what Leslie would have done if left to his own devices. It is possible that he would have interposed his army between Cromwell's army at Perth and Edinburgh, accepting battle on ground of his own choosing with a numerically superior army. But matters were taken out of his hands by Charles and the Royalists: confident of massive support from loyal Cavaliers they determined on a march into England. On 31 July Charles, who was beginning to assume more than nominal command of his army, broke camp and headed for the border, which the army numbering some 14,000 men crossed on 6 August. Leslie, whose subsequent action at the Battle of Worcester was to make defeat doubly certain, had no confidence in the army or the venture. He is alleged to have said to Charles that 'he well knew that army, how well soever it look'd would not fight'. Nor was the Duke of Hamilton much more encouraging with his written comment: 'We are all now laughing at the ridiculousness of our condition. We have quit Scotland, being scarce able to maintain it: and yet we grasp at all, and nothing but all will satisfy us, or to lose all.' There were others, such as Argyll and his kinsman Lord Loudoun, who deemed it inexpedient to leave Scotland.

Cromwell was in no great hurry to pursue the Royalist army: he had laid his plans well. His army recrossed the Forth on 4

August and Lambert was sent off independently with about 4,000 horse with orders to join Harrison and to harass the Scottish army, but not to risk a serious engagement, while Monck was to be left in Scotland with some 6,000 men to besiege and take Stirling. In England Fleetwood was collecting a force north of London: the Council of State had been advised of the plan and requested to summon the militia, and Cromwell himself wrote to the Northern and Midland County Committees instructing them to raise troops and remove their animals from the advancing Scots. Recent arrests of prominent Royalists throughout England had further strengthened Parliament's chances of concluding the forthcoming business successfully.

Cromwell with the bulk of the infantry left Leith on 6 August and marching rapidly he crossed the Tyne on the 13th. That same day Lambert and Harrison joined forces south of Preston and together they fell back before the Scottish advance and joined the Cheshire militia on the south bank of the Mersey at Warrington. Their combined force numbered at least 9,000 horse and 3,000 infantry, so they were not greatly, if at all, inferior to the Royalists, who had had a most disappointing march through the northern counties gathering remarkably few recruits. They might therefore have disputed the crossing – even though the Royalists had gained the bridge before they could destroy it – but it was not part of Cromwell's plan that Charles should be brought to battle before the full force that he was so carefully assembling could be concentrated. And so Lambert and Harrison withdrew to Knutsford. From there they marched to Warwick, where on 24 August they were joined by Cromwell, whose troops had averaged sixteen miles a day since leaving Leith.

The Royalist 'success' at Warrington was scarcely sufficient to raise their flagging spirits. Lord Derby joined them there from the Isle of Man, but he had with him only 250 foot and sixty horse, and everywhere the militia were responding to Parliament's orders. Any attempt to march on London with hostile forces ringing them round was no longer feasible – but might there not be some hope from the Welsh border and the western counties? It was therefore determined to leave Lord Derby to rally the Lancashire loyalists and Massey, himself a Presbyterian, to try to gain recruits from his own sect, while Charles and his weary Scots continued towards Shrewsbury. Here the governor refused a summons to surrender, and the army moved on south. At Worcester Charles was slightly more fortunate: the Parliamentary Committee had determined to oppose the Royalist entry, but with the approach of the army the mayor and citizens of this consistently loyal Royalist city turned against the committee, and on 23 August Charles entered Worcester unopposed.

It seemed as good a place as any in which to rest his tired troops, who after 300 miles had had more than enough marching. Food and forage were fairly plentiful and Worcester commanded the approaches to Wales and the south-west, from where Charles still hoped to draw reinforcements. The fortifications had fallen into a sad state of disrepair, but men were hastily pressed for what repair work was possible in the time. Particular attention was paid to the earthwork, known as Fort Royal, just outside the city wall at the south-east, and connected to the walls by a rampart. When Massey rejoined them from his abortive attempt to rally the apathetic Presbyterians he was sent with a small force to destroy bridges at Powick, Bransford and Upton. Only the one across the Severn leading from the city to St John's suburb was left intact, allowing troops to be positioned in that suburb and to the south, where the meadows adjoined the Teme at its confluence with the Severn. When this was done Charles probably considered he occupied a fairly strong defensive position – but rivers are seldom a reliable barrier, a fact that he was soon to realize.

Meanwhile, Cromwell was drawing the net round Worcester ever tighter. He was in no particular hurry and had taken every conceivable precaution even down to ordering tools for a siege should this become necessary – though with an army that when finally assembled was almost double the size of that of his opponents he would not have allowed his mind to dwell too long on siege warfare. Colonel Lilburne had been ordered to deal with Lord Derby during the march south, and afterwards to position himself in the Bewdley area to intercept any Royalist retreat. Fleetwood had moved to Banbury and was now marching to join Cromwell, as was Lord Grey of Groby with 1,100 horse, and General Desborough was advancing from Reading with further troops. Cromwell was at Evesham on 27 August, and by the time that Fleetwood and the other commanders had joined him he had amassed an army of about 28,000 men.

His general plan, like all good plans, was simple. The attack was to be made on both sides of the river Severn. Fleetwood was to cross the river at Upton with about 11,000 men and march up the west bank, while Cromwell took the rest of the army via White Ladies Aston and Spetchley to occupy the Perry Wood – Red Hill heights above Worcester with his left on Bund's Hill, above the confluence of the rivers Teme and Severn. Contact between the

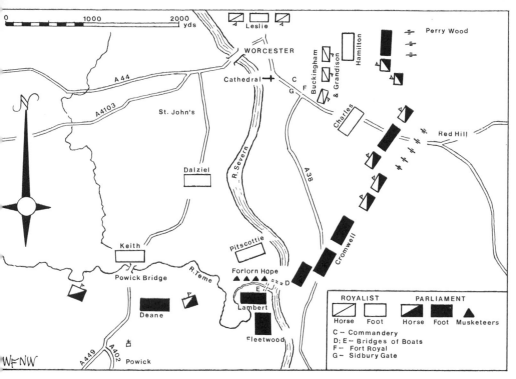

Above and overleaf: Battle of Worcester

two wings was to be effected by means of two bridges of boats –
one across the Teme and the other just above it across the Severn.

Back in Worcester the enthusiasm with which Charles had been
proclaimed king was not matched by any great desire to join his
army. It is doubtful if as many as 2,000 had rallied to his standard
since the army crossed the border, and it cannot now have numbered any more than 16,000 men. Their morale was far from high
and their commanders did little to inspire them. The Duke of
Buckingham had been sulking ever since Charles sternly rebuked
him for his temerity in suggesting he should be given command
of the army; Leslie continued to maunder over the poor fighting
quality of his troops, and to make matters worse he was hardly on
speaking terms with the capable General Middleton. It could not,
therefore, have been a very harmonious council of war that met
in the Commandery on the afternoon of 29 August.

At this council it was decided to mount an attack that night
against the battery on Red Hill, which had just started bombarding
the city, and also upon a post above the river. General Middleton
and Colonel Keith led 1,500 men altogether on these sorties, but
surprise was lost through the plan's being betrayed by a Puritan
tailor called Guise (who was hanged next day), and both parties

Leslie

St. John's

Keith

Dalziel

Powick Bridge (new)

Deane

R. Teme

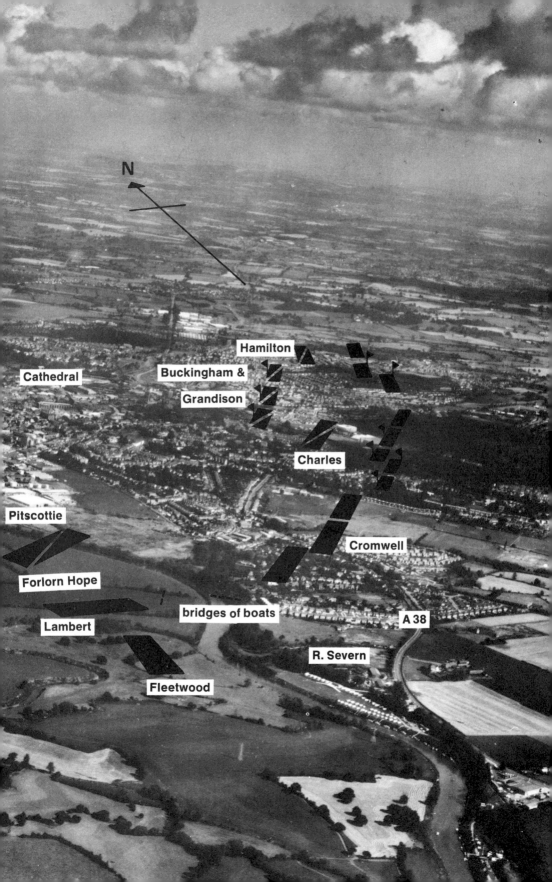

N

Hamilton

Buckingham &

Grandison

Cathedral

Charles

Pitscottie

Cromwell

Forlorn Hope

Lambert

bridges of boats

A 38

R. Severn

Fleetwood

were repulsed with loss upon reaching their objectives. To add to Charles's discomfiture, three days later Lord Derby arrived wounded in the mouth and with thirty men, almost the only survivors of the 1,200 who had been routed by Lilburne near Wigan on 25 August.

It is difficult to know why General Massey was sent to Upton-upon-Severn with only 300 men. Some rudimentary defences had been constructed around Wick just north of the river Teme, so it looked as though the Royalists considered an attack west of the Severn feasible, and if so Upton was an important outpost, for here the river would most likely be crossed. It was even more surprising that such an experienced soldier as Massey should have been caught napping, and the river crossing forced through the gallantry of eighteen men.

The bridge that spanned the Severn at Upton in 1651 was a little way downstream from the one there now, and a little further down still (just below the present Swan Inn) the river was found to be fordable. This was not known at the time and General Lambert, who was spearheading Fleetwood's army, on finding a plank over the partly broken bridge chose eighteen picked dragoons to carry out the unpleasant crossing high above the swirling water in the early hours of 29 August. It was still dark as the daring eighteen straddled rather than walked the single plank, and scrambled across unseen by a negligent enemy. Once across, however, their presence was quickly discovered and there followed a fierce fight, first in the churchyard and then the church itself,* into which the men barricaded themselves and for some time held out against the 300 Royalists.† To reinforce the eighteen from across the broken bridge was quite impossible, but in desperation Lambert ordered more dragoons, this time mounted, to try the crossing lower down. Half fording and half swimming, they struggled over, and taking the enemy in the rear forced them back against their improvised entrenchments. Massey, who was spending the night at the Lechmeres' house, Severn End, was quickly on the scene and fought bravely, suffering two severe wounds. But soon Lambert hopelessly outnumbered his small force, and Massey broke off the engagement and made for Worcester.

By the next day the bridge was repaired and Fleetwood's army,

* The church exists no longer, but the tower still stands and the churchyard is kept up.
† Most accounts refer to the men of the Upton outpost as Scots, but as Massey commanded Charles's small English contingent they were more probably English.

reinforced by two regiments of horse and two of foot under General Deane, crossed over to the west bank. Now the task was to collect boats and planks for the two bridges, and this did not prove too difficult. By 2 September everything was ready, but the Lord-General had decreed that the attack should not be made until the next day. It was no coincidence that it therefore occurred on the anniversary of his great victory at Dunbar, for Cromwell was becoming increasingly superstitious and it seems almost certain that the auspicious day was predetermined. What could be considered a coincidence, however, was that the first engagement of the Civil Wars, in 1642, and the last, in 1651, were both fought around Powick Bridge. Furthermore, the date of his victories – 3 September – was seven years later to be the date of Cromwell's death.

At about 5 a.m. on Wednesday 3 September Generals Fleetwood, Deane and Lambert began their advance up the west bank of the Severn. It was slow going, for with them they hauled twenty 'great boats' for nearly eight miles against the current – and no doubt there were plenty of mishaps. In the early afternoon they were held up for a short while by an action fought around the church at Powick, but the river Teme was reached at some time between two and three o'clock. We cannot be certain of the exact sequence of events in the fighting west of the river, and it seems incredible that two bridges could be constructed (according to one source* in only half an hour) in the face of a determined enemy. The general plan was for Deane to try to force the bridge at Powick, while Lambert made use of the bridge of boats; meanwhile the batteries on Red Hill and Perry Wood were to keep the Scots in Worcester fully occupied. The bridges were to be thrown across the rivers within pistol shot of each other, the one across the Severn being just to the north of the confluence.

Major-General Robert Montgomery was in charge of the Royalist troops in the Powick meadows, and he had ordered Colonel Keith's brigade to hold the bridge, while Colonel Pitscottie's Highlanders were on the right bank of the Severn in the meadow above the confluence. In reserve was Major-General Dalziel's brigade on the higher ground between Powick and Worcester. Powick Bridge had not been completely destroyed: planks had been left for patrols, and for the rearguard that had held up the advance by the church, but it was a formidable task to force it and certainly the cavalry could cross only by a ford higher up the river.

The fighting all along the river Teme front was very bitter. A

* Henry Cary, *Memorials of the Civil War,* London, 1842, Vol. II, p. 357.

forlorn hope was put across the river (presumably in boats) to cover the construction of the floating bridges. No doubt this made the operation possible, but it nevertheless remains an incredible feat of ingenuity and it is a pity that we have so few details. General Deane could make no headway against Powick Bridge and when Lambert's advance troops did get across their pontoon the Highlanders at first drove them back. It only needed one of the two attacks to succeed and the other brigade would be forced to retire. Charles had been watching the fight from the top of the tower of Worcester Cathedral, and was soon galloping to the river to give personal encouragement. Also watching from the high ground east of the Severn was Cromwell, and now his foresight in throwing the bridge across became apparent. Seeing what little headway Fleetwood's men were making he personally led three brigades across the river.

Pitscottie's Highlanders, tough and desperate, beat off the superior numbers of their opponents for a little while: but attacked in front by Lambert and in the flank by Cromwell they gradually gave ground, fighting every inch of the way with discipline and fury. But these men were at a disadvantage when it came to hedge fighting, and the fields round Powick were much enclosed. The English had considerable experience of this type of in-fighting and pressed the Scots back remorselessly. Their forced withdrawal left Keith's brigade with its left flank in the air, and becoming discouraged by this development they quickly broke, leaving their commander to be captured. Dalziel either could not or would not stem the rapidly accelerating retreat and General Montgomery was severely wounded and out of action. Soon the retreat became a rout and the Scots were streaming back through St John's and across the bridge into Worcester, the English not far behind them.

This river battle lasted for a full two hours, and Charles is usually credited with being personally responsible for the Royalist attack on Cromwell's right. This is quite possible, even though he must have been kept busy riding between Worcester and Powick. Certainly Leslie had nothing to do with it, for neither he nor his large cavalry force stirred from the Pitchcroft just north of the city all day. In crossing the river Cromwell had seriously weakened his position, for although he had great numerical superiority some of the troops left on Red Hill were inexperienced militiamen. Charles was operating on interior lines and had the opportunity of launching an attack on the enemy's right wing while his army was unevenly divided. It was a brilliant conception and executed with a resolution that nearly succeeded.

156

The attack was two-pronged: Charles commanded the right thrust against Red Hill and the Duke of Hamilton the left against Perry Wood, while the Duke of Buckingham and Lord Grandison were in support with cavalry. Leaving the city by the Sidbury Gate and covered by the guns from Fort Royal, both wings met with success, and Hamilton's men were soon among the enemy artillery at Perry Wood. The Parliamentarian foot gave way all along the line in a battle that lasted for three hours. Had Leslie's cavalry not refused to fight, Cromwell's position east of the river might have become desperate. He still had on that side some of Lambert's cavalry and those from Whalley's and Harrison's brigades, who came to the support of the militia, but the issue continued in doubt until Cromwell had recrossed the river ahead of his three brigades and taken personal command. Meanwhile, the Royalist attack was almost spent and Hamilton's men were running short of ammunition, while Hamilton himself was seriously wounded in the leg. The arrival of Cromwell's brigades finally turned the tide and the Royalists were driven back into the city in considerable confusion. It had been a bold attempt that deserved to succeed.

The last phase of the battle was an untidy shambles. From out of the imbroglio there emerged several instances of individual gallantry, but there was no time to organize any proper defence of the city and little desire on the part of the troops to become further involved in the bloody, bewildering business of street fighting. When the Royalists were forced back from Red Hill, they were closely pursued right up to the Sidbury Gate, where the confusion was appalling. Charles, who had displayed great courage throughout the fighting, now found his way blocked by an ammunition wagon whose leading ox had been killed. He was forced to dismount and squeeze through the gate with the enemy close behind him. Discarding his heavy armour and taking a fresh horse he joined with such stalwarts as the Earl of Cleveland, Sir James Hamilton and Colonel Wogan in trying to rally some of the broken regiments and induce them to continue the battle.

Their combined efforts met with only partial success, for by now the enemy were hemming them in on all sides. There had been no time to destroy the bridge across the river from St John's, and Dalziel's brigade, which might have held up the advance on the west for some time, laid down their arms without firing a shot; Leslie's cavalry continued supine on Pitchcroft; and when Sir Alexander Forbes refused to surrender Fort Royal the Essex militia stormed and captured it with great élan, and then proceeded to turn its guns onto the tortured city. There was by now only one gate by which the defeated Royalists could hope to escape: the Bridge Gate was in the hands of Fleetwood's men: the Sidbury and Friars Gates were also held by the enemy, and the Foregate had been blocked up. Everyone converged upon St Martin's Gate and the road to the north. Some panicked, but most were fighting their way at push-of-pike and the slaughter in the city was considerable. On Castle Mound, Lord Rothes, Sir William Hammond and Colonel Drummond continued to hold out until offered terms by Cromwell personally, and the courage of men like Cleveland and Hamilton, and a small party of English Cavaliers, enabled Charles to make his escape from the doomed city. As he started upon what was to be the most thrilling adventure of his life the sound of explosions and the faint patter of musketry were still ringing in his ears.

It was a total disaster: of the 15,000–16,000 men who began the battle – mostly Scots – only a very small proportion made good their escape. Somewhere between 2,000 and 3,000 were slain in battle, and about 10,000 were captured either on the battlefield or as they vainly tried to make their way north, including 640 officers. Save for Charles himself hardly a single officer of consequence survived the battle a free man. The Duke of Hamilton was carried back to the Commandery after the Red Hill sortie and died there on 12 September: the Earls of Derby and Lauderdale were captured in Cheshire – Derby was executed and Lauderdale was a prisoner until 1660. Generals Massey, Montgomery and Sir Alexander Forbes were wounded; and Keith, Pitscottie, Grandison and many others joined those taken in Worcester and herded into the cathedral, whose nave formed a temporary prison. Leslie was caught in Yorkshire and, like Lauderdale, remained a prisoner until 1660. The English army is said to have lost only 200 men. This is probably an underestimate, but there was seldom a Pyrrhic victory in the Civil Wars so it may not be very far out.

In his letter to the Speaker on the day after the battle, Cromwell wrote of it: 'The dimensions of this mercy are above my thoughts. It is, for aught I know, a crowning mercy.' For those who favoured Parliament his words proved true. This battle ended the Civil Wars, and it was the last serious attempt to reinstate the lawful King of England by force of arms – other small risings, such as Penruddock's in 1655, were easily dealt with. The battle is also notable for the spotlight it throws upon Oliver Cromwell. The strategical and tactical brilliance of the Worcester campaign is often compared to the best endeavours of the great masters of war. Certainly the means by which Cromwell dislodged Leslie from an impregnable position at Dunbar, and then organized the pursuit in such a way as to bring the Royalist army to battle at a considerable disadvantage, displayed military talents of the highest capacity. But it must be remembered that in the fight which ensued Cromwell outnumbered his opponents by nearly two to one, and the morale of his army was much higher than that of Charles's. This overwhelming superiority enabled him to violate one of the first principles of war: he not only divided his force, but divided it by one of the largest rivers in England. It was a calculated risk, which had Leslie's cavalry shown any inclination to fight might easily not have come off: it was the measure of the man that he took it.

After Worcester Cromwell sheathed his sword. He had risen from the humblest to the greatest position in the military hierarchy through his own genius, and he had created and trained an army that at that time had not its peer in all Europe. For this and much else he deserves his place in the hall of fame. But it is less easy to number him among the great captains, for his battles were fewer and more restricted in scale than men like Gustavus Adolphus, Turenne, Marlborough, Wellington and Napoleon. If he had less opportunity than those men to display his strategical and tactical skill on a broad canvas, he can proudly fall in beside that other great creator and trainer of a modern army, Sir John Moore.

Left: The Solemn League and Covenant accepted by Parliament and imposed on the British people, 1643

CHAPTER 9

'Let Monmouth Reign!'

Sedgemoor

6 July 1685

The battlefield is still in unspoilt country, although it presents a very different picture from what Monmouth knew: where there were areas of only partially drained moorland, there are now orderly well drained and cultivated fields. But the landscape itself has changed little and the visitor walking the ground has no difficulty in appreciating what a stupendous task Monmouth had in marching an army in absolute silence across this land at night.

The Battle of Sedgemoor was fought about three-quarters of a mile to the north of Westonzoyland church. Westonzoyland is some three miles south-east of Bridgwater on the A372 road. If the visitor wishes to follow Monmouth's line of march on foot it is best to work off the 2½-inch Ordnance Survey map (sheet ST 33). It is not possible to follow the whole route from Bradney to Westonzoyland along public footpaths, but so long as one is prepared for a rather muddy walk (except in mid-summer) a great deal of it can be followed in the first instance by walking down the drove leading south-east from Peasy Farm, and then by driving to Chedzoy and walking down a drove that starts near Parchey and joins the public footpath by the King's Sedgemoor Drain. This was not there at the time of the battle, but may in part mark the line of the Black Ditch. The public footpath follows the drain, and to get to Westonzoyland one has to leave it and strike south across a small field that leads to a drove in which is situated – somewhat obscurely – the memorial stone, which stands about 200 yards to the south of the site of the chief burial pit. This pit was excavated at the end of the last century. Coming from Westonzoyland the route to that part of the battlefield is fairly well signposted.

James Scott, Duke of Monmouth, was born in Rotterdam on 9 April 1649. His mother was Lucy Walter, and despite what was often said to the contrary, both then and later, it is almost certain that Charles II described him accurately in the Duke's marriage contract with Anna Countess of Buccleuch as *'Filio nostro naturali et illegitimo'*. Unfortunately for Monmouth, Charles proved a weak

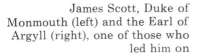

James Scott, Duke of
Monmouth (left) and the Earl of
Argyll (right), one of those who
led him on

and over-indulgent father, who seemed more concerned to heap honours upon the boy than to further his education, which was lamentably neglected. Already transformed from James Crofts to Baron Scott, Earl of Doncaster and Duke of Monmouth, Charles made him Duke of Buccleuch and Earl of Dalkeith on his wedding day (20 April 1663), and conferred upon him the Order of the Garter. Henceforth Monmouth took precedence over every man in the country after the King, the Duke of York and Prince Rupert – small wonder that we find him acting as though he were Prince of Wales, and making sumptuous progresses into the West Country and the north. Nor can we fail to understand the grave displeasure that all this caused the Duke of York.

Monmouth was in many ways an attractive young man. He was a much better-looking edition of his father, with all of Charles's charm; but although often amusing and gay he quickly gave way to flaccid despair whenever anything went wrong. He was a loyal friend, though an unfaithful husband, and a courageous fighter who hated cold-blooded cruelty. Perhaps his greatest fault, which was in the end his undoing, was his weakness and vacillation. He seemed unable to make a decision, and his uncle James spoke the truth when at the end, having granted him an interview at which he refused to pardon him, he said of his victim, 'Poor Monmouth, he was always easy to be imposed upon'.

There was no more obvious choice than the popular 'Protestant Duke' as the fugelman for that growing party of discontented

Whigs and Dissenters who were determined that Catholic James should not ascend the throne. Monmouth, with cries of 'A Monmouth! A Monmouth!' and 'Let Monmouth reign!' still ringing in his ears from his triumphant progress through the western counties, was not averse to being set up as an alternative to James. He became a willing tool in the hands of Shaftesbury, and later of even more dangerous plotters. As a member of the Council of Six he was closely involved in their nefarious schemes to extort from the King, by force if necessary, the summoning of a parliament and an end to what they considered his arbitrary rule, but he never countenanced the designs of the extremists in connection with the Rye House plot. The rejection by the Lords of the second Exclusion Bill in 1680 caused consternation in the City, where Monmouth was given a rapturous reception. This and much else angered James almost beyond endurance. He had every reason to mistrust his nephew, and whether Monmouth was in exile, in Scotland, or in London James laboured for his downfall – and as Charles was determined that the lawful succession should be upheld, James was bound to triumph in the end. Banished from the court, pardoned by a devoted father (although not by a cold, unforgiving uncle, to whom he had made an abject apology), and finally advised to leave the country for a time, Monmouth was at the Hague when on 5 February 1685 Charles died.

His position now was most unenviable: his wisest counsellors had recently perished on the scaffold, he had no friend of importance at court and his uncle wanted him home – but in chains. Monmouth, like the Earl of Argyll and a number of other political agitators, was in exile. Nor could he stay in Holland, for the Prince of Orange found it expedient to placate his father-in-law, although he proved extremely negligent in keeping watch on the movements of his erstwhile guest. At this we are not surprised, for William had all to gain from any attempt on the throne by Monmouth. If he succeeded, which the Prince felt quite certain he would not, there would be a Protestant ally in his quarrels with Louis XIV, and if he failed the succession of the Princess Mary became less complicated. It seems certain that by now Monmouth had no wish to become King of England. He was just beginning to enjoy domestic life with his devoted mistress Henrietta Wentworth (the Duchess was still in England), and they had plans to summer in Sweden – but we know that he was easily imposed upon.

The Earl of Argyll; that arch-plotter and turbulent priest Robert Ferguson; the reprobate Lord Grey of Warke, Monmouth's *eminence grise*; Heywood Dare, a goldsmith from Taunton with

inxit. A. Blooteling *fe.*

COBVS EBORACENSIS ET ALBANIÆ DVX, COMES ULTONIÆ &c.ª

immense influence in the West Country, and others were urging Monmouth, against his better judgement, to head a rebellion in the west that would synchronize with Argyll's landing in Scotland. He knew the difficulties, and although aware that there was a genuine fear for Protestantism, especially in the western and northern counties, he was not so certain that the gentry would rally to him. Moreover, James had begun his reign with caution and summoned a parliament – the first for three years – which was entirely loyal; money was short with which to buy arms and equipment; and above all Monmouth knew, from his own not inconsiderable military experience, the value of a standing army, and that a rabble could never defeat disciplined troops. However, he allowed himself to be overruled. Argyll sailed for the western Highlands on 2 May and a month later Monmouth, in the 32-gun frigate *Helderenburgh,* with two other small ships and eighty-two companions (including some Dutch gunners), left the Texel for the south coast of England.

Finding the money for the hire of the frigate (£5,500) and the purchase of arms and equipment had not been easy. Monmouth had pawned his Great George* and all his jewels, and Henrietta and her mother had added theirs; his friends in Holland had also contributed, but money expected from London had not been forthcoming. He bought four light cannon, about 1,500 back and breast plates (most of which were never used; the money would have been better spent on additional muskets) and a fair quantity of small arms, ammunition and powder. All this left him with very little cash with which to pay his volunteers and buy provisions.

On 11 June, after a voyage of twelve days, the tiny expedition dropped anchor off Lyme Regis. The landing was unopposed, although it seems that had powder been readily available the mayor and at least one loyal citizen would have been prepared to fire upon the small boats bringing Monmouth and his party to the shore. Soon the green standard, inscribed with the words 'Fear nothing but God', was unfurled and it was not long before the eighty-three invaders were joined by a band of eager recruits. Shouts of 'A Monmouth! A Monmouth!' and 'The Protestant religion' greeted the reading of the rebel declaration. This scurrilous document – even for those days when it was customary to use powerful, and often libellous, words to conjure up real or imagined wrongs – was mainly the work of Robert Ferguson.

Not long after the landing there was an unpleasant incident at

* Monmouth received the Garter in 1663.

Lyme that had serious consequences for Monmouth. Andrew Fletcher of Saltoun and old Heywood Dare quarrelled over a horse, and Fletcher killed Dare. The latter's son demanded justice and Monmouth was forced to send Fletcher off to sea. Both these men were a grievous loss, Dare on account of his local standing, and Fletcher because he was a young man with recent battle experience. This unfortunate beginning was followed by a most unsatisfactory affair against the Dorset militia at Bridport. What could have been a successful joint infantry and cavalry operation against a very half-hearted enemy came undone when Lord Grey and his horse turned tail after one volley had been fired at them. Colonel Venner had already been wounded in some house fighting and a complete shambles was only saved by the steadiness of Nathaniel Wade, who was to prove himself Monmouth's most reliable officer.

Although the landing had been unopposed there were those in Lyme ready to speed the news: the local militia commanders had it within the day, and Whitehall knew by 13 June. The King at once despatched Lord Churchill with six troops of horse and dragoons and five infantry companies to keep a close watch on the rebels. Monmouth had no time to lose if he was to avoid being boxed in at Lyme. On Monday 15 June the rebel army, now about 3,000 strong, marched for Axminster. The original plan had been to rally at Taunton on the first stage of a march to Bristol, Gloucester (where it was hoped to link up with the men from Cheshire) and then London. But this plan was to undergo many changes. In addition to a small, shaggy cavalry force under Lord Grey, there were now four regiments: the Duke's (Red) commanded by Nathaniel Wade, the White (Colonel Foukes), Green (Colonel Holmes) and Yellow (formed by Major Fox and later commanded by Colonel Matthews). A fifth regiment, the Blue under Colonel Basset, was added later. There was no shortage of volunteers (a notable newcomer being Daniel Defoe), but many had to be turned away for lack of arms, and some went to war carrying a scythe blade at the end of an eight-foot pole – a formidable weapon at close quarters.

Albemarle's militiamen were encountered at Axminster. Although they outnumbered the rebels by at least a thousand they had no stomach for fighting, and many of them joined Monmouth. The rebel army then went on its way undisturbed to Chard, Ilminster and Taunton. Not taking Exeter at this point was perhaps Monmouth's first mistake: personally brave and popular with his troops, he was not, however, a good general, and although his strategic planning was often sound he was seldom capable of taking a daring decision. Above all he frequently failed to maintain the momentum of success – so essential for an insurgent army. Exeter could have been taken without any difficulty, and with it much needed arms, money and ammunition. A similar opportunity to revitalize the cause was later to be lost before Bristol.

They reached the outskirts of Taunton on 18 June, and the next day Monmouth entered the town to a tumultuous welcome. It was here at the market cross that he was first proclaimed king. Ferguson and Grey had been urging this step upon him ever since the landing, but Monmouth was almost certainly sincere when he said that he wished to leave the matter open for the time being, although he had hinted that he would accept the wishes of his followers. The great majority of these were eager to have him king, and for two principal reasons he agreed: he had become seriously alarmed by the failure of the gentry to enlist, and he was assured that many were holding back because they feared another Commonwealth. This was not the whole truth, but it was a slightly more plausible reason for assuming kingship than the belief that in the event of defeat his followers would be in a more favourable legal position because they were serving a king – if only a *de facto* one – rather than a rebel leader. Treason could not be thus deceitfully veiled.

Leaving Taunton on 21 June Monmouth marched to Bridgwater at the head of almost 8,000 men. But his heart was heavy, for there had been no encouraging sign from London or the north and still the local gentry held back. His objective was Bristol, the second richest city in the country, and could he but capture it the tide might yet flow in his favour. The Duke of Beaufort, in command of the Gloucestershire militia, held the town and Lord Feversham, who had superseded Churchill in command of the royalist forces, was at Bath with some 2,000 troops. Bristol was vulnerable from the Gloucester side and a more determined commander than Monmouth would have taken it. The rebels repaired the bridge over the Avon at Keynsham and crossed the river. Coming back to the town for rest and provisions they were surprised by a body of enemy cavalry, but managed to drive them off after suffering some casualties. However, Monmouth, fearing that he might be caught between Churchill's force, which had been constantly harassing him, and the main royalist army, abandoned the assault. The sunshine days were now gone; the long grey aftermath of disappointment, dejection and defeat lay ahead. And Monmouth knew it.

King James's men – dragoon, gunner and grenadier

His occasional flashes of unbounded optimism were now crowded out by long periods of gloomy pessimism. Indecision had cost him Bristol; now, uncertain of his reception and fearful of Churchill's harassing operations on his slow-moving, badly shod army, he discarded the plan to march north. Instead, as an act of bravado born of despair, he decided to summon Bath to surrender. When the unfortunate herald who was sent upon this forlorn mission was killed, Monmouth bypassed the city and with no apparent plan in mind marched to Philips Norton (now Norton St Philip). As it was in this village, which lies a few miles south of Bath, that on 27 June the first engagement of any consequence was fought between the King's army and his nephew's rebel host, we should briefly turn our attention to the troops that James was able to bring against Monmouth.

At the Restoration Charles II was careful to retain a small standing army, although there were certain alterations to the system. It was an ironical touch that in 1678 Monmouth should have become this army's captain-general. In 1685, when James succeeded, the cavalry comprised three troops of Life Guards, with Grenadier dragoons (mounted infantry) attached to each troop, the King's Regiment of Horse (later the Royal Horse Guards) and the Royal Dragoons (recently the Tangier Horse). On the English establishment there were two regiments of Foot Guards and five other regiments of foot – of which one was called the

167

Admiral's Regiment and served mainly at sea. In addition there were six regiments (three raised in England and three in Scotland) which were maintained by the Dutch and served in Holland, but they could be recalled if needed. The militia had been remodelled shortly before the Restoration, and gentlemen were liable, according to the value of the land they held, to equip and pay a horseman, a pikeman or a musketeer. Under the King the lords lieutenant held the command in their counties and the men could be called up for periods not exceeding fourteen days in one year. It was estimated that the total militia force was around 130,000 men.

With the exception of the 3rd Regiment of Foot (the Buffs) the Admiral's Regiment and some cavalry units, Feversham had under his command the whole of the regular army and sixteen light guns. Companies of the 3rd Guards (who were then on the Scottish establishment) were ordered to join him, but did not arrive until after the rebellion had been quashed. The Prince of Orange was asked to send his six regiments over and offered to lead them himself, but they took no part in the fighting. Weapons and equipment had not changed greatly since the Civil War. The soft hat had replaced the cavalryman's helmet, but troopers still wore the cuirass and in addition to sword and pistol they now carried a carbine. The pikemen no longer wore armour, and indeed by now the infantrymen had been given the long red or blue coats. In most regiments the flintlock had replaced the matchlock, but bayonets issued in 1673 had been withdrawn again. Each regiment of foot now had a Grenadier company, but these played no part in this campaign. Out of a total standing army of about 4,000 all ranks,* Feversham had 1,800 infantrymen and 700 horse. If we discount the militia regiments, which took little part at Philips Norton and none at Sedgemoor, he was inferior in numbers to what Monmouth could bring against him, but in training, discipline and firepower his infantry and artillery were immeasurably superior; while Monmouth's troopers, mounted on country hacks completely unaccustomed to the noise of battle, only added to the incalculable hazards of the battlefield.

---

* The total number of men serving in the standing army at the time of Monmouth's rebellion cannot be accurately given. There are no muster rolls extant for this time, and the annual pay rolls vary enormously. These can be studied in the Public Record Office (War Office Class 24, pieces 7 and 8 and 25/3206). The pay roll for 1 January 1685 (W.O. 24/8 Pt 3) shows a figure greatly in excess of the one given here, but many regiments existed only on paper, and that of 3,617 for the standing army of 1684 (W.O. 24/7) is probably fairly accurate for both that year and the next.

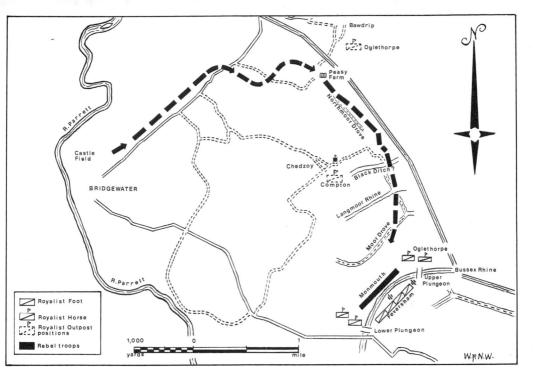

Above: Battle of Sedgemoor, showing Monmouth's night march
Overleaf: Battle of Sedgemoor

The rebel army arrived at Philips Norton on Friday 26 June and Monmouth spent the night in the Old House – now the George Inn. The long drought had at last broken and the rain was pouring down as the infantry sought what shelter they could in fields adjacent to the town; the cavalry took up positions in the town itself. The troops were not alone in their dejection; Monmouth's spirits were rapidly reaching their nadir. He had expected 500 horse to join him here under a Colonel Adlam, and had been confidently assured that many royalist soldiers would come over to him. In both events he was disappointed.

Wandering round the old parts of Norton St Philip now, it is not possible to be certain from contemporary accounts exactly where the fighting took place. There was a lane leading from a ploughed field that ran close to the courtyard of a fair-sized house – possibly near the site of the present house that stands back from the road north of the inn – and Monmouth had placed a barricade in this lane. Throughout the night of 26–7 June there had been alarms, but it was not until the morning of the 27th that Feversham, marching from Bath, made contact. He sent a party of Grenadiers, under Monmouth's half-brother the Duke of Grafton, against the barricade, but they came under sharp fire and Mon-

Royalist Cavalry (Oglethorpe

Upper Plungeon

Chedzoy New Cut

Monmouth

Feversham

Royalist Cavalry

Lower Plungeon

King's Sedgemoor Drain

Bussex Rhine

N

Oxford House

WESTONZOYLAND

mouth immediately led his own regiment through the courtyard of the house and took them in the flank. It was an ill conducted affair on Feversham's part, and although he sent strong reinforcements in support of Grafton they too came under heavy fire from rebels lining the surrounding hedges. Failing to achieve a breakthrough, he withdrew the attacking force, and for the next six hours both armies conducted a brisk cannonade which did no harm to anyone. Eventually Monmouth gave orders to attack, but the royalists did not wait: they withdrew to Bradford having lost about eighty men (some crawled into the standing corn to die, and were not found until the harvest) as against Monmouth's eighteen.

Monmouth had had the best of his first proper engagement with his uncle's army, but it did nothing to raise his morale or remove those bouts of melancholy; and many of his men, no doubt sensing eventual defeat, began to drift away. The army marched to Frome and here the situation was deemed so bad as to warrant a council of war. At this serious conclave it was suggested that the men should be allowed to take the benefit of the pardon offered by James to any who would desert Monmouth, and those exempt from this pardon (Monmouth and all who had come from Holland with him) should make good their escape. It must have been a difficult decision for Monmouth, who had just learned – to add to his other disappointments – that Argyll had been captured and executed in Scotland. But he probably knew that to abandon the enterprise now was to abandon it for good, and he had had experience of the way that James treated plotters and put no faith in his uncle's promises.

Undoubtedly the decision to fight on was the right one. It was decided to revert to the original plan and march north to join up with Lord Delamere in Cheshire; but discovering that Feversham was at Westbury Monmouth retired again on Bridgwater, from where he dispatched his chaplain Nathaniel Hooke to London to urge his supporters there to rise at once, and sent a detachment to Minehead to procure more horses and the guns from the quayside. Meanwhile, chiefly as a bluff, for he had determined to march north on 6 July, some steps were taken to fortify Bridgwater.

Lord Feversham, learning of Monmouth's movements, advanced on Bridgwater, reaching Somerton on 3 July. From here he carried out a personal reconnaissance as far as Middlezoy, where he intended to have his next camp, but when he learned that Westonzoyland, which was less than four miles from Bridgwater, was a much more favourable site, he left his 1,500-strong Wiltshire militia at Middlezoy and marched the rest of the army to Weston.

Between this village and the even smaller one of Chedzoy, less than two miles to the north, was an expanse of open, boggy moorland, which was partially drained by ditches taking the water to the river Parrett. Two of these ditches, known locally as rhines, were formidable obstacles, and even after a long dry spell were impassable to horse except by the recognized crossing places. Any force occupying Westonzoyland had the protection of one of these obstacles, the Bussex Rhine, which ran roughly in a crescent from just across the Bridgwater road at its southern end almost to where the King's Sedgemoor Drain is now situated. There were two crossing places, known as plungeons; one was immediately to the north of the Bridgwater road, and the other about 1,000 yards up the ditch.

The royalist army reached Westonzoyland on Sunday 5 July, and Feversham pitched his newly arrived tents between the village and the Bussex Rhine, leaving room for the infantry to deploy behind the rhine (for the royalist army's order of battle see page 180). Feversham was a naturalized Frenchman and nephew of the great Turenne. He certainly had not inherited his uncle's military talent, and his conduct of the campaign has often been criticized; and in particular he has been blamed for being taken by surprise at Sedgemoor. But in fact his tactics before and during the battle were almost beyond reproach. The outlying picquets may not have been as alert as they should have been, but the dispositions would seem to have been perfectly adequate. The infantry were encamped 100 yards behind the rhine, the cavalry were in the village and were ordered to remain saddled throughout the night, the cannon were on the left guarding the Bridgwater road. Colonel Oglethorpe, with a strong patrol of Life Guards, was sent to Bawdrip to watch the Bristol road, along which it was expected that Monmouth would march north; Sir Francis Compton, with a hundred horse and fifty dragoons, was positioned in Chedzoy; there were further outposts on the Bridgwater road, and to the rear at a ford over the Parrett. The only important place that appears to have been left unguarded was the upper – or right-hand – plungeon.

The Reverend Andrew Paschall, Vicar of Chedzoy, to whom we are indebted for a lively account of the proceedings, was a royalist and was largely responsible for keeping his flock out of trouble; but at least one of them, a farmer called Sparke, held rebel sympathies. And when Sparke, watching through his spyglass from Chedzoy church tower, saw the royalist army taking up position he sent his servant Richard Godfrey to inform Monmouth. Monmouth was painfully aware that his army stood no chance against the royalists in an open fight: but here perhaps was an opportunity for a surprise attack by night. One of the most hazardous operations of war, even with well trained, well disciplined troops, is an approach march over difficult country by night; but it often proves irresistible as a gamble in desperate circumstances. After some discussion it was decided to attempt it, provided Feversham was not dug in. Accordingly Godfrey, who knew every inch of the moor and was prepared to act as guide, was sent off to discover if the enemy were entrenched. He reported that they were not: but he apparently made no mention of the Bussex Rhine – no doubt assuming that everybody knew about rhines and he was only asked to investigate trenches. The night attack was to go forward and the Bussex Rhine would be its undoing.

Not long after the decision to attack had been taken news was brought to Monmouth – certainly exaggerated and probably untrue – that the enemy were in no state to resist, for most of the officers and men were sadly affected by the local cider. At least it pushed up the mercury in Monmouth's personal barometer: 'We shall have no more to do than to lock up the stable-doors, and seize the troopers in their beds' was the over-optimistic remark John Oldmixon tells us he made. No doubt he modified these views on hearing the latest reports of Feversham's outpost positions. These made it necessary for the rebel army to take a wide circuit of almost six miles from their camp in Castle Field, instead of a short three-mile approach along an easy road. The plan was daring, if perhaps dangerously simple, and displayed great confidence. Nathaniel Wade, who with Monmouth and Lord Grey was chiefly responsible for its conception, tells us that the horse were to break into the right flank of the enemy camp and engage the foot, keeping them from coming together before Monmouth's infantry and cannon could engage them from the front. The whole action was to be swiftly accomplished before the enemy's cavalry and cannon could become effective.*

It was 11 p.m. on the night of Sunday 5 July when Wade's regiment led the advance out of Bridgwater. The most savage orders

* Historians are totally unable to agree on whether Monmouth knew about the Bussex Rhine and the plungeons before leaving Bridgwater. Contemporary accounts are mostly silent on the matter, although King James asserts that Monmouth did not know of it. Almost certainly Godfrey made no mention of it, but before marching the presence of the Black Ditch and the Langmoor Rhine seems to have been known, so it is possible that the Bussex Rhine was too. The plan could fit either contingency, so long as the position of the upper plungeon was known.

174

The Duke of Monmouth is defeated at Sedgemoor

had been given to preserve silence; anyone breaking it was to be immediately stabbed by his neighbour. To avoid Sir Francis Compton in Chedzoy the army marched north-east up the Causeway (present A39 road), leaving the baggage wagons and one gun in the Knowle Hill area ready for the march on Bristol after the victory. From here they followed the route shown in the sketch map (p. 169), and somewhere in the area of Peasy Farm the horse passed through the infantry and took the lead.* It was here, too, that the ammunition wagons were parked, for the army was about to debouch onto the open moorland. The night was not completely dark; the moon was almost full, but a thick mist blanketed the moor, restricting visibility to a few feet and to some extent muffling sound. Even so it is difficult to understand how nearly 3,000 infantrymen and 800 horse could have passed within half a mile of Colonel Oglethorpe's patrol without being heard. Great credit must be given to Godfrey, who led the rebels unerringly over a narrow moorland track, and across the Black Ditch; only on reaching the Langmoor Rhine, more a morass than a ditch with one crossing place, did he falter temporarily and miss the ford.

Up till now the march had been carried out with a secrecy and skill that must evoke our admiration. Those who have been

* It is perhaps curious that horse should have led the way on a night march.

engaged in a night march will know how every eye seeks to pierce the darkness, and the strain that it puts upon any sensitive soldier when strange objects distort the vision and unbidden fears leap to the mind. Everyone is tense: any moment the deep silence may be broken by the crash of a volley, or the crack of a single shot. Directly Godfrey had managed to find the crossing place and got the army safely to the other side of the Langmoor Rhine the silence was shattered by that sound that every man had dreaded to hear – a pistol shot.

Almost certainly the pistol was fired by a vedette (a mounted sentinel – and not, as is sometimes asserted, by a traitor in Monmouth's army), who made all haste to Chedzoy to inform his picquet commander that the enemy were at hand and in strength. The Langmoor Rhine was about half a mile to the south-east of Chedzoy and almost exactly a mile from the royalist camp. It is immaterial whether the pistol shot was heard in either place, because it would have conveyed little without the vedette's information. In any event Sir Francis Compton at Chedzoy was not slow in despatching a trooper to inform the main camp, and it was clear to Monmouth that they had been discovered. There was nothing for it but to press on urgently, and hope that an attack might still be launched before the enemy were fully prepared. Lord Grey was therefore ordered to trot forward with his cavalry to engage the enemy in the flank as originally planned, while the infantry, still in column, followed as quickly as they could.

To go back in time an hour or two and to the royalist camp, we find Lord Feversham leaving Westonzoyland around 11 p.m. to visit most of his outposts. He rode first up the Bridgwater road and then struck north to Chedzoy, where he spent some time chatting with Compton. He was back in camp before 1 a.m., and when soon afterwards a messenger came in from Colonel Oglethorpe to say that there was no sign of any movement up the Bristol road and he was marching towards Bridgwater to investigate, Feversham felt fairly sure that there would be no night attack, so retired to his quarters in the village. He could hardly have got into bed when at about 1.45 he clearly heard the alarm being sounded, and pausing – very properly – only to dress himself correctly he was soon back in the camp. Battle had already begun, but Lord Churchill was on the spot and taking the necessary measures to meet the tactical situation.

In the fighting, although great courage was shown by most of the individual combatants, the rebel army as a whole and the officers who led it did not distinguish themselves: the odds against them were far too great. But no praise can be too high for the skill and discipline of their night march. After the Langmoor Rhine had been crossed Godfrey was either dismissed, or more likely left behind in the general scramble that followed the alarm, but the last mile was covered at speed with no guide except the light from the enemy's matchlocks* as they came close to the great ditch. The rebel army had covered almost six miles, much of it across extremely difficult country, in a thick mist, and maintaining absolute silence, in just under three hours. It was a remarkable achievement by any standard.

Before the night march ended and the enemy's main force could be engaged, Lord Grey had a brush with Sir Francis Compton's detachment of Blues and dragoons. As the latter rode from Chedzoy they met the rebel cavalry either by accident or design and a fierce and very confused skirmish took place in the mist. Compton was wounded by a bullet in the chest, but he and his men had given the royalist army time to deploy for battle, and most of the picquet (including Compton) got safely across the Bussex Rhine and took up position at the upper plungeon, which they held with considerable stubbornness against 300 enemy cavalry. For Grey had hit the rhine some distance below the upper plungeon, and split his force. He sent Captain Jones and 300 men up the rhine and they found the plungeon, while Grey with the remainder soon became engaged by the Grenadier battalions. It is not really surprising that these rustic men on their even more rustic animals, after a trying march and a sharp skirmish, should have shrunk before the destructive fire that flared and crackled at them out of the darkness. Cavalry to cavalry before the plungeon they showed some spirit, but Grey was quite unable to control the main body of his horse, who fled from the bullets in a disorderly rabble.

Monmouth, coming up with the infantry, was hampered by the retreating horsemen, but the Dutch gunners got their three remaining pieces into action on the left, and did some damage to the Grenadiers and Dumbarton's regiment. Wade tells us that the last part of the march had been so fast that the infantry arrived in some disorder, and the deployment from column into line was a rather ragged affair. Unfortunately his personal account of the

* James II would seem to have been mistaken in his statement that Dumbarton's regiment was the only one still using matchlocks at this battle. The equipment scale of the Sedgemoor army shows a distinct preponderance of matchlocks over flintlocks in all but the Grenadier companies and dragoons. What few muskets Monmouth's army had would have been mainly flintlocks purchased in Holland.

battle is confused, but there is no doubt that the rebel infantry halted some hundred yards from the enemy and stood, crowded together, firing their muskets at random. Those men lucky enough to be armed with a musket had had little training in its use, and although the weapon had a range of about 400 yards it was not noted for its accuracy; even trained soldiers found it difficult to hit a man at a hundred yards. Monmouth's men discharged a lot of shot – and their ammunition reserve was back at Peasy Farm – but we are told that they were firing high and doing little damage.

As soon as he saw that the rebel left extended beyond Dumbarton's right, Churchill switched Kirke's and Trelawney's regiments to strengthen that flank, and the artillery was hastily moved from the extreme left of the line. Many of the gun team (probably impressed civilians) had already left the field, but the militant Bishop of Winchester, Doctor Mews, who had had more experience with culverins than crosiers, quickly unharnessed the horses from his coach and personally assisted in the movement of the artillery to the right and centre of the line, where he continued to supervise the firing. As soon as he arrived on the scene Feversham issued strict and very sensible orders that no infantryman was to cross the ditch before daylight. Grey had reached the rhine a little

Monmouth pleading with James II

before 2 a.m. and the infantry battle probably started rather less than half an hour later. Not long after it started, and while it was still dark, Feversham led three troops of cavalry across the lower plungeon and positioned them on the rebel right flank with orders to envelop this flank as and when possible. On recrossing the rhine he was met by Colonel Oglethorpe and his Life Guards, who had ridden completely round the battlefield without having seen the enemy. Feversham immediately led these in the rear of the infantry to cross by the upper plungeon – now cleared by the Blues of enemy horse – and positioned them on Monmouth's left flank. At first light the frontal attack went in and the rebel army found itself being relentlessly squeezed on three sides. Nevertheless, perhaps out of desperation, they continued for a little to fight most courageously, even though their leader had fled the field.

As we have seen, it is in pursuit of a defeated army that the heaviest casualties are apt to occur, and this is especially true when that army is little better than an ill-organized rabble. Wade says that he 'made a kind of disorderly retreat to a ditch a great way behind us'. He was Monmouth's best commander and probably held his troops together longer than the others; the ditches and bogs did not help, and the royalist cavalry took a fearful toll of these misguided peasants. Rebel casualties have always been difficult to assess, for they often include those who were hanged out of hand after the battle by orders of the victorious commander, and even those who were the victims of the notorious Judge Jeffreys. Probably no more than 300 were killed in the battle and a further 1,000 in the pursuit. The royalist casualties are usually given at around 400, which is probably too high. Many rebel prisoners were taken on the field and 500 of them spent the night after the fight in Westonzoyland church.

Had Monmouth died on the battlefield he would have been a hero; but although in the heat of battle he always fought with great courage, he was not the stuff of which heroes are made. He knew that he could not save his army and when Grey (who accompanied him) and others suggested that he should try to save himself while there was still time he found it difficult to refuse. We may criticize him for deserting men still fighting his battle, and we may find ourselves unable to excuse him on the grounds that he himself had been deserted, but we can perhaps understand something of the agony of it all. But although in life Monmouth was never a king, in the Tower and on the scaffold he knew how to behave like one. And he died horribly at the hands of a bungling executioner.

Order of Battle for the Royalist Army at Sedgemoor

(Extracted from Viscount Wolseley's *Life of Marlborough,*
Vol. I, p. 319.)

Infantry
From the right of the line to the left:
5 companies of the Royal Regiment (Dumbarton's), now the
Royal Scots, under Lieutenant-Colonel Douglas: one company
was a Grenadier company.
7 companies, of which one was a Grenadier company, of the
1st Battalion of the King's Guards, now the Grenadier Guards,
under the Duke of Grafton.
6 companies of the 2nd Battalion of the King's Guards, now the
Grenadier Guards, under Major Eaton.
6 companies of the 2nd Regiment of Guards, now the Coldstream
Guards, under Lieutenant-Colonel Sackville.
5 companies of the Queen Dowager's Regiment, now the Queen's
or West Surrey Regiment, under Colonel Kirk.
Note: Wolseley places these troops on the extreme left. So does
      Roberts (*Life of Monmouth,* Vol. II, p. 61), but Roberts
      puts 5 companies (of which one was a Grenadier company)
      of Trelawney's regiment, now the King's Own, under
      command of Lieutenant-Colonel Charles Churchill,
      between Sackville and Kirk.

Cavalry
150 men selected from the three troops of Life Guards, and 60
Horse Grenadiers, under Lieutenant-Colonel the Honourable
F. Villiers.
7 troops (about 400 men) of the King's Regiment of Horse, now
the Royal Horse Guards (Blues and Royals), under Sir Francis
Compton, who was senior cavalry officer in command of horse.
3 troops of Churchill's dragoons, now the Royal Dragoons (about
150 men under Lord Cornbury). The fourth troop of this regiment
was at Langport watching the passage over the river Parrett.

Artillery
Under the command of Mr Shere, helped by the Bishop of
Winchester, Dr Mews, 2 twelve-pounders, 8 demi-culverins,
4 six-pounders, 2 minions.

Totals given by various authorities differ slightly, but the
general consensus is that there were 1,800 infantrymen, 700
cavalrymen and with the artillerymen a total force of about
2,700 men.

CHAPTER 10

The First Jacobite Rising

Preston, Sheriffmuir and Glenshiel

12–14 November 1715, 13 November 1715 and 10 June 1719

There is little to be gained from a special visit to Preston, for it has now spread almost to the bridge over the Ribble in the south and beyond the bridge (near the site of the old ford) on the Liverpool road. But a visitor to the town can still pick out some of the main features, which stand on or near the sites occupied in 1715. The parish church (rebuilt in the last century), the market place and the main street (now Church Street and Fishergate) are on their original sites, and the modern bridge across the river is not far from the old site.

Sheriffmuir, on the other hand, remains very much as it was more than 250 years ago. The battlefield lies about five miles north of Stirling between the two minor roads that run from Dunblane and Bridge of Allan to Blackford. It is difficult to be certain exactly where the fighting took place, because there were no recognizable landmarks, such as a road, village, wood or river to feature in the contemporary accounts, and there is more than one ridge to choose from. The site marked on the one-inch Ordnance Survey map (sheet 54) is probably about right. Argyll's line may have crossed the Dunblane road near the site of the MacRae cairn and stretched down towards the Wharry burn, while Mar – whose right over-lapped Argyll's – would have had much of his force north of the road. The present Dunblane–Blackford road therefore runs through the site of the two positions at the outset of the battle, and from the Gathering Stone (just north of the cairn) a view of the battlefield, and the line of Mar's approach from Kinbuck, can be obtained.

Glenshiel is twenty miles west of Fort Augustus (twenty-five by road) in Ross and Cromarty. The A87 runs through the glen and the site of the battle is at the narrow pass immediately to the west of the present Forestry Commission plantations, almost exactly as marked on the one-inch Ordnance Survey map (sheet 35). The whole battle-field can be viewed from the main road, or one can climb the shoulder to the north of the road for a better view of the glen.

When James II died in exile in 1701, Louis XIV of France at once recognized his son, James Francis Edward, as James III of England and VIII of Scotland. Had not James II, and indeed his son too at a later date, refused to abjure his Catholic faith for a throne, the Prince would, in due course, have been recognized as James III in England as well. As it was this young man, who at the death of his father was only thirteen years old, was soon to be known to his supporters as the Chevalier de St George (a blatantly transparent pseudonym given to him when he embarked on his first attempt to regain the throne in 1708), and to his enemies as the Pretender.

By the Act of Settlement (1701) the crown was to pass on the death of Queen Anne to the Electress Sophia of Hanover (the granddaughter of James I) and her descendants, who were Protestants. The Electress died on 28 May 1714 (O.S.) leaving her very unattractive, narrow-minded son as the next in line. Queen Anne died less than two months later. The two men principally concerned with the government of England in the months immediately preceding the Queen's death were Robert Harley, Earl of Oxford, and Henry St John, Viscount Bolingbroke. Both had been secretly working for a Jacobite restoration while outwardly supporting the legitimate Protestant succession; both had realized that Jacobite prospects were gravely diminished, if not completely doomed, when they learned from James some five months before Anne died that he would not consent to change his religion – but Bolingbroke continued right up to the end to run with the hare and hunt with the hounds.

The Queen's death found Bolingbroke unprepared. Some say that he needed only six weeks more, but it is unlikely that he could ever have brought off a *coup de main*. He was not a forceful enough character; unpredictable and unprincipled, he failed to master events and was sadly lacking in drive or purpose. His Whig adversaries had the measure of him, and had taken every precaution to ensure that the Elector of Hanover was proclaimed king without disturbance.

At the time of Anne's death James was at Commercy, for under the terms of the Treaty of Utrecht Louis XIV had accepted the Protestant succession and James had been obliged to leave France for Lorraine. He was now twenty-six, tall, good-looking and almost as dark as his uncle Charles II. He was utterly humourless and inclined to be taciturn and withdrawn, but he was almost always courteous, rarely lost his temper and bore his many reverses with dignity. He was in an unenviable position, for any attempt to cross the Channel was bound to be obstructed. His visit to his

Queen Anne (above left), whose death in 1714 led the way to the first
Jacobite rebellion, and Prince James Francis Edward, the Jacobite
pretender. Both the Earl of Oxford (below left) and Viscount
Bolingbroke (below right), had been intriguing for a Jacobite
restoration even before Anne's death

King George I (left) and the Earl of Mar (right), principal supporter
of the Jacobite cause after the summer of 1715

mother in France was soon discovered and he was ordered to leave
that country at once. He could only issue a manifesto in which
he cautioned his friends in Scotland to have patience, for no foreign
help could be expected at present. On 18 September 1714 King
George entered his kingdom, and soon the principal Scottish clans
had sent a letter to the Earl of Mar (Secretary of State for Scotland)
assuring the government of their loyalty. And yet the chances of
a successful Jacobite rebellion were immeasurably greater than
they were to be thirty years later. Had James been served by a
capable commander in the coming months, the course of English
history might have been quite different and certain disasters
might have been avoided.

George I was little better than a puppet in Whig hands, and
they had many personal scores to pay off. Bolingbroke realized
at once that he could expect no favour under the new regime and
quickly fled the country. The Duke of Ormonde, commander-in-
chief of the army, had been too closely involved with Bolingbroke
at the time of the Treaty of Utrecht not to expect dismissal, but
he stayed on in England for a little while until the threat of impeachment drove him to join Bolingbroke in France. This left
Lord Lansdown and Sir William Wyndham in charge of Jacobite
affairs in England, where it had been intended to raise the standard
of revolt in the summer of 1715. Bath was to be the centre, and it

was planned that James should land at Plymouth. But their plans although well laid were ill concealed, and the government, acting on information and with considerable speed, stamped out this incipient revolt and arrested many of the leaders. This left the principal support for the Cause in the person of the Earl of Mar, whose surprising adherence came about when, in spite of many protestations of loyalty, he had had the seals of office taken from him in a most peremptory way.

John Erskine, sixth Earl of Mar, was a man perfectly prepared to turn his coat according to circumstances, and we may be fairly certain that in spite of a refusal by the Duke of Atholl to lead any rebellion Mar must have reckoned the chances of success to be good. Once he had decided where his interests lay he moved – almost for the only time – with speed. He summoned a number of prominent Scottish chieftains or their sons to what became known as Mar's hunting party, and they met him on 27 August. More than once James had warned him against acting precipitately, for he felt that with the collapse of the English rebellion the time was not opportune. However, at Braemar on 6 September 1715 Mar raised what was called the Restoration Standard, that symbol of hope intended to replace the constant round of intrigue and diplomacy in the council chamber with courage and skill on the battlefield.

Mar's original force at Braemar may not have numbered as many as 500, but it quickly snowballed and very soon almost all Scotland north of the Tay was under Jacobite control. He opened his campaign with a forcefulness that unfortunately was not maintained. An attempt to take Edinburgh Castle through an artifice was a dismal failure, but Lord Kinnoull's younger son John Hay secured Perth with a party of 200 horse, and King James was proclaimed with enthusiasm at Aberdeen, Montrose, Inverness, Forfar, Brechin and Dundee. By the time Mar arrived at Perth towards the end of September he had an army of some 5,000 men, which was increasing every day as more recruits came in from the Highlands. Most of these men lacked any experience, but they were malleable material given competent leadership. Having plunged precipitately into rebellion Mar seems to have thought that he could possess Scotland by sitting passively in Perth. He did not realize that if rebellions are to succeed they must be prosecuted with ruthless vigour. He possessed little military skill, and what he had was of the slow shuffling kind.

In the early autumn of 1715 the English government were rightly more apprehensive of the danger in the south-west, and although they recalled troops from Flanders* the order was rescinded when the French (now ruled by the Duke of Orleans as regent for Louis XV) assured them that they would not permit James to embark. However, in the Duke of Argyll the government possessed an able general whose intention was to block Mar's path to the south at Stirling, even though his garrison when reinforced numbered little more than 3,000. The spirit of rebellion was infectious, and in the Lowlands as well as in the north of England men of import-ance had come out in favour of the Jacobite cause. Mar held all the cards: had he been a man of action and played them with determination he might have gained the kingdom for his new master. With his superior numbers he could have swept Argyll's force, the only obstacle to his joining hands with the southern rebels, out of existence. But instead he stayed at Perth and sent Brigadier Mackintosh of Borlum with 2,000 men on a somewhat vague expedition to the south.

Mackintosh's adventures are a story of their own, which we can pick up only on his arrival at Kelso, where he joined two other Jacobite contingents. Ormonde's hurried flight to France and his subsequent signs of recreancy had produced an atmosphere of uncertainty, if not defeatism, among Jacobite supporters in the south and west of England. It was, however, different in the north, where men like the Earl of Derwentwater, Mr Thomas Forster (the Member for Northumberland) and Lord Widdrington came out in arms. Among the Lowlanders, too, the Cause received considerable support, and the third party now assembled at Kelso included Lords Kenmure, Nithsdale, Carnwath and Winton.

These three forces had united at Kelso by 22 October. A con-temporary chronicler† gives the total as 1,400 foot and 600 horse, but this is clearly wrong and must exclude Mackintosh's men, which even allowing for those he failed to get across the Forth and some subsequent desertions would have numbered a thousand or more. Mar had commissioned Lord Kenmure to command the Scots and Thomas Forster the English contingent. It was con-sidered that the Cause would be best served by giving the command to a Protestant, otherwise there could be no excuse for Forster's commission: he may have been a good Member of Parliament, but he had no conception of the military art.

* Two-thirds of a total army of 22,000 were at this moment serving abroad, and in Scotland there were only some 1,500 men.

† Peter Rae, *The History of the Rebellion rais'd against His Majesty King George I by the Friends of the Popish Pretender*, p. 268.

186

At a council to decide on the next move opinions were divided. The Englishmen under Forster, short of arms and without artillery, had already made a feeble attempt to take Newcastle, and a suggestion that they should try again with the much stronger combined force was ruled out through a quite unjustified fear of General Carpenter's strength. Dumfries was found to be too well guarded, but had there been any coordination by Mar the obvious course of a joint attack from north and south on Argyll at Stirling must have succeeded, and with Scotland secure the advance into England, which was finally decided upon, could have been more easily undertaken.

Thomas Forster was the moving spirit of a bold strike into north-west England. He promised that in Lancashire they would find overwhelming support for the rebellion. However, the Scots were very loath to undertake what they deemed a grave and almost desperate venture: eventually Forster overcame their reluctance, but 500 Highlanders turned for home, only to end their march in an Edinburgh prison. Lord Winton also would not at first conform to the agreed plan and led off a body of his men, but soon seeing where his duty lay turned back upon the road that was to lead him to the Tower. The small (less than 3,000 men) but reasonably well equipped army crossed the border on 1 November and spent that night at Brampton. A large rabble of mainly unarmed peasants had been hastily got together by Lord Lonsdale and the militant Bishop of Carlisle to bar the invaders' way north of Penrith, but on sighting their enemy they quickly dispersed. Thereafter Forster's march through Appleby, Kendal, Kirby Lonsdale and Lancaster was notable only for the few recruits who rallied to the Chevalier's standard. On the night of 9 November the Jacobite horse entered Preston. Two troops of Colonel Stanhope's dragoons, who were in the town, withdrew without offering any resistance.

On 10 November the foot also arrived in Preston, and Forster, who had been assured through his local intelligence system that he could expect ample warning of any enemy approach, intended resting his army for a day or two before proceeding to Manchester. It came as a considerable surprise to him, therefore, to learn on the 12th that General Wills, who commanded the royalist troops in Cheshire, was at hand with five cavalry and three infantry regiments. Moreover, General Carpenter, displaying an offensive spirit that went far to compensate for the inferior material at his disposal, was said to be closing in from the north-east. This information seems to have proved too much for Forster, who issued a series of orders and counter-orders then retired to his lodgings. When, a little later, Colonel Oxburgh and Lords Kenmure and Widdrington reported for orders they found their 'general' in bed.

Preston was a quite unprotected small market town, but a resolute commander could have put up a strong defence. The key point to be held was the bridge over the Ribble and John Farquharson of Invercauld had been sent there by Forster with a small force of picked men. Farquharson had plenty of courage and he and his men would have given a good account of themselves, but at the first hint of danger they were withdrawn to the town. Wills was so amazed at finding the bridge unguarded that he immediately suspected an ambush in the narrow lane with its high hedges that led from the bridge up the hill to the town. He therefore proceeded with caution, which enabled the Jacobites to perfect their dispositions. These were fairly skilfully laid out, and reflect some other hand than Forster's.

Barricades were set up blocking the main entrances to the town, and proper use was made of the houses and narrow lanes as points of defence. The Jacobites possessed six cannon, and if these could have been properly manned the royalists, who were without artillery, would have been more severely mauled than was the case; but without trained gunners what little advantage they offered was chiefly psychological. Brigadier Mackintosh of Borlum commanded the barricade set up to the east of the church in the main street, and was supported by the Earl of Derwentwater's troops, who were in position in the churchyard. Another member of Clan Mackintosh commanded what was known as the windmill barrier, which was situated on the Lancaster road, while the one on the Liverpool road was under a Major Mills. Lord Charles Murray blocked a lane leading into fields across which General Carpenter's troops were expected. By midday on 12 November Preston was in a state of adequate defence.

General Wills, having discovered that the approach lanes to the town were clear and that the Jacobites had decided to make a stand, launched a two-point attack. Brigadier Honywood, commanding his own dragoons, and Preston's foot under Lord Forrester, attacked Borlum's post, while Brigadiers Dormer and Munden led a mixed force of infantry and dismounted cavalry against the Lancaster barricade. Little headway was made against this barrier and the attack does not seem to have been a very spirited affair. But on the Wigan side of the town the battle was fiercely contested and the Jacobites, firing from the protection of houses, inflicted considerable casualties on Wills's men.

The strength of Borlum's position was that between the double

188

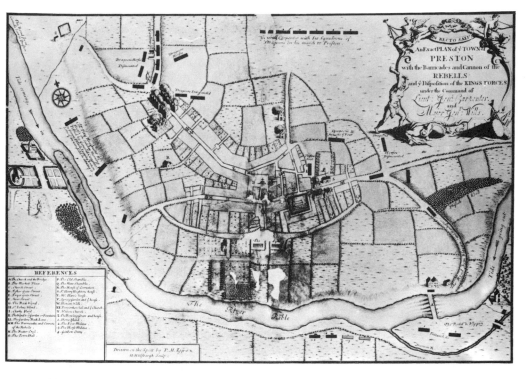

Above: Contemporary town plan of Preston
Below: Battle of Preston

barricade set up to the east of the church there stood two of the largest houses in the town. These belonged to Sir Henry Haughton and Mr Hare; both houses had been occupied by Highlanders. A frontal attack down the road had no chance of success so long as the attackers were subject to enfilade fire from these houses; but when Lord Forrester infiltrated his regiment through the gardens between the church and the two houses the position was dangerous, but by no means critical – that is, until the troops in the larger house (Haughton's) were withdrawn. It is not clear from contemporary accounts of the battle why Mackintosh did this, but it was a fatal error. Before nightfall Preston's regiment was in possession of both these houses, although in getting them they suffered the only heavy casualties of the whole battle.

A third attack had also been launched against Lord Charles Murray's barricade, but this had been held after heavy fighting in the course of which Murray had had to ask for reinforcements from Derwentwater. As night drew on and the whip-lash sound of close-range bullets became less persistent the Jacobites could be well content with the day's work, for all the barriers were still intact, although the one by the church had become dangerously vulnerable. However, all was not well among the rebel soldiery: royalist prisoners taken in the fighting soon dispelled all hopes that any of their colleagues would desert. Some Jacobites with cool heads, and cold feet, made their way out of the town while there was still time – for the next day General Carpenter arrived and immediately sealed off all exits.

Carpenter claimed the credit for the victory, but at the time he commended General Wills for the fighting on the 12th, and the only serious flaw that he could find in his dispositions was that the bridge and ford across the Ribble had been left unguarded. Once these exits had been closed the rebels were bottled up, but there was little doubt that they could have fought their way out. However, much to the disgust of the Highlanders, caitiff counsels in the end prevailed. On 14 November the English marched in and disarmed Forster's men. The number of prisoners taken was about 1,500, of which seventy-five were English noblemen or gentlemen and 143 Scottish. Most of the rank and file taken were Scotsmen and they were treated with considerable savagery. The important prisoners were taken to London and some were sentenced to death. Both Mackintosh of Borlum and Forster escaped from Newgate – but whereas Forster decided that exile in France was preferable to any further military forays, we shall meet Mackintosh again. The Jacobite casualties were only eighteen killed and twenty-five wounded, as opposed to about 200 royalists killed or wounded, most of whom were from Preston's regiment.

The Battle of Preston terminated the Jacobite insurrection in England; but at almost exactly the same time as Forster and his officers were negotiating the surrender in Lancashire an even more disastrous blow to James's cause was struck on a lonely moor near Stirling. Although Mar had scarcely stirred from Perth since his arrival there at the end of September, a constant stream of recruits had doubled his army to around 10,000 men,* and behind him almost the whole of Scotland was held for James. At last even Mar (whom James had made a duke in October) thought that his force was sufficiently formidable to permit him to venture forth, and on 10 November he left Perth with the intention of joining up with the Jacobites in Lancashire. He planned three diversionary crossings of the Forth, each with 1,000 men, in the neighbourhood of Stirling, while he himself crossed the river higher up with the main body. At Auchterarder General Gordon joined him from Doune, and he was put in command of the 3,000 men with orders to secure Dunblane as his first objective.

However, Argyll had quickly learned of Mar's plan, and he was not the man to let his small army be defeated in detail or to sit back in Stirling and await attack. He immediately called in his outlying garrisons and advanced to Dunblane before Gordon could reach the town. On the bitterly cold night of 12 November he had his army encamped on the high ground some two miles east of Dunblane, and on this commanding feature he awaited Mar. On becoming aware of Argyll's advance, General Gordon fell back on the main army, which in the meantime had marched down the drove leading from Greenloaning to Kinbuck. Here the army encamped, and at daybreak the next morning Mar marched for Sheriffmuir, where with a superiority in numbers of three to one he had reason to be confident of the outcome of any engagement.

Argyll was well acquainted with the site, for the name Sheriff-muir derives from the place's use as a training ground for the militia. When he found that the recent hard frosts had enabled his cavalry to ride over the usually wet Lynns he extended his line to reach from the high ground just above the present Dunblane–Blackford road down the slope towards the Wharry burn. He formed his army into two lines. The first comprised six battalions of infantry, with each wing protected by three squadrons of

* This was probably the number after the Frasers had deserted Fraser of Fraserdale shortly before the battle when their chief (Simon Fraser, eleventh Lord Lovat) took the government's side.

dragoons and an additional squadron behind each of the wings; the second line had only two battalions of foot and one squadron of dragoons to each wing. Argyll commanded the right wing, General Wightman the centre and General Whetham the left.

Although Argyll from his vantage point near the Gathering Stone could see a part of the Jacobite army, neither commander was properly aware of the other's dispositions, for much of Mar's approach march from Kinbuck had been in dead ground. Mar also formed his army into two lines. The ten battalions of infantry in the first line were mostly Highlanders, and there were a further ten battalions in the second line with a reserve of 800 men. The Stirling squadron (who had charge of the standard) and two squadrons of Huntly's horse protected the right flank of the first line with the Perthshire and Fifeshire squadrons on the left; the Earl Marischal's squadron was on the right of the second line and the Angus squadrons on the left. The Earl Marischal was in overall command of the cavalry, while General Gordon commanded on the right of the line and General Hamilton on the left. Mar took position at the right centre of the front line.

Thus, shortly before midday on this cold November morning, these two armies formed up for battle within a very short distance of each other without either side being perfectly aware of what the other was about. The Jacobites, confident of victory, were in a mood of great exhilaration, tossing their bonnets in the air and emitting loud huzzas. After Mar had delivered to the heads of clans what even his sternest critics described as a stirring address, the order to advance was given. On the one side of the ridge colourful plaids and kilts, on the other brilliant uniforms with flaunted facings of scarlet and blue: a pageantry of splendour, so soon to become a sorry scene of disarray.

Contemporary accounts of the muddle into which the rebel army got itself as it advanced to the attack are confusing and, as each soldier-scribe is seeking to justify his action, often contradictory. But it appears that as soon as the Jacobites topped the crest of the ridge it was seen that the right wings of both armies overlapped the other's left. Both Mar's lines were advancing in column of battalions, and his hasty attempt to deploy and extend to his left resulted in the front and rear lines of that wing becoming entangled. What was more serious, the cavalry on the left – perhaps on account of the boggy ground – edged to their right, leaving the infantry unprotected.

Argyll was in a position to observe the confusion into which the Jacobite left had been thrown and he wasted no time in exploiting

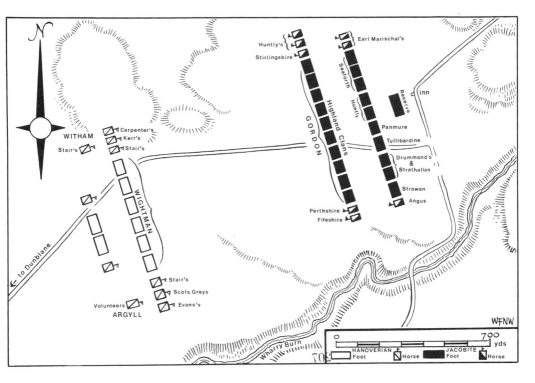

Above and below: Battle of Sheriffmuir

it. He went into the attack at the head of five squadrons of dragoons and five battalions of foot, as well as sixty mounted volunteers under the Earl of Rothes. Taken off balance, the Highlanders nevertheless put up an amazingly stout resistance, more especially when the Fife and Angus squadrons had dislocated themselves from the centre and come to their assistance. Wherever the ground was favourable this retreating left wing stood and fought with much stubbornness, but gradually they were pressed back in a two-mile half-circle to the river Allan, which they crossed – still under pressure – in the neighbourhood of Kinbuck.

Sheriffmuir was an inconclusive and untidy battle, for Argyll, although a greatly superior general to Mar, seems to have been guilty of going into the attack before he had assured himself that his left wing was adequately protected. In fact it too, although to a lesser degree than the Jacobite left, was still getting into position when Mar ordered the Highland clans on his right and two squadrons of horse into the attack. At the same time, unaware of what was happening on his left, he sent an aide-de-camp to General Hamilton with orders to advance that wing. Mar's attack opened with a sharp bout of musketry, both armies firing at almost point-blank range. The ranks shivered like corn in the wind, and among the Highlanders the popular Captain of Clanranald fell, but Glengarry rallied the clan and crying for revenge they discarded their muskets and were quickly among the militia with their broadswords. It was all over in a matter of minutes: Argyll's left was chased from the field and even to the outskirts of Stirling.

The field of battle was now almost deserted, for owing to lack of enthusiasm, if not actual disobedience of orders, the Master of Sinclair and his cavalry remained totally inactive throughout, and this allowed Argyll's centre to join in the pursuit of the Jacobite left. Both commanders learned of the disasters to their respective left wings while two miles from the scene of battle, both having assumed the victory to be theirs. Mar retraced his steps, with his right wing virtually intact, and occupied the high ground from Stonehill to the Gathering Stone. This wing alone was larger than the whole of Argyll's army, and he would have had little difficulty in annihilating the victorious royalist troops, whom he could clearly see from his commanding position above Kippendavie. But Mar in his weak, indecisive way lacked the manhood to dare, and he even allowed some enemy stragglers to pass underneath his hill unscathed. For the rest of the day the two protagonists, with what was left of their troops, remained passively watching each other. Then, as the early darkness closed in, Mar marched his men back

194

to Ardoch and Argyll camped in and around Dunblane.

If a victory was to be claimed by either side Argyll had that slender right, for on the next day he re-occupied the battlefield and gathered up the spoils – which were considerable. The royalists admitted to 290 killed, 187 men wounded and over 100 taken prisoner, most of whom were shortly released for want of means to accommodate them. Mar owned to the loss of only sixty men and eighty-two prisoners. Casualties were not too high, partly because artillery played no part in this battle, but certainly the Jacobites lost more than they admitted to – possibly 300–400 – and very probably the royalists did too. Apart from the Captain of Clanranald the Earl of Strathmore was the only Jacobite of importance to be killed, while the government troops lost the Earl of Forfar.

For the Jacobites anything less than a victory was a defeat. Loss of prestige was serious, resulting in many of the clansmen going home – Seaforth's people being hastened on their way by the news that the government had taken Inverness. There was now no chance of joining up with the army in England, and indeed the simultaneous defeat at Preston virtually brought the rebellion to a close, even though James was to arrive in Scotland in just over a month's time. The Hanoverian hand fell heavily on all who had come 'out' for the Chevalier. Nineteen Scottish and two English peerages were attainted; the Earl of Derwentwater* and Lord Kenmure were executed in 1716, and Lords Nithsdale and Winton saved their heads only through daring escapes.

The French did what they could to obstruct James's attempt to reach Scotland – even unloading the ship carrying a large quantity of arms that he had bought – and when he found their efforts unavailing Lord Stair (English ambassador in Paris) made his own arrangements to have the Chevalier murdered. The intended victim, however, having disappeared in the night from the court of Lorraine and run the gauntlet through France in a series of exciting adventures, eventually took ship from Dunkirk on 16 December and arrived in Peterhead harbour on the 22nd.

James's six-week stay in Scotland was one of almost continual disappointment. Tired and dispirited, ill and fevered, he made his way incognito through Aberdeen to Feteresso Castle, where he took to his bed for nine days. Then by way of Brechin and Glamis he reached Scone on 8 January 1716. Plans were made for his

* His brother Charles Radclyffe was imprisoned, but escaped and
  assumed the title—even though it had been attainted. He was
  captured at sea in 1746 and executed for his part at Preston.

coronation to take place there on 23 January, but by that time Argyll (and his difficult second-in-command General Cadogan) was stirring with an army three times the size of the one he commanded at Sheriffmuir, and the Jacobite court was preparing to move north.

James had not required the constant prompting of Bolingbroke and his nephew the Duke of Berwick to come to Scotland, but the latter's persistent refusal to accompany his uncle and the news – received just before he sailed – of Ormonde's second failure to invade England, were grievous blows, which he knew greatly diminished his prospects of success. Nothing occurred in Scotland to make him think otherwise. General Hamilton, whom he sent to France with an urgent appeal for help, had no luck there; Argyll, recently superseded and rightly considered to be discontented, nevertheless disregarded a letter from James, and Huntly was busy coming to terms with the Hanoverians. There were some still willing to join the pathetic remnants of the Jacobite army in Perth had James called them to arms, but many more would have done so had he arrived at the head of a well equipped French army. Mostly his Scotsmen were disappointed in him, and his weakness in agreeing to his advisers' foolish scorched earth policy before Perth did him personally, and the Cause generally, much harm.

By the end of January winter had the country in its firm grip, but Argyll commandeered the local people to clear the roads of snow and advanced on Perth. The Jacobite army retreated through Dundee to Montrose and here Mar persuaded James to embark for France in a ship that he had conveniently at hand. Mar said that the retreating army could make better terms without James – but he had no intention of staying himself to make these terms. James sailed for France on 4 February with Mar, the Earl of Melfort and Lord Drummond. A second boat sailed shortly afterwards with some other gentlemen.

The Jacobite army, now abandoned by both its sovereign and its commander-in-chief, continued its sorrowful way north in surprisingly good order. Argyll made what haste he could – although Cadogan thought otherwise – but he was never able to come to grips with the rebel army and probably took no more than 100 prisoners. Once into the Highlands this undaunted but sadly disillusioned band of men was safe from pursuit, and able to melt away to the comparative security of their remote fastnesses. The process of cleaning up, as it was euphemistically called, continued for over a year until with the Act of Pardon, passed in May 1717, Scotland was considered to be pacified.

The defeat at Preston, the fiasco of Sheriffmuir, the disheartening performance of James in Scotland, and the flight of many prominent Jacobite leaders to France had torn the entrails out of the movement for the time being. And when, just over three years later, an attempt was made to rekindle the flames of rebellion it quickly died of its own inanition.

The prime mover in the 1719 rising was the Spanish Cardinal Alberoni, whose policy had become increasingly hostile to England, France and Austria as a result of the Treaty of Utrecht in 1713, through which Spain lost both land and prestige. Matters went from bad to worse and on 17 December 1718 Britain declared war on Spain. Cardinal Alberoni decided to strike at England through the Jacobite movement; he was willing to supply money and what troops he could spare. The Duke of Ormonde was once more to attempt an invasion, landing on the south-west coast, and there was to be a smaller subsidiary landing on the west coast of Scotland. For this latter purpose the Earl Marischal and his brother James Keith were summoned to Spain and given instructions to return to France and recruit such prominent exiles as the Marquess of Tullibardine, his brother Lord George Murray, the Earl of Seaforth, John Cameron of Lochiel and Macdonald of Keppoch.

The main expedition under Ormonde, comprising 5,000 men and 15,000 arms in twenty-nine ships, sailed from Cadiz on 27 March (N.S.).* Two days later the fleet met with the usual Stuart weather at sea and was driven back to port with sufficient loss to incapacitate it. The smaller fleet, carrying the Jacobite leaders, 307 Spanish soldiers and a good quantity of arms and ammunition, sailed on varying dates and from different French ports. After an unpleasant and dangerous journey round the north coast, and a certain amount of island-hopping on the west coast, the fleet was finally united off Eilean Donan Castle at the head of Loch Alsh on 2 April (O.S.), but owing to the difficulty of finding boats it was not until 17 April that all the arms, powder and supplies had been safely landed.

Here the small force remained for several weeks while the leaders engaged in argument and recrimination. Tullibardine disputed the command with the Earl Marischal, basing his claim to leadership on an outdated commission from King James. Keith gave way so far as the land troops were concerned, but insisted

* The difference between dates prevailing on the continent to those in England was at this time eleven days, owing to our not adopting the Gregorian calendar (New Style (N.S.)) until 1752. The fleet would have left Cadiz on 6 April by Old Style (O.S.) dating.

on keeping command of the fleet. Two consequences of this dis-agreement were that Tullibardine and Keith set up camps separated by some two miles, which only increased existing difficulties, and that when Tullibardine showed signs of wishing to re-embark the troops and withdraw (which in the event would have been the wiser course) Keith sent the ships away. Lochiel and the Captain of Clanranald were sent to their own country to see how matters were, and letters were despatched to other clans urging them to rise. But most of the clansmen were loath to do so without some positive sign that numbers, so woefully misused at Sheriffmuir, were once more on their side.

The consensus among the leaders was that as theirs was only a diversionary operation no advance inland should be made before news of Ormonde's landing was received, but before the fate of the Duke's fleet was known matters at Eilean Donan had become critical. On 9 May three government warships appeared in Loch Alsh, and information (false as it turned out) was received that enemy troops were within twenty miles. It was clearly time for action to replace argument: an advance base for ammunition and stores was established at the Crow of Kintail,* and letters were urgently sent for Lochiel and Macdonald to rendezvous with as many men as they could. Soon some encouraging news was brought from Edinburgh: although the Duke of Ormonde had failed in his enterprise, he sent word from Spain that the Scottish rising should proceed and he promised to support it with arms and money. Now prodded from behind by the royalist navy and fed with vague promises from the front, the Jacobite force moved towards Glen-shiel by two different routes. One party marched down the east bank of Loch Duich, while another went via Loch Long and then over the high ground north of Loch Duich.

About six miles south-east of Loch Duich the high hills on each side of the present road almost join; here the road, then nothing more than a cattle drove, winds through a pass not fifty yards wide. It was a place where a handful of resolute men might have held up an army for days. The Jacobites arrived at this pass towards the end of May. On 4 June Lochiel joined them with 150 men, Seaforth had raised 400 of his clan, and there were perhaps a further thousand Highlanders assembled. Three days later a party of Chisholm's men came in with information that a royalist army under General Wightman had passed through Fort Augustus

* A small garrison of forty soldiers and two officers left at Eilean Donan in charge of the main ammunition supply were forced to surrender to the men-of-war, and the castle was destroyed.

and was now marching down Glen Moriston. The Jacobites had had plenty of time in which to prepare their dispositions (some sangars had been constructed in the pass), and when on the 9th they learned that the enemy was encamped for the night at the head of Loch Cluanie they were ready to give battle the next day.

The narrow pass is just to the west of where there is now a conifer plantation. The Jacobite right, under Lord George Murray, took up a position on the foothills immediately to the south of the drove, with advance patrols some way forward. The 250 Spaniards held the rocky hillside immediately north of the drove, and above them came Lochiel and his 150 clansmen, then forty of Rob Roy's rascals, and further up were men under commanders such as Sir John Mackenzie, Brigadiers Campbell of Ormidale and Glendaruel, and Brigadier Mackintosh of Borlum. Lord Seaforth, with 200 of his best men, was in a commanding position about half a mile up the steep hill.

Against this Jacobite force of 1,600 Highlanders and 250 Spaniards, General Wightman had 850 foot, 120 dragoons and 136 Highlanders. This was no country for cavalry, so the dragoons had been dismounted on entering the glen. They, together with the six coehorn mortars advanced along the line of the drove. On the extreme right Wightman placed his Mackays from Sutherland, then came some 200 Grenadiers under Major Richard Milburn, the 11th

Battle of Glenshiel

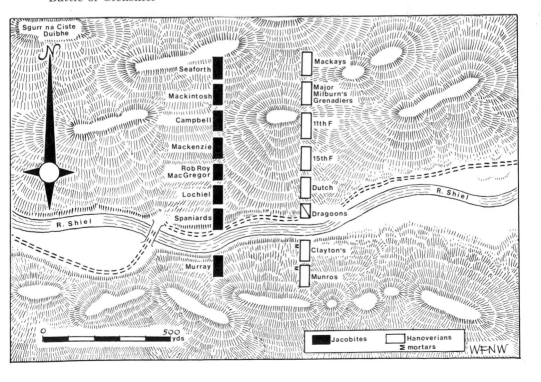

and 15th Foot, and a Dutch contingent. This right wing was commanded by Colonel Clayton, whose own regiment, under Lieutenant-Colonel Reading, formed part of the left wing which advanced south of the drove with the Monros on the extreme left.

The engagement began on the Jacobite right soon after midday., when Lord George Murray's advance picquets contested ground as they gradually fell back onto the main position, but it was not until after 5 p.m. that the battle proper began. Undoubtedly the mortars played an important part in this short fight. They were used in the first instance against Lord George's men, who promptly withdrew from the very exposed hillock to the south of the drove, thus leaving the pass virtually unguarded. They were then turned upon the Spaniards, and firing at extreme range they probably did little harm, but they set the heather on fire, which must have caused confusion in the ever-narrowing funnel of attack. Meanwhile the Mackays, having made light of the steep and rocky ascent, had got round Seaforth's flank, and in the short bout of musketry that followed the Earl got a ball in the arm. Soon the Jacobite left was in retreat, and although the Earl Marischal and Brigadier Campbell of Ormidale held the centre steady for a while it was not long before these men, and then Lord Tullibardine with the Spaniards, were seen to be scampering up the hillside and away through the pass that leads round the north side of the Sgurr na Ciste Duibhe. Before darkness fell on 10 June 1719 the Jacobite army had disintegrated and the Pretender's troops in Scotland had suffered the last of the repeated blows of fortune.

The surprising ease with which the King's army rolled up the rebels is no indication of the Highlanders' inability to hold an almost impregnable position. The fact is that this was just a face-saving affair. The will to win was lacking, for no one would have known what to do with the victory had it been gained. The battle was chiefly notable in that it was probably the only one in which Highlanders fought without charging or engaging in hand-to-hand grapple. The Spaniards, being unable to melt into the countryside, had to surrender, but the battle casualties were quite insignificant. Wightman lost twenty-one killed and perhaps double that number wounded, while there is no reliable record of any Jacobites being killed. However, some there must have been; and no doubt the figure of less than ten mentioned in Field-Marshal Keith's memoir is about right. Lord George Murray was among those wounded, but he soon recovered and almost thirty years later, when another and more romantic Jacobite prince resolved to venture upon the hazards of invasion, he was to play a most important part.

200

CHAPTER 11

The Second
Jacobite Rebellion

Prestonpans, Falkirk and Culloden

21 September 1745, 23 January 1746 and 16 April 1746

Prestonpans and Falkirk were fought not far from Pinkie Cleuch and Falkirk (1298) respectively. The Prestonpans site is not very rewarding, as too much of it is now built over. About half a mile south of the crossed swords on the one-inch Ordnance Survey map (sheet 62) the local authority has marked the site of the battle with a notice and a useful description and plan, but sadly this has been greatly defaced. This noticeboard stands beside the A198 road between the road and the railway line, and is backed by some hideous slag heaps. The ruin of Colonel Gardiner's house still stands about half a mile north-west of Tranent church, where the Colonel was buried.

At Falkirk a stone stands on the side road just off the B803 road leading out of Falkirk to the south-west. This monument is close to where the fight took place; from it a footpath leads north along the side of the ravine which was such an important feature on the Hanoverian right and Jacobite left. The ground on either side of the ravine is still open country, as it is to the south of the stone where the battle was chiefly fought – although what was wet moorland is now good agricultural land. One can get a fair idea of the lie of the land either from an open field about a quarter of a mile down the footpath, or from vantage points just off the B803 road south of the stone.

The field of Culloden is very accessible, being only a little east of Inverness, off the Inverness–Perth road (A9). The B9006, which runs east from the A9 to Nairn, takes the visitor to the National Trust for Scotland's Information Centre on the site of the battle. It is possible to walk over much of the battlefield, but the Forestry Commission plantations prevent one from seeing the ground as a whole – no trees obscured the superb views of the Moray and Beauly Firths at the time of the battle. However, what disadvantages there may be from the restricted view of the site are compensated for by the National Trust for Scotland, who have at their centre a very useful audio-visual exhibit running during the summer season which supplements an excellent guidebook and most interesting museum.

On 23 July 1745 the little frigate *La Doutelle* dropped anchor off the island of Eriskay. After an eventful and exciting sea journey of eighteen days Prince Charles Edward Louis Philip Casimir Stuart had come home.

For the past two years messengers had been travelling between Edinburgh and Paris, and the hopes of Jacobites were high. The political climate was far less favourable for their cause than it had been thirty years before (see chapter 10); nevertheless there was reason for cautious optimism. The French defeat at Dettingen in June 1743 had so infuriated Louis XV that he at last agreed to mount a full-scale invasion of England and Scotland with a force of 13,000 troops under Marshal Saxe, and the Chevalier de St George, himself no longer fit for active service, sent his eldest son from Rome to accompany the Marshal on his important enterprise. But the weather, which never ceased to play scurvy tricks on the Stuarts, battered and scattered the warships and transports before they had even left Dunkirk and other embarkation ports: the invasion was off.

Prince Charles Edward returned to Paris, and after a year of frustration as a seemingly unwanted pawn on Louis's political chessboard he decided that he could wait no longer on the whims of the French king. Without French aid his prospects were doubtful, but he was well aware that time was running out: the Stuart flame

Entry of Prince Charles Edward Stuart into Edinburgh

was flickering and might soon be extinguished. Therefore with a handful of companions, who became known as the Seven Men of Moidart, for it was on the borders of Arisaig and Moidart that the party first stepped ashore on the Scottish mainland, he set forth on a venture that was hazardous in the extreme.

At the time that he landed in Scotland the Prince was not quite twenty-five years old; he was a tall, good-looking young man much more given to the field than the drawing room. He possessed many outdoor accomplishments and great physical stamina; his courage was undoubted and his capacity to endure hardships unrivalled, but although his charm and debonair manner have in retrospect irradiated the last years of a doomed dynasty, these and other popular qualities tend to be exaggerated. History has clothed his name with a romantic aura, but in truth this prince was seldom 'bonnie', and although he contrived to behave with fortitude and dignity in times of misfortune his mercurial temperament quickly plunged him from the pinnacle of optimism to the depths of despair, and he found it more difficult than his father had to bear the disappointments and disillusionments that crowded upon him.

The immediate response of the Highlanders to their prince's landing was not encouraging – indeed even at the height of his success he never commanded more than 9,000 men out of an estimated warrior strength, if the clans could ever be united in a common cause, of some 32,000. The romantic conception of the Forty-five as a popular and glorious crusade is misplaced. Charles, arriving unaided, was in the main unwanted, and only his determination and an early display of loyalty by Lochiel and one or two other chiefs saved the day. When Alexander Macdonald of Boisdale, almost the first chief to meet him, advised the Prince to go home, Charles replied, 'I am come home, sir, and I will entertain no notion at all of returning to that place from whence I come; for that I am persuaded my faithful Highlanders will stand by me.' And in the event a great many of them did. By 19 August, when the huge white, red and blue silk standard was broken at Glenfinnan, there had gathered some 200 Clanranald Macdonalds, and Alexander Macdonald of Keppoch was on his way with 300 more men. And we can readily imagine what joy there must have been in that little valley flanked by mountains of timeless antiquity when the sound of the Cameron pipers could be heard in the distance leading 700 of their clansmen towards the royal standard. Donald Cameron of Lochiel had been one of those who advised the Prince to return, but when he saw the spirit of the man he declared, 'I'll share the fate of my prince; and so shall every man over whom nature or fortune hath given me any power.' And, like many others, he never wavered in his loyalty to the very end.

The march to Edinburgh and the south had begun. The road was not to be broad and easy, and in the many hazards that lay ahead only success would keep the clans together and hold the wolves at bay – and at first success attended them everywhere. General Cope, with an English army of not more than 3,000 men, most of them raw recruits in whom he could place little trust, failed to intercept the Highlanders or prevent them from taking Edinburgh. But shipping his army from Aberdeen to Dunbar, he set off immediately on disembarkation to oppose them. At a council of war held in the Highlanders' camp near Duddingston it was agreed that their army should not wait for the English to attack, but should march against them. By now the Prince had a fighting force of about 2,500 men, although he was completely without artillery and his cavalry arm consisted of only some forty horsemen under Lord Strathallan. Against this force General Cope mustered 2,300 men, which included the 13th and 14th Dragoons, and six cannon – the latter manned by a team of very inadequate nautical gunners.

On the morning of 20 September, when the clans had been assembled and were ready to leave camp, the Prince addressed the chiefs. Having reminded them of the good cause for which they were about to fight he ended by dramatically drawing his sword from its scabbard and declaring, 'Gentlemen, I have flung away the scabbard; with God's help I will make you a free and happy people.' Shortly afterwards Lord George Murray,* the Prince's most able commander, led the army out of camp, across the river Esk and on towards the enemy. Soon they reached Fawside Hill, and moving along its crest they were within half a mile of the village of Tranent when the English army came into view. Sir John Cope was in the vicinity of Seton when Lord Loudoun brought him the news that the Jacobites were on the march. But he was in no way alarmed, for he reckoned he had reached the ideal battleground for his horse and foot. Certainly his first position facing west was a very strong one, being protected on three sides – to the north the sea and villages, to the west a ten-foot boundary wall

* Lord George Murray, who as a young man had fought at Glenshiel (see pp. 198–200), joined the Prince at Perth; he was the younger brother of William Murray, the Jacobite Duke of Atholl. Made a lieutenant-general in the army, he usually held the most important command in the field, although the Prince was titular commander-in-chief. He had many enemies among the Prince's cronies, and there was often friction between him and the Prince with most unfortunate consequences to the Cause.

surrounding Preston House park, and south of that Colonel Gardiner's house, which was almost surrounded by what Cope believed to be an impenetrable marsh. When he discovered that the rebel army was facing him from the south and not the west he swung his army round to what was an even stronger position, for the marsh was then on his immediate front.

The Forty-five campaign was throughout bedevilled by the fractious conduct of the senior officers, and the fact that command was based on the principle of limited liability. Only at Culloden did the Prince take actual command of the army, and nearly every decision – even after he had stopped holding councils – was imposed upon him, often against his better judgement, by a cabal of ill assorted advisers. One of the Seven Men of Moidart was an Irishman called Colonel John William O'Sullivan, who on account of his supposed military knowledge had been made adjutant-general and quartermaster-general of the army; this man disliked Lord George Murray intensely, and the dislike was reciprocated. Their incapacity to cooperate manifested itself for the first time just before the battle began, when Lord George, who on this occasion shared the command with the Duke of Perth, proceeded to make and execute a plan without informing either the Prince or the Adjutant-General.

Earlier Lord George had sent Colonel Ker of Graden to reconnoitre the enemy position, and on learning from him that it was almost impregnable he decided that the enemy could only be attacked from the east. Accordingly he led off with the Camerons, sending a message back to the Prince asking him to follow with the remaining front line troops, less the Atholl brigade and a reserve to be temporarily left on Fawside to confuse the enemy. This exposure of his flank to the enemy in broad daylight violated all the principles of O'Sullivan's military training – but his protests were in vain. Cope was certainly somewhat confused, but until he knew what Murray was about he was determined not to be taken by surprise, and he had outposts guarding the narrow defile between Preston and Bankton Houses and all other approaches. But although the Athollmen and the reserves did not rejoin the main army until after dark the barking of the dogs as they passed through Tranent clearly indicated the design. Cope then swung his line round once more, this time to face almost due east. He now prepared for battle with the 44th regiment on the right, the 46th on the left, and eight companies of the 47th and two of the 6th in the centre (for table of regiments in the English army see page 224). His guns were all on the right of the line. On the right of the foot were two squadrons of the 13th Dragoons, and on the left two squadrons of the 14th. In reserve there was a single squadron from each cavalry regiment.

The Jacobite army, having passed through Tranent and round the front of the enemy, still had to cross the marsh before reaching suitable ground over which to attack. One of their number, a local man called Robert Anderson, volunteered to show them a track that he knew well from snipe-shooting, and in the early hours of the morning he led the way. The mist swirled up from the bog as the wraith-like army wound its silent way through a defile near Riggonhead Farm and on through the morass. Suddenly there was a challenge from an enemy patrol, who scurried back to give the alarm, but as day was breaking Anderson had the army safely across the bank that divided the marsh from an open stubble field. The Duke of Perth led the van, and in the half-light he mistook the distance he had to go to ensure that the rear was clear of the bog before facing left. In consequence there was a large gap between the two halves of the army which might have proved serious had the English cavalry been able to exploit it – but the dragoons, who had already made an undignified exit from Edinburgh, were again to be found unworthy of their calling. This need to clear the end of the marsh also meant that the Jacobite left was not exactly opposite the English right, and the greatly extended line not only gave Cope a mistaken idea of the enemy numbers but posed a threat to his left flank. He therefore sent his aide-de-camp to fetch two guns from the right of the line. But he was too late: the civilian drivers and nautical gun crews had already left the field.

Murray, in personal command of the left wing, went into the attack somewhat before the right half of the Jacobite army. The sun was just rising, drawing more vapours from the marshes, as with a great yell 500 Camerons, 250 Appin Stewarts and 200 men of the Duke of Perth's charged obliquely to their left across the 200 yards that separated them from the English line. At once Colonel Whitefoord and another officer manipulated the guns so shamefully abandoned by their recreant crews; they managed to discharge five of the 1½-pounders and all the mortars, although the latter were of little effect. For a moment the Highland line reeled and there were a few casualties, but without trained gun crews the artillery was powerless against the irresistible charge of the clansmen. When the outposts had been called in there had been insufficient time to send the men to their regiments, so they had been told to fall in on the right of the line. This cramped the 13th Dragoons for space and necessitated one squadron being formed

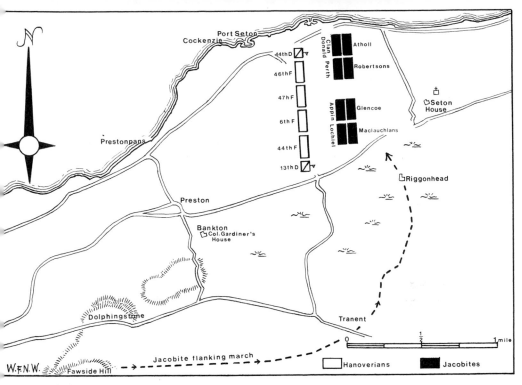

Battle of Prestonpans

up in the rear. The crowded position in which they found themselves may also have had some bearing on their refusal to charge. Both Colonel Whitney's squadron, and Colonel Gardiner's which was in the rear, failed to obey their commanders, one volley from the Highlanders being sufficient to put the troopers to flight.

The position for the English was as grim at the other end of the line. Here the Macdonalds were coming on in steadier formation than the Camerons and Stewarts, who had charged with equal élan but in small groups, and as they swung in towards the English left the 14th Dragoons, in spite of the courageous example of their commander, soon panicked and left the field without inflicting any damage on the enemy. The royalist infantry now had the unenviable task of facing the full fury of a Highland charge. Both wings came on remorselessly, and, as was their wont, having discharged a volley the Highlanders threw away their muskets and relied upon their broadswords, which, wielded with accuracy and vigour, bit deeply into the heads and limbs of the badly shaken redcoats. General Cope and Lords Loudoun, Drummore and Home did their best to rally the terrified royalists: parties of dragoons were rounded up, and infantrymen urged at pistol point to stand again and dirty their muskets and blood their bayonets. But all was chaos and confusion, and in a white heat of undisciplined passion the Highlanders laid about them, scattering the English army, until eventually the few officers and men who had tried to stem the flood joined the broad stream of fleeing men.

In the rout that followed considerable execution was done by the wildly excited and triumphant Highlanders and the fields around were strewn with wounded soldiers and severed limbs. The Battle of Prestonpans, or Gladsmuir as it at first came to be called, was a disaster for King George's army and a tremendous morale-raiser for the Jacobites: the former probably lost no more than 300 dead, most of whom were killed in flight, but eighty officers and more than a thousand men, together with all the baggage, were captured. The Jacobites lost six officers and somewhere around forty men. The English death roll might well have been heavier had not the Duke of Perth and Lord George Murray, acting under the Prince's orders, made sure that all the wounded got the best medical attention available.

After the battle Charles returned to Edinburgh and Cope hastened to Berwick, where Lord Mark Kerr remarked somewhat unkindly that he must be the only general in Europe to be the first to bring the news of his own defeat. Both sides now gathered strength for the next round. The Jacobites more than doubled their numbers and Lords Elcho and Pitsligo had around 500 horse under command. Moreover, there was better news from France: arms and ammunition (including six four-pounders) had recently been landed and the Marquis d'Aiguilles, Louis's unofficial ambassador, held out promise of further aid. To meet this formidable threat the Whig government hurried troops across from Flanders, including 6,000 Dutch, and sent General Handasyde to replace Cope.

Charles favoured a march on Newcastle to meet General Wade's force before it could be strengthened. Had this been done soon after Prestonpans who could say that he was not right? English morale was low – in fact it had almost reached panic proportions in certain circles – and once the fortified area of Newcastle was overcome the road to London would be virtually open. But by the end of October, when the need for a decision had become imperative if the daily desertions were to be halted, it may have been too late, and Lord George's advice, backed by many of the Highland chiefs, was probably the best. He argued that to march by Carlisle was a sounder plan: the route was better and the capture of Carlisle would rally English Jacobite support, making it easier to defeat Wade's newly reinforced army. The Prince reluctantly agreed.

Carlisle and its castle surrendered on 14 November after a siege lasting no more than six days. Wade had moved slowly towards its relief, but got no further than Hexham, and after Carlisle Penrith, Lancaster, Preston and Manchester were quickly occupied. Except in Manchester, where some 300 volunteers had been formed into a special regiment (later to be sacrificed in garrisoning Carlisle), the English response to the Jacobite cause had been disappointingly small, and when the army entered Derby on 4 December it numbered only about 4,500 men. The decision taken at Derby to return to Scotland was perhaps the most momentous of the whole campaign, and the rights and wrongs of it have long been argued. It could be said that the Stuart dynasty died at Derby. Certainly the Prince, whose earnest entreaties were overruled by Murray and most (but not quite all) of the chiefs, was convinced that the decision to retreat had irreparably marred his fortunes, and from that time of torment there emerged a deeply disappointed and slightly embittered man.

The return to Scotland was not entirely uneventful. The Duke of Cumberland, whose attempt to intercept the army on its way south had been cleverly foiled by Murray's tactical competence, was now in close pursuit with a force of 4,000 men. At Clifton, near Penrith, his cavalry caught up with the Jacobite rearguard under Lord George. By the light of a partially obscured moon three dragoon regiments were put to rout in a short, sharp engagement by the Glengarry Macdonalds, the Stewarts of Appin and Cluny Macpherson's men. There were no more than fifty casualties altogether, but this fierce little skirmish effectively checked Cumberland's pursuit. Carlisle was reached on 19 December. Here it was decided to abandon all the artillery, less three field guns, and on the Prince's insistence a garrison of 400 men was left there – soon to fall victims of Cumberland's avenging army.

The Highlanders crossed the Esk into Scotland on 20 December 1745. It was, by the English Old Style of reckoning, the Prince's twenty-fifth birthday. Charles spent a week in Glasgow trying to maintain some state amongst a population that for the most part had never been sympathetic to the Jacobite cause, and on 3 January he left for Stirling. Welcome reinforcements joined him here, including a contingent from France. While the army had been trekking through England 800 men under Lord John Drummond had landed on the east coast of Scotland (mostly Irish troops in the French service), and with them came two sixteen-pounders, two twelve- and two eight-pounders. However the majority of the new recruits came from all over Scotland: Frasers, Farquharsons,

Macdonells, Grants, Mackenzies and Ogilvys – more than 3,000 in all. The Jacobite army had now reached the moment of its fullest efflorescence: 9,000 warriors, of whom 1,300 were cavalry, and a good train of artillery. Stirling town surrendered on 6 January, but General Blakeney retired to the castle and prepared to withstand a siege. It is doubtful if the futile attempts of Charles's French engineer, M. Mirabel de Gordon, would ever have made any impression on the redoubtable castle perched on its precipitous rock, but events to the south caused the Prince to march to meet the enemy, leaving only a containing force at Stirling.

After capturing Carlisle the Duke of Cumberland returned to London, and his troops were kept in the south against the possibility of a French invasion. Wade was rightly considered too old for his post and was superseded by General Henry Hawley as commander-in-chief in the north, a fierce disciplinarian, but not a general of any particular merit. On arrival at Edinburgh Hawley found that he had under his command twelve battalions of infantry and three regiments of dragoons, but although their paper strength was formidable he complained that many of the men were 'no better than militia', and his artillery was a very scratch lot. Hawley might maunder over an inadequate army, but he was no poltroon refusing to come to grips with the foe. On 13 January his second-in-command, Major-General John Huske, marched from Edinburgh with the vanguard and two days later the whole English army was encamped near Falkirk. Here it was joined by Colonel John Campbell with three companies of Lord Loudoun's regiment, one of Lord John Murray's and twelve of the Argyll militia. The royalist force now numbered 8,000, and as Charles had left 1,000 to contain Stirling Castle the two armies were about equal.

The battle was fought to the west of Falkirk where the ground rises steeply from the Forth and Clyde Canal to a rough plateau called Falkirk Moor. The ascent was over a broken and rugged hillside, and there was a deep ravine that ran up its face for several hundred yards. Lord George Murray pressed upon the Prince the need to seize this high ground before the English, who were encamped only a mile away, got to it first. This was agreed, and after elaborate plans for deception had been worked out Murray, at the head of three Clan Donald regiments, marched out of the camp at Plean about midday on 17 January. He had a fair knowledge of the ground, and took a circuitous route southwards under cover of Torwood, crossing the river Carron (after ignoring O'Sullivan's and the Prince's request that he wait until night) at Dunipace. As the Highlanders advanced towards their objective a heavy

Above: Dragoon, infantry sergeant and private, 1745. The sergeant is armed with a halberd. Below: Highland clansmen, 1745. Left: The belted plaid (large plaid kilted and belted about waist, upper portion pinned on left shoulder) was worn from about 1599. The clansman carries a Lochaber axe. Right: The short kilt (philabeg) was introduced about 1730. The clansman carries broadsword, targe, dirk, Highland dag (slung pistol) and musket (fired and thrown down before the charge)

storm broke across this wild, primeval place of bog and bramble, but the driving rain was on their backs and in the faces of the enemy, who were scrambling unseen up the other side of the hill.

General Hawley, having examined the ground early that morning with Colonel Wolfe (later to gain immortal fame on the Heights of Abraham), retired to his billet apparently confident that the Jacobite army would never dare to attack him. His conduct at this stage was negligent in the extreme, for not only did he prefer the generous hospitality so purposefully plied by his hostess Lady Kilmarnock* to the rigours of the camp, but he failed to see that his army took elementary precautions against surprise even when an officer warned him that the Highlanders would be upon him before dark. When at last he grasped the seriousness of the situation the camp was startled by the sight of their dyspeptic-looking general arriving at the gallop hatless and breathless. However, he wasted no time in sending the three cavalry regiments up the face of the hill, led by Colonel Francis Ligonier in command of the 13th Dragoons. The cavalry was followed by the front line infantry with six regiments forward and six in the second line, with the Glasgow militia in rear of the cavalry and the Argyll militia on the right at the bottom of the hill.

As Lord George Murray breasted the hill at the head of the army, with the three Macdonald regiments in the van, the rain was lashing down, and on such an afternoon darkness would come early. It was already after half past three. The Highlanders formed line with the Macdonalds on the right with their flank protected by an impenetrable bog; the long front line extended to the edge of the ravine where the Appin Stewarts held the left. In between them and the Macdonalds were the Camerons, Frasers, Macphersons, Mackintoshes, Mackenzies and Farquharsons. The second line was made up of two battalions each of Lord Lewis Gordon's and Lord Ogilvy's together with three battalions of the Atholl brigade. Lord John Drummond, whose troops had taken part in the deception march, was in command of the reserve. It is sometimes said that he commanded the left of the Jacobite line, but in fact no one was appointed to this post, an oversight that could have proved disastrous. The artillery of both armies found immense difficulties in the terrain they were attempting to cross and played little part in the battle. No sooner had the line been formed than the acidulous adjutant-general was, as usual, criticizing Murray's

* She was the wife of the fourth Earl of Kilmarnock, who was captured at Culloden and later executed. A staunch Jacobite herself, she did what she could to keep the not unwilling Hawley from his command.

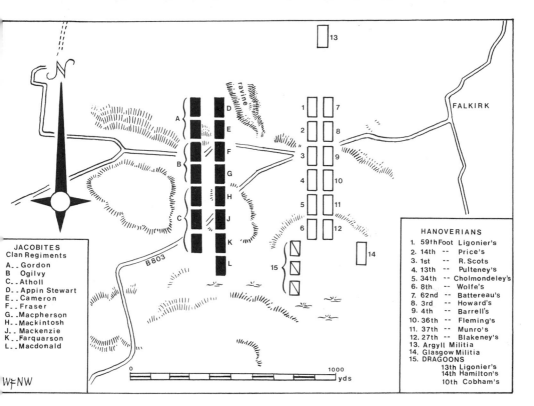

Battle of Falkirk

dispositions and – also as usual – getting a markedly cold response.

Displaying a confidence in the ability of his cavalry to defeat Highlanders which was not shared by their commander nor borne out by events at Prestonpans, General Hawley ordered them into the attack unsupported by the infantry, who were still forming up. Colonel Ligonier's three regiments of dragoons were on the left of the English line, and as they advanced Murray ordered the Highland right to hold their fire until the horsemen were within about fifteen paces. At least eighty horses went down under that first murderous volley which thundered down the line from the Macdonalds to the Frasers. The terrified cavalrymen, with their unenviable record of past failures, were again thrown into confusion; a few reached the Jacobite line only to be hacked and stabbed by Scottish dirks, but most of them wheeled about and only Cobham's regiment took any further part in the fighting.

The shattering volley that repulsed the dragoons was fired at about 4 p.m.; the rest of the battle, which lasted for less than half an hour, was an untidy, muddled affair. Murray tried in vain to hold the Highland right steady, but two of the Macdonald regiments could not be restrained and were soon lost to the battle in pursuit of the dragoons, who had themselves ridden down and scattered men of their own left. The centre Jacobite regiments then swung in on these hard-pressed men. Attacked from the front and the flank, their cartridges damp and their muskets misfiring, it was not long before both the first and second lines gave way. But on the Highlanders' left, where there was no one in overall command, the position was very different. Here three royalist regiments, whose front was protected by the ravine, stood firm, and poured a withering fire into the flank of the advancing Jacobites. The left of the rebel army, unable to close with the English across the ravine, suddenly found Cobham's dragoons taking them in the rear. The situation looked dangerous, and in the confusion of order and counter-order some of the clansmen were leaving the field thinking the battle lost. But the Prince, realizing the position, ordered up the Irish picquets, and on the appearance of these fresh troops the English right fell back towards Falkirk, the dragoons covering this comparatively orderly retreat.

The royalist army, abandoning most of their camp, seven cannon and a quantity of ammunition, made for Linlithgow. The Prince, in spite of English denials, had won another victory. It was to be his last. Jacobite losses amounted to only about fifty killed and seventy or eighty wounded, while General Hawley left some 300 men dead on the field, including at least twelve officers of which five were of field rank, and upwards of 200 prisoners were taken by the Scots. That night the Prince entered Falkirk in triumph.

But the Jacobite leaders had never displayed that spirit of concord so essential for ultimate success, and now recriminations for the conduct of the battle soured victory and laid the foundation for future disaster. Opinions were divided as to how to proceed. There were those in favour of pursuing Hawley's demoralized army and striking it a decisive blow while it was off balance; success would have been almost certain, but the road to London was no longer open. Others advocated the need to reduce Stirling Castle. The Prince was hesitant, but finally agreed upon a continuance of the siege. It was a forlorn enterprise in spite of all Monsieur Mirabel's gasconades, for the castle was well provisioned and from its commanding position the royalist armament was quickly able to silence the Jacobite batteries. Highlanders could never be inactive for long, and while preparations for the siege were going on many drifted away. They did not all intend to desert – but a sufficient number disappeared to seriously alarm the chiefs. Once again Lord George Murray and his colleagues presented their prince with a memorial (written representation), this time urging upon him the necessity to retire northwards for the winter and to recoup their strength. Charles was bitterly disappointed, although

214

as before he had to comply: he offered no reproaches, but he made it clear that it was a decision taken against his wishes. On 1 February the Jacobite army crossed the Forth and marched north.

The march to Inverness, in appalling weather conditions through a poverty-stricken countryside, whose primitive agriculture was far less capable of supporting an army than the Lowlands now abandoned to the enemy, was carried out under the Prince and Lord George Murray along separate routes. On 21 February the two divisions were reunited at Inverness, which had been evacuated by Lord Loudoun's troops a few days earlier, and Colonel Grant of Rothiemurchus was not long in surrendering the castle. During the next six weeks, while their prince amused himself shooting and enjoying the social life of Inverness, his troops were busy on a variety of military ventures. Fort Augustus was taken and Lord George, aided by Macpherson of Cluny, conducted a most successfull raid on the English outposts in Atholl territory, although he failed to take Blair Castle. At the insistence of the Camerons Fort William was besieged, but this was found to be too hard a nut to crack. Neither did the cause gain much from the exertions of Lord Cromarty. This nobleman was no soldier, and having failed (until supported by the Duke of Perth) to make headway against Lord Loudoun's force in the north, he later allowed himself to be ambushed and captured while endeavouring to rescue the valuable contents of the *Prince Charles,* which had been seized by Lord Reay's troops when that vessel was disabled in the Pentland Firth.

At the beginning of April, when the net was inexorably tightening around them, the Jacobite army was still scattered and in poor shape. The Duke of Perth and Lord John Drummond, with a totally inadequate force, were watching the Spey in the neighbourhood of Fochabers, Murray was still besieging Blair Castle, Cluny was in Badenoch with at least 300 clansmen, the Camerons were before Fort William, the Master of Lovat was said to be marching towards Inverness with a second Fraser regiment, and Lord Cromarty was still in the north with the Mackenzies and MacGregors. Urgent messages to these distant clansmen succeeded in rallying them just in time, save for those men with Cluny, Lord Cromarty and the Master of Lovat, all of whom took no part in the coming battle. When the Prince at the head of his shrunken army moved to Culloden House he had under command somewhere around 5,000 men. His artillery was not worthy of the name, and his cavalry was scarcely any better – Lord Elcho's Life Guards, originally formed as a *corps d' élite* of landed gentry but now sadly diminished, and all that was left of a squadron of FitzJames's horse that had landed from France in February: in all two troops numbering perhaps 150 horse. The morale of the whole army was at a low ebb: the treasure chest was empty and the men were lamentably short of pay and food. Yet there is a touch of grandeur in the death throes of this Jacobite army, desperate, demoralized but in a strange way still undaunted.

Meanwhile, how did the Whig government set about repairing the disaster of Falkirk? The answer was provided in the person of the King's second son, William Augustus Duke of Cumberland, 'Billy the Martial Boy' or 'the Butcher', depending which side you were on. Only a few months younger than Prince Charles, this unattractive Hanoverian had gained rapid military promotion, even allowing for his position and the times. Although by no means a brilliant commander he was not without ability: his courage and powers of leadership had been tested and proved at Dettingen and Fontenoy, and he was certainly a considerable improvement on his three predecessors. Now that the French threat to the south had been removed Cumberland was sent north at the end of January. He immediately set out to relieve Stirling, and pursued the Jacobite army as far as Perth. From here he marched to Aberdeen, where he arrived on 27 February and where he was to remain until 8 April. Before he left Perth his command had been reinforced by some 5,000 Hessian troops, who had landed at Leith under Prince Frederick of Hesse-Cassel. These troops were of great assistance in guarding Cumberland's lines of communication.

In March Cumberland had sent one division under Major-General Bland into Strathbogie, and on 11 April he joined him at Cullen with the rest of the army. The Spey was crossed unopposed* on 12 April, and the English army reached its camp at Balblair (a mile south-west of Nairn) on 14 April. Cumberland had under command fifteen infantry battalions, three regiments of horse and a formidable train of artillery; there were also several companies of Argyll militia (Campbells), bringing his total force up to not far short of 9,000, of whom 2,400 were cavalrymen. Since the introduction, in about 1720, of the iron ramrod the infantryman's rate of fire had been greatly increased – and these men, who had spent the last two months perfecting their musketry, could probably fire

---

* It is sometimes argued that the Jacobite army would have had more chance of success had they opposed the crossing of the Spey in strength. But apart from the fact that Cumberland had moved too quickly for them, their armament and method of fighting were quite unsuitable for this sort of action.

216

three effective volleys in a minute. It is also noteworthy that the battle about to be fought was the first major action on British soil in which the cannon were manned by men of the Royal Regiment of Artillery, which had been formed in 1716.

The fifteenth of April was Cumberland's twenty-fifth birthday and the English troops, well provisioned by the fleet, were permitted a day's rest to celebrate the event. Twelve miles away, however, all was bustle in the Jacobite camp. Lochiel's men had only come in from Fort William the previous day, and many of the clansmen were still being rounded up from fighting and foraging expeditions near and far. But the Prince was determined to give battle, and ordered his men to move into position on the high ground to the south of Culloden House known as Drummossie Moor. This almost flat, gently rolling piece of land is some 470 feet above sea level; it is about a mile in width at the place where the Prince elected to deploy, falling quite steeply to the river Nairn on its south edge. There were few trees on the ground, but some of the small cultivated areas that existed were enclosed by turf or loose stone walls, particularly on either side of the Jacobite battle position where parts of Culloden park were enclosed.

Murray, who was well aware of the limitations of the Highland army, was violently opposed to offering battle on this open expanse, so suitable for properly equipped, well trained troops to operate on. He had been sent, a few days earlier, to reconnoitre the ground between Culloden and Nairn and had found near Dalcross some much rougher and more suitable terrain, but had been overruled by O'Sullivan. Now, on his own initiative, he had sent Brigadier Stapleton and Colonel Ker to examine the ground to the south of the Nairn. Their report was most encouraging for the land being steep and rugged was useless for cavalry and ideal for Highlanders. However, Lord George's advice went unheeded.

He did, however, gain approval for a night march against the enemy camp. His argument, that the army could cover the distance in time to deliver a two-pronged surprise attack in the early hours of the morning, when the English could be expected to be suffering from the aftermath of their commander's birthday celebrations, had some merit. If the march had been undertaken with a full force of fit men it might well have succeeded and – as at Sedgemoor – a surprise attack certainly offered more chance of success than taking on the powerful English army on open ground. But in the circumstances it was asking too much of the troops.

When the time came to set off (about 8 p.m.) many of the Highlanders were absent in search of food, and no man in the two columns had eaten more than a biscuit or small loaf all that day. The commissariat under John Hay of Restalrig had completely broken down. Murray led the first and largest column, and the Duke of Perth was with the Prince at the head of the second one. The night was dark, the route extremely rough, and few save the Mackintosh guides had any sense of direction. As the hungry men trudged through the heather in black silence many fell out 'by faintness from want of food', and Murray's column had constantly to halt to allow those in the rear to catch up. By 2 a.m. the leading men had only reached Knockanbuie, some three miles from their objective, and it was obvious that the attack could not go in under cover of darkness; moreover, drums could be heard in the English camp, clearly indicating loss of surprise. There was nothing for it but to return, and although the Prince was at first eager to proceed he came to see that the decision was inevitable. It was 5 a.m. on 16 April when the dismayed and utterly exhausted troops got back to Drummossie Moor. Here many weary and faithful feet that had tramped through half England and most of Scotland were soon to find their final rest.

No one thought of anything but sleep. For some reason the Jacobite leaders considered it most unlikely that the English would advance to the attack that day. But no sooner had Cumberland learned of the disastrous night march than he ordered his troops forward. The first news reached the Jacobite camp at about 10 a.m., when a patrol announced that the enemy were within four miles. Even before Charles had laid down to rest the Marquess d'Aiguilles had sought an interview and besought him not to offer battle, but to retire – even if it meant abandoning Inverness – and recoup his strength, later to offer battle on better ground. This sensible plea was joined by those of Murray, Macdonald of Keppoch and Lochiel. Alas, that stubborn streak of Stuart obstinacy asserted itself and no further mention of retreat was permitted.

When the Highland army deployed for battle Lord George begged the right for his Atholl brigade and the Prince, perhaps as an emollient for his earlier rebuttal over choice of ground, granted it to him. The Macdonalds are said to have been greatly offended at being denied their time-honoured position in the line, and it is often suggested that their performance in the battle suffered in consequence. However, there is reason to believe that this thorny question was first raised before Prestonpans, and that the Macdonalds – albeit reluctantly – agreed that the right should be taken in rotation. In any case many other factors weighed heavily against the Macdonalds in the confusion of the battle, and

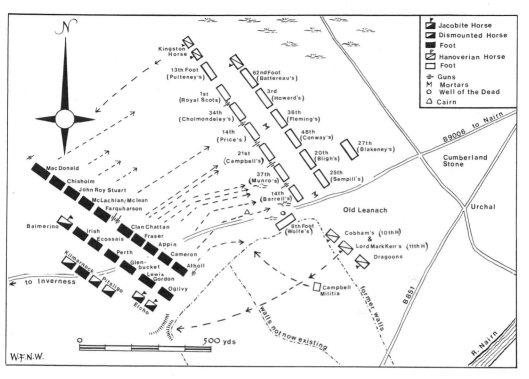

Legend

Jacobite Horse	
Dismounted Horse	
Foot	
Hanoverian Horse	
Foot	
Guns	
Mortars	M
Well of the Dead	O
Cairn	△

N

Kingston Horse

13th Foot (Pulteney's)

62nd Foot (Battereau's)

1st (Royal Scots)

3rd (Howard's)

34th (Cholmondeley's)

36th (Fleming's)

14th (Price's)

48th (Conway's)

27th (Blakeney's)

Cumberland Stone

21st (Campbell's)

20th (Bligh's)

37th (Munro's)

25th (Sempill's)

14th (Barrell's)

MacDonald

Chisholm

John Roy Stuart

McLachlan/Mclean

Farquharson

Old Leanach

Urchal

8th Foot (Wolfe's)

Balmerino

Irish Ecossais

Clan Chattan

Fraser

Cobham's (10th H) & Lord Mark Kerr's (11th H)

Appin

Dragoons

Perth

Cameron

Kilmarnock

Glen- bucket

Lewis Gordon

Atholl

Pitsligo

Campbell Militia

to Inverness

Ogilvy

former walls

Elcho

walls not now existing

R. Nairn

B9006 to Nairn

B851

0   500 yds

W.F.N.W.

Above and below: Battle of Culloden

Cumberland Stone

Urchal

HANOVERIAN ARMY

Information Centre
Old Leanach

Well of the Dead

Cairn

N

JACOBITE ARMY

King's Stables

Irish Memorial

it cannot be definitely said that their courage and loyalty suffered from wounded pride.

The Camerons formed up on the left of the Athollmen and then came the Stewarts of Appin and the Frasers; this wing was commanded by Murray. In the centre of the front line were the Mackintoshes and Farquharsons (Clan Chattan), the combined MacLachlan–Maclean regiment, John Roy Stuart's regiment and the Chisholms, all under the command of Lord John Drummond. And the left, commanded by the Duke of Perth, comprised the Clanranald, Keppoch, Glencoe and Glengarry Macdonalds. The exact composition of the second line remains uncertain, but it seems to have been widely spaced with Lord Elcho's and Fitz-James's horse and Lord Ogilvy's troops on the right, the Irish picquets and the French regiment known as the Royal Scots (under Lord Lewis Drummond) together with Lord Lewis Gordon's regiment in the centre, and on the left another Gordon regiment under the septuagenarian John Gordon of Glenbucket. Brigadier Stapleton commanded the second line. The Prince assumed overall command, and having inspected both lines took up his position initially just to the rear of the second line. His ineffectual cannon, manned mostly by inexperienced Highlanders, was placed in batteries of four on the right, centre and left of the front line.

The Duke of Cumberland's army reached their final position, with their left on the Leanach Farm enclosure, a little after midday. There was then about 500 yards separating the two armies. Cumberland had already halted some way back and deployed his columns into line, originally with six regiments in each of the first two lines and three in reserve; but on finding that he had advanced beyond the protective bog to his right he ordered up two battalions from the reserve to take position on the right of the first and second lines respectively. He also ordered Wolfe's regiment, who were on the left of the second line and standing ankle-deep in water, to take position immediately on the left of the front line and at right angles to that line (*en potence*), so that they could pour flanking fire into any attack. The English artillery, which was in the capable hands of Colonel Belford and had with difficulty been manhandled over the boggy ground, was now placed at intervals between the front line regiments. The Duke also had six coehorn mortars which were formed into batteries of three and posted in advance of the regiments forming the right and left wings of the second line. The cavalry, under General Hawley, was divided and placed on the right and left of the front lines.

The cold north-east wind now began to blow rain and sleet into the Highlanders' faces, and there could have been few among those weary, wasted men who were not to some degree awed by the long lines of red- and blue-coated soldiers that confronted them, bristling with bayonets fixed and sabres drawn. Soon to the drums and fifes that they heard – yes, and even their own music from the Campbell pipes – would be added the terrifying accompaniment of Belford's blazing batteries.

It was just after 1 p.m. that the cannonade started. The Prince's feeble guns fired first, but without any noticeable effect. Then the royalist pieces took up the challenge, and firing in one great roll the noise was deafening and the damage devastating. As the Highlanders stood straining at the leash waiting for the order to charge – the order that seemed never to come – the English guns kept up their remorseless pounding. Through the dust and smoke drifting across on the wet wind the gunners could be dimly seen sponging out their reeking barrels and ramming home more powder and shot. Opinions differ as to how long this fearful bombardment lasted. John Home* puts it at almost an hour, but this must be wrong, for the whole battle was over in forty minutes. Almost certainly it was no more than fifteen minutes before the High-landers charged; but then Belford switched from ball to grape and the air was thick with pieces of iron, nails and small shot that burst from the flimsy canisters.

It is difficult to know why the Prince was so dilatory in giving the order to charge: it was the one very slender chance that his men had of victory. By the time the order eventually reached the front line troops Cumberland's guns had made defeat inevitable. Maybe he was convinced that the English would come at him and thereby close the gap over which his men had to charge, but more probably he was too far back to have proper control of the battle and did not see to what extent the Highland lines were being torn apart. When at last he did give the order his aide, young Lachlan MacLachlan, was struck down as he rode across to the left, for these troops being somewhat retarded should have got the order to advance first. But the right and centre could be restrained no longer, and whether the Prince's order ever reached them is of small consequence: they had waited too long and now they were off.

Once the Highlanders were committed to the charge the story is soon told. The short fight was contested with fearful savagery, but the odds against the rebel army were too great. Indeed, we cannot but be amazed at the courage and determination which

* John Home, *The History of the Rebellion in the Year 1745*, p. 230.

carried their right and centre into the second line of English infantrymen. The actual fighting casualties were heaviest on this front, and in the mêlée that ensued once the two sides had closed in hand-to-hand combat it is probable that Wolfe's men did as much damage to their own ranks as to those of the enemy. The impact upon the English left, which almost overwhelmed them at this point, was caused by the Clan Chattan swerving to their right as they charged up the drier ground of the old road. The unwieldy mass thus formed momentarily pushed back the English by sheer weight of numbers, but made it impossible for the clansmen to use their firearms and exposed them to the pitiless fire of Cholmondeley's and Price's regiments in the English centre.

The Highland casualties were grievous in the extreme: eighteen officers of Clan Chattan fell before they even reached the English line, and the Atholl brigade lost more than twenty, most of them shot down by Wolfe's men as the swerving centre pressed them against the park wall. Nevertheless, the Highlanders with their broadswords did great damage to Barrel's and Munro's regiments, and it was not until Cumberland ordered Major-General Huske to bring forward Sempill's and Bligh's regiments that the Highlanders were finally repulsed. Lord George Murray, who was soon unhorsed, continued fighting ferociously on foot until borne away in the stream of retreating men. The heroic and legendary Alexander MacGillivray of Dunmaglas, commanding the centre in Lord John Drummond's absence, stormed his way through the first line only to be shot down by men of Sempill's or Bligh's.

The Macdonalds, on the left of the Jacobite line, never reached the English right. There is no doubt that at first they paid little heed to the exhortations of the Duke of Perth and his brother, and even when Alexander Macdonald of Keppoch, so soon to meet his death, appealed to their honour they advanced only in short rushes firing their muskets at random. The usual explanation for this is, as we have noted, that they were aggrieved at their position in the line; but other possibilities must be considered. They had by far the furthest distance to charge, and they had already been devastated by the enemy artillery. As soon as they advanced, their left, now protected by the Culloden enclosures, would be exposed, just as their right already was because of the swerving of the centre. Moreover, before the reserve could plug this gap Kingston's Dragoons were through it and in the rear of the Macdonalds. When these clans did eventually get near enough to Pulteney's and the Royals they were shot down like rabbits, and seeing the right and centre give way they too fell back. The Irish picquets and the

Royal Scots under Brigadier Stapleton ably covered their withdrawal and fought bravely in this closing stage of the battle.

Even before the cannonade had begun Lochiel and Murray had espied a party of Campbells and dragoons making their way round the Jacobite right flank. This flank was protected by the park walls, but dry-stone walls are not difficult to pull down and this the Campbells set about doing. As soon as he realized the danger Murray ordered some of Lord Lewis Gordon's men to face that front, but they were not able to prevent the Campbells from making a passageway for Hawley's cavalry. In the rout that followed the breaking of the Highland line the Campbells were able to pour volley after volley into their Cameron enemies from the protection of the walls, and the dragoons, charging through the gaps, added to the general destruction.

There are many conflicting accounts of the Prince's action at the end of the battle. Lord Elcho put it on record that as soon as the left broke Charles, escorted by a party of FitzJames's horse, rode quickly to safety; but this was probably only a half-truth. By nature an optimist, he must at last have seen defeat outstaring him. He seems to have made some effort to rally the regiments on the left wing, but realizing the impossibility of the task he allowed himself to be taken from the field by Sir Thomas Sheridan, Hay of Restalrig and a few others. No doubt he never envisaged retreat, but the event should have been catered for and a rallying point made. As it was most of those on the right who survived made across the Nairn and into Badenoch, while those on the left took the road to Inverness. The Prince first drew rein some four miles from the battlefield at Faillie, and again Lord Elcho tells us that he had no word for the Scots, but seemed only concerned for the welfare of his Irish and exile French troops.

The carnage of the field was appalling, and Cumberland's men had orders not to spare the wounded. The exact number of casualties on both sides has long been in dispute, but the Highlanders certainly lost 1,000 men killed in battle or murdered on the field – and probably more. Most of the English casualties occurred in Barrel's, Munro's, Bligh's and Sempill's regiments, for they were virtually the only infantry seriously engaged, and were said to number 364 killed and wounded. Vast quantities of muskets, broadswords and ammunition fell to the victors, as well as fourteen standards.

The destiny of a dynasty flowed with the blood of these proud Jacobite warriors. The victories that had been gained in the past, the final disaster at Culloden and the hardships that they and their prince were still to endure, ensure for them a lasting renown.

Table Showing the Regiments of the English Army (1746: Culloden)

Name of the commander	Number of regiment	What the regiment later became
CAVALRY		
Gardiner's ⎫ Ligonier's ⎬	13th Dragoons	13th Hussars
Hamilton's	14th Dragoons	14th Hussars
Cobham's	10th Dragoons	10th Hussars
Lord Mark Kerr's	11th Dragoons	11th Hussars
Kingston's horse	—	Disbanded
REGIMENTS OF THE LINE		
The Royals (or the Royal Regiment of Foot)	1st	The Royal Scots
Howard's	3rd	The Buffs (Royal East Kent Regiment)
Barrell's	4th	The King's Own Royal Regiment (Lancaster)
Wolfe's	8th	The King's Regiment (Liverpool)
Pulteney's	13th	Somerset Light Infantry
Price's	14th	West Yorkshire Regiment
Bligh's	20th	Lancashire Fusiliers
Campbell's	21st	Royal Scots Fusiliers
Sempill's	25th	King's Own Scottish Borderers
Blakeney's	27th	1st Battalion Royal Inniskilling Fusiliers
Cholmondeley's	34th	1st Battalion The Border Regiment
Fleming's	36th	2nd Battalion Worcestershire Regiment
Munro's	37th	1st Battalion Hampshire Regiment
Conway's	48th	1st Battalion Northamptonshire Regiment
Battereau's	62nd	Disbanded 1748
Argyll militia	—	Disembodied after suppression of rising
Guise's	6th	Royal Warwickshire Regiment
	44th ⎫ 46th ⎬ 47th ⎭	These regiments were marine regiments and were disbanded in 1748

At the time of Culloden all regiments would usually have been known by the colonel's name—and this was constantly changing. The Clothing Regulations of 1747 required regiments to bear their precedence numbers on their colours, and from this date onwards regiments began to refer to themselves by numbers rather than by names of colonels.

Bibliography

Chapter 1: The First Civil War
Barrett, C. R. B., *Battles and Battlefields in England*, A. D. Innes, 1896.
Burne, A. H., and Peter Young, *The Great Civil War*, Eyre and Spottiswoode, 1959.
Clarendon, Edward, Earl of, *The History of the Rebellion*, Clarendon Press, 1704.
Firth, Charles, *Cromwell's Army*, Methuen, 1912.
Fortescue, J. W., *History of the British Army*, Vol. I, Macmillan, 1899.
Fraser, Antonia, *Cromwell—Our Chief of Men*, Weidenfeld and Nicolson, 1973.
Gardiner, S. R., *History of the Great Civil War, 1642-1649*, 4 vols, Longmans, 1911.
Rogers, H. C. B., *Battles and Generals of the Civil Wars, 1642–1651*, Seeley Service, 1968.
Roper, H. R. Trevor-, *Archbishop Laud 1573–1645*, Macmillan, 1962.
Trench, Charles Chevenix, *A History of Horsemanship*, Longmans, 1970.
Wedgwood, C. V., *The Great Rebellion, Vol. I: The King's Peace*, Collins, 1955.
Wedgwood, C. V., *The Great Rebellion, Vol. II: The King's War*, Collins, 1958.
Woolrych, Austin, *Battles of the English Civil War*, Batsford, 1961.
Young, Peter, *Edgehill 1642*, Roundwood Press, 1967.
Young, Peter, *The British Army 1642–1970*, William Kimber, 1967.
Young, Peter, and John Adair, *Hastings to Culloden*, G. Bell, 1964.

Chapter 2: Edgehill
Burne, A. H., *Battlefields of England*, Methuen, 1950.
Burne, A. H., and Peter Young, *The Great Civil War*, Eyre and Spottiswoode, 1959.
Davies, Godfrey, 'The Battle of Edgehill', *English Historical Review*, XXXVI, 1921.
Firth, Charles, *Cromwell's Army*, Methuen, 1912.
Gardiner, S. R., *History of the Great Civil War, 1642–1649*, Vol. I, Longmans, 1911.
Rogers, H. C. B., *Battles and Generals of the Civil Wars, 1642–1651*, Seeley Service, 1968.
Wedgwood, C. V., *The Great Rebellion, Vol. II: The King's War*, Collins, 1958.
Young, Peter, *Edgehill 1642*, Roundwood Press, 1967.
Young, Peter, and John Adair, *Hastings to Culloden*, G. Bell, 1964.

Chapter 3: The First Battle of Newbury
Barrett, C. R. B., *Battles and Battlefields in England*, A. D. Innes, 1896.
Burne, A. H., *Battlefields of England*, Methuen, 1950.
Burne, A. H., and Peter Young, *The Great Civil War*, Eyre and Spottiswoode, 1959.
Clarendon, Edward, Earl of, *The History of the Rebellion*, Book VII, pp. 205–14, Clarendon Press, 1704.
Firth, Charles, *Cromwell's Army*, Methuen, 1912.
Gardiner, S. R., *History of the Great Civil War, 1642–1649*, Vol. I, Longmans, 1911.
Money, Walter, *The First and Second Battles of Newbury*, Simpkin, Marshall, 2nd edition, 1884.
Rogers, H. C. B., *Battles and Generals of the Civil Wars, 1642–1651*, Seeley Service, 1968.
Wedgwood, C. V., *The Great Rebellion, Vol. II: The King's War*, Collins, 1958.
Young, Peter, and John Adair, *Hastings to Culloden*, G. Bell, 1964.

Primary Sources
Codrington, Robert, *The Life and Death of the Illustrious Robert, Earle of Essex*, London, 1646.
Thomason Tracts, E.69 and E.70 (which include Sir John Byron's account of the battle).

Chapter 4: Cheriton
Adair, John, *Cheriton 1644*, Roundwood Press, 1973.
Burne, A. H., *More Battlefields of England*, Methuen, 1952.
Burne, A. H., and Peter Young, *The Great Civil War*, Eyre and Spottiswoode, 1959.
Clarendon, Edward, Eurl of, *The History of the Rebellion*, Book VIII, Clarendon Press, 1704.
Gardiner, S. R., *History of the Great Civil War*, Vol. I, Longmans, 1911.
Godwin, G. N., *The Civil War in Hampshire*, revised edition, Southampton, 1904.
Rogers, H. C. B., *Battles and Generals of the Civil Wars, 1642–1651*, Seeley Service, 1968.
Walker, Sir Edward, K. G., *Historical Discourses upon Several Occasions*, London, 1705.
Wedgwood, C. V., *The Great Rebellion, Vol. II: The King's War*, Collins, 1958.
Woodward, B. B., T. C. Wilks and C. Lockhart, *A General History of Hampshire*, Vol. II, London, 1861-9.

Primary Sources
Healey, Charles, ed., *Bellum Civile* (Hopton's account of the battle), Somerset Record 18, 1902.
Military Memoir of Colonel John Birch, written by Roe, his secretary, ed. Rev. T. W. Webb, Camden Society, 1873.
Thomason Tracts, E.40 (including Elias Archer's and Harley's accounts of the battle).

Chapter 5: Marston Moor
Barrett, C. R. B., *Battles and Battlefields in England*, A. D. Innes, 1896.
Burne, A. H., *Battlefields of England*, Methuen, 1950.
Burne, A. H., and Peter Young, *The Great Civil War*, Eyre and Spottiswoode, 1959.
Firth, Charles, *Cromwell's Army*, Methuen, 1912.
Fraser, Antonia, *Cromwell—Our Chief of Men*, Weidenfeld and Nicolson, 1973.
Gardiner, S. R., *History of the Great Civil War, 1642–1649*, Vol. I, Longmans, 1911.
Leadman, A. D. H., *Battles Fought in Yorkshire*, London, 1891.
Rogers, H. C. B., *Battles and Generals of the Civil Wars, 1642–1651*, Seeley Service, 1968.
Wedgwood, C. V., *The Great Rebellion, Vol. II: The King's War*, Collins, 1958.
Young, Peter, *Marston Moor 1644*, Roundwood Press, 1970.
Young, Peter, and John Adair, *Hastings to Culloden*, G. Bell, 1964.

Primary Sources
Thomason Tracts, E.54 (7, 8, 19: Watson, *A Full Relation of the Late Victory*), E.2 (14: Stewart, *A More Exact Relation of the Late Battell*).

Chapter 6: Naseby
Buchan, John, *Oliver Cromwell*, Hodder, 1934.
Burne, A. H., *Battlefields of England*, Methuen, 1950.
Burne, A. H., and Peter Young, *The Great Civil War*, Eyre and Spottiswoode, 1959.
Clarendon, Edward, Earl of, *The History of the Rebellion*, Book IX, Clarendon Press, 1704.
Dore, R. N., 'Sir William Brereton's Siege of Chester and the Campaign of Naseby', *Transactions of the Lancashire and Cheshire Antiquarian Society*, Vol. 67, 1957.
Firth, Charles, *Cromwell's Army*, Methuen, 1912.
Fortescue, J. W., *History of the British Army*, Vol. I, Macmillan, 1899.
Fraser, Antonia, *Cromwell—Our Chief of Men*, Weidenfeld and Nicolson, 1973.
Gardiner, S. R., *History of the Great Civil War, 1642–1649*, Vol. II, Longmans, 1911.
Markham, C. R., *The Life of the Great Lord Fairfax*, Macmillan, 1870.
Rogers, H. C. B., *Battles and Generals of the Civil Wars, 1642–1651*, Seeley Service, 1968.
Walker, Sir Edward, K. G., *Historical Discourses upon Several Occasions*, London, 1705.
Wedgwood, C. V., *The Great Rebellion, Vol. II: The King's War*, Collins, 1958.
Woolrych, Austin, *Battles of the English Civil War*, Batsford, 1961.
Young, Peter, 'The Northern Horse at Naseby', *Journal of the Society for Army Historical Research*, 1954.

Young, Peter, and John Adair, *Hastings to Culloden*, G. Bell, 1964.

Primary Sources
Sprigge, Joshua, *Anglia Rediviva*, London, 1647.
Thomason Tracts, E.288.

Chapter 7: Montrose's Battles
Buchan, John, *The Marquis of Montrose*, Nelson, 1913.
Clarendon, Edward, Earl of, *The History of the Rebellion*, Book 9, Clarendon Press, 1704.
Gardiner, S. R., *History of the Great Civil War, 1642–1649*, Vols II and III, Longmans, 1911.
Morris, Mowbray, *Montrose*, Macmillan, 1901.
Wedgwood, C. V., *Montrose*, Collins, 1952.

Chapter 8: Charles II's Civil War
Abbott, W. C., *The Writings and Speeches of Oliver Cromwell*, Vol. II, Harvard University Press, 1939.
Barrett, C. R. B., *Battles and Battlefields in England*, A. D. Innes, 1896.
Blount, Thomas, *Boscobel*, London, 1660: revised edition Tylston and Edwards, 1894.
Buchan, John, *Oliver Cromwell*, Hodder, 1934.
Bund, J. W. Willis, *The Civil War in Worcestershire*, Birmingham, 1905.
Burne, A. H., *Battlefields of England*, Methuen, 1950.
Clarendon, Edward, Earl of, *The History of the Rebellion*, Book XIII, Clarendon Press, 1704.
Firth, Charles, *Cromwell's Army*, Methuen, 1912.
Fortescue, J. W., *History of the British Army*, Vol. I, Macmillan, 1899.
Fraser, Antonia, *Cromwell—Our Chief of Men*, Weidenfeld and Nicolson, 1973.
Rogers, H. C. B., *Battles and Generals of the Civil Wars, 1642–1651*, Seeley Service, 1968.
Young, Peter, 'The Northern Horse at Naseby', *Journal of the Society for Army Historical Research*, 1954.
Young, Peter, and John Adair, *Hastings to Culloden*, G. Bell, 1964.

Primary Sources
C.S.P. Domestic Series, 1651.
Hobman, D. L., *Memoirs of Captain Hodgson*.
Thomason Tracts, E.641.

Chapter 9: 'Let Monmouth Reign'
Burne, A. H., *Battlefields of England*, Methuen, 1950.
Churchill, Winston S., *Marlborough: His Life and Times*, Vol. I, Harrap, 1947.

D'Oyley, Elizabeth, *James, Duke of Monmouth,* Bles, 1938.
Fea, Allan, *King Monmouth,* John Lane, 1902.
Fortescue, J. W., *History of the British Army,* Vols I and II, Macmillan, 1899.
Macaulay, Lord, *The History of England,* Vol. I, Macmillan, 1914.
Page, Maurice, *The Battle of Sedgemoor,* Page, 1930.
Roberts, George, *The Life, Progress, and Rebellion of James, Duke of Monmouth,* Vols I and II, Longmans, 1844.
Trench, Charles Chenevix, *The Western Rising,* Longmans, 1969.
Wolseley, Viscount, *The Life of John Churchill, Duke of Marlborough,* Richard Bentley, 1894.
Young, Peter, and John Adair, *Hastings to Culloden,* G. Bell, 1964.

Primary Sources
Dalrymple, Sir John, *Memoirs of Great Britain and Ireland,* Vol. I, revised edition, 1790.
Manuscripts of Mrs Stopford Sackville, Historical Manuscripts Commission, 9th Report, Parts I to III, London, 1883.
Mr Nathaniel Wade's Confession, Harleian MSS. 6845, Folio 264.
Paschall, Andrew: facsimiles of his account of the battle are in Weston Zoyland church and the Blake Museum, Bridgwater.

Chapter 10: The First Jacobite Rising
Anon, *The Battle of Sheriffmuir,* Eneas Mackay, 1898.
Cunningham, Audrey, *The Loyal Clans,* Cambridge University Press, 1932.
Duke, Winifred, *Lord George Murray and the 'Forty-five,* Milne and Hutchinson, 1927.
Fortescue, J. W., *History of the British Army,* Vol. II, Macmillan, 1899.
Petrie, Charles, *The Jacobite Movement,* Eyre and Spottiswoode, 1959.
Shield, A., and Andrew Lang, *The King Over the Water,* Longmans, 1907.
Tayler, Alistair and Henrietta, *1715: Story of the Rising,* Nelson, 1936.
Tayler, Alistair and Henrietta, *The Old Chevalier,* Cassell, 1934.
Terry, Charles Sanford, ed., *The Jacobites and the Union,* Cambridge University Press, 1922.

Chapter 11: The Second Jacobite Rebellion
Anderson, Peter, *Culloden Moor,* William Mackey, 1920.
Duke, Winifred, *Lord George Murray and the 'Forty-five,* Milne and Hutchinson, 1927.

Duke, Winifred, *Prince Charles Edward and the 'Forty-five,* Robert Hale, 1938.
Fortescue, J. W., *History of the British Army,* Vol. II, Macmillan, 1899.
Home, John, *The History of the Rebellion in the Year 1745,* p. 230, London, 1802.
Paton, Henry, ed., *The Lyon in Mourning,* 3 vols, Edinburgh, 1895.
Petrie, Charles, *The Jacobite Movement,* Eyre and Spottiswoode, 1959.
Porcelli, Baron E. G. M., *The White Cockade,* Hutchinson, 1949.
Prebble, John, *Culloden,* Secker and Warburg, 1961.
Taylor, Iain Cameron, *Culloden,* National Trust for Scotland, 1970.
Terry, Charles Sanford, ec., *The 'Forty-five,* Cambridge University Press, 1922.
Tomasson, Katherine, and Francis Buist, *Battles of the '45,* Batsford, 1962.
Wilkinson, Clennell, *Bonnie Prince Charlie,* Harrap, 1932.
Young, Peter, and John Adair, *Hastings to Culloden,* G. Bell, 1964.

List of books studied in connection with armour, weapons and uniforms
Ashdown, C. H., *British and Foreign Arms and Armour,* T. C. and E. C. Jack, 1909.
Barnes, R. M., *History of Regiments and Uniforms of the British Army,* Seeley Service, 1957.
British Military Uniforms, Stamp Publicity, 1971.
ffoulkes, Charles, *Armour and Weapons,* Clarendon Press, 1909.
Hunter, Edmund, *Arms and Armour,* Wills and Hepworth, 1971.
Laver, J., *British Military Uniforms,* King Penguin, 1948.
Lawson, C. C. P., *History of the Uniforms of the British Army,* Kaye and Ward, 1967.
Luard, J. L., *History of the Dress of the British Soldier,* Clowes, 1852.
Martin, Paul, *Armour and Weapons,* H. Jenkins, 1968.
Maxwell, S., and Hutchinson, R., *Scottish Costumes 1550–1850,* A. and C. Black, 1958.
Norman Vesey, *Arms and Armour,* Weidenfeld and Nicolson, 1964.
North, Rene, *Military Uniforms,* Hamlyn, 1970.
Potter, R., and Embleton, G. A., *The English Civil War,* Almark Publications, 1973.
Talbot-Booth, E. C., *British Army Customs, Traditions and Uniforms,* Sampson Low, Marston, 3rd edition, 1941.
Tylden, Major G., *Horses and Saddlery,* J. A. Allan, 1965.
Wilkinson, F., *Arms and Armour,* Hamlyn, 1972.
Wilkinson, F., *Small Arms,* Ward Lock, 1965.
Wilkinson Lathan, R. and C., *Cavalry Uniforms of Britain and the Commonwealth Including Other Mounted Troops,* Blanford Press, 1969.

Index

229

230

231

The BATTLE of

This View of the Glorious Victory obtained over the Rebels, shews His MAJESTIES Army commanded by His Royal Hig
Body of Reserve, composed of Four – Part of the Highland Army is here represented as furiously attempting with Swo
Bainonets of Barrels & Munro's intrepid Regiments. The right wing of the Rebels being cover'd by a stone Wall, Kerr & C
Rebels in put them into immediate confusion Kingstons Horse wheel'd off at the same time by the right of y Kings for

Published 1st November 1797 b